THE THEORY OF CATERING

Ronald Kinton
BEd (Hons), FHCIMA
Formerly of
Garnett College, College for Teachers in Further and Higher Education

Victor Ceserani
MBE, MBA, FHCIMA
Formerly Head of
The School of Hotelkeeping and Catering, Ealing College of Higher Education

Editorial Consultant: David Foskett BEd (Hons), MHCIMA

Sixth Edition

Edward Arnold
A division of Hodder & Stoughton
LONDON NEW YORK MELBOURNE AUCKLAND

First published in Great Britain 1964
Second edition 1970
Third edition 1973
Fourth edition 1978
Fifth edition 1984
Sixth edition 1989

British Library Cataloguing in Publication Data

Kinton, Ronald
The theory of catering – 6th ed.
1. Catering
I. Title II. Ceserani, Victor
642.47

ISBN 0–340–49653–3

Typeset in Great Britain by Wearside Tradespools Limited, Fulwell, Sunderland
Printed and bound in Great Britain for Edward Arnold, the educational, academic and medical publishing division of Hodder and Stoughton Limited, 41 Bedford Square, London WC1B 3DQ by Richard Clay Ltd, Bungay, Suffolk

Contents

Introduction to sixth edition **ix**

Acknowledgements x

1 **Food and society 1**
An introduction to food and society 1
Some factors which affect what we eat 1
Ideas about food 2
Images of food 3
Resources 3
Information 4
Food changes in British society 5

2 **Influences of ethnic cultures 8**
Introduction to ethnic cookery 8
Religious influences 8
European cookery 10
Mediterranean and Middle Eastern 13
American 14
Caribbean 15
Indian, Pakistani and Bangladeshi 16
Chinese 17
Japanese 18
South East Asian 19
African 20

3 **The catering industry 21**
Various types of catering establishments 21
Welfare catering 23
School meals service 29
Residential establishments 33
Catering for industry 33

4 **Menu planning 36**
Introduction 36
Kinds of menus 37
Structure of menus 39
Planning the menu 41
Writing menus in French 43
Examples of different menus 55

5 Commodities 82
1 Meat 83
2 Offal 97
3 Poultry 100
4 Game 103
5 Fish 106
6 Vegetables 122
7 Fruits 130
8 Nuts 135
9 Eggs 136
10 Milk 140
11 Fats and oils 144
12 Cheese 147
13 Cereals 150
14 Raising agents 155
15 Sugar 157
16 Cocoa 158
17 Coffee 159
18 Tea 160
19 Pulses 161
20 Herbs 162
21 Spices 164
22 Condiments 167
23 Colourings, flavourings, essences 169
24 Grocery, delicatessen 170
25 Confectionery and bakery goods 175

6 Purchasing, costing, control and storekeeping 181
Purchasing of commodities 181
Portion control 182
Methods of purchasing 186
Cost control 188
Food cost and operational control 191
Storekeeping 195

7 Kitchen equipment 207
Large equipment 208
Mechanical equipment 222
Food processing equipment 223
Refrigeration 227
Small equipment and utensils 233

8 Gas, electricity and water 243
Gas 243
Electricity 252
Comparison of fuels 257
Energy conservation 260
Water 262

9 Kitchen organisation and supervision 277
Kitchen organisation 277
Kitchen supervision 285

10 Food production systems 293
Standards of hygiene 294
Cook-chill system 296
Overall benefits of cook-chill/cook-freeze 303
Centralised production – an introduction 307
Small centralised operations 310

11 Health and safety 311
Legislation 312
Environmental health officer 312
Accidents 313
Accident prevention 314
First aid 317
Fire precautions 319
Use of portable fire extinguishers 323
Working methods 327

12 Hygiene 332
Personal hygiene 332
Kitchen hygiene 340
Food hygiene 347
Food Hygiene Regulations 367
Definition of terms 371

13 Elementary nutrition and food science 372
Food and nutrients 372
Proteins 374
Fats 376
Carbohydrates 377
Vitamins 380
Mineral elements 382
Water 385
The cooking of nutrients 385
Food requirements 386
Basal metabolism 387
Value of foods in the diet 388
Balanced diet and healthy eating 394
Food additives 394

14 Preservation of food 396
Food spoilage 396
Methods of preservation 398

15 Service of food 406
Types of service 407

16 The use of computers 414
Introduction 414
Catering controls 417
Hotel management software 421
Glossary 423

17 Industrial relations 425
Legal aspects 426
Glossary 429

18 Guide to study and employment 432
Successful studying 432
Examination advice 435
Obtaining employment and building a career 436

Index 441

Introduction to sixth edition

This book is designed to meet the needs of all those involved in the catering industry, particularly students on all of the many catering courses. In it we emphasise the importance of realising and developing the relationship between theoretical knowledge and understanding, and practical experience.

The sixth edition has been completely revised and updated to keep in line with the continuing changes both in the industry and in catering education: new chapters have been added on 'Food production systems', 'Food and society' and 'Influences of ethnic cultures'.

As in previous editions we have not attempted to write a completely comprehensive book, but rather have set out a simple outline as a basis for further study. In this way we hope to assist students at all levels, and, for those who wish to study at greater depth, further references are suggested where appropriate. To assist students in their learning and to help them test their knowledge we recommend the use of the companion book *Questions on the Theory of Catering*.

In preparing this edition we were assisted by David Foskett BEd (Hons), MHCIMA, Head of Department of Hotel and Catering Operations, Ealing College of Higher Education. David Foskett trained at Westminster Technical College, gained experience at the Dorchester and Savoy Hotels, and at the head office of British Petroleum. He has qualifications in food technology and as a chef technologist has worked in test kitchens for food manufacturers.

Acknowledgements

The authors and publishers gratefully acknowledge the contribution of the following people and organisations: Gardner Merchant; British Gas; Michael Harrison, Electricity Council; Sea Fish Industry Authority; Coffee Information Service; British Egg Information Service; Milk Marketing Board's Dairy Product Advisory Service; National Association of Catering Butchers; Energy Efficiency Office; Refrigeration and Unit Air-Conditioning Group; Timothy F Burgess, TFB (Management) Ltd, for the chapter on Computers; Mrs F Cable, Principal Lecturer, Ealing College of Higher Education, for the chapters on Hygiene and Nutrition; Michael Wellman, Kingston-upon-Thames College, for the chapter on Water.

The publishers would also like to thank the following for permission to include copyright material and photographs:

(*Copyright material*) British Gas for Figs. 8.4–8.9; Buderus Küchentechnik GmbH for Figs. 7.3 and 7.4; *Caterer and Hotelkeeper* for Figs. 9.2 (by Stuart Knight, sponsored by TICC) and 5.14; Chubb Fire Security Limited for Fig. 11.8; Electricity Council for Figs. 7.5, 7.11, 7.12, 7.14(b), 7.17, 7.18 and 11.10; the Controller of Her Majesty's Stationery Office for the Ten Point Code on Health and Hygiene from *Clean Catering* on p. 333; Highfield Publications for Fig. 12.9 and 'Definition of terms' on pp. 370–71 from *The Food Hygiene Handbook* by the Institute of Environmental Health Officers; Hotel and Catering Training Board for Fig. 12.7; Macdonald and Company (Publishers) Limited for Fig. 2.2, taken from *Cuisines of Asia* by Jennifer Brennan.

(*Copyright photographs*) The Automatic Vending Association of Britain for Fig. 15.5; Bartec for Fig. 8.26; *Birmingham Post and Mail* for Fig. 9.9; *Caterer* for Figs. 7.32, 9.7 and 15.7; *Caterer and Hotelkeeper* for Figs. 3.1, 3.2, 3.3, 5.9, 9.3, 9.8, 9.9, 11.3, 11.11, 11.12, 12.5, 12.6, 12.16, 15.1, 15.2 and 17.1; *Catering Management* and Dawsons for Fig. 12.3; Chubb Fire Security Limited for Figs. 11.5, 11.7 and 11.8; Convotherm Limited for Fig. 10.6; Corporation of London for Figs. 5.1 and 5.11; John Crocker for Figs. 7.24–7.30 (Ferrari Brothers, 60 Wardour Street, London, for loan of equipment); Dexion Limited for Fig. 6.5; Alex Dufort for Fig. 2.1; Electricity Council for Figs. 10.3, 15.3 and 15.6; Excel Equipment Limited for Fig. 8.10; Food (and other) Matters for Fig. 5.12; Garland Catering Equipment Limited for Fig. 7.14(a); Hobart Manufacturing Company Limited for Fig. 7.16; Insect-o-Cutor Limited for Fig. 12.15; MV Jackson for Fig. 7.19; Ronald Kinton for Fig. 2.3; Mareno Industriale SpA for Fig. 7.31; Meat and Livestock commission for Fig. 5.10; Microwave Products for Fig. 7.6; Ted Poole, The College, Swindon, for Fig. 11.2; The Portman Intercontinental Hotel for Figs. 12.1 and 14.2; Rank Hotels for Fig. 7.1; Rentokil Limited for Fig. 12.13; Ritz Hotel, Piccadilly, London for Fig. 15.4;

Rowlett Catering Appliances Limited for Fig. 7.15; Sevenoaks District Council for Fig. 12.2; Stangard Induction for Fig. 7.7; Stott Benham for Fig. 7.8; Thomson Regional Newspapers for Fig. 7.13; XI Data Systems for Figs. 16.1–16.4; Zanussi Grandi Impianti for Fig. 7.10.

Every effort has been made to trace copyright holders of material reproduced in this book. Any rights not acknowledged here will be acknowledged in subsequent printings if notice is given to the publisher.

1

Food and society

General objectives To understand that people in society are affected by what they eat. To realise that society influences what people eat, and to develop an awareness of the social background to food.

Specific objectives To specify the factors that affect what people eat and to state the main influences on eating habits.

An introduction to food and society

Why do we eat what we eat, select one dish from the menu in preference to another, choose one particular kind of restaurant or use a take-away? Why are these dishes on the menu in the first place? Is it because the chef likes them, the customer or the consumer wants them or is this the only food available – what dictates what we eat?

Catering reflects the eating habits, history, customs and taboos of society but it also develops and creates them. You have only to compare the variety of eating facilities available on any major street today with those of a short while ago.

Some factors which affect what we eat

The individual

Everyone has needs and wants these to be met according to his or her own satisfaction.

1 *Tastes* and *habits* in eating are influenced by three main factors: upbringing, peer group behaviour, and social background. For example, children's tastes are developed at home according to the eating patterns of their family, as is their expectation of *when* to eat meals; teenagers may frequent hamburger or other fast food outlets; and adults may eat out once a week at an ethnic or high class restaurant, steakhouse or pub.
2 Degree of *hunger* will affect what is to be eaten, when, and how much to eat – although some people in the western world over-eat, food shortages cause under-nourishment in poorer countries. Everyone ought to eat enough to enable body and mind to function efficiently; if you are hungry or thirsty it is difficult to work or study effectively.
3 *Health* considerations may influence choice of food, either because a special diet is required for medical reasons, or (as the current emphasis on healthy eating shows) because everyone needs a nutritionally balanced diet. Many

people nowadays feel it is more healthy not to eat meat or dairy products. Others are vegetarian or vegan on moral or religious grounds.

Relationships

Eating is a necessity, but it is also a means of developing social relationships.

The needs and preferences of the people you eat with should be considered. This applies in the family or at the place of study or work. School meals can be a means of developing good eating habits, both by the provision of suitable foods and dishes and by creating an appropriate environment to foster social relationships. Canteens, dining rooms and restaurants for people at work can be places where relationships develop.

Often the purpose of eating, either in the home or outside it, is to be *sociable* and to meet people, or to renew or provide the opportunity for people to meet each other. Frequently there is a reason for the occasion (such as birthday, anniversary, wedding, awards ceremony), needing a special party or banquet menu – or it may just be for a few friends to have a meal at a restaurant.

Business is often conducted over a meal, usually at lunch-time but also at breakfast and dinner. Eating and drinking help to make work more enjoyable and effective.

Emotional needs

Sometimes we eat not because we need food but to meet an emotional requirement:

(a) because of sadness or depression – eating a meal can give comfort to oneself or to someone else. After a funeral people eat together to comfort one another;
(b) a meal can also be used as a reward, a treat, or to give encouragement to oneself or to someone else. An invitation to a meal is a good way of showing appreciation.

Ideas about food

People's ideas about food and meals, and about what is and is not acceptable, vary according to where and how they were raised, the area in which they live and its social customs.

Different societies and cultures have had in the past, and still have, conflicting ideas about what constitutes good cooking and a good chef, and about the sort of food a good chef should provide. The French tradition of producing fine food and highly respected chefs continues to this day – whereas other countries may traditionally have less interest in the art of cooking, and less esteem for chefs.

What constitutes people's idea of a *snack*, a *proper meal* or a *celebration* will depend on their backgrounds, as will their interpretation of terms such as *lunch* or *dinner*. One person's idea of a snack may be another person's idea of a main meal; a celebration for some will be a visit to a hamburger bar; to others, a meal at a fashionable restaurant.

The idea of what is 'the right thing to do' regarding eating varies with age, social class and religion. To certain people it is right to eat with the fingers, others use only a fork; some will have cheese before the sweet course, others will have cheese after it; it is accepted that children and often elderly people need food to be cut up into small pieces, and that people of some religions do not eat certain foods. The ideas usually originate from practical and hygienic reasons although sometimes the origin is obscure.

Images of food

Fashions, fads and fancies affect foods and it is not always clear if catering creates or copies these trends.

1 Nutritionists inform us what foods are good and necessary in the diet, what the effect of particular foods will be on the figure and how much of each food we require. This helps to produce an 'image' of food. This image changes according to research, availability and what is considered to constitute healthy eating.
2 What people choose to eat says something about them as a person – it creates an image. We are what we eat, but *why* do we choose to eat what we do when there is *choice*? One person will perhaps avoid trying snails because of ignorance of how to eat them, or because the idea is repulsive, whilst another will select them deliberately to show off to guests. One will select a dish because it is a new experience, another will choose it because it was enjoyed when eaten before. The quantity eaten may indicate a glutton or a gourmand; the quality selected, a gourmet.

The food itself

Crop failure or distribution problems may make a food scarce or not available at all. Foods in season are now supplemented by imported foods, so that foods out of season at home are now available much of the time. It means that there is a wide choice of food for the caterer and the customer.

(a) Food is *available* through shops, supermarkets, cash and carry, wholesalers and direct suppliers. People at home, and caterers, are able to purchase, prepare, cook and present almost every food imaginable due to rapid air transport and food preservation. Food spoilage and wastage are minimised; variety and quality are maximised.
(b) It is essential that food looks attractive, has a pleasing smell and tastes good. Food which is nutritious but does not look, smell or taste nice is less likely to be eaten. When cooking, these points must be considered, but it should be remembered that people's views as to what is attractive and appealing will vary according to their background and experience.

Resources

Money, time and facilities affect what people eat – the economics of eating affects everyone.

1 *How much money* an individual is able, or decides to spend on food is crucial to what is eaten. Some people will not be able to afford to eat out, others will

only be able to eat out occasionally, but for others eating out will be a frequent event. The money individuals allocate for food will determine whether they cook and eat at home, use a take-away (eg fish and chips, Chinese), go to a pub, eat at a pancake house, or at an ethnic or other restaurant.

2 The *amount* of *time* people have to eat at *work* will affect whether they use any facilities provided, go out for a snack or meal, or bring their own food to work.

3 The *ease* of *obtaining food*, the use of convenience and frozen food and the facility for storing foods, has meant that in the home and in catering establishments the range of foods is wide. Foods in season can be frozen and used throughout the year, so if there is a glut then spoilage can be eliminated.

Information

The media influences what we eat – television, radio, newspapers, magazines and literature of all kinds have an effect on our eating habits. See table on p. 5.

(a) Healthy eating, nutrition, hygiene and outbreaks of food poisoning are publicised; experts in all aspects of health including those extolling exercise, diet and environmental health state what should and should not be eaten.

(b) Information regarding the content of food packets, and the advertising of food, influences our choice. Knowledge about eating and foods is learnt from the family, through teachers, at school meals, at college, through the media, and through the experience of eating at home and abroad.

The following examples illustrate how these factors can affect what people eat.

A TV programme shows the effects of a drought in Africa, in a region where political factions are at war, thus preventing food distribution. Money is given by people morally concerned that others are starving, so air transport is used to deliver foods that have been preserved to provide adequate nutrition. The food should also be in keeping with the religious beliefs and cultural background of those in need.

Another example is related to planning a menu. The first thing to consider is who it is for; therefore it must not conflict with the consumer's religious beliefs or ethnic origin. The price must be affordable and the items on the menu obtainable. To illustrate further: let us say that a restaurant owner has advertised in the local paper, and a family decide to go to this restaurant to celebrate an anniversary. The food they select will be in keeping with their taste, and it may include dishes they are familiar with or new dishes on the menu (which, perhaps, are prepared off the premises and reheated in the owner's new technological equipment). Some of the items available on the menu may have been brought in by air, where the climate allows the production of foods not grown here. In addition, it might so happen that the restaurant is part of a pub which was, say, an original coaching inn named after Bonnie Prince Charlie – so perhaps Scottish dishes are always available, particularly on special occasions such as Burns night, when the local Scots celebrate and eat haggis which is traditional, nutritionally beneficial and flown down from Scotland. (Also, the host and his wife may have relations in Ireland and Wales, so perhaps national dishes of these countries feature on the menu as well.)

We are all creatures of habit conditioned by customs and restrictions, as much in what we do or do not eat, as in what we will or will not wear. Variety is not only the spice of life: it is the ingredient which makes catering and cooking so fascinating.

Further information
Vegetarian Society, Parkdale, Durham Road, Altrincham, Cheshire WA14 4OG.

Influences on what people eat

Media TV books newspapers journals	*Transport* transport of foods by: sea rail air transport of people	*Religious* taboos festivals
Geographical climate indigenous: fish birds animals plant life	*Historical* explorations invasions trade routes establishment	*Economic* money to purchase goods to exchange
Sociological family school work place leisure fashion and trends	*Political* tax on food policies on food mountains export and import restrictions	*Cultural* ethnic tribal celebrations
Psychological appearance of food smell taste aesthetics reaction to new foods	*Physiological* nutritional healthy eating illness additives	*Scientific* preservation technology

These influences are separated for convenience but in reality overlap. Only when sufficient food is available for survival can pleasure from food develop.

Food changes in British society

In the past, inns catered for people travelling by coach, with coffee houses in the towns. Later, with the development of railways, the hotel and catering industry expanded rapidly.

The twentieth century has brought sweeping changes in eating patterns and health. A hundred years ago, most people ate plenty of fibre from bread and potatoes, but they lacked an adequately varied diet. Diseases caused by a lack of vitamins and minerals were common. Today, the problems are different. Many people eat too much meat, dairy produce and sugar, and too little fibre for good health. New methods of farming and food processing, food selling and storage have helped to alter what we eat.

1900s

As the population grew rapidly at the turn of the century, so food imports rose. By 1914 British farmers met less than a quarter of the country's food needs.

New manufacturing processes created new products – for example, people began to eat less bread and potatoes as the new shops brought in cheap cod packed in ice. Flour, margarine and tinned condensed milk were cheap and popular, biscuits, jam, chocolate and cheese also began to be factory-made. Such products were often cleaner and purer than those previously available, but sometimes of less nutritional value. In towns the first grocery store chains appeared, and new co-operative retail societies also flourished. Eating out was limited to fish and chip shops, chop houses and pubs.

Beneath the outward prosperity of Edwardian England were various social problems. One-third of the population was poor and undernourished, a situation that led eventually to free school milk, school medical inspections and clinics.

1930s

The First World War had brought home just how dependent Britain was on imported food, and how unfit the nation was – thousands of men had been graded unfit for active service. Measures were taken to boost British food production such as subsidies and import restrictions. However, cheap meat, wheat and butter from abroad encouraged farmers to specialise in milk, eggs and vegetables.

More of almost every type of food was eaten, but even so researchers found that less than half the population could afford a healthy diet. Rickets, TB, anæmia and physical under-development were common among the poor, leading eventually to the introduction of free school milk and infant welfare clinics to help combat these problems.

A number of companies started to dominate food processing and retailing during the 1930s, and shops increasingly sold pre-prepared brand-name goods. Eating out also became more popular with the introduction of milk bars and modestly priced restaurants such as Lyons Tea Shops and ABC (Aerated Bread Company) Tea Shops.

1950s

The Second World War had created food shortages but rationing and other Government action meant that on average the nation's diet was better than before the war. When rationing ended, consumers splashed out on foods that had been in short supply: meat, eggs, butter, chocolate, sugar and canned fruit. However, only half the population ate a cooked breakfast, and breakfast cereals became fashionable.

At the time, health experts were concerned to ensure that people were eating a balanced diet, with sufficient vitamins and protein. However, these years of plenty were laying down the foundations for increasing obesity and heart disease. Other changes were that shops began to convert to self-service due to rising labour costs, and Chinese restaurants became popular for eating out, due both to their cheapness and because they offered a take-away service; and because people were becoming more adventurous in their choice of foods.

1970s

By now UK farmers produced two-thirds of the nation's food, due to increasing use of technology and pesticides, fertilizers and hormones. Joining the EEC gave farmers new subsidies and guaranteed prices, which resulted in over-production of some foods. Most people began the day with a cereal breakfast and approximately 18 per cent ate nothing. Fewer midday meals were taken at home. Tea shops went out of fashion and were replaced by burger bars. There was growing interest in foreign food: curry, kebabs, chow mein, pizza and chilli con carne became familiar dishes. Health experts' attention shifted from the problems of inadequate nutrition to the new health risks of eating too much of certain types of food.

1980s onwards

Supermarkets continue to expand and, due to air-cargo transport, almost all foods from around the world are now available. Partly because of the development of tourism, the demand for ethnic dishes continues, leading to the opening of many ethnic restaurants. *Nouvelle cuisine* became fashionable, but has tended to give way to healthy eating which is popularised not only in *haute cuisine* but also in the home and school meals. British chefs and cooking are now earning respect. The microwave oven has greatly affected people's eating habits at home, and supermarkets have responded by popularising products which can be cooked or re-heated in the microwave. The 1970s saw the expansion of the use of the freezer; in the 1980s it is the expansion of the use of the microwave.

2

Influences of ethnic cultures

General objectives To become aware of the number of styles of cooking and foods available in different parts of the world. To stimulate an interest in the topic. To know where to obtain further information.

Specific objectives To be able to explain some of the religious influences which affect what people eat. To be able to state examples of foods and dishes of various cultures and countries in the world.

Introduction to ethnic cookery

The races and nations of the world represent a great variety of cultures each with their own method of cooking. Knowledge of this is essential in catering because:

(a) There has been a rapid spread of tourism, creating a demand for a broader culinary experience.
(b) Many people from overseas have opened restaurants using their own foods and styles of cooking.
(c) The development of air-cargo means perishable foods from distant places are readily available.
(d) The media, particularly television, has stimulated an interest in world-wide cooking.

A few years ago it was necessary for a chef to be knowledgeable about traditional classical French cooking; today chefs must also be aware of the foods and dishes of many other races. It is not within the scope of this book to deal in depth with gastronomy, but it is hoped that this brief introduction will stimulate an interest in terms and food associated with ethnic cooking. A list of books for reference is given at the end of this section.

Religious influences

Throughout the world religion always has, and still does, affect what many people eat. Some people's diets are restricted daily by their religion; others are influenced by what they eat on special occasions. Fasts, feasts, celebrations and anniversaries are important happenings in many people's lives. It is necessary for those involved in catering to have some basic knowledge of the requirements and restrictions associated with religions.

Christian

For most Christians, eating habits are not affected – though some will be vegetarians, usually for moral reasons, and some will refrain from eating meat on Fridays. Some sects, for instance Mormons, have many rules and restrictions regarding eating and drinking, for example complete abstinence from tea, coffee and alcohol, and an emphasis on wholesome eating. Many Christians refrain from eating certain foods during Lent – usually something they like very much. Other religious days often observed are: Shrove Tuesday, the day before the start of Lent, when pancakes are on many menus – traditionally to use up ingredients prior to Lent; Good Friday, when hot cross buns are often eaten as a reminder of Christ's crucifixion; Easter Sunday, when simnel cakes are made with marzipan and chocolate, and Easter eggs (decorated boiled or chocolate eggs) are eaten as a symbol of new life and the Resurrection; Christmas, 25 December, is celebrated with feasting, with roast turkey today often replacing the traditional roast beef and boar's head, followed by Christmas pudding and mince pies.

Other predominantly Christian countries celebrate different saints days by special events. For example, St Nicholas, patron saint of children, is celebrated on 6 December in Holland (and other countries) by eating Dutch St Nicholas biscuits; in Spain the Three Kings are remembered with a special crown cake on 6 January. The fourth Thursday of November in the USA is Thanksgiving Day which celebrates the first harvest of the Pilgrim Fathers, when traditionally turkey and pumpkin pie are served.

Muslim

Muslims celebrate the birth of Mohammed at the end of February or early in March. Alcohol and pork are traditionally forbidden in their diet. Only meat that has been prepared according to Muslim custom by a halal butcher is permitted. During *Ramadan*, which lasts for one month and is the ninth month of the Muslim Calendar, Muslims do not eat or drink anything from dawn to sunset. The end of the fast is celebrated with a feast called *Idd-ul-Fitar*, with special foods. Muslims from Middle Eastern countries would favour a dish like lamb stew with okra, those from the Far East, curry and rice.

Hindu

Most Hindus do not eat meat (strict Hindus are vegetarians) and none eat beef since the cow is sacred to them. *Holi* is the festival which celebrates the end of winter and the arrival of spring. *Raksha Bandha* celebrates the ties between brothers and sisters at the end of July or in August, and *Janam Ashtami* celebrates the birth of Krishna, also in August. *Dussehra* is the festival of good over evil; *Divali* is the festival of light, celebrating light over darkness, held in October or November. Samosas (triangles of pastry containing vegetables), banana fudge and vegetable dishes of all kinds, as well as favourite foods, are eaten to celebrate.

Sikh

The Sikhs do not have strict rules regarding food but many are vegetarians. *Baisakhi Day* in April celebrates the new year and is the day Sikhs are baptised into their faith.

Buddhist

Strict Buddhists are vegetarians and their dishes vary since most live in India and China, where foods available will be different. *Vesak* in May is the festival to celebrate the life of the Buddha.

Judaism

The religion of the Jews has strict dietary laws. Shellfish, pork and birds of prey are forbidden. Acceptable foods are fish with scales and fins, animals that have 'cloven hoof' and birds killed according to the law. Strict Jews eat only meat that has been specially slaughtered known as *kosher* meat.

Milk and meat must neither be used together in cooking nor served at the same meal, and three hours should elapse between eating food containing milk and food containing meat.

The Jewish Sabbath, from sunset on Friday to sunset on Saturday, is traditionally a day of rest. In the evening, plaited bread called *chollah* is broken into pieces and eaten. *Matzo*, an unleavened crispbread, is served at Passover as a reminder of the exodus of the Jews from Egypt. *Pentecost* celebrates the giving of the ten commandments by Moses on Mount Sinai; cheesecake is now a traditional dish served at this celebration. *Hanukkah*, the Jewish Festival of Lights in December, is a time of dedication when pancakes and a potato dish, potato latkes, are usually eaten.

European cookery

British

Due to the climate, British cooking tends to be warming and filling. Breakfast, afternoon tea and high tea are examples of meals peculiar to Britain. Selections of some British foods and dishes are given below.

English

Fried cod and chips.
Roast beef and Yorkshire pudding with horseradish sauce.
Roast lamb with mint sauce.
Steak and kidney pie – a pie covering of short or puff pastry.
Steak and kidney pudding – a suet paste meat pudding.
Cornish pasty – a pastry containing potatoes, vegetables and meat.
Apple pie – apples covered with short paste.
Trifle – layers of fruit, sponge, custard and cream.
Treacle pudding – a steamed sponge pudding.
Fool – a purée of mixed fruit with whipped cream.
Chelsea buns – a yeast bun containing dried fruit.
Worcestershire sauce – a bottled spicy sauce used in meat dishes.

Welsh

Welsh lamb pie.
Welsh rarebit – a cheese savoury dish.
Welsh cake – a flat scone-like griddle cake.
Lava bread.
Leek pie.

Scottish

Haggis – chopped sheep's liver, lights and heart with oatmeal and seasoning, cooked inside a sheep's stomach which has been thoroughly cleaned and turned inside-out.
Finnan Haddie – smoked haddock.
Cock-a-leekie – a soup of leek and chicken garnished with prunes.
Venison – the flesh of deer.
Scotch eggs – hard boiled eggs covered in sausage meat, crumbed and deep fried.

Irish

Irish Stew – a stew of many vegetables and potatoes and lamb.
Colcannon – mashed potatoes and cabbage with butter and milk.
Irish herring soup.
Bacon and cabbage.
Carageen moss pudding – a sweet made from milk, eggs, sugar and dried seaweed.

French

Many famous dishes have been created in France, the home of classical cooking, but only a few examples are given here (recommended reading is given at the end of the chapter). Each region of France has its specialities and styles of cooking.

Choucroûte – a dish from Alsace of white cabbage, bacon, and frankfurter sausage.
Bouillabaisse – a stew or soup of assorted fish and shellfish of many varieties with vegetables.
Tournedos Rossini – a cut from a fillet of beef, shallow fried and garnished with *foie gras* (fat goose liver) and a slice of truffle and madeira sauce.
Snails (escargots) – snails served in their shells with garlic butter.

Italian

The Italians brought their culinary skills to France in 1533 and justifiably claim to have influenced French cooking. Italy is noted for its pastas, risottos, cheeses, pizzas and much more. Examples of some food and dishes are:

Gnocchi – there are several kinds made from choux paste, potatoes or semolina.
Minestroni – a vegetable soup containing pasta and served with cheese.
Parma ham (proscuitto) – this ham is mostly cut into thin slices and eaten raw.

Mortadella – a cured pork sausage which is cut into very thin slices.
Parmesan cheese – a very hard cheese which is grated and used for cooking.
Osso buco – a stew of the shin of veal cut across, with the bone.
Risotto – a moist rice dish cooked in stock and finished with cheese.

German and Austrian

German and Austrian dishes are filling, meat being used extensively. Sausages (wursts) are produced in a great many varieties and braised red and green cabbage is popular, whilst Austrian pastries are renowned:

Apfelstrudel – a special thin pastry with apples, dried fruit and spice.
Sauerkraut – a pickled white cabbage served hot.
Wiener schnitzel – a thin slice of veal, crumbed and shallow fried Vienna style.
Sachertorte – a chocolate cake with bitter sweet chocolate filling.

Russian

Russian cooking – cooking in that part of the USSR situated in Europe, including the Ukraine – has provided one of the most popular classical dishes, namely Chicken à la Kiev. Borsch, a famous Russian beetroot soup, originated in the sixteenth century. Other foods and terms associated with Russia include:

Blinis – thin pancakes served with caviar, roe etc.
Coulibiac – puff or brioche pastry with layers of flaked fish, sturgeon or salmon, pancakes cut in strips, and hard boiled eggs.
Zabuska or Zabuski (hors-d'oeuvre) – introduction to the meal beginning with salted or pickled fruits, vegetables and mushrooms.
Shashlyk – meat marinated, skewered and grilled.
Chicken à la Kiev – supreme of chicken stuffed with butter and egg, crumbed and deep fried.
Caviar – raw, slightly salted sturgeon's roe from the Baltic and Caspian seas.
Stroganoff – a sauté of prime beef with a sauce of soured cream.

Eastern European

Hungary – *Goulash* (Gulyas), which is a stew using paprika.
Poland – *Baba*, which is yeast savarin paste soaked in syrup containing rum, which originated in Poland.

Swiss

French, Italian and German cookery influences the cooking of Switzerland, a country famous for its cheeses:

Rösti potatoes – shredded potatoes cooked to a golden brown cake.
Raclette – a melted cheese dish (also the name of the dish in which the cheese is melted).
Fondue – cheese melted with white wine, eaten off chunks of bread.
Emmental and gruyère – two of the best known cheeses.

Spanish

The dishes in this country are varied because of its geographical situation, each area having its own specialities. Some of them are well known:

Paella – rice with shellfish, chicken, vegetables and saffron simmered in stock and olive oil in a paella pan.
Gazpacho – a cold soup of tomatoes, peppers, cucumber, garlic etc.
Tortilla – a flat omelet of potatoes, onions and garlic served hot or cold.
Tapas – snacks, usually served at bars, of omelet, squid, shellfish etc.

Scandinavian

Denmark, Norway and Sweden, due to their proximity to the sea, eat a large amount of fish particularly herrings. Dairy produce from butter, blue cheese and bacon are imported into Britain in considerable quantities. Rye which grows in northern climates is used for crispbreads which are popular, particularly for low-calorie diets:

Smörgäsbord – term for 'buffet', including many dishes particularly those using fresh, smoked and pickled herrings and other fish, shrimps and prawns.
Smørrëbrod – Danish open sandwiches.
Gravlax (Gravad lax) – marinated, filleted salmon coated with dill sugar from Sweden.

Mediterranean and Middle Eastern

Cooking in this area is affected by religious, as well as by geographical and historical influences, sometimes making it unclear where certain dishes originated. Foods from the Mediterranean area include olives, aubergines, lemons, squid, octopus, yogurt and lamb; from the Middle East, wheat, rice, beans, chick peas, lentils, figs, dates and citrus fruits. Burghul, known as 'cracked wheat', is whole wheat grains partially cooked, dried and cracked, and used in many soups, stews and salads.

Greece

Greek cooking (see Fig. 2.1 overleaf) has the most ancient traditions of the world, and some of the best known foods and dishes are:

Feta – a semi-soft, crumbly, salted white goat or sheep's milk cheese.
Avgholemono – egg, lemon and chicken soup or sauce.
Dolmathes (Dolmandes, dolma) – vine leaves stuffed with rice.
Filo (phyllo) – a very thin paste used for sweet and savoury dishes.
Baklava – layers of filo paste with nuts, sugar and spice baked and finished with sugar and lemon syrup.
Moussaka – a dish of minced meat, aubergines, tomatoes and cheese sauce.
Taramasalata – a first course dish or dip of fish roes blended with bread, olive oil and lemon sauce.
Spanakopitta – spinach pie with filo pastry and cheese.
Pitta bread – small, flat, round yeast breads.

Fig. 2.1 Greek pastry cooks

Couscous – north African dish of cracked wheat, resembling semolina, cooked by steaming over stews.
Kebabs – skewered lamb with peppers, tomatoes, mushrooms and onions grilled and served on rice pilaff.
Börek – Turkish dish of filo pastry wrapped around garlic flavoured goat cheese, lamb or vegetables.
Keftedes – fried minced meat balls with onion, oregano, mint and parsley.
Hummus – a purée of chick peas.
Tahina – a paste made of sesame seeds used as a dip or a condiment giving a nutty flavour.
Ful medames – an Egyptian dish of small purple dried beans cooked and mashed with olive oil, lemon juice and garlic.

American

Although English is spoken in the USA some culinary terms are not the same as in the UK, for example:

cornstarch = cornflour
granulated sugar = caster sugar
confectioner's sugar = icing sugar
superfine = caster sugar
cookies = biscuits
heavy cream = double cream
molasses = treacle
powdered sugar = icing sugar

Another difference is that many American recipes are given using *cupfuls* as a means of measuring. The fast food industry is immense; but in a country as cosmopolitan as the USA, cooking is influenced by many European and Asian cookery traditions:

Gumbo – a soup or stew of okra with smoked meat, shellfish and vegetables from Louisiana.
Burgoo – an 'all-in' stew of beef, pork, poultry and vegetables.
Chowder – a fish soup usually with a shellfish base.
Cheesecake – a biscuit base with a cream cheese filling, usually topped with blueberries or other fruits.
Baked Alaska – ice cream coated with meringue and baked.
Strawberry shortcake – shortbread or scone base topped with strawberries, with whipped cream between.
Succotash – butter beans and sweetcorn vegetarian dish.
Corned beef hash – corned beef and potato.
Chicken Maryland – deep fried battered or crumbed chicken pieces with corn fritters and bacon.
Jambalaya – Creole dish of rice, wine, chicken, shellfish etc. The consistency of thick soup.
Eggs Benedict – a muffin base, slice of ham and poached egg coated with hollandaise sauce.
Club sandwich – usually three layers of toast with filling of chicken, bacon, lettuce, tomato and mayonnaise.
Pecan pie – a shortcrust pastry with pecan nuts and maple syrup filling.
Waldorf salad – celery, walnuts and apple bound with mayonnaise served on lettuce leaves.

Mexican and South American

Mexican cookery shows the country's Aztec roots and Spanish influence. It is noted for the hot flavour of its dishes which contain chillies, and for the use of unsweetened chocolate.

Tortilla – unleavened cornmeal dough, flattened to a pancake shape, and griddled.
Tacos – a tortilla with minced meat or chicken filling. A crisp version is deep fried.
Enchiladas – tortilla dipped in chilli sauce, fried and filled with cheese, turkey or chicken, topped with chilli sauce and cheese.
Guacamole – a purée of avocado, chillies, onion and lemon juice used as a dip or garnish.
Mole – a chilli sauce enriched with unsweetened chocolate.

South American cooking is influenced by Spanish and Portuguese cookery:

Cerviche – Peruvian dish of raw fish 'cooked' by the acid of citrus fruit.
Feijoada – Brazilian dish of smoked and fresh meats with black beans and spices.

Caribbean

African and European settlers on the Caribbean Islands have greatly influenced the cooking of this area. Yams, coconut, guavas, mango and paw paw are ingredients readily available.

Calaloo – soup made of the vegetable called 'calaloo', originating in Africa,

with okra, garlic, onions, cloves, herbs, chillies and coconut milk.
Blaff – white fish poached in wine and water with hot chillies, allspice, garlic and peppercorns.

Indian, Pakistani and Bangladeshi

Indian cookery is noted for its use of spices, herbs and flavourings but the sub-continent should not be associated only with curry. Northern India's speciality, tandoori cooking, is named after the unusual oven called the *tandoor* (see Fig. 2.2) which produces slightly charred spiced chicken and lamb dishes.

Fig. 2.2 A traditional tandoor oven

Southern India features vegetarian dishes and *vindaloo*. Bangladesh favours seafood. Pakistan uses yogurt extensively, and kebabs are common. Examples of some terms and dishes are:

Chapati – a wholewheat unleavened bread-like pancake.
Ghee – clarified butter.
Poppadums – a very thin round biscuit made from dhal, deep fried or grilled and served with curry etc.
Bombay duck – a salted dried fish.
Vindaloo – very hot curry.
Tandoor – a clay oven heated by wood or charcoal.
Samosas – small deep-fried pastries containing vegetables and meat.
Pakoras – deep fried dumplings.

Garam masala – literally a mixture of spices: hot spices, black cardamom, cinnamon, cloves, peppercorns and nutmeg.

Chinese

China is a vast country with a wide climatic variation, and therefore many kinds of foods are available. Because of its size, four major styles of cooking have developed over the centuries, and foods produced in these areas predominate. The areas are divided into:

Eastern Shanghai – wide variety of fruit, vegetables and fish; light and delicate seasoning; stir fry and steaming are favoured cooking methods. Soy sauce from this area is considered the best in China.

Northern Beijing (Peking) – wheat and corn are produced in this area, not rice, so noodles, pancakes and dumplings are served. Due to the climate many foods are preserved. Less meat is available. Garlic, leeks, onions and sesame seeds are used extensively.

Western Sichuam (Szechuan) – strong flavourings and hot spices predominate, eg red chillies, peppercorns, ginger. Fruit, vegetables, meat and fish are plentiful.

Southern Guangdong (Canton) – foods are not overcooked, and less use is made of garlic. Rice is the staple food. Sweet and sour dishes and dim sums are renowned. Stir fry and steaming are the most common methods of cooking.

Chinese cooking is based on five flavours which affect parts of the body:

Flavour	*Organ*	*Flavour*	*Organ*
sweet	spleen	bitter	heart
acid	liver	sharp	lungs
sour	kidneys		

The Chinese diet is characterised by cooking methods which preserve vitamins, the absence of dairy produce, and little meat. Foods are divided into: yin – cooling food; yang – heating foods; yin yang – neutral foods. Yin foods include crab and duck, and yang foods beef, coffee and smoked fish; yin yang foods include rice, fruit and vegetables. (See Fig. 2.3 overleaf.)

All parts of animals and birds, other than the fur and feathers, are used for food.

Some of the following are items and dishes associated with Chinese cooking:

Soy sauce – made from soya beans, flour and water. Light soy sauce is best and is known as *superior soy*. Dark soy sauce is suitable for stews and is known as *soy superior sauce*.

Bean curd – doufu or tofu (Japanese). Bland nutritious curd made from soya beans. Used extensively in soup, meat and vegetable dishes.

Water chestnuts – this sweet root vegetable is white and crunchy, and is used particularly in southern Chinese dishes.

Bamboo shoots – these edible shoots are pale yellow and are used in vegetable dishes.

Fig. 2.3 Chinese chefs eating Chinese food

Fresh coriander (Chinese parsley) – the flat, feathery leaves have a citrus-like flavour used in sauces etc.

Root ginger – fresh root ginger is used in soups and meat and vegetable dishes.

Peking duck – specially raised ducks, firstly basted with a honey mixture then roasted and served with Chinese pancakes.

Dim sum – savoury and sweet, steamed, baked or fried tea delicacies, eg spring roll filled with bean sprouts on pork, and small sweet egg custard tartlets.

Japanese

Japanese cookery is unique in its artistic presentation and the wide variety of small amounts of different dishes served to please the eye as well as the appetite (see Fig. 2.4). Fish, rice, noodles and vegetables as well as soy sauce predominate. Raw fish which is exceptionally fresh is used extensively.

Sushi – cooked cold rice seasoned with rice vinegar, with raw or cooked fish.

Teriyaki – a cooking technique of glaze grilling, using the marinade.

Yakitori – grilled chicken kebabs basted with soy sauce containing sake and mirin.

Mirin – a type of sweet cooking wine.

Tofu – soya bean curd used extensively.

Sukiyaki – sautéed sliced beef with vegetables, tofu, noodles and soy sauce.

Sake – an alcoholic beverage made from rice.

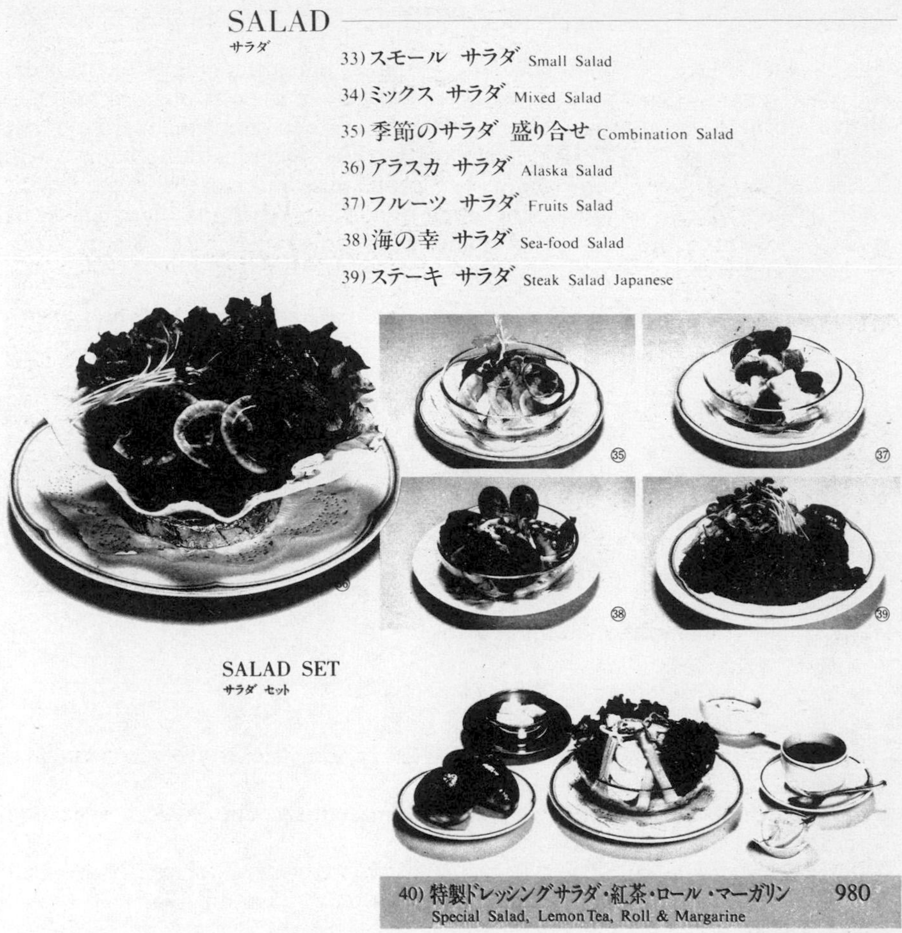

SALAD
サラダ
33) スモール サラダ Small Salad
34) ミックス サラダ Mixed Salad
35) 季節のサラダ 盛り合せ Combination Salad
36) アラスカ サラダ Alaska Salad
37) フルーツ サラダ Fruits Salad
38) 海の幸 サラダ Sea-food Salad
39) ステーキ サラダ Steak Salad Japanese
SALAD SET
サラダ セット
40) 特製ドレッシングサラダ・紅茶・ロール・マーガリン 980
Special Salad, Lemon Tea, Roll & Margarine

Fig. 2.4 Selection of salads from a Japanese menu

South East Asian

South East Asia is influenced by both Chinese and Indian cooking. Singapore, Indonesia, Burma and Thailand use rice extensively as well as pineapples, pomelos, mandarins, bananas, coconut, mangoes and paw paws.

Gado gado – vegetables with peanut sauce; salad of vegetables, beans, carrots and cauliflowers, cooked *al dente* with salad vegetables; hard boiled eggs with hot dressing of peanut butter, sugar, chillies and coconut milk.

Satay – Indonesian kebabs; skewered, grilled meat served with spicy peanut sauce.

This area produces many spices such as nutmeg, cloves, ginger etc. Coconuts, rice and other tropical fruits including pineapples and bananas are common.

African

The climate of Africa enables bananas, paw paws, mangoes, grapes, citrus fruits and sugar-cane to grow well. From north Africa comes couscous, the national dish of Morocco, Tunisia and Algeria, which is a fine semolina made from wheat steamed over soup, stew or fish. East Africa, which includes Ethiopia, is where coffee originated. Both coffee and tea are grown here and maize is an important crop. In west Africa *cassava* is the staple food, and Ghana is the main cocoa producing country in the world. Groundnut is grown in Nigeria. South Africa produces sugar-cane and maize and cattle and sheep are raised.

Bobotie – a South African dish of curried minced meat with nuts and raisins covered with a savoury custard.
Groundnut stew – a chicken stew enriched with peanut butter.
Ugali – maize porridge served with soups and stews.

Suggested books

British
British Cookery, Jane Grigson, Mermaid Books 1986.
Farmhouse Cookery, Readers' Digest 1980.

French
Larousse Gastronomique
The New Cuisine, Paul Bocuse, Granada 1985.
Cuisine of the Sun, Roger Vergé, Papermac 1981.

Greek
Best Book of Greek Cooking, C. Paradissis, Efstatiadis Group 1983.

Middle Eastern
A New Book of Middle Eastern Food, Claudia Roden, Penguin 1986.

Chinese
Chinese Cookery, Kenneth Hom, BBC 1984.
Chinese Cooking, Zhaohva Publishing House, Guanghwa Company, 7–9 Newport Street, London WC2.

Japanese
Japanese Cookery, Jon Spayde, Century.

Asian
The Complete Asian Cookbook, Charmaine Soloman, Windward.
The Cuisines of Asia, Jennifer Brennan, Macdonald 1984.

See also *Contemporary Cookery* (Ceserani, Kinton and Foskett) and *Practical Cookery* (Ceserani and Kinton).

3

The catering industry

Having read the chapter, these general objectives should be achieved.

General objectives Be aware of the various types of catering establishments and know of the particular characteristic peculiar to each.

Various types of catering establishments

Students need to be aware of the scope for employment in the industry, and should realise both the social and economic importance of the industry. The economic health of a nation is reflected by the food served in the home and in the eating establishments of the country. With full employment, businesses boom; with the expansion of overseas tourism, the catering industry also expands.

The UK needs an industry capable of contributing to the health of the national economy, therefore all aspects of the catering industry have an important part to play.

The provision of food for people of all ages, in all walks of life, at all times of the day or night, and in every situation, shows the scope and variety to be found in the catering industry.

One thing is common to all – *the need for food to be cooked and served well*. Certain groups of people, however, have special food requirements; for example, some old people, due to poor digestion and because they may have dentures, require foods which are easily digested and need little chewing. Likewise when catering for young people it is particularly important to consider the nutritional needs of those who are still growing. An adequate supply of protein and calcium is essential.

In a world of increased travel and better communications, it is increasingly important to be aware of the social and religious requirements of others. Social customs involving the use of certain foods or dishes often originated because of religious events such as fasts, feasts (or other significant reasons). Many of the traditional observances are declining and the origins forgotten. Fish on Friday and pancakes on Shrove Tuesday have less significance today. This is not only because of the changing influence of religion, social attitudes and customs, but is also due to increased use of technology. Perishable foods are now refrigerated; fish does not have to be dried and salted so as to meet religious demands.

The geographical situation dictates what constitutes national diet. In certain areas of the world rice will be commonplace; in other areas yams, or sweet potatoes, and elsewhere wheat. Nationals from other countries, either visiting or working in the UK, should be considered so that their foods are available to them.

People restrict themselves to a vegetarian diet on religious grounds, for ethical reasons (because they consider it morally wrong) or because they are concerned with their physical well being. The provision of vegetarian foods should be available for those needing them.

An awareness of people's food requirements and how to meet them is the responsibility of those employed in the catering industry.

The various types of catering establishments are listed in the table following.

Various types of catering establishments

Hotels and restaurants	*Welfare and industrial*	*Transport*	*Other aspects*
hotels	Residential establishments	railways	contracts
restaurants	eg	motorways	outdoor
cafés	schools and colleges	airlines	the Services
clubs	halls of residence	at sea	Navy
public houses	hostels		Army
wine bars	old people's homes		Air Force
speciality restaurants	hospitals		police
departmental stores	nursing homes		prisons
chainstore cafeterias	workers in industry and		
ethnic	commerce		

Hotels and restaurants

The great variety of hotels and restaurants can be demonstrated by comparing the palatial, first-class luxury hotel with the small hotel owned and run as a family concern. With restaurants, a similar comparison may be made between the exclusive top-class restaurant and the small one which may just serve a few lunches.

Hotels are residential and most of them will provide breakfasts, lunches, teas, dinners and snacks. In some hotels banquets will be an important part of the business.

Restaurants will vary with the kind of meals they serve. Some will serve all types of meals whilst others will just serve lunch and dinner or lunch and tea. Again, banqueting may form an important part of the restaurant's service.

In some cases special types of meal service, such as grill rooms or speciality restaurants, may limit the type of foods served – eg smörgåsbord or steaks will be provided.

Wine bars, fast foods, take-away

Customer demand has resulted in the rapid growth of a variety of establishments offering a limited choice of popular foods at a reasonable price, and with little or no waiting time, to be consumed either on the premises or taken away. See p. 411 on speciality restaurants.

Clubs

These are usually administered by a secretary or manager appointed by a management committee formed from club members. Good food and drink with an informal service in the old English style are required in most clubs, particularly of the St James's area of London – see Fig. 3.1.

Night clubs and casinos usually have the type of service associated with the restaurant trade.

Fig. 3.1 A men's club – Great Gallery Restaurant, The RAC Club

Chain-catering organisations

There are many establishments with chains spread over wide areas and in some cases over the whole country. Prospects for promotion and opportunities are often considerable, whether it is in a chain of hotels or restaurants. These are the well-known hotel companies, restaurant chains, the popular type of restaurant, chain stores and the shops with restaurants – which often serve lunches, teas and morning coffee, and have snack bars and cafeterias.

Welfare catering

The fundamental difference between welfare catering and the catering of hotels and restaurants is that the hotel or restaurant is run to make a profit and provide a service. The object of welfare catering is to provide a service without necessarily making a profit. The standards of cooking should be equally good, though the types of menu will be different.

Hospital catering

Hospital catering is classified as welfare catering, the object being to assist the nursing staff to get the patient well as soon as possible. To do this it is necessary to provide good quality food which has been carefully prepared and cooked to retain the maximum nutritional value, and presented to the patient in an appetising manner.

It is recognised that the provision of an adequate diet is just as much a part of the patient's treatment as careful nursing and skilled medical attention (see Fig. 3.2).

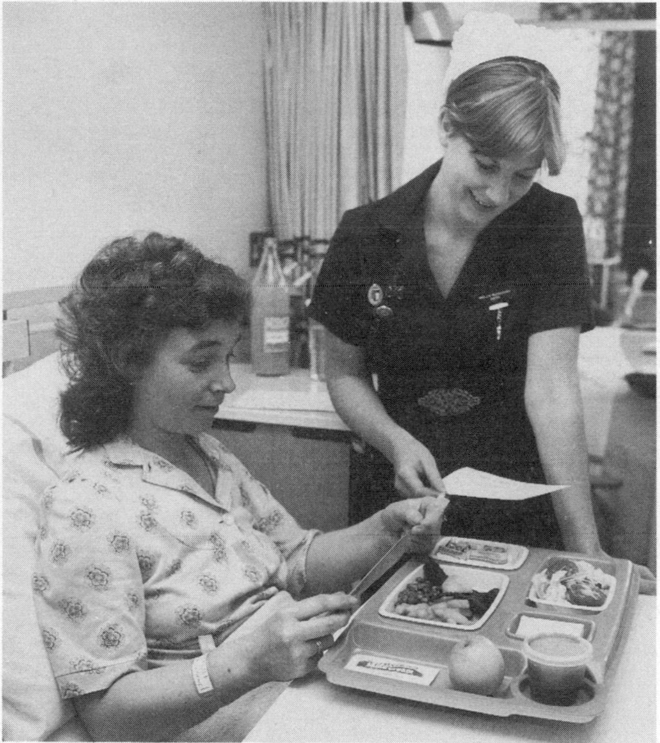

Fig. 3.2 Pre-plated hospital meal being served

Within the health service approximately two million meals are served every 24 hours and the number served in one establishment can vary from 50 to 3000 people. In many hospitals patients are provided with a menu choice. The staff in the hospital catering service are organised as follows:

Catering managers plan menus, obtain supplies and supervise the preparation, cooking and service of the meals, and are also responsible for training and safety. They visit the wards to advise on the service of food to the patients, and control the provision of the catering facilities for the doctors, nurses and other hospital employees.

Assistant catering managers assist and deputise for the catering managers with all or part of their duties, or they may be responsible for a small hospital.

Catering supervisors have responsibility for dining rooms.

Kitchen superintendents are responsible to the catering manager or the assistant catering manager for the running of one or more hospital kitchens.

Cooks are graded: 1 – assistant cook, 2 – assistant head cook, 3 – head cook. The head cook would be in charge of a kitchen under the control of the kitchen superintendent or catering manager.

Dining room supervisors are in charge of the staff during meal service and they are responsible to the catering manager.

People interested in being of service to the community and gaining job satisfaction could find this aspect of catering rewarding. Conditions, hours of work and pay as well as promotion prospects are factors which contribute to making this a worthwhile career.

Dietitians

In many hospitals a qualified dietitian is responsible for:

(a) collaborating with the catering manager on the planning of meals;
(b) drawing up and supervising special diets;
(c) instructing diet cooks on the preparation of special dishes;
(d) advising the catering manager and assisting in the training of cooks with regard to nutritional aspects;
(e) advising patients.

In some hospitals the food will be prepared in a diet bay by diet cooks.

Diets

Information about the type of meal or diet(s) to be given to each patient is supplied daily by the ward sister to the kitchen. The information will give the number of full, light, fluid and special diets, and with each special diet will be given the name of the patient and the type of diet required. (See tables overleaf.)

The main hospital kitchen

All food, except diets and food cooked in the ward kitchens, is cooked here. In this kitchen all meals for patients, doctors, nurses, clerical and maintenance staff are prepared. In hospitals where a canteen is provided for out-patients and visitors this will come under the control of the catering officer.

Hospital routine

Hospital catering has its own problems, which often make it very difficult to provide correctly served meals. Wards are sometimes spread over a wide area, and, in a large hospital, where there are long distances for the food to travel, provision of effective, silent trolleys is essential to keep the food hot.

The routine of a hospital is strictly timed and meals have to fit in with the duties of the nursing staff.

The amount of money the catering manager has to spend on food and drink is

Hospital menu for one week: lunches and suppers, patients and staff (P/S)

Tuesday	*Wednesday*	*Thursday*	*Friday*	*Saturday*	*Sunday*	*Monday*
Home-made vegetable soup	Home-made potato and leek soup	Home-made scotch broth	Home-made spiced lentil soup	Minestrone soup	Scotch broth	Home-made carrot and onion soup
Chicken Maryland (S) Roast chicken (P)	Cottage pie (P/S)	Roast leg of pork and apple sauce (P/S)	Fried haddock (S) Grilled plaice (P)	Shepherd's pie (P/S)	Roast beef, Yorkshire pudding and horseradish sauce (P/S)	Gammon and pineapple (P/S)
Courgette and mushroom pasta bake (P/S)	Wholemeal pizza (P/S)	Cauliflower cheese (P/S)	Home-made vegetable pie (P/S)	Sweetcorn and mushroom vol-au-vent (P/S)	Macaroni cheese (P/S)	Mild vegetable curry with boiled rice
Bacon roll and tomato sauce (S)	Toad in the hole (S)	Mild chicken curry and rice (S)	Chilli con carne and boiled rice (S)	Scotch egg salad	Tuna fish salad	Lasagne (S)
Edam cheese salad	Ham and peach salad	Corned beef salad	Sardine and egg salad	Parsley potatoes Creamed potatoes	Roast potatoes Creamed potatoes	Cold meat and salad
Chipped potatoes Creamed potatoes	Jacket potatoes Creamed potatoes	Roast potatoes Creamed potatoes	Chipped potatoes Creamed potatoes	Courgettes Side salad	Sprouts Peas	Sauté potatoes Creamed potatoes
Cabbage Peas	Baby carrots Spinach Baked beans (S)	Diced swede Broccoli	Peas Cauliflower	Steamed jam pudding and custard	Apple and blackberry pie and custard	Diced carrots Broad beans
Wholemeal raspberry and apple pie and custard	Bread pudding and custard	Wholemeal apple crumble and custard	Spotted dick and custard	Fruit yogurt	Ice cream	Semolina and jam
Ice cream	Fruit yogurt	Strawberry whip	Fruit jelly	Dessert banana	Dessert apple	Pear Condé
Dessert banana	Dessert apple	Dessert orange	Dessert apple			Dessert orange

Tuesday	*Wednesday*	*Thursday*	*Friday*	*Saturday*	*Sunday*	*Monday*
Home-made vegetable soup	Home-made potato and leek soup	Home-made scotch broth	Home-made spiced lentil soup	Minestrone soup	Scotch broth	Home-made carrot and onion soup
Home-made cornish pasty (P/S)	Cod Portugaise (P/S)	London pie (P/S)	Sausage and egg pie and tomato sauce (P/S)	Breaded plaice fillet (P/S)	Chicken pilaff and curry sauce (P/S)	Quiche Lorraine (P/S)
Stuffed tomatoes (P/S)	Baked jacket potato with cheese (P/S)	Fish fingers (P/S)	Celery and ham au gratin (P/S)	Beef curry and boiled rice (P/S)	Fish cakes (P/S)	Savoury mince (P/S)
Liver sausage and lettuce sandwich	Corned beef and tomato sandwich	Cheese and chutney sandwich	Tuna fish and cucumber sandwich	Salad sandwich	Egg and cress sandwich	Cream cheese and cucumber sandwich
Jacket potatoes Side salad	Parsley potatoes Side salad	Creamed potatoes Side salad	Creamed potatoes Side salad	Chipped potatoes Side salad	Parsley potatoes Side salad	Jacket potatoes Side salad
Courgettes	Mixed vegetables	Baked beans	Sweetcorn	Mixed vegetables	Runner beans	Spinach
Chocolate blancmange Ice cream	Pineapple whip Ice cream	Crème caramel Ice cream	Milk jelly Ice cream	Cheesecake Ice cream	Fruit salad Ice cream	Apricot fool Ice cream
Cheese and biscuits	Cheese and biscuits	Cheese and biscuits	Cheese and biscuits	Cheese and biscuits	Cheese and biscuits	Cheese and biscuits

Patient's request form for following day's meal

Breakfast Large ( ) Normal ( ) Small ( )			*Lunch* Large ( ) Normal ( ) Small ( )			*Supper* Large ( ) Normal ( ) Small ( )		
1	Porridge*	1	10	Braised liver and onions*	10	22	Cream of tomato soup*	22
2	Cornflakes*	2	11	Grilled beef sausages	11	23	Fish cake and lemon	23
3	Weetabix*	3	12	Creamed chicken*	12	24	Shepherd's pie	24
4	Boiled egg*	4	13	Sardine salad*	13	25	Egg and cress sandwich	25
5	Hot roll	5	14	Carrots*	14	26	Corned beef salad*	26
6	Wholemeal bread*	6	15	Purée of vegetables*	15	27	Green beans	27
7	White bread*	7	16	Boiled potatoes*	16	28	Purée of vegetables*	28
8	Butter*	8	17	Creamed potatoes*	17	29	Chipped potatoes*	29
9	Marmalade	9	18	Lemon sponge pudding	18	30	Creamed potatoes	30
			19	Custard	19	31	Peach trifle	31
			20	Ice cream and wafers*	20	32	Baked tapioca pudding*	32
			21	Cheese and biscuits*	21	33	Cheese and biscuits*	33
						34	Ice cream	34
WARD NAME *Suitable for diabetic diets			WARD NAME *Suitable for diabetic diets			WARD NAME *Suitable for diabetic diets		

stated as so much per head. Good, wholesome varied meals can only be provided by careful buying and the elimination of waste. The cost of providing the hospital catering service is periodically reviewed by the Government.

Further information
Hospital Caterers Association, 356 Fell Lane, Keighley, Yorkshire; and about dietetics from the British Dietetic Association, 103 Daimler House, Paradise Street, Birmingham.

School meals service

The provision of a midday meal at school for children up to and including secondary school age has been a statutory duty of local education authorities since 1941, and the policy governing this provision is laid down by the Department of Education and Science.

Fig. 3.3 School meals being served

Over the years however, this policy has varied, generally due to the economic situation of the country at the time. At the present time local education authorities may decide for themselves:

(a) their own free school meals policy, subject to free meals being provided to pupils from families in need;

Four-weekly menu for primary schools

	Monday	*Tuesday*	*Wednesday*	*Thursday*	*Friday*
Week beginning	Spaghetti bolognese Carrots, potatoes Pineapple shortbread Fresh fruit	Cod au gratin Peas, mashed potatoes Fruit sponge and custard Fresh fruit	Sausages Spaghetti rings, sauté potatoes Baked rice pudding Fresh fruit	Meat pie Cabbage, potatoes Yogurt Fresh fruit	Turkey grill Baked beans, chips Apple crumble with custard Fresh fruit
Week beginning	Cheese and egg flan Jacket potatoes, salad Fruit and custard Fresh fruit	Sausages Beans, chips Apple and raisin stir up with custard Fresh fruit	Lancashire flan Carrots, potatoes Yogurt Fresh fruit	Beefburgers Jacket wedges, green beans Iced buns Fresh fruit	Wholemeal ham pizza Corn or peas, potatoes Choc. chip sponge with choc. sauce Fresh fruit
Week beginning	Beef stew with pasta Cabbage, potatoes Yogurt Fresh fruit	Fish fingers Beans, chips Apricot crumble with custard Fresh fruit	Ham salad Jacket potatoes Delaware pudding with custard Fresh fruit	Chicken pie Peas, potatoes Stewed fruit with custard Fresh fruit	Sausages Green beans, potatoes Peach shortbread Fresh fruit
Week beginning	Boiled ham with parsley sauce Carrots, potatoes Iced sponge with custard Fresh fruit	Wholemeal pasta with mince Peas or carrots Plum pie with custard Fresh fruit	Egg and cheese salad Jacket potatoes Milk pudding Fresh fruit	Beefburgers Beans, chips Stewed fruit with evaporated milk Fresh fruit	Cornish pasty Cabbage, potatoes Yogurt Fresh fruit

1 Meats (must include 2 pasta dishes)
2 Ham
3 Beefburgers
2 Beefburgers
1 Turkey grill
2 Cheese and egg
1 Fish fingers
1 Fish
1 Pizza (with meat topping)

(b) the kind of meals service they wish to provide;
(c) the charge they wish to make for meals.

The school meals service is controlled by school meals organisers responsible for the catering service, including control of finance within the budget, menu planning, advice on food purchasing, kitchen planning and general administration. Supervision of the school meals kitchens is undertaken by catering officers or cook supervisors and in smaller units by a cook-in-charge. Many women are employed in this area; they find that working in the school meals service can be fitted in with their responsibilities at home. Many work only for two or two-and-a-half hours each day during the actual meal service, although kitchen staff at all levels receive training.

Many schools now offer a multi-choice menu, with up to a dozen choices of both courses, which is operated on a cash cafeteria system as exists in most departmental stores. In recent years cook-freeze and cook-chill systems have been introduced by some authorities to reduce labour costs.

School kitchens are well equipped. The highest standard of personal and kitchen hygiene is demanded.

Staff training 'in service' and by day and block release are the accepted methods of ensuring a high standard of efficiency in the kitchens.

There is continuing emphasis on healthy eating which is reflected in the menus and recipes used, and attention is paid to the special needs of children of various cultural and religious backgrounds.

The staff supervising the children at mealtimes, particularly in primary and junior schools, have the responsibility of ensuring good behaviour and table manners and also encouraging children to develop the right attitude to healthy eating (see Fig. 3.4 overleaf).

For up-to-date information on the School Meals Service obtain the current circulars issued by the Department of Education and Science, Elizabeth House, York Road, London SE1, or contact the local education authority's school meals organiser.

An interpretation of the healthy sample menu cycle (as seen in table opposite)

Main course items (no soya used)

Spaghetti bolognese	–	Wholemeal spaghetti, low fat meat and beans
Fried fish	–	Pure white cod, fried in unsaturated oil
Sausages	–	Low fat, high pork content
Meat pie	–	Wholemeal flour, low fat meat, pulses added
Beefburgers	–	High beef content, reduced saturated fat content
Cheese and egg flan	–	Wholemeal pastry, skimmed milk used
Lancashire flan	–	Wholemeal pastry, low fat meat, pulses added
Beef stew	–	Low fat meat, pulses added and pasta
Fish fingers	–	Additive free crumbs, pure cod only used
Ham salad	–	Best hocks of ham, boiled and sliced
Chicken pie	–	Low fat meat, wholemeal pastry used, pulses added to meat mix
Cornish pasty	–	Low fat meat, wholemeal pastry, pulses added

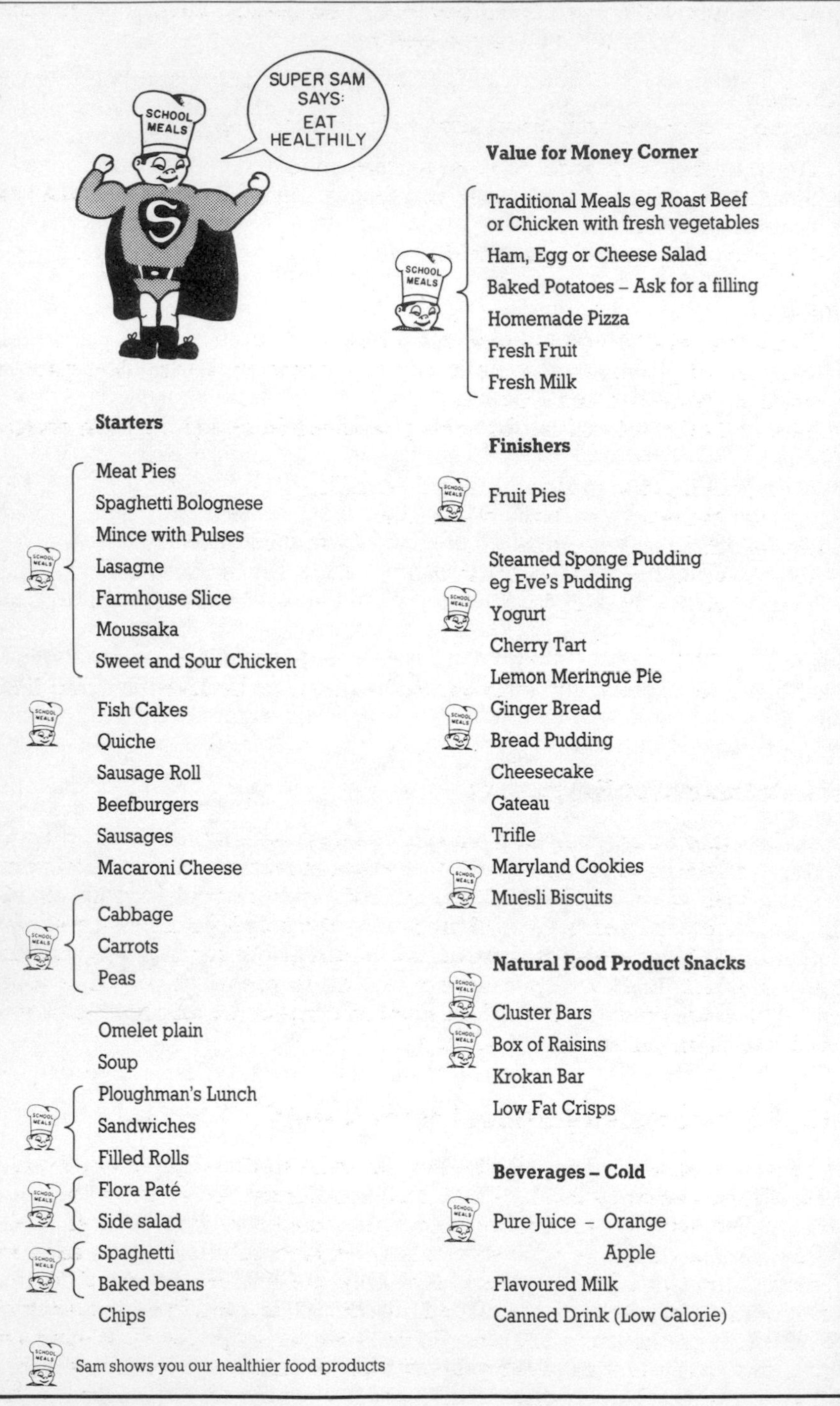
SCHOOL MEALS

SUPER SAM SAYS: EAT HEALTHILY

Starters

- Meat Pies
- Spaghetti Bolognese
- Mince with Pulses
- Lasagne
- Farmhouse Slice
- Moussaka
- Sweet and Sour Chicken
- Fish Cakes
- Quiche
- Sausage Roll
- Beefburgers
- Sausages
- Macaroni Cheese
- Cabbage
- Carrots
- Peas
- Omelet plain
- Soup
- Ploughman's Lunch
- Sandwiches
- Filled Rolls
- Flora Paté
- Side salad
- Spaghetti
- Baked beans
- Chips

Value for Money Corner

- Traditional Meals eg Roast Beef or Chicken with fresh vegetables
- Ham, Egg or Cheese Salad
- Baked Potatoes – Ask for a filling
- Homemade Pizza
- Fresh Fruit
- Fresh Milk

Finishers

- Fruit Pies
- Steamed Sponge Pudding eg Eve's Pudding
- Yogurt
- Cherry Tart
- Lemon Meringue Pie
- Ginger Bread
- Bread Pudding
- Cheesecake
- Gateau
- Trifle
- Maryland Cookies
- Muesli Biscuits

Natural Food Product Snacks

- Cluster Bars
- Box of Raisins
- Krokan Bar
- Low Fat Crisps

Beverages – Cold

- Pure Juice – Orange, Apple
- Flavoured Milk
- Canned Drink (Low Calorie)

Sam shows you our healthier food products

Fig. 3.4 School cafeteria menu

Egg and cheese salad – Salad would include lettuce, cucumber, tomato, carrot, beetroot etc.

Vegetables
Only fresh or frozen vegetables are used with the exception being:

(a) Baked beans – with reduced sugar and fat content.
(b) Spaghetti – with reduced sugar and fat content and use of a wholemeal variety.
(c) Chips are only served once a week.

Puddings
(a) Fresh fruit available for all school children.
(b) Majority of puddings do contain a fruit percentage, either solid pack or dried, eg plate pies and crumbles.
(c) Suet and other animal fats have been removed from puddings, eg spotted dick.
(d) Milk puddings are made with skimmed milk.
(e) Popular fruits with custard are available.
(f) Fruits will be served on biscuits, eg pineapple shortbread.
(g) Reduced sugar content, eg custard.
(h) Yogurt may be provided daily.

Additives
All additives considered by some medical experts to be harmful have been removed.

Residential establishments

Under this heading are included schools, colleges, halls of residence, hostels, etc, where all the meals are provided. It is essential that in these establishments the nutritional balance of food is considered, and it should satisfy all the residents' nutritional needs, as in all probability the people eating here will have no other food. Since many of these establishments cater for students, and the age group which leads a very energetic life, these people usually have large appetites, and are growing fast. All the more reason that the food should be well cooked, plentiful, varied and attractive.

Catering for industry (industrial catering)

The provision of staff dining rooms for industrial workers has allowed many catering workers employment in first-class conditions. Apart from the main lunch meal, tea trolley rounds and/or vending machines may be part of the service. In some cases a 24 hour service is necessary and it is usual to cater for the social activities of the workers. Not only are lunches provided for the manual workers but the clerical staff and managerial staff will in most cases have their meals from the same kitchen. There is ample scope for both men and women, and in this branch of the industry there are many top jobs for women.

Many industries have realised that output is related to the welfare of the employees. Well-fed workers produce more and better work and because of this a great deal of money is spent in providing first-class kitchens and dining-rooms and in subsidising the meals. This means that the workers receive their food at a price lower than its actual cost, the rest of the cost being borne by the company.

Further information
Industrial Catering Association, 1 Victoria Parade, 331 Sandycombe Road, Richmond, Surrey TW9 3NB.

Luncheon clubs

Clerical staffs in large offices are provided with lunching facilities, usually called a luncheon club or staff restaurant. These are often subsidised and in some instances the meal may be supplied without charge. The catering is frequently of a very high standard and the kitchen or kitchens will provide meals for the directors, which will be of the very best English fare or international cuisine.

Business lunches are served in small rooms so that there is privacy; the standard of food served will often be of the finest quality since the company will probably attach considerable importance to these functions. The senior clerical staff may have their own dining-room, whilst the rest of the staff will in some cases have a choice of an à la carte menu, a table d'hôte menu, waitress service or help-yourself and snack-bar facilities.

Luncheon clubs are provided by most large offices belonging to business firms, such as insurance head offices, petroleum companies, banks, etc. When luncheon facilities are not provided many firms provide their employees with luncheon vouchers.

Large stores also provide lunching arrangements for their staff as well as the customers' restaurants.

Transport catering

Aircraft

Aircraft catering is concerned with the provision of meals during flights and this form of catering presents certain problems. Owing to very limited space on the plane special ovens are provided to heat the food, which may be frozen or chilled. The food is prepared by the aircraft company or by an outside contract company.

Railway catering

Meals on trains may be served in restaurant cars, and snacks from buffet cars. The space in a restaurant car kitchen is very limited and there is considerable movement of the train, which causes difficulty for the staff.

Catering at sea

The large liners' catering is of similar standard to the big first-class hotels and many shipping companies are noted for the excellence of their cuisine. The kitchens on board ship are usually oil-fired and extra precautions have to be taken in the kitchen in rough weather. Catering at sea includes the smaller ship, which has both cargo and passengers, and the cargo vessels and this includes the giant tankers of up to 100 000 tonnes.

Other aspects of catering

The Services

Catering for the armed services is specialised and each branch has its own training centre; details of catering facilities and career opportunities can be obtained from career information offices.

Contract catering

There are many catering concerns which are prepared to undertake the catering for businesses, schools or hospitals, leaving these establishments free to concentrate on the business of educating or nursing, etc. By employing contract caterers and using the services of people who have specialised in catering, organisations can thus relieve themselves of the worry of entering a field outside their province. Contract caterers are used by nearly every type of organisation, including the armed forces. The arrangements made will vary – the contractor may meet certain operating costs or receive a payment from the company employing the contractor. Often the cost of food, wages and light equipment is the responsibility of the contractor, whilst the cost of fuel and heavy equipment maintenance is borne by the company.

Outside catering

When functions are held where there is no catering set-up or where the function is not within the scope of the normal catering routine then certain firms will take over completely. Considerable variety is offered to people employed on these undertakings and often the standard will be of the very highest order. A certain amount of adaptability and ingenuity is required, especially for some outdoor jobs, but there is less chance of repetitive work. The types of function will include garden parties, agricultural and horticultural shows, the opening of new buildings, banquets, parties in private houses, etc.

Licensed house (pub) catering

There are approximately 70 000 licensed houses in England and Wales and almost all of them offer food in some form or another. To many people the food served in public houses is ideal for what they want, that is, often simple, moderate in price and quickly served in a congenial atmosphere.

There is great variety in public-house catering, from the ham and cheese roll operation to the exclusive à la carte restaurant. Public-house catering can be divided into four categories:

(a) the luxury-type restaurant;
(b) the speciality restaurant, eg steak bar, fish restaurant;
(c) fork dishes served from the bar counter where the food is consumed in the normal drinking areas;
(d) finger snacks, eg rolls, sandwiches, etc.

Further information

Pub Caterer magazine, *Caterer and Hotelkeeper*.

4

Menu planning

Having read the chapter these learning objectives, both general and specific, should be achieved.

General objectives Understand the principles of menu planning and know how to compile menus suitable for a wide variety of establishments.

Specific objectives Apply the principles of menu planning to special parties, table d'hôte and à la carte menus. Specify suitable dishes for various courses. Compile menus taking account of all the factors – costs, season, staff capabilities, equipment, facilities, suppliers, nutritional value, types of customer. Demonstrate by correctly writing menus in English and, where appropriate, in French.

Introduction

A menu, or bill of fare, is a means of *communication*, informing the customer what the caterer has to offer. The compiling of a menu is one of the caterer's most important jobs – whether for establishments such as restaurants aiming to make a profit, or for those working to a budget, such as hospitals and schools.

The function of a menu is twofold. It informs:

(a) the catering staff of what is to be prepared;
(b) the customer or consumer of what is available.

The staff need to know in advance what is to be ordered, prepared and served; the customer or consumer needs to know what the food is, how it is cooked and, where appropriate, how much it will cost. The information needs to be clearly stated and set out in courses so that the menu is easily comprehensible.

The content of the menu creates an image which reflects the overall style of the restaurant. The printed menu should match the decor of the restaurant and be attractive and well laid-out, as it helps to promote sales, especially if dishes are described in an appetising way. Some caterers see the menu as a means of marketing, particularly when photographs are used of 'specials' or dishes of the day, or to advertise speciality evenings etc.

Traditional cookery methods and recipes form a sound foundation of knowledge for the craftsman and the caterer. However, it should be remembered that fashions in food change and customers look for new dishes, different combinations of food and fresh ideas on menus. This does not mean that the wide range of popular dishes of the past should be ignored as some of the most successful menus contain a sensible balance of traditional and contemporary dishes.

Students should be both aware of changes in contemporary cooking and prepared to experiment and create new and original recipes so that the caterer can continue to offer the customer fresh interest, variety and pleasure in his or her menus.

It is necessary to make certain that terms are accurately expressed so that the customer receives exactly what is stated on the menu; otherwise it may mean that the *Trade Descriptions Act* is being contravened. In the words of the act 'Any person who in the course of a trade or business:

(a) applies a false trade description to any goods or
(b) supplies or offers to supply any goods to which a false trade description is applied shall be guilty of an offence.'

For example, 'Paté maison' should really be home-made paté, not factory made. If fried fillets of sole are offered on the menu, then more than one must be offered, and the fish must be sole; and if an 8 oz rump steak is given as the portion on the menu, then it must be 8 oz *raw* weight.

If the sole is advertised as 'fried' and the steak as 'grilled' then these processes of cooking should be undertaken; if the soles are named as *Dover soles* and the steak as *rump steak* then this is what must be served. Likewise, if the sole is stated to be served with a *sauce tartare* and the steak with a *béarnaise sauce* then the sauces should be correctly and accurately made.

The description on the menu should give an indication, as appropriate, of the quality, size, preparation and composition of the dish.

In some types of establishments it may be good practice to offer certain dishes eg pasta, steak, etc, in varying sizes of portions.

Kinds of menus

It must be clearly understood that there are several kinds of menus:

1 Table d'hôte – a set menu forming a complete meal at a set price. A choice of dishes may be offered at all courses; the choice and number of courses will usually be limited to two, three or four.
2 À la carte – a menu with all the dishes individually priced. The customers can therefore compile their own menu. A true à la carte dish should be cooked to order and the customer should be prepared to wait for this service.
3 Special party or function menus – are for banquets or functions of all kinds. As all the guests start the meal at the same time it is generally unsuitable to place items such as steak or soufflé on the menu for large numbers. Care needs to be taken with seasonable foods to ensure they will be available if the menu is printed well in advance thus avoiding difficulty and embarrassment.
4 Ethnic or speciality menus – can be table d'hôte or à la carte specialising in the food (or religion) of the country or in a specialised food itself. For example, ethnic: Chinese, Indian, kosher, Afro-Caribbean, Greek etc; speciality: steak, fish, pasta, vegetarian, pancakes etc. The kitchen staff must know how to find and use the ingredients, and important in this respect is the ambience of the restaurant reflecting the menu.
5 Hospital menus – usually take the form of a menu card given to the patient

the day before service so that his or her preferences can be ticked. Both National Health Service and private hospitals cater for vegetarians and also for religious requirements. In many cases a dietitian is involved with menu compilation to ensure nothing is given to the patients that would be detrimental to their health. Usually hospital meals are of two or three courses.

6 Menus for people at work – these are menus which are served to people at their place of work. Such menus vary in standard and extent from one employer to another due to company policy on the welfare of their staff and work-force. Progressive companies ensure that their employees are well looked after; some may charge for meals and some ask for a token sum and offer meals at a sudsidised rate. A number of staff restaurants charge a price that covers the cost of food and labour with all other charges being subsidised. In most of these places, whether or not it is a factory canteen or head office staff restaurant, the menu often offers at least a two or three course meal with a selection of items – a table d'hôte style menu. There may also be a call-order à la carte selection charged at a higher price. The food will usually be mainly British with some ethnic dishes and a vegetarian dish. The menu consists of soup, main meat and/or dish with vegetables, followed by sweets, cheese and yogurts. According to the policy of the management and employee requirements, there will very often be a salad bar and healthy eating dishes included on the menu. When there is a captive clientele who face the same surroundings daily and meet the same people, then no matter how long the menu cycle or how pleasant the people, or how nice the decor, boredom is bound to set in and staff then long for a change of scene. So, a chef or manager needs to vary the menu constantly to encourage customers to patronise the establishment rather than going off the premises to eat. The decor and layout of the staff restaurant plays a very important part in satisfying the customer's needs. The facilities should be relaxing and comfortable so that he or she feels that the restaurant is not a continuation of the work-place. Employees who are happy, well-nourished and know that the company has their interests and welfare at heart will tend to be well-motivated and work better. (See menu examples at the end of this chapter.)

7 Menus for children – in schools there is an emphasis on healthy eating and a balanced diet in boarding schools. Those areas with children of various cultural and religious backgrounds have appropriate items available on the menu. Many establishments provide special children's menus which concentrate on favourite foods and offer suitably sized portions. (See menu example given on p. 32.)

Cyclical menus

These are menus which are compiled to cover a given period of time, ie one month, three months etc. They consist of a number of set menus for a particular establishment: for example, industrial catering restaurant, cafeteria, canteen, director's dining-room, hospital or college refectory. At the end of each period the menus can be used again thus overcoming the need to keep compiling new ones. The length of the cycle is determined by management policy, by the time of the year and by different foods available. These menus must be monitored carefully to take account of changes in customer requirements and any variations in weather conditions which are likely to affect demand for certain dishes. If cyclical menus are designed to remain in operation for long periods of time, then they must be carefully compiled so that they do not have to be changed too drastically during operation.

Advantages of cyclical menus

1 They save time by removing the daily or weekly task of compiling menus, although they may require slight alterations for the next period.
2 When used in association with cook/freeze operations, it is possible to produce the entire number of portions of each item to last the whole cycle, having determined that the standardised recipes are correct.
3 They give greater efficiency in time and labour.
4 They can cut down on the number of commodities held in stock, and can assist in planning storage requirements.

Disadvantages

(a) When used in establishments with a captive clientele, then the cycle has to be long enough so that customers do not get bored with the repetition of dishes.
(b) The caterer cannot easily take advantage of 'good buys' offered by suppliers on a daily or weekly basis unless such items are required for the cyclical menu.

Pre-planned and pre-designed menus

Advantages

1 Pre-planned or pre-designed menus enable the caterer to ensure that good menu planning is practised.
2 Before selecting dishes that he or she prefers, the caterer should consider what the customer likes, and the effect of these dishes upon the meal as a whole.
3 Menus which are planned and costed in advance allow banqueting managers to quote prices instantly to a customer.
4 Menus can be planned taking into account the availability of kitchen and service equipment, without placing unnecessary strain upon such equipment.
5 The quality of food is likely to be higher if kitchen staff are preparing dishes that they are familiar with and have prepared a number of times before.

Disadvantages

(a) Pre-planned and pre-designed menus may be too limited to appeal to a wide range of customers.
(b) They may reduce job satisfaction for staff who have to prepare the same menus repetitively.
(c) They may limit the chef's creativity and originality.

Structure of menus

1 Length – there is no relationship between the length and quality of a menu.

If the menu is too short the customer may be disappointed at having insufficient choice; if the menu is too long it may consist of a large number of dishes of mediocre quality. In general, it is better to offer fewer dishes of a good standard and aim to give the customer what he wants (always remembering it is the customer who pays the bill).

2 Design – the design of the printed menu should complement the image, atmosphere and decor of the restaurant or dining room. The management policy on the frequency of menu change determines the design, and can give the appearance of daily change. It must be remembered that design should not dominate practicality. A poor design, however, can be detrimental to the product and the image of the establishment.

3 Language – traditional menus use French, and in some cases French with an English translation, but it is unwise to use a mixture of French and English. It is important when describing dishes to be accurate so that the customer can identify the dish. Over-elaboration should be avoided as it may cause disappointment. If we believe that menus are means of communication then we should use the language which is easily understood, that is English. As the majority of customers are English-speaking then it seems logical that caterers should be encouraged to use the national language. As an example, 'Poulet sauté chasseur' or 'Sautéd chicken Hunter style' is less informative to the customer than 'Chicken pieces fried and served in a white wine, mushroom, tomato and tarragon flavoured sauce'.

4 Presentation – the way the menu is presented to the customer will often determine initial reaction to it – whether it is on the wall before entering a staff dining room, handed to a patient in a hospital bed or presented by a waiter or waitress. An off-hand, brusque presentation (either written or oral) can be off-putting and can lower expectations of the meal.

Essential considerations prior to planning the menu

1 The location of an establishment should allow easy access for both customers and suppliers as and when required. A difficult journey can be off-putting no matter how good the quality of food on offer and can affect repeat business and profitability. If the establishment is in an area noted for regional speciality foods or dishes, the inclusion of a selection of these on the menu can give extra menu appeal.

2 Competition in the locality – it is important to be aware of what is offered by competitors, including their prices and, particularly, their quality. As a result, it may be wiser to produce a menu quite different to those of nearby establishments.

3 Suitability of a particular establishment to a particular area – a self-service restaurant situated in an affluent residential district, or a very expensive sea-food restaurant in a run down inner-city area may not be very successful.

4 Anticipate and analyse the type of people you are planning to cater for – it may be sensible to create a menu to satisfy, for example, office workers in the city, with a fast lunch service. Also opportunities may exist for outdoor catering.

5 The spending power of the customer – a most important consideration is how much the potential customer is able and willing to pay. This is

particularly important when catering for the needs of nurses in hospitals, children in schools and workers in industry and in offices. Whatever level of catering or type of establishment, a golden rule should be to offer 'value for money'.

6 Customer requirements – it is the customer not the caterer who selects his menu, so analysis of dish popularity is necessary, and those dishes which are not popular should not stay on the menu. Customer demand must be considered, and traditional dishes and modern trends in food fashions need to be taken into account.

7 Number of items and price-range of menus – it is essential to determine the range of dishes, and whether table d'hôte or à la carte menus are to be offered. Decisions regarding the range of prices have to be made. A table d'hôte menu may be considered with an extra charge or supplement for more expensive dishes, or more than one table d'hôte menu of different prices may be more suitable.

8 Seat turnover – if space is limited, or there are many customers (and control of the time the customer occupies the seat is needed) then the menu can be adjusted to increase turnover eg more self-service items, separate service for coffee etc.

9 Space and equipment in kitchen – these will influence the composition of the menu and production of dishes. The menu-writer must be aware of any shortcomings or deficiencies in equipment and may be wary of offering dishes that are difficult to produce. Also, certain items of equipment should not be overloaded by the menu requirements eg salamander, steamers, fritures, etc.

10 Amount and capability of labour – the availability and capability of both the preparation and service staff must be considered when planning a menu. Enough able and willing staff, both in the kitchen and the restaurant, are necessary to achieve customer satisfaction with any menu.

11 Supplies and storage – menu planning is dependent on availability of supplies – that is, frequency of deliveries of the required amounts. Storage space and seasonal availability of foods need to be taken into account when planning menus.

12 Cost factor – when an establishment is run for profit the menu is a crucial consideration; *but*, even when working to a budget, the menu is *no less crucial*. Costing is the crux of the success of compiling any menu.

Planning the menu

1 Type of establishment – there will be considerable variation, for example, in menus for five star hotels and restaurants, school meals, heavy manual workers' canteens or hospitals.

2 Type of customer – especially for private parties, eg 21st birthday party, senior citizens' conference, football players after an international, visiting overseas students and a mayor's banquet, all need personal consideration.

3 Religious rules if applicable – important, as lack of knowledge or understanding can easily lead to innocently giving offence, eg kosher catering or a Muslim occasion.

4 Meat or non-meat preferences – as the number of non-meat eaters steadily increases this becomes more important.

5 Time of the year:
(a) the prevailing temperature should be considered as certain dishes suitable for cold weather may not be acceptable in mid-summer;
(b) foods in season are usually in good supply and more reasonable in price;
(c) special dishes on certain days, eg Shrove Tuesday, Christmas, Hogmanay.
6 Time of day – whether breakfast, brunch, lunch, tea, high tea, dinner, supper, snack or special function.
7 Price range – unless fair prices are charged (so that customers are satisfied that they have received good value for money) repeat business may not occur and the caterer may go out of business.
8 Number of courses – will vary according to all prior considerations.
9 Correct sequence of courses – important if the menu is to achieve a good balance.
10 Appropriate languages – always use languages customers can understand. If writing in French, support each item with an English description.
11 No repetition of wines – if using wine for more than one course, ensure that a different type is used.
12 Sensible nutritional balance – if a selection of dishes with varying nutritional contents are offered then customers can make their own choices.
13 No repetition of commodities – never repeat basic ingredients eg mushrooms, tomatoes, peas, bacon etc on one menu. If a basic ingredient is used in one course it should not reappear in any other course on the same menu.
14 No repetition of flavours – if using strong seasoning like onion, garlic or herbs such as thyme, sage or bay-leaf, do not repeat in more than one course.
15 No repetition of colours – colour of food is important to give unusual appeal, but avoid repetition of colour eg:

Celery soup	Tomato soup
Fricassée of chicken	Goulash of veal
Buttered turnips, creamed potatoes	Vichy carrots, Marquise potatoes
Meringue and vanilla ice-cream	Peach Melba

16 Texture of courses – ensure variation is given, eg food should not be all soft or all crisp, but balanced.
17 Sauces – if different sauces are served on one menu, the foundation ingredient of each sauce should vary. For example, reduced stock, demi-glace, velouté, cream, butter thickened, yogurt, quark etc.

Menu policy – summary

(a) Provide a means of communication.
(b) Establish the essential and social needs of the customer.
(c) Accurately predict what the customer is likely to buy and how much he is going to spend.

Aim

Customer satisfaction; remember who pays the bill.

(d) Purchase and prepare raw materials to pre-set standards in accordance with predictions – purchasing specifications.

(e) Skilfully portion and cost the product in order to keep within company profitability policy.
(f) Effectively control the complete operation from purchase to service on the plate.

Writing menus in French

French has been the traditional international language of professional chefs and the kitchen just as Italian has been the traditional language for music. This means that many French words cannot be exactly translated into English, particularly kitchen and menu terms. Examples such as *hors-d'oeuvre*, *roux*, *canapé* and *fleuriste* prove the point. It may or may not be considered worth while to maintain this French tradition; but, if French is used it must be used *correctly*. Not only should the spelling, grammar and pronunciation be accurate, but, if a dish is named traditionally then it must be authentic; for example, if 'meunière' is stated then it should be shallow fried, served with lemon, chopped parsley and nut-brown butter.

As a rule it is better to use correct English than incorrect French and it should be acknowledged that the function of language on the menu is to inform the customers, the kitchen and the serving staffs. It follows therefore that choice of French or English will depend upon the establishment. If the work-force consists of many nationalities or if the clientele is sophisticated or international, this will have a bearing on the language used.

Every trade or industry has its own particular terminology, and the student of catering would be wise to get to know basic French words and phrases, since students cannot predict what situations may arise when some knowledge of French would be invaluable. This is why the following information is included. It is *not* intended to perpetuate the use of French; indeed we would encourage the increased use of English.

The grammar of French menu terms

There are few rules for the writing of menus, but accuracy of gender, agreement and spelling are required. 'The' in French is translated by different words according to the gender and number (ie singular and plural):

	Singular	*Plural*
Masculine	le melon	les melons
	l'abricot	les abricots
	l'hôtel	les hôtels
Feminine	la tomate	les tomates
	l'orange	les oranges

If the singular noun begins with a vowel then the *le* or *la* changes to *l'*:

Eau (f)	l'eau	the water
Ail (m)	l'ail	the garlic

In some cases the noun begins with an 'h' and the same rule applies:

Hôtel (m)	l'hôtel	the hotel

Note Words that begin with an 'h' and do not take an 'l' are usually marked with an asterisk in the dictionary, eg le homard.

When the noun is plural – that is, when more than one item is considered, the French for 'the' is 'les':

Les saumons	les homards	les hôtels

When using 'le', 'la' or 'les' on the menu before a cut, part or joint then the gender used is *that of the cut*, *part* or *joint* and *not* that of the food of which it is part:

La darne de	la selle de	le tronçon de
La coeur de	le suprême de	le ris de
Le délice de	les goujons de	la paupiette de

The *method of cooking* the cut or piece must also agree with the cut or piece:

Les filets de sole frits	la selle d'agneau rôtie	le gigot d'agneau rôti

Verbs are often used to describe the cooking method. In the dictionary the verb is given in the *infinitive*, eg brouiller – to scramble; sauter – to toss. On the menu, they are given in the *past tense* (past participles) and follow the noun and agree with it, like an adjective, in gender and number:

Sauter – to toss	sauté – tossed, Pommes sautées
Flamber – to set alight	flambé – set alight, Pêche flambée
Concasser – to cut roughly	concassé – cut roughly, Tomates concassées

With a masculine singular noun the verb is left unaltered:
Saumon fumé
With a masculine plural noun add 's':
Champignons grillés
With a feminine singular noun add 'e':
Anguille fumée
With feminine plural noun add 'es':
Pommes persillées

Most verbs to do with cooking will end in 'er' but some end in 'ir', 're', or 'ire', and these take different spellings in the past tense, for example:

Frire – to fry	frit – fried
Fondre – to melt	fondu – melted
Bouillir – to boil	bouilli – boiled
Farcir – to stuff	farci – stuffed

The agreement rule still applies:

Cabillaud (Masc. sing.)	Cabillaud frit
Pommes (Fem. pl.)	Pommes frites
Beurre (Masc. sing.)	Beurre fondu
Boeuf (Masc. sing.)	Boeuf bouilli
Tomates (Fem. sing.)	Tomates farcies

The word 'à' has several meanings, but on the menu the usual ones are 'with' and 'in'. Changes in the translation of 'with the' and 'in the' take place according to the gender and number of the noun used:

à le becomes *au*

à la is not changed
à l' is not changed
à les becomes *aux*

Therefore 'tart with apples' (tarte à les pommes) must be written: *Tarte aux pommes*
'Skate with black butter' (raie à le beurre noir) must be written: *Raie au beurre noir*
'Homard à la Américaine' becomes *Homard à l'Américaine*
'Crêpes à le citron' becomes *Crêpes au citron*
'Chou-fleur à la grecque' remains *Chou-fleur à la grecque*

Nouns (eg as used below, apple, butter and chocolate) when following the name of the main ingredient of a dish can be singular or plural:

Raie au beurre noir	Profiteroles au chocolat	Tarte aux pommes

'De' means 'of', and the 'e' is replaced by an apostrophe before words beginning with a vowel or 'h' as with 'le' and 'la':
'Gigot de agneau' becomes *Gigot d'agneau*
'Table de hôte' becomes *table d'hôte*
'Rable de lièvre' is unchanged
'Longe de veau' is unchanged
'Filet de boeuf' is unchanged
'Bisque de homard' is unchanged

When translating 'of' between two nouns, 'de' is the only correct form:

Darne de saumon	Tronçon de barbue	Suprême de turbot
Délice de sole	Paupiette de boeuf	Beignets de pommes
Raviers de hors-d'oeuvre	Purée de marrons	Salade de tomates

On the menu the term 'of' ('de') or 'with' ('au') is used to describe the composition of a dish. If the main ingredient of the dish is described, 'de' is used:
Beignets de pommes
Salade de tomates

If the term is only part of the dish, 'au' is usually used:

Crêpes au citron	Dinde aux marrons	Omelette au jambon

The phrase 'à la mode' means 'in the style of' or 'fashion of' and is often left out of the name of the dish – but the word following which describes the fashion must agree with the noun 'la mode', which is feminine:
'Petits pois à la mode française' becomes *Petits pois à la française*.

The shortening of the phrase is even taken so far that it is not even written, but understood:
'Chou-fleur à la mode polonaise' becomes *Chou-fleur polonaise*.
'Polonaise' is feminine because it is describing a 'mode', which is feminine; it is not describing 'chou-fleur' which is masculine.

When a dish is dedicated to a particular place or person the 'à la' is omitted:

Pêche Melba	Poire Condé

'A la' can also describe a method of cooking:

Bifteck à la poêle	Pommes à la vapeur	Haddock au four

'En' used on the menu means 'in':

En tasse – Consommé en tasse	Consommé in a cup
En branche – Epinards en branche	Leaf spinach
En goujons – Sole en goujons	Sole in small strips
En colère – Merlin en colère	Curled whiting (with tail in mouth)

'Pommes purée' is written in this way because the full name would be 'pommes de terre en purée'. The purée remains singular because it is not an adjective but a noun.

Care should be taken to ensure that 'various hors-d'oeuvre' is translated as 'hors-d'oeuvre variés'.

Capital letters

Capital letters should be used sensibly when writing menus in French. Trade practice, both in France and Britain, is to capitalise all major words in the dish. However, more accurately, a capital letter should be used for the first word and for names of people, eg 'Pêche Melba', and places, 'Crème Crecy'. If it is in the style of a place eg 'Petits pois à la française' then a small letter is used.

The words used to describe a dish on a menu must agree in gender and number, for example:

A fillet of sole	Le filet de sole
Two fillets of sole	Deux filets de sole
Two fried fillets of sole	Deux filets de sole frits
Lamb	Agneau (m)
Lamb cutlet	La côtelette d'agneau
Two lamb cutlets	Deux côtelettes d'agneau
Grilled lamb cutlet	Côtelette d'agneau grillée
Two grilled lamb cutlets	Deux côtelettes d'agneau grillées

It will be noticed that the agreement is made with the cut or joint. The definite article, 'le' or 'la', if used with one dish on a menu should be used on all dishes; for example, the menu on the left is correct (see below), the one on the right is not:

Le saumon fumé	Le saumon fumé
La selle d'agneau rôtie	Selle d'agneau rôtie
Le chou-fleur; sauce hollandaise	Le chou-fleur; sauce hollandaise
Les pommes parisienne	Les pommes parisienne
La Pêche Melba	Pêche Melba

Care should be taken over the use of the term 'à la', which means 'in' or 'after the style of'. This means that it can be used when a dish is prepared in the style of a certain place, town or country, for example:

Hors-d'oeuvre à la grecque	Poulet sauté à la portugaise
Filets de sole frits à la francaise	Petits pois à la flamande

(As stated, the last word does not have a capital letter.)

When a dish of food is named after a person or place the name usually follows the food, and a capital letter is used:

Pêche Melba	Named after Dame Nellie Melba
Crème Dubarry	Named after Madame Dubarry
Salade Waldorf	Named after Waldorf Astoria Hotel, New York

When using classical garnish names, see that any vegetable which is included in the garnish is not repeated as a vegetable. For example: 'Chou-fleur Mornay' would not be put on the menu as a vegetable to be served with 'Selle d'agneau Dubarry'.

The list which follows includes some of the terms used on a menu, which signify that a specific item of food will be served. For example: 'parmentier' indicates that potatoes will be used; therefore 'purée parmentier' is potato soup; 'omelette parmentier' is an omelet garnished with potatoes:

Dubarry	cauliflower	Lyonnaise	onions
Bruxelloise	brussels sprouts	Florentine	spinach
Clamart	peas	Portugaise	tomatoes
Doria	cucumber	Princesse	asparagus
Provençale	tomato and garlic	Washington	sweet corn

Glossary of French menu and kitchen terms

l'aile (f)	wing of poultry or game birds
à la	in the style of (*à la mode*)
à la française	dishes prepared in the French way
à l'anglaise	in the English style
à la broche	cooked on a spit
à la diable	devilled, a highly seasoned dish
à la carte	dishes on a menu prepared to order and individually priced
l'aloyau (m)	sirloin of beef (on the bone)
en aspic (m)	in savoury jelly
assorti	an assortment, eg *Fromages assortis*
au bleu	when applied to meat it means very underdone. When applied to trout it is a specific dish – *Truite au bleu*
au four	cooked in the oven, eg *Pomme au four*
au gratin	sprinkled with breadcrumbs and/or cheese and browned
au vin blanc	with white wine
la blanquette	a white stew cooked in stock from which the sauce is made, eg *Blanquette de veau*
la bombe	an ice cream of different flavours in the shape of a bomb
la bordure	a ring, sometimes of rice or potatoes
les bouchées	small puff-pastry cases
bouilli	boiled
le bouquet garni	a faggot or bundle of herbs, usually parsley stalks, thyme and bay leaf, tied inside pieces of celery and leek
braisé	braised
la braisière	braising pan
en branche	a term denoting vegetables, such as spinach, cooked and served as whole leaves
la brioche	a light yeast cake
la broche	a roasting spit
la brochette	a skewer

brouillé	scrambled, eg *Œufs brouillés*
le buffet	a sideboard of food, or a self-service table
le canapé	a cushion of toasted or fried bread on which are served various foods. It is used as a base for savouries. When served cold as 'Canapé moscovite' the base may be toast, biscuit or short or puff-paste pieces with the food on top and finished with aspic
la carte du jour	menu, or bill of fare for the day
en casserole	in a fireproof dish
Chantilly	sweetened, whipped vanilla-flavoured cream
la charlotte	name given to various hot and cold sweet dishes which have a case of biscuits, bread, sponge, etc
le chateaubriand	the head of the fillet of beef
chaud	hot
le chaud-froid	a creamed velouté or demi-glace with gelatine or aspic added, used for masking cold dishes
le civet	a brown stew of game, usually hare
clair	clear
la cloche	a bell-shaped cover, used for special *à la carte* dishes, eg *Suprême de volaille sous cloche*
la cocotte	porcelain fireproof dish
la compote	stewed fruit, eg *Compote des poires*
concassé	coarsely chopped, eg parsley and tomatoes
le consommé	basic clear soup
le contrefilet	boned sirloin of beef
le cordon	a thread or thin line of sauce
la côte	rib, eg *Côte de bœuf*
la côtelette	cutlet
coupe	cut; also ice-cream dish
le court-bouillon	a cooking liquor for certain foods, eg oily fish, calf's brains, etc. It is water containing vinegar, sliced onions, carrots, herbs and seasoning
la crème fouettée	whipped cream
la crêpe	pancake
le croquette	cooked foods moulded cylinder shape, egg and crumbed and deep fried, eg *Croquette de volaille*
la croûte	a cushion of fried or toasted bread on which are served various hot foods, eg savouries, game stuffing, etc.
le croûton	cubes of fried bread served with soup, also triangular pieces which may be served with spinach and heart-shaped ones which may be served with certain braised vegetables and entrées
les crustacés (m)	shellfish
la cuisse de poulet	leg of chicken
la darne	a slice of round fish cut through with the bone, eg *Darne de saumon*
le déjeuner	lunch
le petit-déjeuner	breakfast
le dîner	dinner
doré	golden
du jour (plat du jour)	special dish of the day
duxelles	finely chopped mushrooms cooked with chopped shallots

émincé	sliced
l'entrecôte (f)	a steak from a boned sirloin
l'escalope (f)	thin slice of meat
étuvée	cooked in its own juice
la farce	stuffing
farci	stuffed
le feuilletage	puff paste
les fines herbes	chopped parsley, tarragon and chervil
flambé	flamed or lit, eg *Poire flambée*
le flan	open fruit tart
le fleuron	small crescent pieces of puff paste used for garnishing certain dishes, eg fish and vegetable
le foie	liver
le foie gras	fat goose liver
le fondant	a kind of icing
fondu	melted
le four	oven
frappé	chilled, eg *Melon frappé*
les friandises	petits fours, sweetmeats, etc
la fricassée	a white stew in which the poultry or meat is cooked in the sauce
frisé	curled
fumé	smoked, eg *Saumon fumé*
le fumet	a concentrated stock or essence
la garniture	the trimmings on the dish
le gâteau	cake
la gelée	jelly
le gibier	game
la glace	ice or ice cream
glacé	iced
glacer	to glaze under the salamander
gratiner	to colour or gratinate under the salamander or in a hot oven using grated cheese or breadcrumbs
grillé	grilled
hacher	to chop finely or very finely dice – to mince
les herbes (f)	herbs
hors-d'œuvre	preliminary dishes of an appetising nature, served hot or cold
le jambon froid	cold ham
jardinière	cut into batons
julienne	cut into fine strips
le jus-lié	gravy thickened with arrowroot or cornflour or *fécule*
le kari	curry
liaison	name given to yolks of eggs and cream when used as a thickening
lier	to thicken
la longe	loin
losange	diamond shaped
macédoine	(a) a mixture of fruit or vegetables, eg *Macédoine de fruits* – fruit salad (b) cut into 6 mm dice

macérer	to steep, to soak, to macerate
la marinade	a richly spiced pickling liquid for enriching the flavour and tenderness of meats before braising
mariné	pickled
la madère	madeira wine
marbré	marbled
masquer	to mask
médaillon	foodstuffs prepared in a round, flat shape
le menu	bill of fare
mignonette	coarse ground or crushed pepper
les mille-feuilles (f)	'thousand leaves', a puff-pastry cream slice
à la minute	cooked to order
mirepoix	roughly cut onions, carrots, celery and a sprig of thyme and bay leaf
mollet	soft, eg *Œuf mollet*
le moule	mould
la mousse	a hot or cold dish of light consistency, sweet or savoury
la moutarde	mustard
moutarder	to smear with mustard, or to add mustard to a sauce
mûr	ripe, mature
natives (f)	a menu term denoting English oysters
navarin	a brown lamb or mutton stew
le nid	nest – imitation nest made from potatoes or sugar etc.
la noisette *or* **noisette**	(a) a hazelnut used in confectionery (b) small round potatoes cut with a special scoop (c) as for noisette butter (nut-brown butter) (d) a cut of loin of lamb
la noix	nut, also the name given to the cushion piece of the leg of veal (*Noix de veau*)
les nouilles (f)	noodles, a flat Italian paste
œuf brouillé	a scrambled egg
œuf en cocotte	egg cooked in an egg cocotte
œuf à la coque	egg boiled and served in its shell
œuf dur	a hard-boiled egg
œuf mollet	a soft-boiled shelled egg
œuf poché	a poached egg
œuf sur le plat	egg cooked in an egg dish
œuf à la poêle	a fried egg
l'oignon (m)	onion
l'olive farcie	stoned and stuffed olive
l'olive tournée (f)	a stoned olive
l'orge (f)	barley
oseille (f)	sorrel
les pailles (f)	straws (*Pommes pailles*, straw potatoes)
les paillettes de fromage (f)	cheese straws
le pain	bread
panaché	mixed
pané	crumbed
panier	basket
papain	a proteolytic enzyme sometimes called vegetable pepsin

papillote	foods cooked *en papillote* are cooked in greased greaseproof paper in their own steam in the oven
la pâte	a dough, paste, batter, pie or pastie
la pâtisserie	a pastry
la paupiette	a strip of fish, meat or poultry stuffed and rolled
paysanne	cut into even thin triangles, round or square pieces
le pilon	the drumstick of a leg of chicken
le piment	pimento
piquant	sharp flavour
piqué	studded
poivre	pepper
poêlé	pot roasted
la pointe d'asperge	asparagus tip
la praline	chopped grilled almonds or hazelnuts or crushed almond toffee
primeurs	early vegetables
printanière	garnish of spring vegetables
profiteroles	small balls of *choux* paste for garnishing soups or as a sweet course
la purée	a smooth mixture obtained by passing food through a sieve
la quenelle	forcemeat of poultry, fish, game or meat, pounded, sieved and shaped, then usually poached
la râble	the back, eg *Râble de lièvre* – the saddle of a hare
le ragoût	stew
le ravioli	an Italian paste, stuffed with various ingredients including meat, spinach and brains
le risotto	Italian rice stewed in stock
le ris	sweetbread
rissolé	fry to a golden brown
rôti	roast
le sabayon	yolks of eggs and a little liquid cooked till creamy
sauté	tossed in fat or turned in fat; also a specific meat dish
soubise	an onion purée
le soufflé	a light dish, sweet or savoury, hot or cold. Whites of egg are added to the hot basic preparation and whipped cream to the cold
le suprême	when applied to poultry it means whole wing and half the breast of the bird (there are two *suprêmes* to a bird). For other foods it is applied to a choice cut
table d'hôte	a meal of several courses, which may have a limited choice, served at a fixed price
la terrine	an earthenware utensil with a lid. A terrine also indicates a pâté cooked and served in one
tomaté	preparations to which tomato purée has been added to dominate the flavour and colour
tourné	turned, shaped (barrel or olive shape)
la tranche	a slice
le tronçon	a slice of flat fish cut with the bone, eg *Tronçon de turbot*
le velouté	(a) basic sauce (b) soup of velvet or cream consistency

vert	green, eg *Sauce verte*
voiler	to veil or cover with spun sugar
la volaille	poultry
le vol-au-vent	puff pastry case

Further information

Schneider and Powrie, *Le Français dans L'Hôtellerie* (Edward Arnold); Grisbrooke, *French for Catering Students* (Edward Arnold); Atkinson, *Menu French* (Pergamon, 1980).

Names used in traditional fish cookery to indicate garnishes and the mode of cooking and serving

Name of classical garnish	*Composition of garnish*	*Menu example*
Bercy	poached with chopped shallots, parsley, fish stock and white wine; finished with white wine sauce and glazed	Filets de sole Bercy
bonne-femme	as for Bercy, with the addition of sliced mushrooms, glazed	Suprême de turbot bonne-femme
Bréval or d'Antin	as for bonne-femme, with the addition of chopped tomatoes, glazed	Suprême de barbue Bréval
Véronique	poached with white wine and fish stock; coated with white wine sauce; glazed and garnished with grapes	Sole Véronique
dieppoise	poached; coated with white wine sauce, garnished with mussels, shrimps' tails and mushrooms	Suprême de carrelet dieppoise
Dugléré	poached with chopped shallots, parsley, tomatoes, fish stock; coated with a sauce made from the cooking liquor	Filet d'aigrefin Dugléré
Mornay	poached; coated with cheese sauce and glazed	Coquille de cabillaud Mornay
florentine	poached; dressed on a bed of leaf spinach; coated with Mornay sauce and glazed	Suprême de turbotin florentine
hollandaise	plain boiled; served with hollandaise sauce and plain boiled potatoes	Tronçon de turbot hollandaise
meunière	shallow fried on both sides; garnished with slice of lemon; coated with nut-brown butter, lemon juice and parsley	Truite de rivière meunière
belle meunière	as meunière, with the addition of grilled mushroom, a slice of peeled tomato, and a soft herring-roe (passed through flour and shallow fried) (all neatly dressed on each portion of fish)	Sole belle meunière
Doria	as for meunière, with a sprinkling of small, turned, cooked pieces of cucumber	Suprême de flétan Doria
grenobloise	as for meunière, with the lemon in peeled segments and capers	Rouget grenobloise
bretonne	as for meunière, with picked shrimps and sliced mushrooms	Filet d'aigrefin bretonne
princesse	poached; coated with white wine sauce; garnished with asparagus heads and slices of truffle	Délices de sole princesse
Saint-Germain	filleted white fish dipped in butter, breadcrumbed, grilled; served with béarnaise sauce and noisette potatoes	Filets de plie St-Germain
Orly	deep fried and served with tomato sauce	Filet de cabillaud à l'Orly

Some traditional meat and poultry garnishes with suitable menu examples

Name of classical garnish	*Composition of garnish*	*Use of garnish*	*Menu term: example using garnish*
boulangère	onions and potatoes	for roast lamb joints	Gigot d'agneau boulangère
bouquetière	artichoke bottoms, carrots, turnips, peas, French beans, cauliflower, château potatoes	for roast joints, usually beef	Filet de bœuf bouquetière
bourgeoise	carrots, onions, dice of bacon	for large joints	Bœuf braisé bourgeoise
bruxelloise	braised chicory, brussels sprouts, château potatoes	for large joints	Noix de veau bruxelloise
Clamart	artichoke bottoms filled with peas à la française or purée of peas and château potatoes	for large joints	Carré d'agneau Clamart
Dubarry	small balls of cauliflower Mornay, château potatoes	for large joints	Contrefilet de bœuf Dubarry
fermière	paysanne of carrot, turnips, onions, celery	for large joints	Poulet en casserole fermière
fleuriste	tomatoes filled with carrots, turnips, peas, French beans; château potatoes	for tournedos and noisettes	Noisette d'agneau fleuriste
Henri IV	pont-neuf potatoes and watercress	for tournedos and noisettes	Tournedos Henri IV
jardinière	carrots, turnips, French beans, flageolets, peas and cauliflower coated with hollandaise sauce	for joints	Selle d'agneau jardinière
judic	stuffed tomatoes, braised lettuce, château potatoes	for joints	Longe d'agneau judic
mascotte	quarters of artichoke bottoms, cocotte potatoes, slices of truffle	for joints and poultry	Poulet sauté mascotte
Mercédès	grilled tomatoes, grilled mushrooms, braised lettuce, croquette potatoes	for joints	Selle de veau mercédès
Parmentier	1 cm dice of fried potatoes	for tournedos, noisettes and poultry	Poulet sauté Parmentier
portugaise	small stuffed tomatoes, château potatoes	for tournedos, noisettes and poultry	Tournedos à la portugaise
printanier	turned carrots and turnips, peas, dice of French beans	for entrées, stews	Navarin d'agneau printanier
Réforme	short batons of beetroot, white of egg, gherkin, mushroom, truffle and tongue	for lamb or mutton cutlets	Côtelette d'agneau Réforme
Sévigné	braised lettuce, grilled mushrooms, château potatoes	for tournedos, noisettes and joints	Carré de veau Sévigné
Soubise	onion purée or sauce	for cuts of mutton	Côte de mouton Soubise
tyrolienne	French fried onions, tomate concassé	for small cuts of meat	Noisette d'agneau tyrolienne
vert pré	straw potatoes and watercress	for grilled meats	Entrecôte vert pré
Vichy	with Vichy carrots	for entrées	Blanquette de veau Vichy
Washington	sweetcorn	for eggs and poultry	Poularde poêlé Washington
duxelle	finely chopped shallots and chopped mushrooms	this is a basic culinary preparation with many uses – for example, stuffed vegetables, sauces, etc	

Names used in traditional sweet dishes to indicate a particular ingredient

Name	*Composition*	*Menu example*
Chantilly	whipped, sweetened, vanilla-flavoured cream	Meringue Chantilly
glacé	with ice cream	Meringue glacé Chantilly
meringuée	finished with piped meringue and glazed	Flan aux pommes meringuées
normande	with apple	Crêpes normande
Rubané	with different flavours and colours	Bavarois Rubané
Montmorency	with cherries	Coupe Montmorency
Condé	with rice	Poire Condé
Moka	coffee flavour	Glace moka
Suchard	chocolate flavour	Profiteroles, sauce Suchard
praliné	with chopped almond and hazel-nut toffee	Gâteau praliné
Melba	with vanilla ice cream and raspberry purée or sauce	Pêche Melba
cardinal	with strawberry ice cream and raspberry sauce, sliced almonds	Fraises cardinal
Hélène	vanilla ice cream, hot chocolate sauce	Poire Hélène
Jamaïque	rum flavour	Coupe Jamaïque

Examples of different menus

Breakfast menus

A breakfast menu can be compiled from the following foods:

1 *Fruits:* Grapefruit, orange, melon, apple.
Fruit juices: Grapefruit, orange, tomato, pineapple.
Stewed fruit: Prunes, figs, apples, pears.
Yogurt: A selection.
2 *Cereals:* Cornflakes, shredded wheat, etc, porridge.
3 *Eggs:* Fried, boiled, poached, scrambled; omelets with bacon (streaky, back or gammon) or tomatoes, mushrooms or sauté potatoes.
4 *Fish:* Grilled herrings, kippers or bloaters; fried sole, plaice or whiting; fish cakes, smoked haddock, kedgeree.
5 *Meats (hot):* Fried or grilled bacon (streaky, back or gammon), sausages, kidneys, calves' liver, with tomatoes, mushrooms or sauté potatoes, potato cakes or bubble and squeak.
6 *Meats (cold):* Ham, bacon, pressed beef with sauté potatoes.
7 *Preserves:* Marmalade (orange, lemon, grapefruit, ginger), jams, honey.
8 *Fresh fruits:* Apple, pear, peach, grapes, etc.
9 *Beverages:* Tea, coffee, chocolate.
10 *Bread:* Rolls, croissants, brioche, toast, pancakes, waffles.

Fruit Juice — Orange, Grapefruit or Tomato
Fresh Grapefruit or Orange Segments

Stewed Fruits — Prunes, Figs or Apricots

Fresh Fruit Selection, Fresh Fruit Salad

Yogurts

Choice of Cereals, Porridge or Mix your own Muesli

Baker's Selection

Croissant, White and Wholemeal Rolls, Continental Pastry

Your choice of White or Brown Toast

Marmalade, Preserve, Honey, Country Butter or Flora Margarine

Cold Ham and Cheese

English Breakfast Tea with Milk or Lemon

Coffee — Freshly Brewed or Decaffeinated
with Milk or Cream

Hot Chocolate, Cold Milk
Chilled Ashbourne Water

Fig. 4.1 Example of a continental breakfast menu

A LA CARTE

FRUITS & JUICES

Fresh Orange or Grapefruit Juice £. . . .Large £. . . .
Pineapple, Tomato or Prune Juice £. . . .Large £. . . .
Chilled Melon £. . . . Stewed Prunes £. . . .Half Grapefruit £. . . .
Stewed Figs £. . . . Fresh fruit in Season £. . . .

BREAKFAST FAVOURITES

Porridge or Cereal £. . . .
Eggs, any style: One £. . . . Two £. . . .
Ham, Bacon, Chipolata Sausages or Grilled Tomato £. . . .
Omelette, Plain £. . . . with Ham or Cheese £. . . .
Grilled Gammon Ham £. . . . Breakfast Sirloin Steak £. . . .
A Pair of Kippers £. . . . Smoked Haddock with a Poached Egg £. . . .
Pancakes with Maple Syrup £. . . .

FROM OUR BAKERY

Croissants or Breakfast Rolls £. . . . Brioche £. . . .
Assorted Danish Pastries £. . . . Toast £. . . .

BEVERAGES

Tea, Coffee, Sanka, Chocolate or Milk £. . . .

Service Charge 15%

Fig. 4.2 Example of an English à la carte breakfast menu

Points to consider when compiling a breakfast menu:

(a) It is usual to offer three of the courses previously mentioned on p. 55. For example see menu below:

Fruit, Yogurt, or Cereals
Fish, Eggs or Meat
Preserves, Bread, Coffee or Tea

(b) As large a menu as possible, should be offered, depending on the size of the establishment, bearing in mind that it is better to offer a smaller number of well-prepared dishes than a large number of hurriedly prepared ones.

(c) A choice of plain foods such as boiled eggs or poached haddock should be available for the person who may not require a fried breakfast.

Breakfast menus may be table d'hôte or à la carte; a continental breakfast does not include any cooked dish. A typical continental breakfast would offer: rolls and butter, croissants, toast, preserves, tea or coffee.

Luncheon menus

A luncheon table d'hôte menu may offer a choice of dishes or may be a set meal with little or no choice, depending on the type of establishment. If a special party luncheon menu is required, three or four courses are usually offered, for example:

LUNCHEON MENU

Cocktail of Melon and Exotic Fruits

☆☆☆

Steak, Kidney and Mushroom Pudding
Creamed Potatoes
Fresh Market Vegetables

☆☆☆

Stilton and Cheddar
Biscuits and Celery

☆☆☆

Coffee
Petits Fours

Fig. 4.3 Luncheon menu

MENU

Filet de Truite de Rivière Fumé
Raifort Chantilly
Fillet of Smoked Trout with Horseradish Mousse

***

Consommé Julienne
Beef Consommé with Vegetable Julienne

***

Escalope de Veau à la Crème de Fenouil
Veal Escalope in a Fennel Cream Sauce

Légumes du Marché
Seasonal Vegetables

Riz Pilaf
Pilaf Rice

***

Salade de Fruits Frais Refraîchis au Kirsch
Crème Fraîche
Fresh Fruit Salad with Kirsch and Cream

***

Café

Fig. 4.4 Luncheon menu

Served throughout 24 hours

SANDWICH SELECTIONS

Club House: Sliced Turkey Breast, Bacon, Lettuce, Tomato and Mayonnaise £. . . .
Ham and Swiss Cheese £. . . . Tuna Fish Salad £. . . .
Cold Roast Beef £. . . . Turkey Breast £. . . .
Chicken Breast £. . . .

HOT SPECIALITIES

The following are served with French Fried Potatoes

Grilled Chopped Steak on a Toasted Bun £. . . .
Grilled Chopped Steak accompanied by a Fried egg,
Bacon, and a Grilled tomato £. . . .
Calf's Liver and Bacon £. . . . Omelettes to Choice £. . . .
Vegetables and Side Salads to Choice £. . . .

BREADS, PASTRIES AND ICE CREAMS

Gateaux £. . . . Toast and Butter £. . . .
Assorted Danish or French Pastries £. . . . Brown Bread and Butter £. . . .
Assorted Ice Creams £. . . . Assorted Biscuits £. . . .
Full Afternoon Tea £. . . .

BEVERAGES

Tea, Coffee, Sanka, Chocolate or Milk £. . . .

Fig. 4.5 Example of a hotel coffee shop menu

Petite Nage de Coquilles St Jacques au Safran et Petits Légumes
Scallops with Small Vegetables in a light Saffron Sauce

***

Rosette de Boeuf aux Endives Braisées et à l'Ail Doux
Fillet of Beef with Braised Belgium Endives and Sweet Garlic in a Red Wine Sauce

Pommes Tournées au Fond de Volaille
Turned Potatoes in Chicken Bouillon

Panaché de Légumes en Saison
Panaché of Vegetables in Season

***

Quenelle de Blanc d'Oeuf, Sauce Vanille
Poached Italian Meringue in a Vanilla Sauce

***

Café
Petits Fours

Fig. 4.6 Special lunch party menu

Almost all foods are suitable for serving at luncheon. In warm weather cold dishes are popular and a cold buffet could be available.

Only offer the number of courses and the number of dishes within each course that can be well prepared, cooked and served.

Luncheon menus, both table d'hôte and à la carte, can be compiled from the following foods:

Fruit cocktails: Melon, grapefruit, orange, Florida.
Fruits: Melon, grapefruit, avocado pear.
Fruit juices: Grapefruit, orange, pineapple, tomato.
Shellfish, etc: Potted shrimps, prawns, oysters, caviar, snails, crabmeat.
Shellfish cocktails: Lobster, crab, prawn, shrimp.
Smoked fish or meat: Salmon, trout, eel, sprats, buckling, mackerel, roe, ham, salami.
Hors-d'œuvre: Assorted or simple items, light salads with a vegetable, fish, meat or game content.

Soup: Consommé with simple garnish. Cold in summer.
Vegetable soups, cream soup, eg mushroom. Also chicken, minestrone, Scotch broth etc.

Farinaceous: Spaghetti, macaroni, ravioli, canneloni, gnocchi (romaine, parisienne), nouilles, risotto, pizza and quiche.

Eggs: When served for a luncheon menu egg dishes are usually garnished.
Scrambled, poached, soft boiled, en cocotte, sur le plat, omelet.

Fish: (Nearly all kinds of fish can be served, but without complicated garnishes. They are usually steamed, poached, boiled, grilled, deep or shallow fried.)
Mussels, scallops, herrings, skate, whiting, plaice, cod, turbot, brill, sole, scampi, trout, salmon trout, salmon, monkfish, whitebait, kedgeree. Dishes to include various fish in light sauces.

Entrée: (This is a dish of meat, game or poultry which is not roasted or grilled.)

Brown stews (ragoût de bœuf, navarin de mouton).
Braised steaks, braised beef, civet de lièvre.
Goulash, braised oxtail, salmis of game.
Hot pot, Irish stew.
Meat pies, chicken pies.
Meat puddings.
Boiled meat (French and English style).
Fricassé, blanquette.
Calves' head, tripe, sautéd kidneys.
Vienna and Hamburg steaks, hamburgers.
Sausages, minced meat, chicken émincé.
Fried lamb, veal or pork cutlets or fillets.
Fried steaks (entrecôte, tournedos, fillets, etc).
Veal escalopes, sweetbreads.
Vol-au-vent of chicken or sweetbreads or both.
Sauerkraut, pilaff, kebab, chicken cutlets.
Vegetarian and ethnic dishes

Roasts: Beef, pork, veal, lamb, mutton, chicken.

Grills: Steaks (chateaubriand, fillet, tournedos, point, rump).
Porterhouse, entrecôte.
Cutlets (single, double).
Chops (loin, chump).
Kidneys, mixed grill, chicken, chicken legs, kebabs.

Cold buffet: Salmon, lobster, crab.
Pâté or terrine.
Beef, ham, tongue, lamb.
Chicken, chicken pie, raised pies.
Vegetarian dishes.
Salads.

Vegetables: Cabbage, cauliflower, French beans, spinach, peas, carrots, tomatoes, etc. Asparagus, globe artichoke (hot or cold with suitable sauce).
Potatoes: Boiled, steamed, sautéd, fried, roast, creamed, croquette, lyonnaise, etc.

Sweets: Steamed puddings (fruit and sponge).
Milk puddings.
Fruit (stewed, fools, flans, salad, pies, fritters).
Egg custard sweets (baked, bread and butter, cream, caramel, diplomat, cabinet).
Bavarois, savarin, baba.
Charlottes, profiteroles, gâteaux.
Pastries (mille-feuille, éclairs, etc).
Various ices and sorbets.

Savouries: Simple savouries may also be served: for example, Welsh rarebit.

Cheese: A good selection of cheese. Biscuits, celery and radishes.

Dessert: Fresh fruit of all kinds and nuts.
Coffee or tea.

A vegetarian menu may be offered as an alternative to or as a part of the à la carte or table d'hôte menus.

VEGETARIAN MENU

Iced Cucumber Soup
(Flavoured with mint)

Avocado Waldorf
(Filled with celery & apple bound in mayonnaise, garnished with walnuts)

***

Vegetable Lasagne
(Layers of pasta & vegetables with melted cheese, served with salad)

Mushroom Stroganoff
(Flamed in brandy, simmered in cream with paprika & mustard, served with rice)

Chilli con Elote
(Seasonal fresh vegetables in a chilli & tomato fondue, served with rice)

Poached Eggs Elizabeth
(Set on buttered spinach, coated in a rich cream sauce)

Fig. 4.7 Example of a vegetarian menu

Tea menus

These vary considerably, depending on the type of establishment. The high-class hotel will usually offer a dainty menu. For example:

Sandwiches (smoked salmon, ham, tongue, egg, tomato, cucumber) made with white or brown bread.

HIGH TEA

A very popular meal in Scotland, eaten late afternoon in lieu of dinner.
Often enjoyed by the highland farmer who afterwards
would secure the animals for the night.

☆☆☆☆☆

Fried Haddock in Breadcrumbs
served with Chipped Potatoes

or

Traditional Scottish Mixed Grill
Consisting of
Two Rashers Ayrshire Bacon, 1 slice of Black Pudding,
1 slice of Beef Sausage, Fried Egg, Grilled Liver
served with Chipped Potatoes

☆☆☆☆☆

Brown Bread and Butter

☆☆☆☆☆

Choice of Assorted Scottish Tea Breads
(Girdle Scones, Pancakes, Crumpets)

or

Selection of Scottish Cakes
(Dundee Cake, Gingerbread, Shortbread)

☆☆☆☆☆

Scottish Preserves
(including Wild Bramble Jelly, and Blackcurrant)

☆☆☆☆☆

The Scottish High Tea
is reckoned to be the most pleasant hour of the day

Fig. 4.8 Example of a high tea menu

Bread and butter (white, brown, fruit loaf).
Jams, honey, lemon curd.
Small pastries, assorted gâteaux.
Fruit salad and cream, ices.
Tea (Indian, China, Russian, iced).

The commercial hotels, public restaurants and canteens will offer simple snacks, cooked meals and high teas. For example:

Assorted sandwiches.
Buttered buns, scones, tea cakes, Scotch pancakes, waffles, sausage rolls, assorted bread and butter, various jams, toasted tea-cakes, scones, crumpets, buns.
Eggs (boiled, poached, fried, omelets).

Fried fish; grilled meats; roast poultry.
Cold meats and salads.
Assorted pastries; gâteaux.
Various ices, coupes, sundaes.
Tea; orange and lemon squash.

Dinner menus

A list of some of the foods suitable for dinner menus is given below, and both table d'hôte and à la carte menus should offer a sensible choice, depending upon the size of the establishment, and the capabilities of the staff.

The number of courses on special party menus can be from three upwards. The occasions for special dinner parties are often very important for the guest attending, therefore the compiling of such a menu is extremely important, calling for expert knowledge and wise judgement on the part of the caterer. The following are some traditional and classical dishes which may be used with light contemporary style dishes:

Cocktail: Fruit and shellfish.
Fruit: Melon, fresh figs, avocado pear.
Delicacies: Caviar, oysters, snails, potted shrimps, prawns, foie gras.
Smoked: Salmon, trout, ham, salami, sausages, sprats, eel.
Hors-d'œuvre.

Soup: Clear and consommé based, petite marmite, shellfish bisques and cream soups, turtle soup, Germiny, velouté Agnès Sorel, soupe à l'oignon, etc.
Cold soups include vichyssoise and consommé.

Fish: Poached salmon, turbot, trout (au bleu).
Shallow poached: Sole, turbot, brill, halibut, with a classical or contemporary style sauce and garnish.
Hot shellfish: Scampi, oyster, crab, lobster.
Meunière: Sole, fillets of sole – grenobloise, belle meunière.
Fried: Sole, fillets of sole, goujons, scampi.
Grilled: Lobster, sole, salmon.
Cold: Salmon, salmon trout, trout, sole.
Combinations of several fish in delicately flavoured sauces.

Entrée: Light entrée dishes are used which are small and garnished. Vegetables are not served with an entrée if it is followed by a relevé or roast with vegetables. Examples are:

Sweetbreads, quail.
Sauté of chicken, tournedos, noisettes or cutlets of lamb.
Suprême de volaille sous-cloche, etc.
Saddle of hare, filet mignon, vol-au-vent.

Relevé: This is usually a joint which is carved and is cooked by braising or poêler such as:

Poularde poêlée aux champignons.

Starters

Terrine of duck liver with muscat
jelly and toasted butter bread

South coast seafood bouillabaisse flavoured
with fennel, saffron and tomato

Tart of asparagus with sweet onions,
chives and scented with lemon

Oysters spiked with oriental spices
and glazed under a light curry and
mango sauce

Crottin of wood pigeon bound with
wild mushroom, thyme, savoy cabbage
and wrapped in filo pastry

A salad of mixed spring leaves
with scallops and artichokes

Main Courses

Rossette of Angus beef with roasted
shallots, caramelised in ruby wine

Canon of new season lamb with a
tartlet of crayfish glazed under a
mint scented sabyon

Veal sweetbreads braised with
baby onions and smoked bacon

Pot roasted baby guinea fowl with potato
and onion galette served with a sauce
of pink grapefruit spiked with grey pepper

Steamed fillet of veal with poppy
seed mustard, spring vegetables
and a tarragon butter fondue

Seabass steamed in a sauce of
ginger and lime

Fillet of halibut panfried with leek,
woodland mushrooms and tomato

Desserts

Wild crispy tuille with Devonshire ice cream
and fresh fruit

Gratin of oranges encircling a brandy
snap basket with an orange sherbet

British unpasteurised farmhouse cheeses
from James of Beckenham

Rich chocolate slice layered with pistachio
ice cream and pear sorbet

A mirror of blackcurrants served with
its own puree

Hot apple tart with calvados ice cream
and vanilla custard

Coffee, teas, tisanes served with
homemade chocolates
£2.50

All prices are inclusive of VAT & Service

Fig. 4.9 Example of a dinner menu

LES DESSERTS

Flan au Trois Fruits
Trio de Coulis
Glazed Sponge Flan filled with Pastry Cream, Strawberries, Kiwi and Mango
Served on a Strawberry, Kiwi and Mango Coulis

Summer Pudding
Pudding made from soft fruits
Served on a Coulis of Red Fruits

Oeuf à la Neige Regane
Poached Meringues topped with fresh poached Apricots and Vanilla Sauce Anglaise

Kahlua Imperial
Coulis d'Ananas
Cream Torte made with pure Kahlua Coffee Liqueur and chopped Pineapple
Served on a fresh Pineapple Coulis

Mille-Feuilles au Myrtilles
Coulis de Mirabelle
Puff Pastry and Chocolate Sponge filled with Blackberries and Cream and served on a Mirabelle Plum Coulis

Parfait à l'Orange au Chocolat
Sauce Chocolat au Lait
Frozen Parfait flavoured Orange with Chocolate pieces
Served on a Milk Chocolate Sauce scattered with Orange Chocolate Flakes

Chef Patissier

Fig. 4.10 Dessert menu

Poulet en casserole bonne-femme.
Selle d'agneau poêlée bouquetière.
Contrefilet de bœuf poêlé.
Braised ham, tongue, duck, pheasant, pigeon.

The relevé is served with a good quality vegetable and potatoes.

Vegetable: French beans, broccoli, asparagus points, peas, broad beans, button brussels sprouts, aubergine, cauliflower, etc.

Potatoes: Parmentier, noisette, olivette, dauphine, nouvelles, rissolées, Mireille, duchesse, Byron, Rösti, etc.

Sorbet: This is a lightly frozen water ice sometimes flavoured with a liqueur or champagne and served with a wafer. Sorbets are served when several courses are offered to refresh the palate before proceeding with the remainder of the meal.

DINNER MENU

Cocktail de Crevettes et Avocat
(Prawn and Avocado Cocktail)

***

Consommé de Volaille en Surprise
(Clear Chicken Soup cooked under a Pastry Case)

***

Tournedos Soufflé 'Melton Mowbray'
(Fillet Steak topped with a Stilton Mousse)
Pommes Nouvelles Rissolées
(Roasted New Potatoes)
Légumes du Marché
(Fresh Market Vegetables)

***

Mousse au Chocolat Noir et Blanc
(Chocolate Mousse)

***

Café
Friandises

Fig. 4.11 Example of a dinner menu

DINNER MENU

Viande de Grisson et Melon
(Cured Ham and Melon)

***

Darne de Saumon Pochée, Sauce aux Fines Herbes
(Poached Salmon Steak with a Fine Herb Sauce)
Pommes Nouvelles
(New Potatoes)
Légumes du Marché
(Fresh Market Vegetables)

***

Biscuit Roulé aux Noisettes
(Home Made Hazelnut Ice Cream)

***

Galette au Fromage
(Puff Pastry filled with Hot Cheese and Mustard)

***

Café
Petits Fours

Fig. 4.12 Example of a dinner menu

Roast: The roast may be served with a compound salad.
Examples of roasts are:

Saddle of lamb or veal, fillet or sirloin of beef.
Poultry or game such as chicken, turkey, duck, goose, grouse, partridge, pheasant, snipe, woodcock, guinea fowl, wild duck, plover, teal, venison, saddle of hare.

Cold dish: Such dishes as chicken in aspic or mousse de foie gras or jambon may be served.

Vegetarian dishes should be a regular feature on menus.

Sweet: Light sweets, eg soufflés, pancakes.
Cold, iced soufflé, bombes, coupes with fruit such as peaches, strawberries, raspberries, sorbet, posset, syllabub, mousse, bavarois.
Friandises, mignardises or frivolités (these are different names for very small pastries, sweets, biscuits, etc also known as 'petit fours').
Coffee or tea.

Savoury: Any hot savouries prepared in neat, small portions may be used on dinner menus.

Cheese: All varieties may be offered.

Dessert: All dessert fruits and nuts may be served.

Banquet menus

When compiling banquet menus certain points should be considered:

1 The food, which will possibly be for a large number of people, must be dressed in such a way that it can be served fairly quickly. Heavily garnished dishes should be avoided.
2 If a large number of dishes have to be dressed at the same time certain foods deteriorate quickly and do not stand storage, even for a short time in a hot plate – for example, deep-fried foods.

Banquet luncheon menus

A normal luncheon menu is used, bearing in mind the number of people involved. It is not usual to serve farinaceous dishes, eggs, stews or savouries. A luncheon menu could be drawn from the following and would usually consist of three or more courses.

First course
Soup, cocktail (fruit or shellfish), hors-d'œuvre, assorted or single item.

Second course
Fish, usually poached fillets with a sauce.

LUNCHEON MENU

Filet de Saumon d'Ecosse Parisienne
(Cold Fillet of Scotch Salmon with Salad garnish)

***

Suprême de Pintade Poêlé au Calvados
(Breast of Guinea Fowl with Calvados Sauce)
Pommes de Jersey
(Jersey Potatoes)
Légumes du Marché
(Fresh Market Vegetables)

***

Parfait Glacé aux Noisettes
(Home Made Parfait Ice Cream with Hazelnuts

***

Café
Petits Fours

Fig. 4.13 Example of a luncheon banquet menu

Third course
Meat, hot or cold, but not a stew or made-up dish. Vegetables and potatoes or a salad would be served.

Fourth course
If the function is being held during the asparagus season, then either hot or cold asparagus with a suitable sauce may be served as a course on its own.

Fifth course
Sweet, hot or cold, and/or cheese and biscuits.

Banquet dinner menus
Here the caterer has the opportunity to excel, as can be seen from the example given in Fig. 4.14.

Functions and banquets

It will be necessary to know the nature of function, as special facilities may be required. The type of function could be a wedding breakfast, silver or golden wedding anniversary, coming of age, retirement, presentation, conference, etc.

Avocat farci au fromage avec ses deux coulis
Avocado filled with cream cheese and two fruit sauces

***

Timbale de fruits de mer, sauce écrevisses
A seafood filled fish mousse with crayfish sauce

***

Tournedos sauté au beurre Romanos
A butter cooked fillet of beef with sliced mushrooms and tongue in Madeira sauce
Maraîchère des légumes
A selection of market vegetables
Pommes Byron
Potatoes garnished with cream cheese

***

Petite Pavlova aux fruits
A light soft meringue topped with fruit

***

Frivolités des dames

***

Café

Fig. 4.14 Example of a dinner banquet menu

If there are any special diet requirements of guests, such as vegetarian dishes in place of meat, then the kitchen should know of them in advance.

The type of meal for functions can vary from a formal sit-down meal to a buffet – which can be light, hot, fork, or cold. Foods may be served from behind the buffet or guests may help themselves. Many buffets consist of a selection of hot and cold foods (see Fig. 4.15 on pages 70–71).

The cost of the menu is agreed with the organiser of the function, and if any of the following are required then they will be charged as extras:

Floral decorations
Special menu printing
Orchestra
Cabaret
Invitation cards
Place-name cards
Table plan
Toastmaster or MC
Hire of rooms
Special decorations

BUFFET MENU SELECTOR

The following are a selection of dishes that are available for Buffet Menus.
Each dish is individually priced and may be ordered in minimum quantities
of 20 portions to allow you to select a menu of your choice.
All prices are inclusive of service charge and VAT.

Hors-d'Oeuvre

Melon et Jambon de Parme
Melon and Parma Ham
Gravlax, Sauce Moutarde
Marinated Salmon, Mustard Sauce
Pâté de Canard en Croûte
Duck Pate in Pastry
Saumon d'Ecosse Fumé au Citron
Smoked Scotch Salmon
Cocktail d'Avocat aux Crevettes Rose
Avocado and Prawn Cocktail
Mousse de Haddock Fumé Mimosa
Mousse of Smoked Haddock

Cocktail de Melon de la Saison à la Menthe
Melon Cocktail flavoured with Mint
Terrine de Saumon à l'Aneth
Salmon Terrine flavoured with Dill
Filet de Truite Fumée, Sauce Raifort
Fillet of Smoked Trout, Horseradish Sauce
Perles Grises – 14 grammes
Half an ounce of Beluga Caviar
Saumon Froide en Belle Vue
Whole decorated Salmon

Soupes

Avocat Vichyssoise sur Glace
Chilled Avocado flavoured with Vichyssoise Soup
Gaspacho
Chilled Tomato Soup with traditional dressing
Crème Cressonnière Froide
Chilled Cream of Watercress Soup

Bortsch Givré
Chilled Beetroot Consomme
Crème de Champignons
Cream of Mushroom Soup
Consommé aux Julienne de Légumes
Beef Consomme garnished with shredded Vegetables

Buffet Froid

Turbot Tiède, Sauce Gribiche
Warm Turbot with a Tomato Tartare Sauce
Filet de Sole Duglèré Froid
Fillets of Sole in White Wine Sauce
Dinde de Norfolk Rôti
Roast Norfolk Turkey
Vitello Tomato
Veal and Tuna Fish
Veal and Ham Pie
Poulet Froid à la Gelée
Chicken in Aspic
Cochon de Lait
Suckling Pig

Langue de Boeuf à l'Ecarlate
Ox-tongue
Aiguillette de Caneton Hawaïenne
Wing of Duckling with Pineapple
Contrefilet de Boeuf
Roast Sirloin of Beef
Saumon d'Ecosse aux Crevettes
Whole Salmon decorated with Prawns
Selle de Veau Parisienne
Saddle of Veal
Boeuf Salé
Salt Beef

Buffet Chaud

Emincé de Veau Zurichoise
Sliced Veal with Mushrooms
Curry de Crevettes
Prawn Curry
Curry d'Agneau
Lamb Curry
Riz Pilaff
Pilaff Rice
Spaetzle au Beurre
Homemade Pasta
Nouilles au Beurre
Buttered Noodles

Strogonoff de Boeuf
Beef Strogonoff
Goujons de Baudroie Amoureuse
Monk Fish in Pernod Sauce
Chicken à la King
Salmon Kedgeree

Fig. 4.15 Example of a buffet menu

Salades

Verte
Green

Tomates
Tomato

Niçoise
Green Bean and Anchovy

Panachée
Tossed

Russe
Vegetable

Parmentier
Potato

Betterave et l'Oignon
Beetroot and Onion

Waldorf
Celery, Apples, Walnuts and Mayonnaise

Concombre et Laitue
Cucumber and Lettuce

Pommes de Terre

Pommes au Four
Jacket Potatoes

Pommes en Robe de Chambre
Steamed New Potatoes

Desserts

Savarin Fruitière Crème Chantilly
Fruit Filled Baba

Gratin de Pêches Milady
Peaches Glazed in Cream

Profiteroles au Chocolat
Chocolate Profiteroles

Orange à l'Orientale
Sliced Orange with Water Ice

Croquembouche
Croquembouche

Tranche d'Ananas au Kirsch
Fresh Pineapple in Kirsch

Tarte aux Pommes
Apple Tart

Tranche de Millefeuille
Millefeuille Pastry

Gâteau Moka
Coffee Gateau

Gâteau Forêt Noir
Black Forest Gateau

Apple Strudel

Walnut Cheesecake

Fromages

Cheddar, Stilton, Green Sage Derby, Caerphilly, Double Gloucester
Your choice of English Cheeses

Café et Petits Fours

Brie, Camembert, Roquefort, Danish Blue, Emmental, Gouda
Your Choice of Continental Cheeses

Light buffets (including cocktail parties)

Light buffets can include:

1 Hot savoury pastry patties of lobster, chicken, crab, salmon, mushrooms, ham, etc.
2 Hot sausages (chipolatas), various fillings, such as chicken livers, prunes, mushrooms, tomatoes, etc, wrapped in bacon and skewered.
3 Bite-sized items: quiche and pizza, hamburgers, meat balls with savoury sauce or dip, scampi, fried fish en goujons, tartare sauce.
4 Savoury finger toast to include any of the cold canapés. These may also be prepared on biscuits or shaped pieces of pastry. On the bases the following may be used: salami, ham, tongue, thinly sliced cooked meats, smoked salmon, caviar, mock caviar, sardine, eggs, etc.
5 Game chips, gaufrette potatoes, fried fish balls, celery stalks spread with cheese.
6 Sandwiches, bridge rolls open or closed but always small.
7 Fresh dates stuffed with cream cheese, crudités with mayonnaise and cardamom dip, tuna and chive Catherine wheels, crab claws with garlic dip, smoked salmon pin wheels, choux puffs with camembert.
8 Sweets such as trifles, charlottes, jellies, bavarois, fruit salad, strawberries and raspberries with fresh cream, ice creams, pastries, gâteaux.
9 Beverages, coffee, tea, fruit-cup, punch-bowl, iced coffee.

COCKTAIL PARTY MENU

CANAPES MOSCOVITE
(A selection of Cold Canapes to include:)

Jambon Crû et Melon
(Melon and Cured Ham)

Petites Tomates farçies aux Pavés de Truite Fumée
(Tomato stuffed with Smoked Trout)

Contrefilet de Boeuf au Raifort
(Roast Beef flavoured with Horseradish)

Mousseline de Foie de Volaille au Xérès
(Chicken Liver Mousse flavoured with Sherry)

Crevettes Marie Rose
(Prawns in Cocktail Sauce)

* * * * *

HORS D'OEUVRE CHAUDS
(A selection of Hot Canapes to include:)

Ramequins au Saumon Fumé
(Small Smoked Salmon Tartelettes)

Goujons de Baudroie Frits, Sauce Tartare
(Deep fried Monk Fish with Tartare Sauce)

Saucisses Assorties Diablées
(Beef, Pork and Veal Chipolatas with Devil Sauce)

Pizza Napolitaine
(Homemade Baby Pizza)

Kéftèdes à l'Orientale
(Lamb Meatballs in Sweet and Sour Sauce)

Fig. 4.16 Example of a cocktail party menu

Fork buffets

For these functions individual pieces of fish, meat and poultry are prepared so that they can be eaten by the guests standing up and balancing a plate in one hand. Salads should also be sensibly prepared so that they can be easily handled by the guest using only a fork; the lettuce should be shredded and kept in short lengths. Chicken or ham mousse, galantine, terrine, pâté, mayonnaise of salmon, lobster and chicken are all suitable dishes.

BUFFET

Cold or Hot Soup
Melon Boats
Fruit Cocktail

***

Egg and Vegetable Salad
Ratatouille
Red and Green Peppers with Anchovies
Potato Salad
Selection of Smoked Fish
Selection of Herrings
Steak Tartar and Garnish (made à la minute)
Prawn Cocktail
Crab Salad
Waldorf Salad
Whole Scotch Salmon

***

York Ham, Chicken, Turkey, Beef Wellington,
Leg of Lamb, Breast of Duckling

Salads:
Mushroom, Tossed, Tomato, Onion, Cucumber in Dill,
French Bean, Endive in Cream, Artichoke bottoms,
Asparagus, Celery

Sauces:
Roquefort, French Dressing, Mayonnaise, Cocktail,
Mint, Creamed Horseradish, Thousand Island

***

Croquembouche
Fruit Salad and Cream
Chocolate Mousse
Vanilla Gâteau
Meringue with Fruit
Cream Caramel
French Apple Tart
Ice Cream Gâteau
Petits Fours
Fruit Basket
Cheese Board

Fig. 4.17 Example of a buffet menu

ROOM SERVICE

DAILY DINING

These specially selected dishes are available served to your room from 12.00 noon until 10.30 pm

☆ ☆ ☆ ☆ ☆

APPETIZERS AND SALADS

Cocktail of Prawns Oceanique
Set on crisp lettuce, masked with a piquant marie rose sauce

Gravlax
Marinated wild Scotch Salmon accompanied by a light salmon caviar dressing

Hot Garlic Mushrooms
Served with a savoury tomato and fresh herb sauce

Tortellini Alla Romana
Small meat filled pasta hoops bound in a creamy cheese sauce

Chef's Homemade Soup of the Day

Chef's Salad
Choice tossed seasonal salad topped with fine strips of ham and gruyere cheese

☆ ☆ ☆ ☆ ☆

MAIN MEALS

Prime Scottish Sirloin Steak
Accompanied by grilled tomato and mushrooms

Deep Fried Jumbo Scampi
Served with French fried potatoes and tartare sauce

Beef Casserole
A prime hot pot of best Scottish beef braised with root vegetables

Lasagne Verdi
Piping hot spinach lasagne flavoured with tomato, garlic and cheese

Tandoori Chicken
Served with spiced Indian rice

Chicken Imperial
A creamy supreme of chicken casserole served with pilaff rice

Selection of fresh vegetables and potatoes

☆ ☆ ☆ ☆ ☆

DESSERTS

Fresh fruit salad with cream

Slice of homemade gâteau

Profiteroles with chocolate sauce

Selection of dairy ices and sorbets

Cheese and biscuits

Fig. 4.18 Hotel room service menu

MENU

Melon
Assorted Hors d'oeuvre
Prawn Cocktail
Tomato Soup

***

Roast Prime Rib of Beef, Yorkshire Pudding and Horseradish Sauce
Roast Leg of Lamb and Mint Sauce
Roast Leg of Pork, Sage and Onion Stuffing and Apple Sauce
Cold Roast Joints

***

Roast Potatoes
Buttered Garden Peas
New Carrots
Ratatouille
Salads in Season

***

Meringue Gâteau
Fruit Salad
Strawberry Fool
Chocolate Gâteau
Cheeseboard

***

Coffee

Fig. 4.19 A carvery menu

Fast food menus

Although some people are scornful of the items on this type of menu, calling them 'junk food', nevertheless their popularity and success is proven by the fact that from the original McDonald's, opened in Chicago in 1955, there are now over 10000 outlets world-wide. McDonald's offer customers a nutrition guide to their products, and also information for diabetes sufferers.

FAST FOOD MENU

Chicken Nuggets (6, 9 or 20 pieces)
Big Mac
Hamburger
Cheeseburger
Quarter Pounder
Quarter Pounder with Cheese
Fillet of Fish (Pure Cod)
French Fries – Regular, Large
Barbeque Sauce. Sweet Curry Sauce. Ketchups.
Mild Mustard Sauce. Sweet and Sour Sauce

Drinks/Desserts

Milkshakes – Chocolate, Vanilla, Strawberry
MacDonalds Cola – Regular, Medium, Large
MacDonalds Diet Cola – Regular, Medium, Large
MacDonalds Root Beer – Regular, Medium, Large
MacDonalds Orange Drink – Regular, Medium, Large
Tea, Coffee, Milk
Hot Apple Pie

Breakfast

Big Breakfast – Scrambled Egg, Sausage Pattie,
Hash Brown, English Muffin
Scrambled Egg on English Muffin
Hot Cakes and Sausage
Bacon and Egg McMuffin
Sausage and Egg McMuffin
English Muffin and Jam
Apple Danish
Hash Brown
Pot of Jam
Ketchups

Fig. 4.20 A fast food menu

Other menus

The following are examples of menus from other establishments.

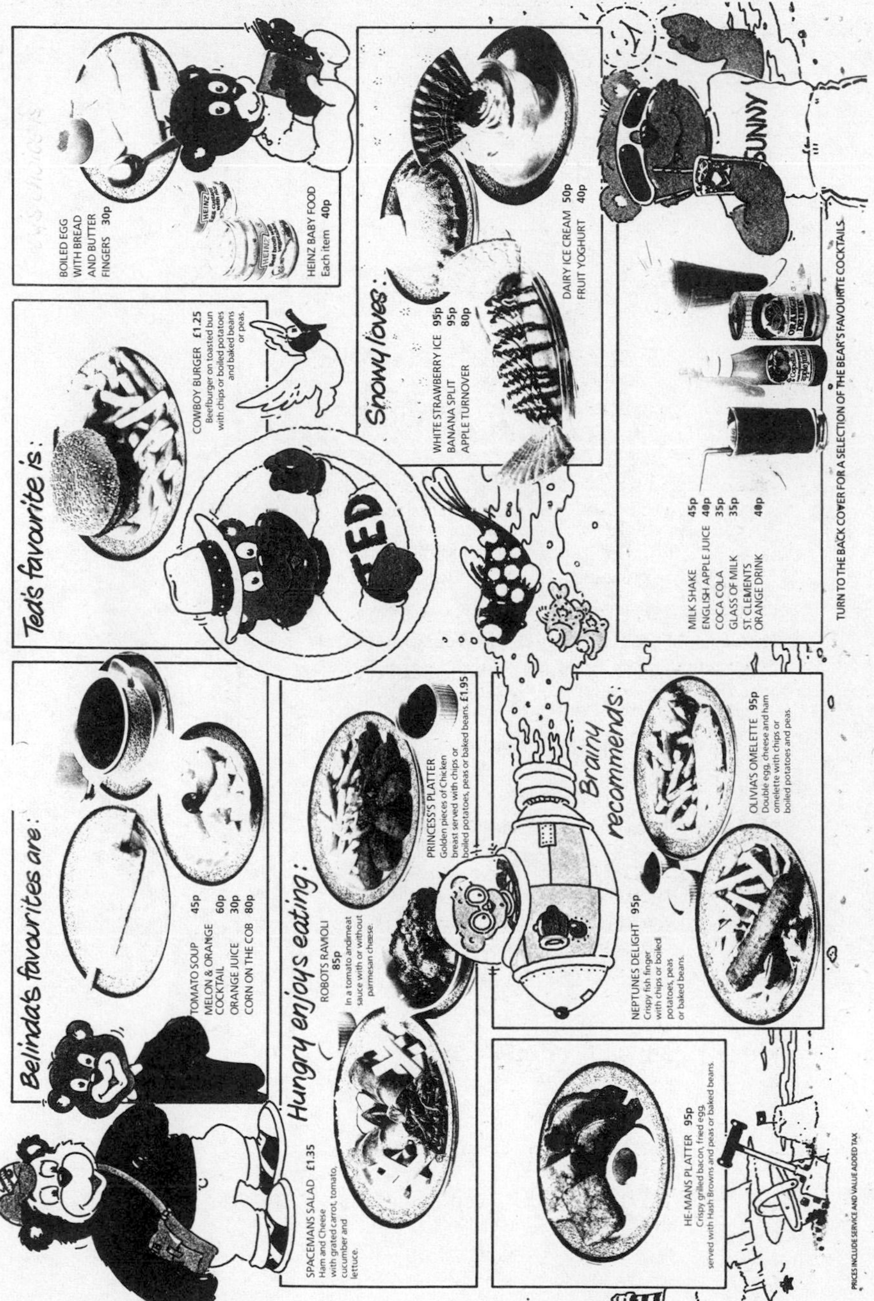

Fig. 4.21 A children's menu

ALL-DAY BRASSERIE

STARTERS

Soup of the day

Pâtés with toast

King prawns, mussels and smoked salmon

Chilled melon

SALADS

Avocado and prawn on a bed of summer leaves and served with raspberry vinaigrette

Walnuts and apple with celery, summer leaves and a light mayonnaise

Mixed side salad with a choice of mayonnaise, French or raspberry dressings

MAIN COURSES

Coq au vin

Chicken Wellington – supreme of chicken in a pastry case with lemon butter

Whole roast poussin cooked with rosemary

Cold smoked chicken garnished with seasonal berries

8 oz sirloin served with blue cheese butter

Fresh salmon cold, poached or grilled

DESSERTS AND CHEESE

Three sorbets

Chocolate truffle cake served with whipped cream

Crème brûlée

Seasonal fresh fruits in puff pastry served with cream

Three cheeses served with celery, grapes and biscuits

Fig. 4.22 Menu for an All-day Brasserie

APPETISERS

Assorted Chilled Fruit Juices
Cream of Cauliflower Soup
with croutons
Pickled Herring and Walnut Salad

* * * * *

CHEF'S SPECIAL DISH OF THE DAY

Grilled Rump Steak Garni

MAIN COURSE

Chinese Style King Ribs
with barbecue sauce

VEGETARIAN FEATURE

Poached Egg Florentine

SERVE YOURSELF SALAD BAR

Ox Tongue, Grated Cheddar, Arbroath Smokies,
Mixed Salad, Shredded Carrot, Red Cabbage

VEGETABLES AND POTATOES

Garden Peas, Creamed Parsnips,
Baked Jacket and Chipped Potatoes

* * * * *

SWEETS

Walnut Sponge
with toffee sauce
Banana Custard
Assorted Cheeses with Biscuits
Fruit and Natural Yoghurts
Fresh Fruit

Fig. 4.23 Industrial catering – luncheon menu

For business meetings we will provide homemade granary bread sandwiches on platters, cheeseboards or fruit baskets.All sandwiches are delivered with a salad garnish.

Bacon and Avocado
Bacon, Avocado and Chicken Mayonnaise
Prawn and Avocado
Chicken Mayonnaise
Ham and Emmental
Ham and Cream Cheese
Breast of Turkey
Curried Turkey
Brie
Pastrami and Gherkins
Italian Salami
Egg and Bacon
Chopped Liver
Tuna Nicoise
Cream Cheese and Smoked Salmon
Scotch Smoked Salmon
Scotch Roast Beef

***

Fresh Fruit Platter
English or French Cheeseboard

***

Spa Drinks / Coke etc.
Fresh Fruit Juices
Cona Coffee

Fig. 4.24 Industrial catering – working lunches menu

MENU

Mousse of Crab
with green vegetables and herb sauce

***

Sliced Breast of Duck
with redcurrants
Glazed Carrots
Cauliflower Florettes
Buttered New Potatoes

***

Platter of English and Continental Cheeses
Fresh Fruits

***

Coffee

Fig. 4.25 Industrial catering – directors' dining room menu

5

Commodities

Having read the chapter, these learning objectives, both general and specific, should be achieved.

General objectives Know how to purchase the various commodities and understand their storage and use. Be aware of the variety available and appreciate their versatility in the practical situation. This applies to all fresh and processed items.

Specific objectives Where appropriate identify the commodity and recognise the points of quality.

List suitable uses in cooking. Specify when in season and explain how the item should be stored. State if and how they may be preserved. Specify purchasing unit and costs.

1 Meat, p. 83
2 Offal, p. 97
3 Poultry, p. 100
4 Game, p. 103
5 Fish, p. 106
6 Vegetables, p. 122
7 Fruits, p. 130
8 Nuts, p. 135
9 Eggs, p. 136
10 Milk, p. 140
11 Fats and oils, p. 144
12 Cheese, p. 147
13 Cereals, p. 150
14 Raising agents, p. 155
15 Sugar, p. 157
16 Cocoa and chocolate, p. 158
17 Coffee, p. 159
18 Tea, p. 160
19 Pulses, p. 161
20 Herbs, p. 162
21 Spices, p. 164
22 Condiments, p. 167
23 Colourings, flavourings, essences, p. 169
24 Grocery, delicatessen, p. 170
25 Confectionery goods, p. 175

When studying commodities, students are recommended to explore the markets to get to know both fresh foods and all possible substitutes such as convenience or ready-prepared foods. Comparison should be made between various brands of foods, and between convenience and fresh unprepared foods. Factors to be considered when comparing should include quality, price, hygiene, labour, cost, time, space required and disposal of waste.

Students are advised to be cost conscious from the outset in all their studies and to form the habit of keeping up to date with current prices of all commodities, equipment, labour and overheads. An in-built awareness of costs is an important asset to any successful caterer. A list of food prices is printed weekly in the *Caterer and Hotelkeeper* (see example on p. 180). A list of other commodities is also given, at the end of this chapter, and students can keep up to date by marking prices in pencil.

The catering student should begin to form opinions as to when and in what circumstances fresh, convenience or possibly a combination of both foods should be used. Convenience or ready-prepared foods are not new and have been in use for many years. However, there are many more products on the market today, and the wise caterer will make a thorough study of all types available and, if and when they are suitable, incorporate them into the organisation.

The most important factor when considering the use of convenience (ready) foods is the same as for traditional foods; who is the food intended for? What price are they able to pay? Having considered these points, it is possible to predict whether the customer will accept, reject or possibly even prefer convenience foods.

1 Meat (*la viande*)

Meat is probably our most important food, accounting as it does for a major share of our total expenditure on food.

Cattle, sheep and pigs are reared for fresh meat and certain pigs are specifically produced for bacon. The animals are humanely killed and the meat prepared in hygienic conditions. The skins or hides are removed, the innards are taken out of the carcass and the offal is put aside.

Carcasses of beef are split into two sides and those of lambs, sheep, pigs and

Fig. 5.1 Wholesale purchasing of meat

calves are left whole; they are then chilled in a cold room before being sent to market.

To cook meat properly it is necessary to know and understand the structure of meat. Lean flesh is composed of muscles, which are numerous bundles of fibres held together by connective tissue. The size of these fibres is extremely small, especially in tender cuts or cuts from young animals, and only the coarsest fibres may be distinguished by the naked eye. The size of the fibres varies in length, depth and thickness and this variation will affect the grain and the texture of the meat.

The quantity of connective tissue binding the fibres together will have much to do with the tenderness and eating quality. There are two kinds of connective tissue, the yellow (*elastin*) and the white (*collagen*). The thick yellow strip that runs along the neck and back of animals is an example of elastin. Elastin is found in the muscles, especially in older animals or those muscles receiving considerable exercise. Elastin will not cook, but it must be broken up mechanically by pounding or mincing. The white connective tissue (collagen) can be cooked, as it decomposes in moist heat to form gelatine. The amount of connective tissue in meat is determined by the age, breed, care and feed given to the animal.

The quantity of fat and its condition are important factors in determining eating quality. Fat is found on the exterior and interior of the carcass and in the flesh itself. Fat deposited between muscles or between the bundles of fibres is called marbling. If marbling is present, the meat is likely to be tender, of better flavour and moist. Much of the flavour of meat is given by fats found in lean or fatty tissues of the meat. Animals absorb flavour from the food they are given, therefore the type of feed is important in the final eating quality of the meat.

Extractives in meats are also responsible for flavour. Muscles that receive a good deal of exercise have a higher proportion of flavour extractives than those receiving less exercise. Shin, shank, neck and other parts receiving exercise will give richer stock and gravies, and meat with more flavour than the tender cuts.

Tenderness, flavour and moistness are increased if beef is hung after slaughter or pre-tenderised (see Beef, opposite). Pork and veal are hung for 3–7 days according to the temperature. Meat is generally hung at a temperature of 1°C.

Butchers' meat

Main sources of supply

Lamb and mutton: England, Scotland, New Zealand and Australia.
Beef: England, Ireland and Scotland.
Veal: England, Scotland and Holland.
Pork: England.
Bacon: England and Denmark.
Farmed venison: Scotland.

Storage

Fresh meat

1 Fresh meat must be hung to allow it to become tender.
2 Ideal storage temperature for fresh meat is −1°C (30°F) at a relative

humidity of 90 per cent. Safe storage times, under hygienic conditions, at these temperatures are:

beef up to 3 weeks
veal up to 1–3 weeks
lamb up to 10–15 days
pork up to 7–14 days.

3 Meat should be suspended on hooks.

Bacon

1 Bacon is kept in a well-ventilated cold room.
2 Joints of bacon should be wrapped in muslin and hung, preferably in a cold room.
3 Sides of bacon are also hung on hooks.
4 Cut bacon is kept on trays in the refrigerator or cold room.

Beef (*le boeuf*)

Approximately 80 per cent of beef used in Britain is home produced.

The hanging or maturing of beef at a chill temperature of 1°C for up to 14 days has the effect of increasing tenderness and flavour. This hanging process is essential as animals are generally slaughtered around the age of 18–21 months, and the beef can be tough. Also a short time after death an animal's muscles stiffen, a condition known as *rigor mortis*. After a time chemical actions caused by enzymes and increasing acidity relax the muscles and the meat becomes soft and pliable. As meat continues to hang in storage *rigor mortis* is lost and tenderness, flavour and moistness increase. (Pork, lamb and veal are obtained from young animals so that toughness is not a significant factor.)

Tenderness can also be achieved by injecting an enzyme, such as papain, into the live animal before slaughter. When the cooking temperature of the meat reaches a certain degree, the enzyme is activated and when the temperature has reached a high level the enzyme is destroyed. This pre-tenderising process has two advantages: it can reduce the period of hanging thus saving both storage space and time, and it can double the amount of meat from the animal that can be grilled or roasted.

Large quantities of beef are prepared as chilled boneless prime cuts, vacuum packed in film. This process has the following advantages: it extends the storage life of the cuts, and allows the tenderising process to continue within the vacuum pack, because the action of the enzyme does not require air; the cuts are boned and fully trimmed thus reducing labour cost and storage space.

It is essential to store and handle vacuum packed meat correctly. Storage temperature should be 0°C with the cartons the correct way up so that the drips cannot stain the fatty surface. A good circulation of air should be allowed between cartons.

When required for use, the vacuum film should be punctured in order to drain away any blood before the film is removed. On opening the film a slight odour is usually discernable, but this should quickly disappear on exposure to the air. The vacuum packed beef has a deep red colour, but when the film is broken the colour should change to its normal characteristic red within 20–30 minutes. Once the film is punctured the meat should be used as soon as possible.

Quality

1 Lean meat should be bright red, with small flecks of white fat (marbled).
2 The fat should be firm, brittle in texture, creamy white in colour and odourless.
3 Home-killed beef is best.

Veal (*le veau*)

Originally most top quality veal came from Holland, but as the Dutch methods of production are now used extensively in Britain, supplies of home-produced veal are available all the year round. Good quality carcasses weighing around 100 kg can be produced from calves slaughtered at 12 to 24 weeks. This quality of veal is necessary for first-class cookery. Calves which are not considered by the producer to be suitable for quality veal or beef are, however, slaughtered within 10 days after birth and are known as 'Bobby' calves. The meat obtained is suitable for stewing, pies, casseroles, etc.

1 The flesh of veal should be pale pink, firm, not soft or flabby.
2 Cut surfaces must not be dry, but moist.
3 Bones in young animals should be pinkish white, porous and with a small amount of blood in their structure.
4 The fat should be firm and pinkish white.
5 The kidney ought to be firm and well covered with fat.

Lamb and mutton (*l'agneau et le mouton*)

In Britain, five times as much lamb and mutton is eaten than in any other European country. Approximately 40 per cent of the lamb and mutton consumed is home produced and the balance comes from Australia and New Zealand. As the seasons in Australia and New Zealand are opposite to those in Britain these supplies can be integrated with our own. Most lamb carcasses imported are from animals aged between 4–6 months.

1 Lamb is under one year old – after one year it is termed mutton.
2 The carcass should be compact and evenly fleshed.
3 The lean flesh of lamb and mutton ought to be firm and of a pleasing dull red colour and of a fine texture or grain.
4 The fat should be evenly distributed, hard, brittle, flaky and clear white in colour.
5 The bones should be porous in young animals.

Pork (*le porc*)

Approximately 95 per cent of pork used in Britain is home produced. The keeping quality of pork is less than that of any other meat, therefore it should be handled, prepared and cooked with great care. Pork must always be *well* cooked, because *Trichinae* (parasitic worms) may be present and must be destroyed by heat. If they are present in the meat and are not destroyed in cooking they will find their way into the voluntary muscles of those who eat pork and they will continue to live in the human body.

1 Lean flesh of pork should be pale pink.
2 The fat should be white, firm, smooth and not excessive.
3 Bones must be small, fine and pinkish.

4 The skin, or rind, ought to be smooth.

Suckling pigs weigh 10 to 20 lbs dressed and are usually roasted whole.

Bacon (*le lard*)
Bacon is the cured flesh of a baconer pig.

A baconer pig is the type that is specifically reared for bacon because its shape and size yield economic bacon joints.

The curing process consists of salting either by a dry method and smoking, or by soaking in brine followed by smoking.

Green bacon is brine cured but not smoked, it has a milder flavour and does not keep as long as smoked bacon.

1 There should be no sign of stickiness.
2 There must be no unpleasant smell.
3 The rind should be thin, smooth and free from wrinkles.
4 The fat ought to be white, smooth and not excessive in proportion to the lean.
5 The lean meat of bacon should be deep pink in colour and firm.

Ham (*le jambon*)
Ham is the hind leg of a pig cut round from the side of pork with the aitch bone; it is preserved by curing or pickling in brine and then dried and smoked. York, Bradenham (Wiltshire) and Suffolk are three of the most popular English hams.

Bradenham is easily distinguished by its black skin. The Bradenham and Suffolk hams are sweet and mildly cured. Imported hams include the Parma, Bayonne and Westphalian, all of which are carved paper thin and eaten raw as hors-d'œuvre.

Food value
Meat, having a high protein content, is valuable for the growth and repair of the body and as a source of energy.

Preservation
Salting: Meat can be pickled in brine, and this method of preservation may be applied to silverside, brisket and ox-tongues. Salting is also used in the production of bacon, before the sides of pork are smoked. This also applies to hams.

Chilling: This means that meat is kept at a temperature just above freezing-point in a controlled atmosphere. Chilled meat cannot be kept in the usual type of cold room for more than a few days, and this is sufficient time for the meat to hang, enabling it to become tender.

Freezing: Small carcasses, such as lamb and mutton, can be frozen and the quality is not affected by freezing. They can be kept frozen until required and then thawed out before being used.

Some beef is frozen, but it is inferior in quality to chilled beef.

Canning: Large quantities of meat are canned and corned beef is of importance since it has a very high protein content. Pork is used for tinned luncheon meat.

Further information

Institute of Meat, Third Floor, 50–60 St John St, London EC1M 4DT; Meat and Livestock Commission, PO Box 44, Queensway House, Bletchley MK2 2EF.

Textured vegetable protein (TVP)

This is a meat substitute manufactured from protein derived from wheat, oats, cotton-seed, soya bean and other sources. The major source of TVP is the soya bean, due to its high protein content.

TVP is used chiefly as a meat extender, varying from 10–60 per cent replacement of fresh meat. Some caterers on very tight budgets make use of it, but its main use is in food manufacturing.

By partially replacing the meat in certain dishes, eg casseroles, stews, pies, pasties, sausage rolls, hamburgers, meat loaf, paté etc, it is possible to reduce costs, provide nutrition and serve food acceptable in appearance.

A meat substitute is being produced from a plant which is a distant relative of the mushroom. This myco-protein contains protein and fibre and is the result of a fermentation process similar to the way yogurt is made. It may be used as an alternative to chicken or beef or in vegetarian dishes, eg quorn.

See following pages for diagrams of cuts of meat, French and English terms, uses and menu examples.

Meat cuts and joints

For economic reasons of saving on both labour and storage space very many caterers purchase meat by joints or cuts rather than by the carcass.

The Meat Buyer's Guide to Caterers is a manual which has been designed to assist caterers who wish to simplify and facilitate their meat purchasing.

The following lists (but not the tables) are taken from the manual and illustrate the various ways in which meat can be ordered. Some of the terminology varies slightly from that in more general use by many caterers, but this should not be a major problem.

Beef joints

Topside and silverside – whole or rolled.
Rump – whole or boneless.
Sirloin – with rump, fillet and wing rib.
Sirloin – short cut, thin flank removed.
Sirloin – boned and rolled, fillet removed.
Sirloin – boneless.
Sirloin – with rump and fillet (known as chump end).
Sirloin – chump end, boned and rolled.
Wing rib – on the bone or boned and rolled.
Striploin – boned, fillet and thin flank removed.
Striploin – special trim boned; fillet, thin flank removed and trimmed.
Fillet, standard – untrimmed.
Fillet, larder trim – all skin, fat and muscle removed.
Fore rib – untrimmed, oven prepared, carvery prepared or boned and rolled.

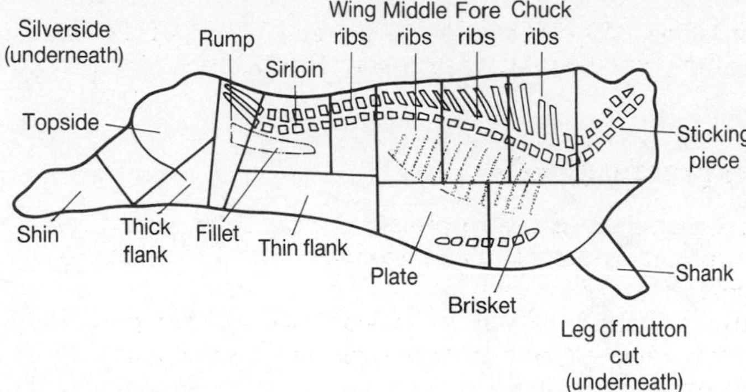

Fig. 5.2 Side of beef

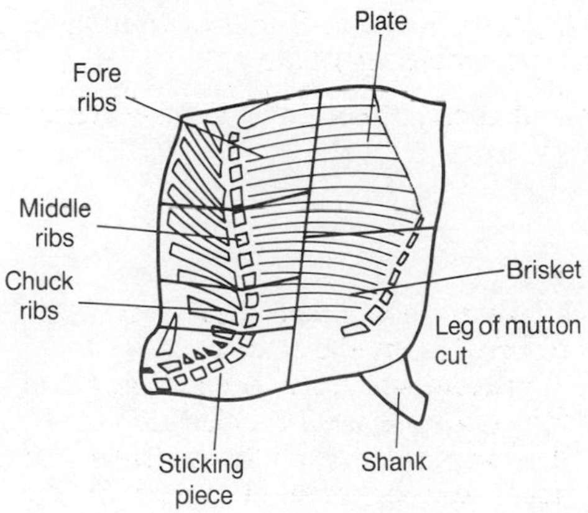

Fig. 5.3 Forequarter of beef

Rib-eye roll – prepared from the fore-rib. The main eye of meat with cartilage, muscle, fat and gristle removed.

Brisket – boneless and rolled.

Pony – prepared from fore-rib after brisket, shank and sticking piece are removed.

Back, top or middle ribs – prepared joints.

Chuck steak – boneless.

Shin – boneless.

Full baron – consists of a pair of rumps, loins and wing ribs.

Short baron – consists of a pair of rumps and loins.

Baron (double sirloin) – consists of a pair of sirloins.

Roastings – consists of half a full baron cut lengthwise.

Loin and rib – consists of half a full baron cut lengthwise with rumps removed.

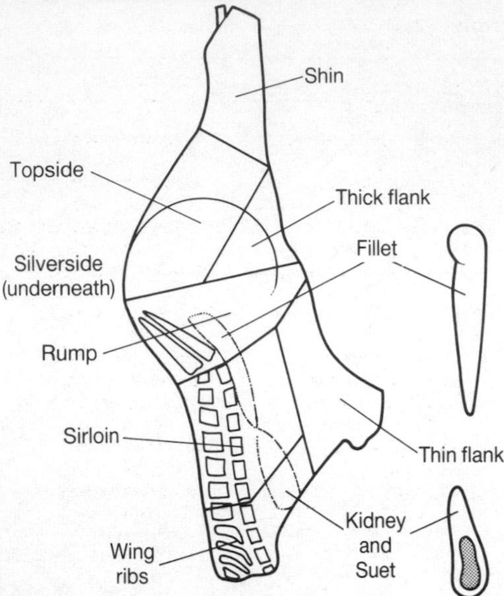

Fig. 5.4 Hindquarter of beef

Beef cuts

These include:

Beef olives, braising steaks, rump steaks.
'T' bone steaks (standard).
'T' bone steaks short-cut – flank removed.
Club steaks – prepared from the sirloin and wing rib.
Sirloin steaks (standard).
Sirloin steaks short cut – flank removed.
Sirloin steaks special trim – flank removed and trimmed.
Sirloin steaks larder trim – flank removed.
Minute steaks.
Fillet steaks (standard).
Fillet steaks, special trim.
Fillet steaks, larder trim.
Fillet tails.
Rib steaks – bone in, prepared from fore rib.
Rib-eye steaks – bone removed.
Braising steaks.
Beefburgers – pure.
Beefburgers – seasoned.
Beefburgers – economy.

Beef (le bœuf): uses and menu examples

Joint	*French*	*Use*	*Menu example*
Hindquarter:			
shin	la jambe	consommé, beef tea, stewing	Consommé royale
topside	la tranche tendre	braising, stewing, second-class roasting	Braised beef with noodles, *bitok*
silverside	la gite à la noix	pickled and boiled	Boiled silverside, carrots and dumplings
thick flank	la tranche grasse	braising and stewing	Ragoût de bœuf aux légumes
rump	la culotte de bœuf	grilling and frying as steaks	Grilled rump steak
sirloin	l'aloyau de bœuf	roasting, grilling and frying as steaks	Roast sirloin of beef, entrecôte grillé
wing ribs	la côte de bœuf	roasting, grilling and frying as steaks	Côte de bœuf rôti à l'anglaise
thin flank	la bavette	stewing, boiling, sausages	Bœuf bouilli à la française
fillet	le filet de bœuf	roasting, grilling, frying	Tournedos chasseur Filet de bœuf bouquetière
Forequarter:			
fore-ribs middle ribs	les côtes	roasting, braising	Roast Beef and Yorkshire pudding
chuck ribs	les côtes du collier	stewing, braising	Beef steak pie
sticking piece	la collier	stewing, sausages	Sausage toad in the hole
plate and brisket	la poitrine	pickled and boiled	Pressed beef, hamburgers
leg of mutton cut	la tallon du collier	braising and stewing	Savoury minced beef
shank	la jambe	consommé, beef tea	Clear soup with vegetables

Veal joints

Hind and end – as a pair, the remaining portion of the carcass after removing the breasts. Can be supplied singly.
Hind – as above with the best ends removed, singly or as a pair.
Haunch – as above with the loins removed, singly.
Haunch – boned and rolled.
Leg – the haunch with the chump-end removed.
Leg – boned and rolled.
Topside – prepared from the leg after removing the knuckle.
Cushion – a prepared muscle block of meat cleared of fat and sinew.
Top rump – thick flank.
Silverside – under cushion.
Whole rump.
Chine and end – remaining portion of the hind and end after removing the haunches.
Long striploin – prepared from the single chine and end.
Long striploin – special trim.
Long striploin – larder trim (further trimmed).
Saddle.
Loin – boneless or with bone in.
Short striploin – prepared from the loin.
Short striploin – special trim.

Short striploin – larder trim (further trimmed).
Fillet.
Knuckle.
Best-end.
Rack – a prepared single best end.
Breast.
Shoulder – bone-in, or boned and rolled.
Diced veal.
Minced veal.

Veal cuts

Escalopes (ex cushion) – prepared from the cushion.
Escalopes – prepared from topside, top rump and silverside.
Chops (standard) – prepared from the loin.
Chops (short cut) – as above with the flank removed.
Steaks – prepared from short striploin (larder trim).
Osso buco – cuts across the skin including bone approximately 2 cm (1 in).
Cutlets – prepared from the best end.
Cutlets (larder trim).

Veal (le veau): uses and menu examples

Joint	*French*	*Use*	*Menu example*
leg	le cuissot de veau	See p. 240 *Practical Cookery*	Roast leg of veal
loin	la longe de veau	roasting, frying, grilling	Veal chops with spaghetti
best end	la carré de veau	roasting, frying, grilling	Côte de veau milanaise
shoulder	l'épaule de veau	braising, stewing	Goulash of veal
neck end	le cou de veau	stewing	Fricassée de veau à l'ancienne
scrag	le cou de veau	stock, stewing	
breast	la poitrine de veau	stewing, roasting	Blanquette de veau aux nouilles
Leg of veal:			
knuckle	le jarret de veau	stewing	Osso buco
cushion	la noix de veau	escalopes, roasting, sauté, braising	Noix de veau braisé Belle Hélène
under cushion	la sous noix	escalopes, roasting, sauté, braising	Escalope de veau viennoise
thick flank	le quasi	escalopes, roasting, sauté, braising	Sauté de veau Marengo

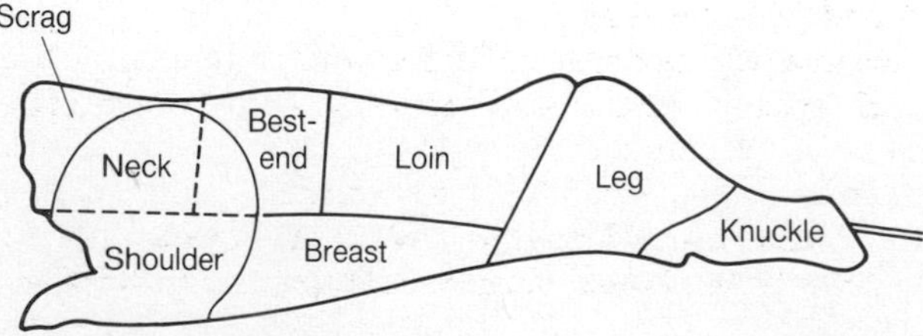

Fig. 5.5 Side of veal

Lamb joints

Hind and end (long) – the remainder of the carcass after the breast, neck and shoulders are removed.

Hind and end (short) – as above with the middle neck also removed.

Hind – consists of two legs and loins, uncut.

Haunch – a leg with the chump end.

Haunch – boneless.

Leg – a leg with the chump end removed.

Leg – boneless or boned and rolled.

Leg (carvery cut) – prepared from the leg or haunch with the aitch bone, cool fat and tail removed, excess fat and shank end removed, the knuckle bone cleaned and the joint tied.

Chine and end (long) – the remainder of the carcass after removing the breasts, neck, shoulders and legs.

Chine and end (short) – the remainder of the carcass after removing the breasts, neck, shoulders, legs and middle neck.

Saddle – an uncut pair of loins and chump ends.

Saddle (oven-prepared) – the flanks, kidney knobs, bark and all internal fat removed.

Saddle (boned and rolled) – oven-prepared, boned and tied or netted.

Short saddle – an uncut pair of loins without chump ends.

Short saddles are also available oven-prepared or boned and rolled.

Best-end (long) – a pair of uncut ends with eleven rib bones each side.

Best-end (short) – a pair of uncut ends with seven rib bones each side.

Best-end (split and chined) – prepared from short best-ends.

Rack – best-end split and chined and trimmed ready for cooking.

Rack (larder-trim) – a rack further trimmed with $1\frac{1}{2}$ cm, $\frac{3}{4}$ in. of the ends of the rib-bones cleaned.

Fore – the remaining portion of the carcass after removing the hind.

Short fore – a fore with the breasts and short best ends removed.

Short-fore – boned and rolled.

Shoulder – also available boneless or boned and rolled.

Neck and middle – short fore with the shoulders removed, five rib bones each side.

Middle neck – neck and middle with the neck removed between the first and second ribs – leaving 4 rib bones each side.

Breast.

Lamb cuts

Diced lamb (stewing) prepared from any combination of cuts.

Diced lamb (kebabs) prepared from the legs.

Minced lamb – the fat content should not exceed 25 per cent.

Economy chops – prepared from the chine and short-end from which the flank has been removed.

Loin chops (trimmed) – prepared from the saddle (two loins).

Noisettes – prepared from boned loins, rolled, tied and cut into pieces.

Valentine of lamb – prepared from the boned short saddle, partially sliced to give a butterfly cut.

Crown or Barnsley chops – cut across the short saddle giving an uncut pair of loin chops.

Cutlets (trimmed) – cut from the best end.
Butterfly cutlets – cut across an uncut pair of best ends, producing double cutlets.
Cutlets (French trimmed) – prepared from the rack (larder trimmed).
Band saw chops – prepared from the unacceptable chump ends from loin chops and the unacceptable blade-bone cutlets from the best end.
Pauillac lamb – young milk-fed lambs supplied with head and liver weighing between 7–10 kg, 15–22 lbs.
Dressed saddle – an oven prepared saddle, decorated and embellished for buffet presentation.
Crown of lamb – prepared from two best ends tied in a round shape with the rib bones slanting outwards.

Lamb and mutton (l'agneau et le mouton): uses and menu examples

Joint	*French*	*Use*	*Menu example*
shoulder	l'épaule d'agneau ou de mouton	roasting, stewing	Epaule d'agneau boulangère
leg	le gigot d'agneau	roasting (mutton – boiled)	Roast leg of lamb, mint sauce Boiled leg of mutton, caper sauce
breast	la poitrine	stewing, roasting	Irish stew
middle neck	le cou	stewing	Navarin d'agneau printanier
scrag end	le cou	broth	Mutton broth
best end	le carré d'agneau	roasting, grilling, frying	Carré d'agneau persillé
saddle	la selle d'agneau	roasting, grilling, frying	Selle d'agneau niçoise
loin	la longe d'agneau	roasting, grilling, frying	Roast stuffed loin of lamb
chop	la côte d'agneau	grilling, frying	Grilled loin chop
cutlet	la côtelette d'agneau	grilling, frying	Côtelette d'agneau Réforme
fillet	le filet mignon	grilling, frying	Filet mignon fleuriste

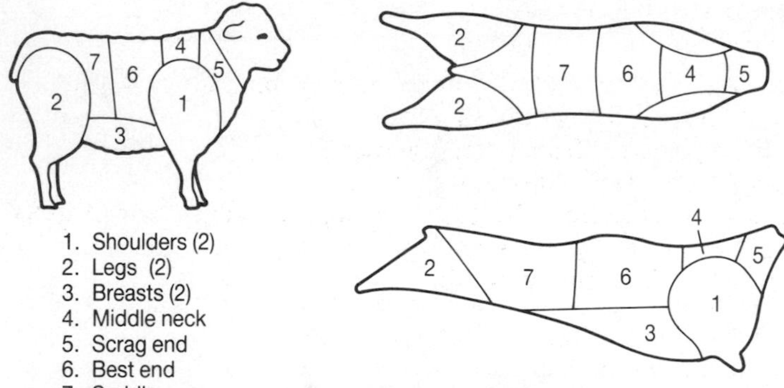

Fig. 5.6 Side of lamb

Pork joints

Side – half a carcass split down the middle lengthwise, available with or without the head.
Leg and long loin – a side with head, hand and belly removed.
Leg and short loin – as above with the neck-end removed between fourth and fifth ribs.

Leg – available with bone-in, boned, boned and rolled and carvery cut.
Long loin – the portion remaining after removing the leg.
Long loin – available boneless or boned and rolled.
Short loin – the portion remaining after removing the leg.
Short loin – available boneless or boned and rolled.
Middle loin – short loin with chump end removed, available with bone-in or boned and rolled.
Long hogmeat – long loin with skin and excess fat removed, available with bone-in or boned and rolled.
Short hogmeat – short loin with skin and excess fat removed, available with bone-in or boned and rolled.
Middle hogmeat – middle loin prepared and available as above.
Neck-end – the remaining portion of long loin after removing short loin, available as above.
Fillet – also known as tenderloin.
Belly.
Hand – the remaining portion of a side when the leg and long loin are removed. Available bone-in, boned and boned and rolled.
Shoulder – the shoulder is removed from a side by a perpendicular cut between fourth and fifth ribs. Available as above.
Spare rib – the remaining portion of the neck-end after removing the blade-bone.
Boneless neck – spare-rib with bones removed.
Blade bone – the remaining portion of the neck-end after removing the spare rib. Available boneless.
Barbecue spare ribs – the rib bones and related meat removed from the belly.
Diced pork – produced from any combination of cuts.
Minced pork – fat content should not exceed 25 per cent.
Suckling pig – young piglet which is slaughtered prior to weaning which normally takes place 5–7 weeks after birth. Supplied as a carcass with head weighing between 5–10 kg, 10–20 lbs.

Pork cuts

Escalopes – cut from the leg or chump end, trimmed and battened out.
Chops (rind-on) – prepared from the short loin.
Chops (trimmed) – prepared from short hogmeat.
Steaks – prepared from middle hogmeat.
Neck-end chops – prepared from the neck-end, supplied rind-on or trimmed.
Sliced belly – cut from the prepared belly.
Spare ribs chops – cut from the spare rib.

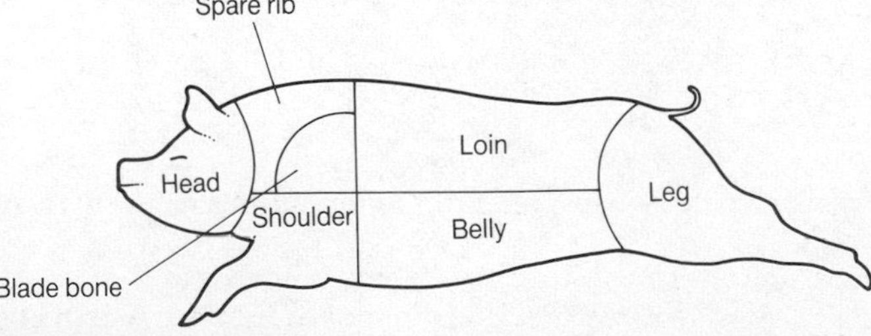

Fig. 5.7 Side of pork

Pork (le porc): uses and menu examples

Joint	*Use*	*Menu example*
leg	roasting, boiling	Roast leg of pork, apple sauce
loin	roasting, frying, grilling	Roast loin of pork
spare rib	roasting, pies	Pork pie
blade bone	roasting, pies	Boiled belly of pork and pease pudding
shoulder	roasting, sausages, pies	Saucisse de porc grillé, sauce charcutière
head	brawn	

Bacon (le lard): uses and menu examples

Joint	*Use*	*Menu example*
collar	boiling, grilling	Boiled bacon, pease pudding and parsley sauce
hock	boiling, grilling	
back	grilling, frying	Egg and bacon
streaky	grilling, frying	Canapé Diane
gammon	boiling, grilling, frying	Braised gammon, Madeira sauce Grilled gammon and pineapple

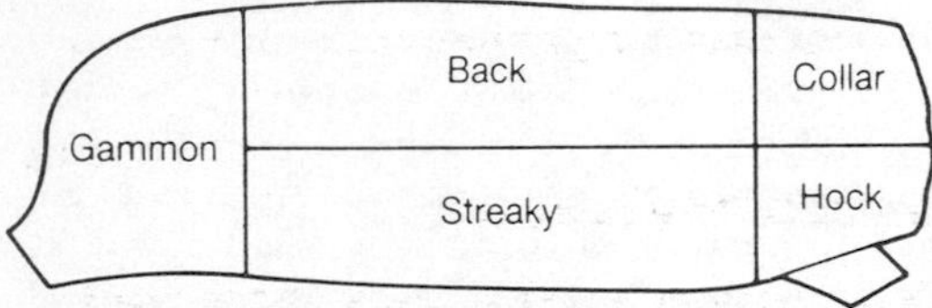

Fig. 5.8 Side of bacon

Fig. 5.9 Inspecting a freshly delivered hindquarter of beef

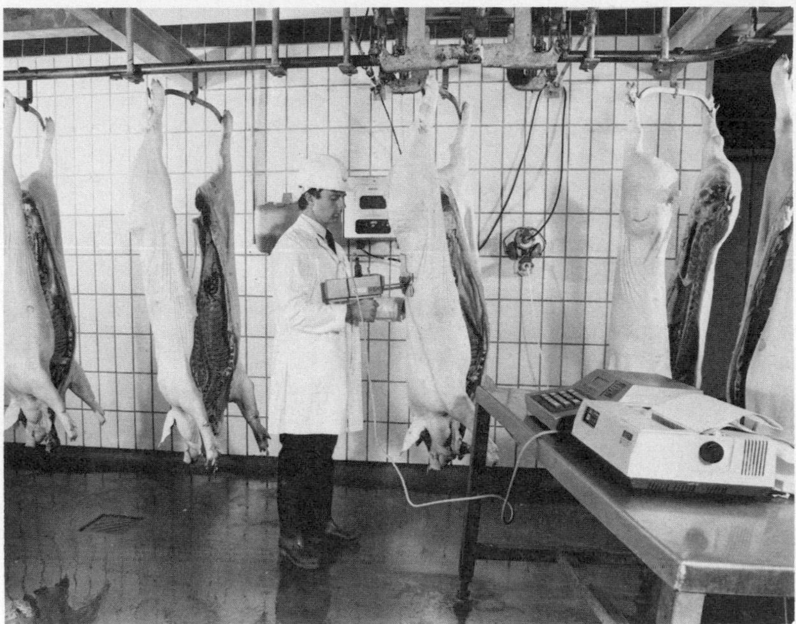

Fig. 5.10 Measuring depth of fat in pig carcass using probe meter (connected to computer print-out)

2 Offal and other edible parts of the carcass

Offal is the name given to the edible parts taken from the inside of the carcass: liver, kidney, heart, sweetbread. Tripe, brains, oxtail, tongue and head are sometimes included under this term. Fresh offal (unfrozen) should be purchased as required and can be refrigerated under hygienic conditions at a temperature of −1°C (30°F), at relative humidity of 90 per cent for up to seven days. Frozen offal should be kept frozen until required.

Tripe (*la tripe*)
Tripe is the stomach lining or white muscle of the ox. Honeycomb tripe is the second compartment of the stomach and considered the best. Smooth tripe is the first compartment of the stomach, and is not considered to be as good as honeycomb tripe. Sheep tripe, darker in colour, is obtainable in some areas. It may be boiled or braised.

Menu example: Tripe and onions.

Oxtail (*la queue de bœuf*)
Oxtails should be 3–5 lbs, lean and with no signs of stickiness. They are usually braised or used for soup.

Menu examples: Oxtail soup; Braised oxtail.

Head (*la tête*)
Sheep's heads can be used for stock, and pigs' heads for brawn. The calf's head

is used for soup and certain dishes such as calf's head vinaigrette.

Sheep's and calves' heads should not be sticky; they should be well fleshed and odourless.

Suet (*la graisse de rognon*)

Beef suet should be creamy white, brittle and dry. It is used for suet paste. Other fat should be fresh and not sticky. Suet and fat may be rendered down for dripping.

Marrow (*la moelle*)

Beef marrow is obtained from the bones of the leg of beef. It should be of good size, firm, creamy white and odourless. It may be used as a garnish for steaks and for savouries.

Menu example: Toast baron.

Brains (*la cervelle*)

Calf's brains are those usually used; they must be fresh.

Menu example: Calf's brain with black butter sauce.

Bones (*les os*)

Bones must be fresh, not sticky; they are used for stock.

Liver (*le foie*)

Calf's liver is the most expensive and is considered the best in terms of tenderness and delicacy of flavour and colour.

Lamb's liver is mild in flavour, tender and light in colour.

Sheep's liver, being from an older animal, is firmer in substance, darker in colour and has a stronger flavour than lamb's or calf's liver.

Ox or *beef* liver is the cheapest and if taken from an older animal can be coarse in texture and strong in flavour.

Pig's liver is full flavoured and used in many pâté recipes.

Quality

1 Liver should appear fresh and have an attractive colour.
2 It must not be dry or contain tubers.
3 The smell must be pleasant.
4 It should be smooth in texture.

Food value: Liver is valuable as a protective food; it consists chiefly of protein and contains useful amounts of vitamin A and iron.

Kidney (*le rognon*)

Lamb's kidney is light in colour, delicate in flavour and is ideal for grilling and frying.

Sheep's kidney is darker in colour and has a stronger flavour than lamb's kidney.

Calf's kidney is light in colour, delicate in flavour and can be used in a wide variety of dishes.

Ox kidney is dark in colour, strong in flavour and is generally used mixed with beef, for steak and kidney pie or pudding.

Pig's kidney is smooth, long and flat by comparison with sheep's kidney; it has a strong flavour.

Quality

1 Ox kidney:
(a) Ox kidney should be fresh.
(b) The suet is left on the kidney until it is prepared for cooking.
(c) If the suet is removed, the kidney dries out.
(d) The kidney should be deep red.

2 Lamb's kidney:
(a) Lamb's kidney should be covered in fat which is removed just before use.
(b) The fat should be crisp and the kidney moist.
(c) Both fat and kidney should have a pleasant smell.

Food value: The food value of kidney is similar to liver, ie a protective food containing vitamin A and iron.

Hearts (*le coeur*)

Ox or *beef* hearts are the largest used for cooking. They are dark-coloured, solid and tend to be dry and tough.

Calf's heart, coming from a younger animal, is lighter in colour and more tender.

Sheep's heart is dark and solid and can be dry and tough unless cooked carefully.

Lamb's heart is smaller and lighter and is normally served whole. Larger hearts are normally sliced before serving.

Quality

Hearts should not be too fatty and should not contain too many tubes. When cut they should be moist.

Food value: They have a high protein content and are valuable for growth and repair of the body.

Tongue (*la langue*)

1 Tongues must be fresh.
2 They should not have an excessive amount of waste at the root-end.
3 They must smell pleasant.
4 Ox tongues may be used fresh or salted.
5 Sheep's tongues are used unsalted.

Sweetbreads (*le ris*)

There are two kinds, unequal in shape and quality. The heart bread is round and plump and of much better quality than the throat or neck breads, which are longer and uneven in shape. Calf's heart bread weighs up to $1\frac{1}{2}$ lbs ($\frac{3}{4}$ kg); lamb's heart bread up to 4 oz (100 g).

Quality

1 Heart and neck breads should be fleshy and large.
2 They ought to be creamy white in colour.
3 They must smell pleasant.
4 Heart breads are of better quality than neck breads.

Food value: Sweetbreads are valuable foods, particularly for hospital diets. They are very easily digested and useful for building body tissues. See table.

Different kinds of offal: uses and menu examples

English	*French*	*Use*	*Menu example*
LIVER	LE FOIE		
calf's liver	le foie de veau	frying	Calf's liver and bacon
lamb's liver	le foie d'agneau	frying	Shish kebab
pig's liver	le foie de porc	frying, pâté	Liver pâté
ox liver	le foie de bœuf	braising, frying	Braised liver and onions
KIDNEY	LE ROGNON		
calf's kidney	le rognon de veau	grilling, sauté	Mixed grill
lamb's kidney	le rognon d'agneau	grilling, sauté	Rognons sautés Turbigo
pig's kidney	le rognon de porc	grilling, sauté	Grilled kidneys and bacon
ox kidney	le rognon de bœuf	stewing, soup	Kidney soup
HEART	LE CŒUR		
sheep's heart	le cœur d'agneau	braising	Stuffed braised sheep's heart
ox heart	le cœur de bœuf		Braised ox heart
TONGUE	LA LANGUE		
lamb's tongue	la langue d'agneau	boiling, braising	Langue d'agneau poulette
ox tongue	la langue de bœuf	boiling, braising	Braised tongue with Madeira sauce
SWEETBREADS	LE RIS		
lamb's sweetbreads	le ris d'agneau	braising, frying	Ris d'agneau braisé Clamart
calf's sweetbreads	le ris de veau	braising, frying	Ris de veau bonne-maman

3 Poultry (*la volaille*)

Poultry is the name given to domestic birds specially bred to be eaten and for their eggs.

Season

Owing to present-day methods of poultry production by the battery method, and to deep freezing, poultry is available all the year round.

Food value

The flesh of poultry is more easily digested than that of butchers' meat. It contains protein and is therefore useful for building and repairing body tissues and providing heat and energy. Fat content is low and contains a high percentage of unsaturated acids.

Fig. 5.11 Wholesale purchasing of poultry and game

Storage

Fresh poultry must be hung by the legs in a well-ventilated room for at least 24 hours, otherwise it will not be tender, and the innards are not removed until the bird is required.

Frozen birds must be kept in a deep-freeze cabinet until required; they are then allowed to thaw out completely before cooking.

Chicken

Quality

1 The breast of the bird should be plump.
2 The vent-end of the breast-bone must be pliable.
3 The flesh should be firm.
4 The skin ought to be white and unbroken, with a faint bluish tinge.
5 The legs should be smooth, with small scales and small spurs.
6 Old birds have large scales and large spurs on the legs.

Types of chickens

Broiler chickens, so called after the American word for roasting, are reared until they reach the required weight (averaging between 1½–2 kg, 3–4½ lbs), which takes approximately 6–7 weeks.

Whole chickens weighing up to 3 kg (6 lbs) are also available.

Oven-ready fresh chickens are sold completely eviscerated, normally chilled, with or without giblets.

Frozen chickens are first cleaned and then quickly frozen.

Poussins, or spring chickens as they used to be known, are 4–6 weeks old, weighing about 0.5 kg (1 lb) and are available fresh or frozen.

Corn-fed chickens are reared on a diet of maize which gives them their distinctive yellow hue. Mostly available fresh, but some are frozen.

Chicken portions, both fresh and frozen, are available in a wide variety of packs including breasts, drumsticks, thighs or packs of mixed portions.

Use

Chickens are suitable for cooking whole by roasting, grilling (split open), pot-roasting and braising. They can also be cooked in pieces as supremes, ballottines, sautés, pies, galantines, and in vol-au-vents, salads and sandwiches. Also stocks, soups and sauces.

Boiling fowl are either smaller, less meaty birds weighing 1–2 kg (2–4 lbs) or large tough old hens which have finished laying. They are chiefly used for stocks, soups and sauces.

Further information

British Chicken Information Service, Bury House, 126–128 Cromwell Road, London SW7 4ET.

Duck, duckling (*le canard, le caneton*)

Goose, gosling (*l'oie (f), l'oison (f)*)

Quality

1 The feet and bills should be bright yellow.
2 The upper bill should break easily.
3 The web feet must be easy to tear.

Use: Ducks and geese may be roasted or braised.

Menu examples: Roast Aylesbury duckling; Duck with apple sauce and sage and onion stuffing; Braised duck with peas; Roast goose with sage and onion stuffing and apple sauce; Braised goose with turnips.

Turkey (*le dindonneau, la dinde*)

Quality: The breast should be large, the skin undamaged and with no signs of stickiness. The legs of young birds are black and smooth, the feet supple with a short spur. As the bird ages the legs turn reddish grey and become scaly. The feet become hard.

Use: Turkeys are usually roasted.

Menu examples: Roast Norfolk turkey and chestnut stuffing; Emincé de dinde à la king.

Guinea fowl (*le pintarde*)

When plucked these grey-and-white feathered birds resemble a chicken with darker flesh. The young birds are known as squabs.

The quality points relating to chicken apply to guinea fowl.

Menu examples: Braised Guinea fowl with wild mushrooms; Breast of Guinea fowl with noodles and pepper sauce.

Pigeon (*le pigeon*)
Pigeon should be plump, the flesh mauve-red in colour and the claws pinkish. Tame pigeons are smaller than wood pigeons.

Menu examples: Pigeon pie; Breast of pigeon with herb ravioli.

Poultry (la volaille): weights and portions

English	*French*	*Undrawn weight (approx)*	*Number of portions (approx)*
single baby chicken (spring chicken)	le poussin	360 g–½ kg	1
double baby chicken	le poussin double	½ kg–¾ kg	2
small roasting chicken	le poulet de grain	¾ kg–1 kg	3–4
medium roasting chicken	le poulet reine	1 kg–2 kg	4–6
large roasting or boiling chicken	la poularde	2 kg–3 kg	6–8
capon	le chapon	3 kg–4½ kg	8–12
boiling fowl	la poule	2½ kg–4 kg	8–12
young turkey	le dindonneau	3½ kg	**
turkey	la dinde	3½ kg–20 kg	**
duckling	le caneton	1 kg–1½ kg	3–4
duck	le canard	1½ kg–2½ kg	4–6
gosling	l'oison	2 kg–3½ kg	**
goose	l'oie	3½ kg–7 kg	**
guinea fowl	le pintarde	1 kg–1½ kg	3–4
pigeon	le pigeon	¾ kg–1 kg	1–2

Drawn poultry loses approximately 25 per cent of its original weight.
All poultry is bought by number and weight.
** For turkey and goose allow ½ kg undrawn weight per portion.

4 Game (*le gibier*)

Game is the name given to certain wild birds and animals which are eaten; there are two kinds of game:

(a) feathered;
(b) furred.

Food value
As it is less fatty than poultry or meat, game is easily digested, with the exception of water fowl, owing to their oily flesh. Game is useful for building and repairing body tissues and for energy.

Storage

1 Hanging is essential for all game. It drains the flesh of blood and begins the process of disintegration which is vital to make the flesh soft and edible, and also to develop flavour.

2 The hanging time is determined by the type, condition and age of the game and the storage temperature.
3 Old birds need to hang for a longer time than young birds.
4 Game birds are not plucked or drawn before hanging.
5 Venison and hare are hung with the skin on.
6 Game must be hung in a well-ventilated, dry, cold storeroom; this need not be refrigerated.
7 Game birds should be hung by the neck with the feet down.

Game availability

Game is available fresh in season between the following dates and frozen for the remainder of the year:

Grouse	August 12–December 10
Snipe	August 12–January 31
Partridge	September 1–February 1
Wild duck	September 1–January 31
Pheasant	October 1–February 1
Woodcock	October 31–February 1

Venison, hares, rabbits and pigeons are available throughout the year.

Quality points for buying:

Venison
Joints of venison should be well fleshed and a dark brownish-red colour.

Hares and rabbits
The ears of hares and rabbits should tear easily. With old hares the lip is more pronounced than in young animals. The rabbit is distinguished from the hare by shorter ears, feet and body.

Birds

1 The beak should break easily.
2 The breast plumage ought to be soft.
3 The breast should be plump.
4 Quill feathers should be pointed, not rounded.
5 The legs should be smooth.

Venison (*la venaison*)
Venison is the flesh of deer and the lean meat is a dark blood red colour. The surface of the carcass is usually dusted with a mixture of flour, salt and black pepper before being hung in a cold room for 2–3 weeks. The roebuck (*le chevreuil*) is the deer which is frequently used.

Venison is usually roasted or braised in joints. Small cuts may be fried. Before cooking it is always marinaded to counteract the toughness and dryness of the meat.

Menu examples: Roast haunch of venison, Cumberland sauce; Fillet of venison with beetroot.

Hare (*la lièvre*)
Hare is cooked as a red wine stew called jugged hare (*civet de lièvre*) and the saddle (*rable de lièvre*) is roasted.

Menu examples: Jugged hare; Roast saddle of hare with port-wine sauce.

Pheasant (*le faisan*)
This is one of the most common game birds. Average weight 1½–2 kg (2–4 lbs). Young birds have a pliable breast bone and soft pliable feet. Hang for 5–8 days. Used for roasting, braising or pot roasting.

Menu examples: Salmis de faisan; Pot roasted pheasant with celery.

Partridge (*le perdreau*)
The most common varieties are the grey legged and the red legged. Average weight 200–400 g (½–1 lb). Hang for 3–5 days. Used for roasting or braising.

Menu examples: Braised partridge with cabbage; Roast partridge.

Grouse (*la grouse*)
A famous and popular game bird is the red grouse which is shot in Scotland and Yorkshire. Average weight 300 g (12 oz). Young birds have pointed wings and rounded soft spurs. Hang for 5–7 days. Used for roasting.

Menu example: Roast grouse.

Woodcock (*le bécasse*)
Small birds with long thin beaks. Average weight 200–300 g (8–12 oz). Prepare as for snipe.

Snipe (*la bécassine*)
100 g (4 oz). Hang for 3–4 days. The heads and neck are skinned, the eyes removed and they are then trussed with their own beaks. When drawing the birds only the gizzard, gall-bladder and intestines are removed. The birds are then roasted with the liver and heart left inside.

Menu example: Roast snipe.

Quail (*la caille*)
Small birds weighing 50–75 g (2–3 oz) produced on farms, usually packed in boxes of 12. Quails are not hung. They are usually roasted or braised.

Menu examples: Roast quail with grapes; Boned and stuffed quail and salad.

Wild duck (*le canard-sauvage*)
Such as mallard and the widgeon, average weight 1–1½ kg (2–3 lb). Hang for 1–2 days. Usually roasted or braised.

Menu example: Wild duck with orange sauce.

Teal (*la sarcelle*)
The smallest duck, weighing 400–600 g (1–1½ lb). Hang for 1–2 days. Usually roasted or braised. Young birds have small pinkish legs and soft down under the

wings. Teal and wild duck must be eaten in season otherwise the flesh is coarse and has a fishy flavour.

Menu example: Roast teal.

Further information
Practical Cookery (Edward Arnold), sixth edition, pp. 297–302.

Game (le gibier): weights and portions

English	*French*	*Undrawn weight (approx)*	*Number of portions (approx)*
Furred:			
venison	la venaison	15 kg	15–20
hare	le lièvre	$2\frac{1}{2}$–$3\frac{1}{2}$ kg	6–8
rabbit	le lapin	1 kg	4
Feathered:			
pheasant	le faisan	$1\frac{1}{2}$–2 kg	2–4
partridge	le perdreau	$\frac{1}{4}$–$\frac{1}{2}$ kg	1–2
grouse	la grouse	360 g	1–2
woodcock	la bécasse	$\frac{1}{4}$ kg–360 g	1
snipe	le bécassine	120 g	1
quail	le caille	150 g	1
wild duck	le canard-sauvage	1–$1\frac{1}{2}$ kg	2–4
teal	la sarcelle	$\frac{1}{2}$–$\frac{3}{4}$ kg	1–2
wood pigeon	le pigeon	360g	1

5 Fish (*les poissons*)

Fish have formed a large proportion of our food because of their abundance and relative ease of harvesting. It is interesting to note that fish consume the smaller organisms in the sea and are themselves the food of the larger organisms. In addition to providing fresh and processed food for human consumption, other valuable products such as oil and *isinglass*, as well as fertiliser, come from fish.

Unfortunately the fish supply is not unlimited due to overfishing, so it is now necessary to have fish farms (eg for trout and salmon) to supplement the natural resources. This is not the only problem: due to contamination by man, the seas and rivers are increasingly polluted, thus affecting both the supply and the suitability of fish, particularly shellfish, for human consumption.

Fish are valuable, not only because they are a good source of protein, but because they are suitable for all types of menus and can be cooked and presented in a wide variety of ways. The range of different types of fish of varying textures, taste and appearance is indispensable to the creative chef.

Types or varieties

1 Oily fish
These are round in shape (eg herring, mackerel, salmon)

2 White fish
(a) Round (eg cod, whiting, hake).
(b) Flat (eg plaice, sole, turbot).

3 Shellfish
(a) Crustacea (eg lobster, crabs).
(b) Mollusca (eg oysters, mussels).

Purchasing unit

Fresh fish is bought by the kilogram, by the number of fillets or whole fish of the weight that is required. For example, 30 kg of salmon could be ordered as 2 × 15 kg, 3 × 10 kg or 6 × 5 kg. Frozen fish can be purchased in 15 kg blocks.

Source

Fish is plentiful in the UK, because we are surrounded by water, although overfishing and pollution are having a detrimental effect on the supplies of certain fish. Most catches are made off Iceland, Scotland, the North Sea, Irish Sea and the English Channel. Salmon are caught in certain English and Scottish rivers, and are also extensively farmed. Frozen fish is imported from Scandinavia, Canada and Japan; the last two countries send frozen salmon to Britain.

Storage

1 Fresh fish are stored in a fish-box containing ice, in a separate refrigerator or part of a refrigerator used only for fish.
2 The temperature must be maintained just above freezing-point.
3 Frozen fish must be stored in a deep-freeze cabinet or compartment.
4 Smoked fish should be kept in a refrigerator.

Quality points for buying

When buying whole fish the following points should be looked for to ensure freshness.

1 Eyes: bright, full and not sunken; no slime or cloudiness.
2 Gills: bright red in colour; no bacterial slime.
3 Flesh: firm and resilient so that when pressed the impression goes quickly. The fish must not be limp.
4 Scales: these should lie flat, and be moist and plentiful.
5 Skin: this should be covered with a fresh sea slime, or be smooth and moist, with a good sheen and no abrasions.
6 Smell: this must be pleasant, with no smell of ammonia or sourness.

Buying points

1 The flesh should be translucent.
2 It should be firm and not ragged or gaping.
3 The flesh should not retain an indentation when pressed with a finger.
4 There should be no smell of ammonia or sour odours.
5 There must be no bruising or blood clots.
6 There should not be areas of discoloration.
7 Fish should be purchased daily.

8 If possible, it ought to be purchased direct from the market or supplier.
9 The fish should be well iced so that it arrives in good condition.
10 The flesh of the fish should not be damaged.
11 Fish may be bought on the bone or filleted. (The approximate loss from boning and waste is 50 per cent for flat fish, 60 per cent for round fish.)
12 Fillets of plaice and sole can be purchased according to weight. They are graded from 45 g to 180 g per fillet and go up in weight by 15 g.
13 Medium-sized fish are usually better than large fish, which may be coarse; small fish often lack flavour.

Kinds of fish: seasons and purchasing units (a) Oily fish

Oily fish	*French*	*Season*	*Purchasing unit*
anchovy	l'anchois	imported occasionally June to December – home waters	number and weight
common eel	le congre	all year, best in autumn	number and weight
conger eel	l'anguille	March to October	weight
herring	le hareng	all year except Spring	number and weight
mackerel	le maquereau	all year, best February to June	number and weight
pilchard (mature sardines)	la sardine	all year	number and weight
salmon (farmed)	le saumon	all year	number and weight
salmon (wild)	le saumon	February to August	number and weight
salmon trout	le truite saumonée	February to August	number and weight
salmon (Pacific)	le saumon	July to November	number and weight
sprat	le sprat	September to March	number and weight
sardines	les sardines	all year	number and weight
trout	la truite	February to September	number and weight
tuna	le thon	all year	steaks or pieces
whitebait	les blanchailles	when available	weight

Kinds of fish: seasons and purchasing units (b) White flat fish

White flat fish	*French*	*Season*	*Purchasing unit*
brill	la barbue	June to February	number and weight
dab	la limande	March to December	number and weight
flounder	le flét	May to February, best in winter	number and weight
halibut	le flétan	June to March	number and weight or steaks
megrim		April to February	number and weight
plaice	la plie	May to February	number and weight or fillets
skate	la raie	May to February	wings, number and weight
sole, Dover	la sole de Douvre	May to March	number and weight or fillets
sole, lemon	la limande	all year, best in spring	number and weight or fillets
turbot	le turbot	all year	number and weight or fillets
turbot (farmed)	le turbot	when available	number and weight
witch		all year, best in spring	number and weight or fillets

Kinds of fish: seasons and purchasing units (c) Round fish

Round fish	*French*	*Season*	*Purchasing unit*
bass	le bas	June to March	number and weight or fillets
bream, fresh water	la brème	August to April	number and weight or fillets
bream, sea	la brème	June to December	number and weight or fillets
carp (mostly farmed)	la carpe	fluctuates throughout year	number and weight or fillets
cod	le cabillaud	all year, not at best in spring	number and weight or fillets
coley		all year	number and weight or fillets
dogfish (huss, flake, rigg)	la chien de mer	all year, best autumn	steaks or fillets
grey mullet		May to February, best autumn and winter	number and weight
haddock	l'aigrefin	all year, best autumn and winter	number and weight or fillets
hake	le colin	June to February	number and weight or fillets
John Dory	le Saint Pierre	September to May	number and weight or fillets
ling		September to July	number and weight or fillets
monkfish (angler-fish)	la lotte	all year, best in winter	number and weight or tails
pike	le brochet	all year	number and weight
perch	la perche	May to February	number and weight
pollack (yellow, green)	le merlan	May to December	number and weight
redfish	le colin	all year	number and weight or fillets
red gurnard	le grondin	all year, best from July to April	number or weight
red mullet	le rouget	imported, best in summer, UK autumn	number and weight or fillets
sea bream	la brème	June to February	number and weight
smelt	l'eperlan	occasionally	number and weight
shark (porbeagle)	le pèlerin	occasionally	steaks or pieces
snapper, red snapper		check with supplier	
whiting	le merlan	all year, best in winter	number and weight or fillets

Food value

Fish is as useful a source of animal protein as meat. The oily fish, such as sardines, mackerel, herrings and salmon contain vitamins A and D in their flesh; in white fish, such as halibut and cod, these vitamins are present in the liver.

The bones of sardines, whitebait and tinned salmon, when eaten, provide the body with calcium and phosphorus.

Since all fish contains protein it is a good body-building food and oily fish is useful for energy and as a protective food because of its vitamins.

Owing to its fat content oily fish is not so digestible as white fish and is not suitable for cookery for invalids.

Preservation (see also Chapter 14)

Freezing
Fish is either frozen at sea or as soon as possible after reaching port. It should be thawed out before being cooked. Plaice, halibut, turbot, haddock, sole, cod, trout, salmon, herring, whiting, scampi, smoked haddock and kippers are available frozen.

Canning
The oily fish are usually canned. Sardines, salmon, anchovies, pilchards, tuna, herring and herring roe are canned in their own juice (as with salmon) or in oil or tomato sauce.

Salting
In this country salting of fish is usually accompanied by a smoking process.

Cured herrings: Cured herrings are packed in salt.

Caviar: Caviar is the slightly salted roe of the sturgeon which is sieved, tinned and refrigerated. Imitation caviar is also obtainable – see p. 171.

Smoking
Fish to be smoked may be gutted or left whole. It is then soaked in a strong salt solution (brine), and in some cases a dye is added to improve colour. After this it is drained and hung on racks in a kiln and exposed to smoke for five or six hours.

Cold smoking takes place at a temperature of no more than 33°C (to avoid cooking the flesh). Therefore all cold smoked fish is raw and is usually cooked before being eaten, the exception being smoked salmon.

Hot smoked fish is cured at a temperature between 70–80°C in order to cook the flesh, so does not require further cooking.

Quality points for buying
Choose fish with a pleasant smoky smell and a bright glossy surface. The flesh should be firm; sticky or soggy flesh means that the fish may have been of low quality or under smoked.

Storage
Refrigerate before use as the preservative quality of the smoke is only slight. Smoked fish products keep in good condition for a little longer than fresh fish.

Arbroath smokies – are small haddocks smoked in Arbroath, Scotland. The fish is hot smoked and can be eaten uncooked or may be brushed with melted butter and grilled.

Finnan haddock – the name derives from Findon, Scotland. The haddocks are split, left on the bone, lightly brined without a dye, and cold smoked to give a pale-coloured fish. Usually cooked by poaching in milk.

Yellow smoked haddock – the fish is split or filleted, cold smoked and dyed to give a bright yellow colour.

Bloaters – are whole herrings, lightly salted and cold smoked. They are traditionally smoked in Yarmouth and on the East Coast. They only keep for a few days as they are mildly salted and the gut is not removed so that the body swells and has a gamey flavour. Bloaters are usually gutted and grilled.

Buckling – are small, whole, lightly hot-smoked herring served either cold or warmed through.

Kippers – are gutted and flattened herring, salted and cold-smoked. High quality kippers come from Loch Fyne, Craister and the Isle of Man. Mass produced varieties are available filleted and vacuum packed. Kippers are at their best between August and April and are cooked by grilling or simmering in water.

Red or hard smoked herrings – are whole, heavily brined and smoked until very firm.

Smoked cod – is filleted, briefly soaked in brine with bright yellow colouring or dipped into a chemical solution to give colour and a slight smoky flavour. Should be cooked before eating by poaching, grilling or baking.

Smoked eel – smoked whole or in small fillets. Usually served cold as a first course.

Smoked mackerel – is usually hot-smoked so does not require cooking. Cold-smoked mackerel is also available which needs to be cooked, usually by grilling.

Smoked salmon – regarded as the best of the smoked fish, cured in two ways. The London cure involves light smoking and salting to give the salmon a delicate flavour and moist texture; the Scottish cure is a stronger smoking process giving the fish a more pronounced flavour. Traditionally served thinly sliced as a first course.

Smoked sprats – the fish are hot-smoked and may be eaten cold or grilled.

Smoked trout – the fish are hot-smoked whole or in fillets and are usually served cold as a first course.

Cod's roe – is also smoked and usually served as a first course.

Pickling

Herrings: Herrings pickled in vinegar are filleted, rolled and skewered and known as rollmops.

Use

Fish is cooked by boiling, poaching, grilling, baking, shallow and deep frying. Certain fish are not cooked, apart from the smoking or curing process. This applies for example to smoked salmon, smoked eel, smoked trout, and buckling.

Oily fish

Anchovies (*les anchois*)

Anchovies are small round fish used tinned in this country; they are supplied in 60 g and 390 g tins. They are filleted and packed in oil.

They are used for making anchovy butter and anchovy sauce, for garnishing dishes such as Scotch woodcock and Escalope de veau viennoise. They may be used as a dish in a selection of hors-d'œuvre, as a savoury, and they can be used in puff pastry and served at cocktail parties.

Conger eel (*la congre*)

The conger eel is a dark grey sea-fish with white flesh which grows up to 3 metres in length. It may be used in the same way as eels, or it may be smoked.

Menu example: Smoked eel, horseradish sauce.

Common eel (*l'anguille*)
Eels live in fresh water and are also farmed and can grow up to 1 metre in length. They are found in many British rivers and considerable quantities are imported from Holland. Eels must be kept alive until the last minute before cooking and they are generally used in fish stews.

Menu examples: Bouillebaisse; Jellied eels.

Herring (*le hareng*)
Fresh herrings are used for breakfast and lunch menus; they may be grilled, fried or soused. Kippers (which are split, salted, dried) and smoked herrings are served mainly for breakfast and also as a savoury. Average weight is 250 g.

Menu example: Grilled herrings, mustard sauce.

Mackerel (*le maquereau*)
Mackerel are grilled, shallow fried or soused, and may be used on breakfast and lunch menus. They must be used fresh because the flesh deteriorates very quickly. Average weight, 360 g.

Menu example: Grilled mackerel with anchovy butter.

Pilchards (*la sardine*)
These are mature sardines, and can grow up to 24 cm (10 in). They have a good distinctive flavour, and are best grilled or baked.

Salmon (*le saumon*)
Salmon is perhaps the most famous river fish and is caught in British rivers like the Dee, Tay, Severn, Avon, Wye and Spey. It is also extensively farmed. A considerable number are imported from Scandinavia, Canada, Germany and Japan. Apart from using it fresh, salmon is tinned or smoked. When fresh, it is usually boiled or grilled. When boiled it is cooked in a court-bouillon. Frequently, whole salmon are cooked and when cold decorated and served on buffets. Weight varies from 3½–15 kg. Salmon under 3½ kg are known as grilse.

Menu examples: Poached salmon with hollandaise sauce; Salmon mayonnaise.

Salmon trout (sea trout) (*la truite saumonée*)
Salmon trout are a sea fish similar in appearance to salmon, but smaller, and they are used in a similar way. Average weight, 1½–2 kg.

Menu example: Cold salmon trout with mayonnaise sauce.

Sardines (*les sardines*)
Sardines are small fish of the pilchard family which are usually tinned and used for hors-d'œuvre, sandwiches and as a savoury. Fresh sardines are also available and may be cooked by grilling or frying.

Sprats (*le sprat*)
Sprats are small fish fried whole and are also smoked and served as an hors-d'œuvre.

Trout (*la truite*)
Trout live in rivers and lakes and in the UK they are cultivated on trout farms. When served *au bleu*, they must be alive just before cooking; they are then killed, cleaned, sprinkled with vinegar and cooked in a court-bouillon. Trout are also served grilled or shallow fried, and may also be smoked and served as an hors-d'œuvre. Average weight, 180–230 g.

Menu examples: Smoked trout with horseradish sauce; Panfried river trout.

Tunny (*le thon*)
Tunny is a very large fish cut into sections, used fresh or tinned in oil and is used mainly in hors-d'œuvre and salads.

Whitebait (*la blanchaille*)
Whitebait are the fry or young of herring, 2–4 cm long, and they are deep fried.

Menu example: Devilled whitebait.

Fig. 5.12 A wholesale fish market

White fish – flat

Brill (*la barbue*)
Brill is a large flat fish which is sometimes confused with turbot. Brill is oval in shape; the mottled brown skin is smooth with small scales. It can be distinguished from turbot by brill's lesser breadth in proportion to length; average weight, 3–4 kg.

It is usually served in the same way as turbot.

Menu examples: Tronçon de barbue grillé, sauce anchois; Suprême de barbue Mornay.

Dab (*la limade*)
Dab is an oval-bodied fish – its upper skin is sandy brown with green freckles. Usual size is 20–30 cm (8–10 in). It has a pleasant flavour when fresh, and may be cooked by all methods.

Flounder (*le flet*)
This is also oval, with dull brown upper skin (or sometimes dull green with orange freckles). Usual size is 30 cm (12 in). Flesh is rather watery and lacks flavour, needing good seasoning. It can be cooked by all methods.

Halibut (*le flétan*)
Halibut is a long and narrow fish, brown, with some darker mottling on the upper side; it can be 3 metres in length and weigh 150 kg. Halibut is served on higher-class menus as it is much valued for its flavour. It is poached, boiled, grilled or shallow fried.

Menu example: Suprême de flétan belle meunière.

Megrim
Megrim has a very long slender body, sandy-brown coloured with dark blotches. Usual size is 20–30 cm (8–12 in). It has a softish flesh and an unexceptional flavour, so needs good flavouring. It is best breadcrumbed and shallow-fried.

Plaice (*la plie*)
Plaice are oval in shape, with dark brown colouring and orange spots on the upper side, used on all types of menus; they are usually deep fried or grilled. Average weight, 360–450 g.

Menu example: Grilled plaice with lemon and parsley butter.

Larger plaice known in French as 'carrelet' are also used for poached, fried and grilled dishes.

Menu example: Filet de carrelet Dugléré.

Skate (*la raie*)
Skate, a member of the ray family, is a very large fish and only the wings are used. It is always served on the bone and either shallow or deep fried or cooked in a court-bouillon and served with black butter.

Menu examples: Raie au beurre noir; Fried skate.

Sole (*la sole*)
Sole is considered to be the best of the flat fish. The quality of the Dover sole is well known to be excellent.

Soles are cooked by poaching, grilling or frying, both shallow and deep. They are served whole or filleted and garnished in a great many ways.

The usual size is 180–750 g; fillets are taken from sole of 500 g and over. A 180–250 g fish is referred to as a slip sole. When serving a whole fish, a 250–500 g sole may be used, the size depending on the type of establishment and the meal for which it is required.

Menu examples: Sole colbert; Sole dieppoise; Filet de sole Waleska; Paupiette de sole Newburg.

Lemon sole (*la limande*)
This is related to Dover sole, but is broader in shape, and its upper skin is

warm, yellowy-brown and mottled with darker brown. It can weight up to 600 g (1½ lbs), and may be cooked by all methods.

Turbot (*le turbot*)
Turbot has no scales and is roughly diamond in shape; it has knobs known as tubercules on the dark skin. In proportion to its length it is wider than brill; 3½–4 kg is the average weight.

Turbot may be cooked whole, filleted or cut into portions on the bone. It may be boiled, poached, grilled or shallow fried.

Menu examples: Turbot poche, sauce hollandaise; Suprême de turbot florentine; Tronçon de turbot grillé, beurre maître d'hôtel.

Witch
This is similar in appearance and weight to lemon sole, with sandy-brown upper skin. It is best fried, poached, grilled or steamed.

John Dory (*le Saint Pierre*)
John Dory has a thin distinctive body, flattened from side to side, which is sandy beige in colour and tinged with yellow, with a blue silver grey belly. There is a blotch on each side referred to as 'thumbprint of St Peter'. It has very tough sharp spikes. The flavour is considered superb, and the fish may be cooked by all methods but is best poached, baked or steamed. The large bony head accounts for two thirds of the weight. Usual size 36 cm (15 in).

Ling
This is the largest member of the cod family, and is mottled brown or green with a bronze sheen; the fins have white edges. Size can be up to 90 cm (3 ft). Ling has a good flavour and texture and is generally used in fillets or cutlets, as for cod.

Monkfish (also known as angler-fish)
Monkfish has a huge flattened head, with a normal fish-shaped tail. It is brown with dark blotches. The tail can be up to 180 cm (6 ft), weight 1–10 kg (2–20 lbs). It may be cooked by all methods, and is a firm, close textured white fish with excellent flavour.

Pike (*la brochet*)
Pike has a long body usually 60 cm (2 ft) which is greeny-brown, flecked with lighter green, with long toothy jaws. The traditional fish for quenelles, it may also be braised or steamed.

Perch (*la perche*)
Perch has a deep body, marked with about five shadowy vertical bars, and the fins are vivid orange or red. Usual size 15–30 cm (6–12 ins). It is generally considered to have an excellent flavour, and may be shallow-fried, grilled, baked, braised or steamed.

Pollack
This is a member of the cod family, and has a similar shape and variable colours. Its usual size is 45 cm (18 ins). It is drier than cod, and is used for soups and stews.

Redfish
This is bright red or orange-red, with a rosy belly and dusky gills. Usual size is 45 cm (18 ins). It may be poached, baked or used in soups.

Red gurnard (grey and yellow gurnard may also be available) (*le grondin*)
This has a large 'mail-checked', tapering body with very spiky fins. Usual size is 20–30 cm (8–12 ins). It is good for stews, braising and baking.

Red mullet (*le rouget*)
Red mullet is on occasion cooked with the liver left in, as it is thought that they help to impart a better flavour to the fish. Mullet are usually cooked whole, and the average weight is 360 g ($\frac{3}{4}$ kg).

Menu examples: Rouget grenobloise; Rouget en papillote.

Shark (*le pèlerin*)
The porbeagle shark, mako or hammerhead, fished off the British coast, gives the best quality food. It is bluish-grey above with a white belly and matt skin. Size is up to 300 cm (10 ft). It may be cooked by all methods, but grilling in steaks or *en brochette* are particularly suitable.

Smelt (*l'éperlan*)
Smelts are small fish found in river estuaries and imported from Holland; they are usually deep fried or grilled. When grilled they are split open. The weight of a smelt is from 60 to 90 g.

Menu example: Fried breadcrumbed smelts.

Snapper
There are several kinds of snapper all of which are brightly coloured. Deep red or medium sized ones give the best flavour. Snapper may be steamed, fried, grilled, baked or smoked.

Whiting (*le merlan*)
Whiting are very easy to digest and they are therefore suitable for cookery for invalids. They may be poached, grilled or deep fried and used in the making of fish stuffing (farce de poisson). Average weight, 360 g.

Menu example: Merlan en colère.

Rockfish
Rockfish is the fishmonger term applied to catfish, coal-fish, dogfish, and conger eel etc, after cleaning and skinning. It is usually deep fried in batter.

White fish – round

Bass
Bass have silvery-grey backs and white bellies; small ones may have black spots. They have an excellent flavour, with white, lean, softish flesh (which must be very fresh). Bass can be steamed, poached, stuffed and baked, or grilled in steaks. Usual length is 30 cm (1 ft) but they can grow to 60 cm (2 ft).

Bream (*la brème*)
Sea bream is a short, oval-bodied, plump, reddish fish, with large scales and a dark patch behind the head. It is used on many less expensive menus; it is usually filleted and deep fried, or stuffed and baked, but other methods of cooking are employed. Average weight ½–1 kg; size 28–30 cm (11–16 in).

Menu examples: Fillet of bream, tartare sauce; Filet de brème meunière.

Carp
This is a freshwater fish, usually farmed. The flesh is white with a good flavour, and is best poached in fillets or stuffed and baked. The usual size is 1–2 kg (2–4 lbs).

Cod (*le cabillaud*)
Cod varies in colour but is mostly greenish, brownish or olive grey. It can measure up to 5 ft in length. Cod is cut into steaks or filleted and cut into portions; it can be deep or shallow fried or boiled. Small cod are known as codling. Average weight of cod, 2½–3½ kg.

Menu examples: Darne de cabillaud pochée, sauce persil; Grilled cod steak.

Coley (Saith, Coalfish, Blackjack)
Coley is dark greenish-brown or blackish in colour, but the flesh turns white when cooked. It has a coarse texture and a dry undistinctive flavour, so is best for mixed fish stews, soups or pies. Size is 40–80 cm (16–30 in).

Dogfish (Huss, Flake, Rigg)
These are slender elongated small sharks. The non-bony white or pink flesh is versatile, and is usually shallow or deep fried. It has a good flavour when very fresh. Length is usually 60 cm (24 in) and weight is 1¼ kg (2½ lbs).

Grey mullet
This has a scaly streamlined body, which is grey-silver or blue-green. Deep sea or off-shore mullet has a fine flavour, with firm, moist flesh. It may be stuffed and baked or grilled in steaks. Some people believe that flavour is improved if the fish is kept in a refrigerator for 2–3 days, without being cleaned. Length is usually about 30 cm (1 ft); weight 500 g (1¼ lb).

Gudgeon
Gudgeon are small fish found in continental lakes and rivers. They may be deep fried whole. On menus in this country the French term *en goujon* refers to other fish such as sole or turbot, cut into pieces the size of gudgeon.

Menu example: Filets de sole en goujons, sauce tartare.

Haddock (*l'aigrefin*)
Haddock is distinguished from cod by the thumb mark on the side and by the lighter colour. Every method of cooking is suitable for haddock, and it appears on all kinds of menus. Apart from fresh haddock, smoked haddock is used a great deal for breakfast; it may also be served for lunch and as a savoury. Average weight, ½–2 kg.

Finnan haddock is the most popular smoked haddock, which takes its name from a fishing village, Findon, south of Aberdeen. For the smoking process the haddock is cleaned, split and the head removed. Then salting takes place for two hours, after which the fish are dried for two to three hours and finally smoked over peat, hardwood, sawdust or fir cones for 12 hours.

Menu examples: Filet d'aigrefin à l'Orly; Haddock Monte Carlo.

Hake (*le colin*)
Owing to overfishing, hake is not plentiful. It is usually boiled and is easy to digest. The flesh is very white and of a delicate flavour.

Menu example: Boiled hake and egg sauce.

Shellfish

Food value
Shellfish is a good body-building food. As the flesh is coarse and therefore indigestible a little vinegar may be used in cooking to soften the fibres.

Quality, purchasing points and storage

1 With the exception of shrimps and prawns all shellfish, if possible, should be purchased alive, so as to ensure freshness.
2 They should be stored in a cold room.
3 Shellfish are kept in boxes and covered with damp sacks.
4 Shellfish should be cooked as soon as possible after purchasing.

Shrimps and prawns are usually bought cooked and may be obtained in their shell or peeled. They should be freshly boiled, of an even size and not too small. Frozen shrimps and prawns are obtainable in packs ready for use.

Cockles
These are enclosed in pretty cream-coloured shells of 2–3 cm (1–1½ in). Cockles are soaked in salt water to purge and then steamed. They may be used in soups, salads and fish dishes, or served as a dish by themselves.

Shrimps (*les crevettes grises*)
Shrimps are used for garnishes, decorating fish dishes, cocktails, sauces, salads, hors-d'œuvre, potted shrimps, omelets and savouries.

Menu examples: Shrimp cocktail; Shrimp omelet.

Prawns (*les crevettes roses*)
Prawns are larger than shrimps; they may be used for garnishing and decorating fish dishes, for cocktails, canapé moscovite, salad, hors-d'œuvre and for hot dishes like curried prawns.

Menu examples: Crevettes roses; Curried prawns.

Scampi, Dublin bay prawn (*la langoustine*)
Scampi are found in the Mediterranean. The Dublin bay prawn, which is the same family, is caught around the Scottish coast. These shellfish resemble small lobster about 20 cm (8 in) long and only the tail flesh is used.

Menu examples: Fried scampi; Scampi provençale.

Crayfish (*l'écrivisse*)
Crayfish are a type of small fresh-water lobster used for garnishing cold buffet dishes and for recipes using lobster. They are dark brown or grey, turning pink when cooked. Average size is 8 cm (3 in).

Lobster (*le homard*)
Quality and purchasing points

1 Live lobsters are bluish black in colour and when cooked they turn bright red.
2 They should be alive when bought in order to ensure freshness.
3 Lobsters should have both claws attached.
4 They ought to be fairly heavy in proportion to their size.
5 Price varies considerably with size. For example, small ½ kg lobsters are more expensive per kilogram than large lobsters.
6 Lobster prices fluctuate considerably during the season.
7 Hen lobsters are distinguished from the cock lobsters by a broader tail.
8 There is usually more flesh on the hen, but it is considered inferior to that of the cock.
9 The coral of the hen lobster is necessary to give the required colour for certain soups, sauces and lobster dishes. For these, 1 kg hen lobster should be ordered.
10 When required for cold individual portions, cock lobsters of ¼–½ kg are used to give two portions.

Use: Lobsters are served cold in cocktails, hors-d'œuvre, salads, sandwiches and on buffets. When hot they are used for soup, grilled and served in numerous dishes with various sauces. They are also used as a garnish to fish dishes.

Menu examples: Mayonnaise de homard; Homard Mornay; Bisque de homard (lobster soup).

Crawfish (*la langouste*)
Crawfish are like large lobsters without claws, but with long antennae. They are brick red in colour when cooked. Owing to their size and appearance they are used mostly on cold buffets but they can be served hot. The best size is 1½–2 kg (3–4 lbs).

Menu example: Langouste parisienne.

Crab (*le crabe*)
Quality and purchasing points

1 Crab should be alive when bought to ensure freshness and both claws should be attached to the body.
2 The claws should be large and fairly heavy.

Shellfish (les crustacés): seasons and purchasing units

Shellfish	*French*	*Season*	*Purchasing unit*
cockles	les coques (f)	all year, best in summer	
common crab	le crabe	all year, best April to December	number and weight
spider crab		all year	number and weight
swimming crab		all year	number and weight
king crab, red crab		check with supplier	imported frozen, shelled, prepared
soft shelled crab		Check with supplier	
crawfish	la langouste	April to October	number and weight
cuttlefish	la seiche	all year	number and weight
Dublin Bay prawn	la langoustine	all year	number and weight
fresh water crayfish	l'écrevise	mainly imported, some farmed in UK, wild have short season	
lobster	le homard	April to November	number and weight
mussels	les moules	September to March	
octopus	le poulpe	all year	number and weight
oysters	les huîtres	May to August	by the dozen
prawn and shrimp	la crevette grise la crevette rose	all year	number and weight
scallop	la coquille St Jacques	best December to March	number and weight
sea urchin	l'oursin	all year	

3 The hen crab has a broader tail, which is pink. The tail of the cock is narrow and whiter.
4 There is usually more flesh on the hen crab, but it is considered to be of inferior quality to that of the cock.

Use: Crabs are used for hors-d'œuvre, cocktails, salads, dressed crab, sandwiches and bouchées. Soft-shelled crabs are eaten in their entirety. They are considered to have an excellent flavour and may be deep or shallow fried or grilled.

Oysters (*les huîtres*)

Whitstable and Colchester are the chief English centres for oysters where they occur naturally and are also farmed. Since the majority of oysters are eaten raw it is essential that they are thoroughly cleansed before the hotels and restaurants receive them.

Quality and purchasing points

1 Oysters must be alive; this is indicated by the firmly closed shells.
2 They are graded in sizes and the price varies accordingly.
3 Oysters should smell fresh.
4 They should be purchased daily.
5 English oysters are in season from September to April (when there is an R in the month).
6 During the summer months oysters are imported from France, Holland and Portugal.

Storage: Oysters are stored in barrels or boxes, covered with damp sacks and kept in a cold room to keep them moist and alive. The shells should be tightly closed; if they are open, tap them sharply, and if they do not shut at once, discard them.

Use: The popular way of eating oysters is in the raw state. They may also be served in soups, hot cocktail savouries, fish garnishes, as a fish dish, in meat puddings and savouries.

Menu examples: Whitstable natives; Huîtres frits, sauce tartare; Steak, kidney and oyster pudding.

Mussels (*les moules*)

Mussels are extensively cultivated on wooden hurdles in the sea, producing tender, delicately flavoured, plump fish. British mussels are considered good; French mussels are smaller; Dutch and Belgian mussels are plumper. All vary in quality from season to season.

Buying and quality points

1 The shells must be tightly closed.
2 The mussels should be large.
3 There should not be an excessive number of barnacles attached.
4 Mussels should smell fresh.

Storage: Mussels are kept in boxes, covered with a damp sack and stored in a cold room.

Use: They may be served hot or cold or as a garnish.

Menu examples: Moules marinière; Moules vinaigrette.

Scallops (*la coquille St Jacques*)

Great scallops are up to 15 cm (6 ins) in size; Bay scallops up to 8 cm (3 ins); Queen scallops are small-cockle-sized, and are also known as 'Queenies'. Scallops may be steamed, poached, fried or grilled.

Buying and quality points

1 Scallops are found on the sea bed, and are therefore dirty, so it is advisable to purchase them ready cleaned.
2 If scallops are not bought clean the shells should be tightly closed.
3 The orange part should be bright in colour and moist.
4 If they have to be kept, they should be stored in an ice-box or refrigerator.

Use: Scallops are usually poached or fried.

Menu examples: Fried scallops; Coquille St Jacques bonne femme.

Squid (*le calmar*)

The common squid has mottled skin and white flesh, two tentacles, eight arms and flap-like fins. Usual size is 15–30 cm (6–12 ins). Careful, correct preparation is important if the fish is to be tender. It may be stir-fried, fried, baked or grilled.

Cuttlefish (*la seiche*)
They are usually dark with attractive pale stripes and the size can be up to 24 cm (10 ins). Cuttlefish are prepared like squid and may be stewed or gently grilled.

Octopus (*le poulpe*)
Large species are tough to tenderise; they are then prepared as for squid. Small octopus can be boiled, then cut up for grilling or frying. When stewing, long cooking time is needed.

Winkles (*les bigorneau (m)*)
Winkles are small sea snails with a delicious flavour. They may be boiled for three minutes and served with garlic butter or on a dish of assorted shellfish.

Sea-urchin or sea hedgehog (*l'oursin (m)*)
They have spine-covered spherical shells. Only the orange and yellow roe is eaten, either raw out of the shell or removed with a teaspoon and used in soups, sauces, scrambled eggs etc. Ten to twenty urchins provide approximately 200 g (8 oz) roe.

Fish offal

Liver
An oil rich in vitamins A and D is obtained from the liver of cod and halibut. This is used medicinally.

Roe
Those used are the soft and hard roes of herring, cod, sturgeon and the coral from lobster.

Soft herring roes are used to garnish fish dishes and as a savoury. Cod's roe is smoked and served as hors-d'œuvre. The roe of the sturgeon is salted and served raw as caviar and the coral of lobster is used for colouring lobster butter and lobster dishes, and also as a decoration for fish dishes.

Further information
Seafish Industry Authority, 144 Cromwell Road, London SW7 4ET.

6 Vegetables (*les legumes*)

Fresh vegetables and fruits are important foods both from an economic and nutritional point of view. On average, each person consumes 125–150 kg per year of fruit and vegetables.

The purchasing of these commodities is difficult because of:

(a) the highly perishable nature of the products;
(b) changes in market practice owing to varying supply and demand;
(c) the effect of preserved foods, eg frozen vegetables.

The high perishability of fresh vegetables and fruits causes problems not encountered in other markets. Fresh vegetables and fruits are living organisms and will lose quality quickly if not properly stored and handled. Improved transportation and storage facilities can help prevent loss of quality.

Types of vegetables

Roots	*Tubers*	*Bulbs*	*Leafy*
beetroot	Jerusalem artichokes	garlic	chicory
carrots	potatoes	leeks	Chinese leaves
celeriac	sweet potatoes	onions	corn salad
horseradish	yams	shallots	lettuce
mooli		spring onions	mustard and cress
parsnips			radiccio
radish			sorrel
salsify			spinach
scorzonera			Swiss chard
swedes			watercress
turnips			

Brassicas	*Pods and seeds*	*Fruiting*	*Stems and shoots*	*Mushrooms and fungi*
broccoli	broad beans	aubergine	asparagus	ceps
Brussels sprouts	butter or lima beans	avocado	beans	chanterelles
cabbage	runner beans	courgette	cardoon	horn of plenty
calabrese	mange-tout	cucumber	celery	morels
cauliflower	okra	marrow	endive	mushrooms
curly kale	peas	peppers	globe artichokes	
spring greens	sweetcorn	pumpkin	kohlrabi	
		squash	sea kale	
		tomatoes		

Automation in harvesting and packaging speeds the handling process and helps retain quality.

Vacuum cooling, a process whereby fresh produce is moved into huge chambers, where, for about half an hour, a low vacuum is maintained, inducing rapid evaporation which quickly reduces field heat, has been highly successful in improving quality.

Experience and sound judgement are essential for the efficient buying and storage of all commodities, but none probably more so than fresh vegetables and fruit.

The grading of fresh fruit and vegetables within the EEC

There are four main quality classes for produce:

Extra Class – for produce of top quality,
Class I – for produce of good quality,
Class II – for produce of reasonably good quality,
Class III – for produce of low marketable quality.

Food value

Root vegetables: Root vegetables are useful in the diet because they contain starch or sugar for energy, a small but valuable amount of protein, some mineral salts and vitamins. They are also useful sources of cellulose and water.

Green vegetables: The food value of green vegetables is not the same as for root vegetables because no food is stored in the leaves, it is only produced there; therefore little protein or carbohydrate is found in green vegetables. They are rich in mineral salts and vitamins, particularly vitamin C and carotene. The greener the leaf the larger the quantity of vitamin present.

The chief mineral salts are calcium and iron.

Quality and purchasing points

Root vegetables

They must be:

(a) clean;
(b) firm;
(c) sound;
(d) unblemished;
(e) even size;
(f) even shape.

Green vegetables

1 They must be absolutely fresh.
2 The leaves must be bright in colour, crisp and not wilted.
3 Cabbage and brussels sprouts should have tightly growing leaves and be compact.
4 Cauliflowers should have closely grown flowers and a firm, white head; not too much stalk or too many outer leaves.
5 Peas and beans should be crisp and of medium size. Pea-pods should be full, beans not stringy.
6 Blanched stems must be firm, white, crisp and free from soil.

Seasons for home grown vegetables

Spring		
asparagus new carrots	greens cauliflower new turnips	broccoli – white and purple new potatoes
Summer		
artichokes, globe cauliflower beans, broad beans, French sweetcorn	turnips aubergine peas carrots	asparagus cos lettuce radishes sea-kale
Autumn		
artichokes, globe artichokes, Jerusalem beans, runner broccoli salsify celeriac turnips	parsnips aubergine cauliflower celery swedes	field mushrooms peppers red cabbage shallots marrow
Winter		
Brussels sprouts kale cauliflower Savoy cabbage turnips	chicory celery broccoli celeriac	cabbage parsnips red cabbage swedes
All the year round		

Although the following vegetables are available all the year round, nevertheless at certain times, owing to bad weather, a heavy demand or other circumstances, supplies may be temporarily curtailed. However, owing to air transport, most vegetables are available all year round.

beetroot	leeks	cabbage
mushrooms	carrots	onions
cucumber	spinach	lettuce
tomatoes	watercress	potatoes

Storage

1 Root vegetables should be emptied from sacks and stored in bins or racks.
2 Green vegetables should be stored on well-ventilated racks.
3 Salad vegetables can be left in their containers and stored in a cool place.

Preservation

Canning: Certain vegetables are preserved in tins: artichokes, asparagus, carrots, celery, beans, peas (fins, garden, processed), tomatoes (whole, purée), mushrooms, truffles.

Dehydration: Onions, carrots, potatoes and cabbage are shredded and quickly dried until they contain only 5 per cent water.

Drying: The seeds of legumes (peas and beans) have the moisture content reduced to 10 per cent.

Pickling: Onions and red cabbage are examples of vegetables preserved in spiced vinegar.

Salting: French and runner beans may be sliced and preserved in dry salt.

Freezing: Many vegetables such as peas, beans, sprouts, spinach and cauliflower are deep frozen.

Different kinds of vegetables

Roots

Beetroot – two main types, round and long. Used for soups, salads and as a vegetable.

Carrots – are grown in numerous varieties and sizes. Used extensively for soups, sauces, stocks, stews, salads, as a vegetable.

Celeriac – large, light-brown, celery-flavoured root. Used in soups, salads and as a vegetable.

Horseradish – long, light-brown, narrow root, grated and used for horseradish sauce.

Mooli – long, white, thick member of radish family, used for soups, salads or as a vegetable.

Parsnips – long white root tapering to a point. Unique nut-like flavour. Used in soups, added to casseroles and as a vegetable (roasted, purée etc).

Radishes – small summer variety, round or oval, served with dips, in salads or as a vegetable in white or cheese sauce.

Salsify – also called oyster plant because of similarity of taste. Long, narrow root used in soups, salads and as a vegetable.

Scorzonera – long narrow root, slightly astringent in flavour. Used in soups, salads and as a vegetable.

Swede – large root with yellow flesh. Generally used as a vegetable, mashed or parboiled and roasted. May be added to stews.

Turnip – two main varieties, long and round. Used in soups, stews and as a vegetable.

Tubers

Artichokes, Jerusalem – potato-like tuber with a bitter-sweet flavour. Used in soups, salads and as a vegetable.

Potatoes – many varieties are grown, but all potatoes should be sold by name eg King Edward, Desirée, Maris Piper etc. This is important as the caterer needs to know which varieties are best suited for specific cooking purposes. The various varieties fall into four categories: floury, firm, waxy or salad potatoes.

Further information

Potato Marketing Board, 50 Hans Crescent, Knightsbridge, London SW1X 0NB.

Sweet potatoes – long tubers with purple or sand coloured skins and orange flesh. The flavour is sweet and aromatic. Used as a vegetable (fried, puréed, creamed, candied) or made into a sweet pudding.

Yams – similar to sweet potatoes, usually cylindrical, often knobbly in shape. Can be used in the same way as sweet potatoes.

Bulbs

Garlic – an onion-like bulb with a papery skin inside of which are small individually wrapped cloves. Used extensively in many forms of cookery. Garlic has a pungent distinctive flavour and should be used sparingly.

Leeks – summer leeks have long white stems, bright green leaves and a milder flavour than winter leeks. These have a stockier stem and a stronger flavour. Used extensively in stocks, soups, sauces, stews, hors-d'œuvre and as a vegetable.

Onions – there are numerous varieties with different coloured skins and varying strengths. After salt, the onion is probably the most-used flavouring in cookery. Can be used in almost every type of food except sweet dishes.

Shallots – have a similar but more refined flavour than the onion and are therefore more often used in top class cookery.

Spring onions – are slim and tiny like miniature leeks. Used in soups, salads and Chinese and Japanese cookery.

Leafy

Chicory – a lettuce with coarse, crisp leaves and a sharp, bitter taste in the outside leaves. The inner leaves are milder.

Chinese leaves – long white, densely packed leaves with a mild flavour resembling celery. Makes a good substitute for lettuce and can be boiled, braised or stir-fried as a vegetable.

Corn salad – sometimes called lamb's lettuce. Small, tender, dark leaves with a tangy nutty taste.

Lettuce – many varieties: cabbage, cos, little gem, iceberg, oakleaf, Webbs. Used chiefly for salads, but can be cooked as a vegetable or used as a wrapping for other foods, eg fish fillets.

Mustard and cress – small embryonic leaves of mustard and garden cress with a sharp warm flavour. Used mainly in, or as a garnish to, sandwiches and salads.

Radiccio – round, deep red variety of chicory with white ribs and a distinctive bitter taste.

Sorrel – bright green sour leaves which can be overpowering if used on their own. Best when tender and young. Used in salad and soups.

Spinach – tender dark green leaves with a mild musky flavour. Used for soups, garnishing egg and fish dishes, as a vegetable and raw in salads.

Swiss chard – has large, ribbed, slightly curly leaves with a flavour similar to but milder than spinach. Used as for spinach.

Watercress – long stems with round dark tender green leaves and a pungent peppery flavour. Used for soups, salads, and for garnishing roasts and grills of meat and poultry.

Brassicas

Broccoli – various types: white, green, purple-sprouting. A delicate vegetable with a gentle flavour used in soups, salads, stir-fry dishes and cooked and served in many ways as a vegetable.

Brussels sprouts – small green buds growing on thick stems. Can be used for soup but are mainly used as a vegetable, and can be cooked and served in a variety of ways.

Cabbage – three main types: green, white and red. There are many varieties of green cabbage available at different seasons of the year. Early green cabbage is deep green and loosely formed. Later in the season they firm up with solid hearts. Savoy is considered the best of the winter green cabbage. White cabbage is used for coleslaw; green and red as a vegetable, boiled, braised or stir-fried.

Cauliflower – are heads of creamy-white florets with a distinctive flavour. Used for soup and cooked and served in various ways as a vegetable.

Pods and seeds

Broad beans – are pale-green oval-shaped beans contained in a thick fleshy pod. Young broad beans can be removed from the pods and cooked in their shells and served as a vegetable in various ways. Old broad beans will toughen and when removed from the pods will have to be shelled before being served.

Butter or lima beans – butter beans are white, large, flattish and oval-shaped. Lima beans are smaller. Both are used as a vegetable or salad, stew or casserole ingredient.

Runner beans – a popular vegetable that must be used when young. Bright-green colour and a pliable velvety feel. If coarse, wilted, or older beans are used they will be stringy and tough.

Mange-tout – also called snow-peas or sugar peas. They are a flat pea pod with immature seeds which after topping, tailing and stringing, may be eaten in their entirety. Used as a vegetable, in salads and for stir-fry dishes.

Okra – curved and pointed seed pods with a flavour similar to aubergines. Cooked as a vegetable or in creole type stews.

Peas – garden peas are normal size, petits pois are a dwarf variety. Marrow fat peas are dried. Popular as a vegetable, peas are also used for soups, salads, stews and stir-fry dishes.

Sweetcorn – also known as maize or Sudan corn. Available 'on the cob' fresh or frozen or in kernels, canned or frozen. A versatile commodity and used as a first course, in soups, salads, casseroles and as a vegetable.

Fruiting

Aubergine – firm, elongated, varying in size with smooth shiny skins ranging in colour from purple-red to purple-black. Inner flesh is white with tiny soft seeds. Almost without flavour, it requires other seasonings, eg garlic, lemon juice, herbs to enhance its taste. May be sliced and fried or baked, steamed, stuffed and used in ratatouille.

Avocado – a fruit that is mainly used as a vegetable because of its bland, mild, nutty flavour. There are two main types: the summer variety that is green when unripe and purple-black when ripe has golden-yellow flesh; the winter ones are more pear-shaped with smooth green skin and pale green to yellow flesh. Eaten as first courses and used in soups, salads, dips and garnishes to other dishes.

Courgette – a baby marrow, light to dark green in colour, with a delicate flavour becoming stronger when cooked with other ingredients, eg herbs, garlic, spices. May be boiled, steamed, fried, baked, stuffed and stir-fried.

Cucumber – a long smooth-skinned fruiting vegetable, ridged and dark green in colour. Used in salads, soups, sandwiches, garnishes and as a vegetable.

Marrow – long, oval-shaped edible gourds with ridged green skins and a bland flavour. May be cooked as for courgettes.

Peppers – are available in three colours: green peppers are unripened and they turn yellow to orange and then red (they must remain on the plant to do this). Peppers are used raw and cooked in salads, vegetable dishes, stuffed and baked, casseroles and stir-fried dishes.

Pumpkins – vary in size and can weight up to 50 kg (100 lbs). Associated with Halloween as a decoration but may be used in soups or pumpkin pie.

Squash – there are many varieties. The bright golden-brown or green skins have flesh that is firm and floury. They can be boiled, steamed, puréed or baked.

Tomatoes – along with onions, probably the most-used vegetable in cookery. There are several varieties: cherry, yellow, globe, large ridged (beef) and plum. Used in soups, sauces, stews, salads, sandwiches and as a vegetable.

Stems and shoots

Asparagus – three main types: white, with creamy white stems and a mild flavour; French, with violet or bluish tips and a stronger more astringent flavour; and green, with what is considered a delicious aromatic flavour. Asparagus can be used in almost every method of cookery with the exception of pastry dishes.

Bean sprouts – are the slender young sprouts of the germinating soya or mung bean. They are used as a vegetable accompaniment, in stir-fry dishes and salads.

Cardoon – a longish plant with root and fleshy ribbed stalk which is similar to celery, but its leaves are grey-green in colour. Used cooked as a vegetable or raw in salads and dips.

Celery – long stemmed bundles of fleshy, ribbed stalks, white to light green in colour. Used in soups, stocks, sauces, cooked as a vegetable and raw in salads and dips.

Chicory – also known as Belgian endive. Conical heads of crisp white, faintly bitter leaves approximately 15 cm (6 in) long. Used cooked as a vegetable and raw in salads and dips.

Globe artichokes – resemble fat pine cones with overlapping fleshy, green, inedible leaves, all connected to an edible fleshy base or bottom. Used as a first course, hot or cold; as a vegetable, boiled, stuffed, baked, fried or in casseroles.

Kohlrabi – a stem which swells to turnip shape above the ground. Those about the size of a large egg are best for cookery purposes (other than soup or purées). May be cooked as a vegetable, stuffed and baked and added to stews and casseroles.

Sea kale – delicate white leaves with yellow frills edged with purple. Can be boiled or braised or served raw like celery.

Mushrooms and fungi

Ceps – wild mushrooms with short, stout stalks with slightly raised veins and tubes underneath the cap in which the brown spores are produced.

Chanterelles – are wild, funnel-shaped, yellow-capped mushrooms with a slightly ribbed stalk which runs up under the edge of the cap.

Horns of plenty – trumpet-shaped, shaggy, almost black wild mushroom.

Morels – delicate, wild mushroom varying in colour from pale beige to dark-brownish black with a flavour that suggests meat.

Mushrooms – field mushrooms are found in meadows from late summer to autumn. They have a creamy white cap and stalk.

Cultivated mushrooms are available in three types button: small, succulent, weak in flavour; cap mushrooms, and open or flat mushrooms.

All mushrooms both wild and cultivated have a great many uses in cookery eg soups, stocks, sauces, salads, vegetables, savouries, garnishes etc.

Further information

Fresh Fruit and Vegetable Information Bureau, Bury House, 126–128 Cromwell Road, London SW7 4EJ.

7 Fruits (*les fruits*)

For culinary purposes fruit can be divided into the following groups:

Different kinds of fruits

Stone fruits	*Hard fruits*	*Soft fruits*	*Citrus fruits*	*Tropical and Mediterranean fruits*
apricots	apples	bilberries	clementines	bananas
cherries	crab apples	blackberries	grapefruit	cape gooseberries
damsons	pears	blackcurrants	kumquats	carambola
greengages		blueberries	lemons	(star fruits)
nectarines		gooseberries	limes	dates
peaches		loganberries	mandarins	figs
		raspberries	oranges	granadillas
		redcurrants	pomeloes	guavas
		strawberries	tangerines	kiwi fruit
			tangelos	lychees
			(uglis)	mangosteens
				mangoes
				passion fruit
Other fruits				papayas
cranberries				paw-paws
grapes				persimmons
melons				pineapples
rhubarb				sharon fruits

Seasons

The chief citrus fruits (oranges, lemons and grapefruit) are available all the year. Mandarins, clementines, satsumas and tangerines are available in the winter.

Rhubarb is in season in the spring, and the soft and stone fruit become available from June in the following order: gooseberries, strawberries, raspberries, cherries, currants, damsons, plums.

Imported apples and pears are available all the year round; home-grown mainly from August to April. Many varieties of fruits are imported from all over the world and speedy air transport cargo services enable some fruits (eg strawberries) to be in season virtually the whole year round.

Food value

The nutritive value of fruit depends on its vitamin content, especially vitamin C; it is therefore valuable as a protective food.

The cellulose of fruit is useful as roughage.

Storage

Hard fruits, such as apples, are left in boxes and kept in a cool store.

Soft fruits, such as raspberries and strawberries, should be left in their punnets or baskets in a cold room.

Stone fruits are best placed in trays so that any damaged fruit can be seen and discarded.

Peaches and citrus fruits are left in their delivery trays or boxes.

Bananas should not be stored in too cold a place because the skins turn black.

Quality and purchasing points

1 Soft fruits deteriorate quickly, especially if not sound. Care must be taken to see that they are not damaged or too ripe when bought.
2 Soft fruit should appear fresh; there should be no shrinking, wilting or signs of mould.
3 The colour of certain soft fruits is an indication of ripeness (strawberries, gooseberries).
4 Hard fruit should not be bruised. Pears should not be over-ripe.

Preservation

Drying: Apples, pears, apricots, peaches, bananas and figs are dried. Plums when dried are called prunes, and currants, sultanas and raisins are produced by drying grapes.

Canning: Almost all fruits may be canned. Apples are packed in water and known as solid packed apples; other fruits are canned in syrup.

Bottling: Bottling is used domestically, but very little fruit is commercially preserved in this way. Cherries are bottled in maraschino.

Candied: Orange and lemon peel are candied; other fruits with a strong flavour, such as pineapple, are preserved in this way.

The fruit is covered in hot syrup which is increased in sugar content from day to day until the fruit is saturated in a very heavy syrup. It is then allowed to dry slowly until it is no longer sticky.

Glacé: The fruit is first candied and then dipped in fresh syrup to give a clear finish. This method is applied to cherries.

Crystallised: After the fruit has been candied it is left in fresh syrup for 24 hours and then allowed to dry very slowly until crystals form on the surface of the fruit.

Candied, glacé and crystallised fruits are mainly imported from France.

Jam: Some stone and all soft fruits can be used.

Jelly: Jellies are produced from fruit juice.

Quick freezing: Strawberries, raspberries, loganberries, apples, blackberries, gooseberries, grapefruit and plums are frozen and they must be kept below zero.

Cold storage: Apples are stored at temperatures between 1°C–4°C, depending on the variety of apple.

Gas storage: Fruit can be kept in a sealed store room where the atmosphere is controlled. The amount of air is limited, the oxygen content of the air is decreased and the carbon dioxide increased, which controls the respiration rate of the fruit.

Fruit juices, syrups and drinks

Fruit juices such as orange, lemon, blackcurrant are canned.

Syrups such as rose hip and orange are bottled. Fruit drinks are also bottled; they include orange, lime and lemon.

Uses

General use: With the exception of certain fruits (lemon, rhubarb, cranberries) fruit can be eaten as a dessert or in its raw state. Some fruits have dessert and cooking varieties – eg apples, pears, cherries and gooseberries.

Stone fruits

Damsons, plums, greengages, cherries, apricots, peaches and nectarines are used as a dessert; stewed (compote) for jam, pies, puddings and in various sweet dishes. Peaches are also used to garnish certain meat dishes.

Menu examples: Damson pie; Peach Melba; Braised ham with peaches; Braised duck with cherries.

Hard fruits

Apples: the popular English dessert varieties include Beauty of Bath, Discovery, Spartan, Worcester Pearmain, Cox's Orange Pippin, Blenheim Orange, Laxton's Superb and James Grieve. Imported apples include Golden Delicious, Granny Smith and Sturmers. The Bramley is the most popular cooking apple.

Pears: The William Conference and Doyenne du Comice are among the best known pears.

Apples and pears are used in many pastry dishes. Apples are also used for garnishing meat dishes and for sauce which is served with roast pork and duck.

Menu examples: Apple pie; Apple fritters; Pear flan; Pear Belle Hélène; Charlotte aux pommes; Apfelstrudel; Apple and red cabbage salad.

Soft fruit

Raspberries, strawberries, loganberries and gooseberries are used as a dessert. Gooseberries, black and red currants and blackberries are stewed, used in pies and puddings. They are used for jam and flavourings.

Menu examples: Gooseberry fool; Raspberry trifle; Strawberry tartlets; Blackcurrant tart.

Citrus fruits

Oranges, lemons and grapefruit are not usually cooked, except for marmalade. Lemons and limes are used for flavouring and garnishing, particularly fish dishes. Oranges are used mainly for flavouring, and in fruit salads, also to garnish certain poultry dishes. Grapefruit are served for breakfasts and as a first course generally for luncheon. Mandarins, clementines and satsumas are eaten as a dessert or used in sweet dishes. Kumquats look and taste like tiny oranges and are eaten with the skin on. Tangelos are a cross between tangerines and grapefruit, and are sometimes called uglis. Pomelos are the largest of the citrus fruits, predominantly round but with a slightly flattened base and pointed top.

Menu examples: Lime soufflé; Florida cocktail; Lemon pancakes; Orange bavarois; Duck with orange salad.

Different fruits and their seasons

English	*French*	*Season*
apple	la pomme	all year round, cheapest October to December
apricot	l'abricot (m)	May to September
banana	la banane	all year round
blackberry	la mûre de ronce	September to October
blackcurrants	le cassis	July to September
red currants	les groseilles rouges	July to September
cherry	la cerise	June to August
clementine	la clémentine	
cranberries	les airelles	November to January
damson	la prune de damas	September to October
date	la datte	
fig	la figue	July to September
gooseberry	la groseille à macquereau	July to September
grapefruit	la pamplemousse	all year round
grapes	les raisins	all year round, best in autumn
greengage	la reine-Claude	August
lemon	le citron	all year round
mandarin	la mandarine	November to June
melon	le melon	
orange	l'orange (f)	all year round
peach	la pêche	September
pear	la poire	September to March
pear, avocado	l'avocat (m)	
pineapple	l'ananas (m)	all year round, best in summer
plum	la prune	July to October
raspberry	la framboise	June to August
rhubarb	la rhubarbe	December to June
strawberry	la fraise	June to August
tangerine	la tangerine	

Tropical and other fruits

Banana: As well as being used as a dessert, bananas are grilled for a fish garnish, fried as fritters and served as a garnish to poultry (Maryland). They are used in fruit salad and other sweet dishes.

Menu examples: Beignets de bananes; Filet de sole caprice; Banana flan; Chicken Maryland.

Cape gooseberries (physalis): A sharp, pleasant-flavoured small round fruit dipped in fondant and served as a type of petit four.

Carambola: Also known as starfruit, it has a yellowish-green skin with a waxy sheen. The fruit is long and narrow and has a delicate lemon flavour.

Cranberries: These hard red berries are used for cranberry sauce, which is served with roast turkey.

Dates: Whole dates are served as a dessert; stoned dates are used in various sweet dishes and petits fours.

Figs: Fresh figs may be served as a first course or dessert. Dried figs may be used for fig puddings, and other sweet dishes.

Granadillos: These are like an orange in shape and colour, are light in weight and similar to a passion fruit in flavour.

Grapes: Black and white grapes are used as a dessert, in fruit salad, as a sweet meat and also as a fish garnish (véronique).

Guavas: Size varies between that of a walnut to an apple. Ripe guavas have a sweet pink flesh. They can be eaten with cream or mixed with other fruits.

Kiwi fruit: Have a brown furry skin. The flesh is green with edible black seeds which when thinly sliced gives a pleasant decorative appearance.

Lychees: A Chinese fruit with a delicate flavour. Obtainable tinned in syrup and also fresh.

Mangoes: Can be as large as a melon or as small as an apple. Ripe mangoes have smooth pinky-golden flesh with a pleasing flavour. They may be served in halves sprinkled with lemon juice, sugar, rum, or ginger. Mangoes can also be used in fruit salads and for sorbets.

Mangostines: Are apple-shaped with a tough reddish-brown skin which turns purple as the fruit ripens. They have juicy creamy flesh.

Melon: There are several types of melon. The most popular are:

Honeydew: These are long, oval-shaped melons with dark green skins. The flesh is white with a greenish tinge.

Charentais: Charentais melons are small and round with a mottled green and yellow skin. The flesh is orange coloured.

Cantaloup: Cantaloup are large round melons with regular indentations. The rough skin is mottled orange and yellow and the flesh is light orange in colour.

Care must be taken when buying as melons should not be over- or under-ripe. This can be assessed by carefully pressing the top or bottom of the fruit. There should be a slight degree of softness to the cantaloup and charentais melons.

The stalk should be attached, otherwise the melon deteriorates quickly.

Uses: Melon is mainly used as a dessert and for hors-d'œuvre and sweet dishes.

Passion fruit: the name comes from the flower of the plant which is meant to represent the Passion of Christ. Size and shape of an egg with crinkled purple-brown skin when ripe. Flesh and seeds are all edible.

Paw-paw (papaya): green to golden skin, orangey flesh with a sweet subtle flavour and black seeds. Eaten raw sprinkled with lime or lemon juice.

Persimmon: a round orange-red fruit with a tough skin which can be cut when the fruit is ripe. When under ripe they have an unpleasant acid-like taste of tannin.

Pineapple: Pineapple is served as a dessert; it is also used in many sweet dishes and as a garnish to certain meat dishes.

Menu examples: Grilled gammon and pineapple; Pineapple fritters, apricot sauce.

Sharon fruit: A seedless persimmon tasting like a sweet exotic peach.

Rhubarb: Forced or early rhubarb is obtainable from January. The natural rhubarb from April–June.

Used for pies, puddings, fool and compote.

Further information

Fruit and Vegetable Information, Bury House, 126–128 Cromwell Road, London SW7 4ET.

8 Nuts (*les noix (f)*)

Nuts are the reproductive kernel (seed) of the plant or tree from which they come. Nuts are perishable and may easily become rancid or infested with insects. Nuts are used extensively in pastrywork, confectionery, vegetarian cooking and the preparation of some liqueurs.

English	*French*
almond	l'amande (f)
Brazil	la noix de Bresil
chestnut	le marron
coconut	la noix de coco
filbert	
hazel nut	la noisette
pecan	la pacane
pistachio	la pistache
walnut	la noix

Season

Dessert nuts are in season during the autumn and winter.

Food value

Nuts are highly nutritious because of their protein, fat and mineral salts. They are of considerable importance to vegetarians, who may use nuts in place of meat; they are therefore a food which builds, repairs and provides energy. Nuts are difficult to digest.

Storage

Dessert nuts, those with the shell on, are kept in a dry, ventilated store. Nuts without shells, whether ground, nibbed, flaked or whole, are kept in air-tight containers.

Quality and purchasing points

1 Nuts should be of good size.
2 They should be heavy for their size.
3 There must be no sign of mildew.

Use

Nuts are used extensively in pastry and confectionery work and vegetarian cookery, and also for decorating and flavouring.

They are used whole, or halved, and almonds are used ground, nibbed and flaked.

Almonds

Salted almonds are served at cocktail parties and bars.

Ground, flaked, nibbed, are used in sweet dishes and for decorating cakes; they are used for cake mixtures, large and small, such as Dundee cake, Congress tarts, macaroons, for sweet meats and large cakes.

Marzipan (almond paste) is used for covering fruit cakes, frangipane is an almond filling used in Bakewell tarts etc; praline (almond brittle) is used for ice cream and gâteaux; Berny potatoes are coated with chopped almonds.

Brazil nuts

Brazil nuts are served with fresh fruit as dessert and are also used in confectionery.

Chestnuts

Chestnuts are used as stuffing for turkeys; chestnut flour is used for soup, and as a garnish for ice cream.

Coconut

Coconut is used in desiccated form for curry preparations, and in all sizes of cakes and confectionery.

Filberts and hazel nuts

These nuts are used as a dessert and for praline.

Pecans

Pecan nuts are used salted for dessert, various sweets and ice cream.

Peanuts and cashew nuts

These are salted and used in cocktail bars as bar snacks.

Pistachio nuts

These small green nuts, grown mainly in France and Italy, are used for decorating galantines, small and large cakes and petits fours They are also used in ice cream.

Walnuts

Walnuts, imported mainly from France and Italy, are used as a dessert, in salads and for decorating cakes and sweet dishes. They are also pickled, while green and unripe.

9 Eggs (*les oeufs*)

The term eggs applies not only to those of the hen, but also to the edible eggs of other birds, such as turkeys, geese, ducks, guinea fowl, quails and gulls.

Hens' eggs

Cost

Wholesale unit	crate 360 eggs
Retail unit	dozen

Quality points for buying

1 The eggshell should be clean, well-shaped, strong and slightly rough.
2 When broken there ought to be a high proportion of thick white to thin white.
3 The yolk should be firm, round and of a good even colour.

If an egg is kept, the thick white gradually changes into thin white and water passes from the white into the yolk. The yolk loses strength and begins to flatten, water evaporates from the egg and is replaced by air, and as water is heavier than air fresh eggs are heavier than stale ones.

It is possible to determine the freshness of an egg by placing it in a 10 per cent solution of salt (60 g salt to ½ litre water). A two-day-old egg will float near the bottom of the solution with its broad end upward. As the egg ages it becomes lighter and floats closer to the surface of the solution.

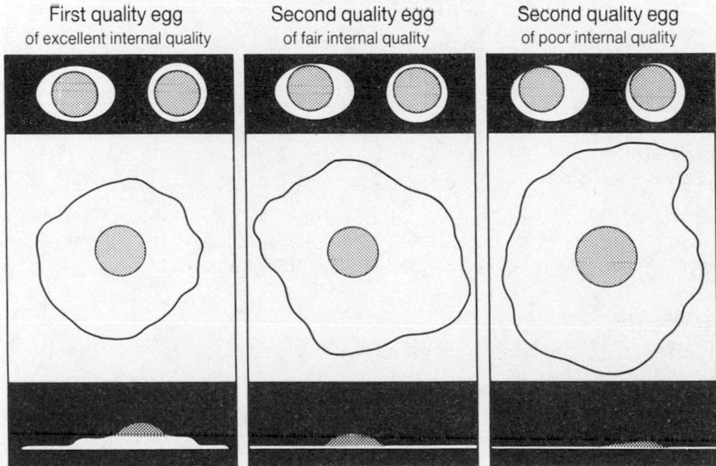

Fig. 5.13 Quality of eggs

Storage

1 Eggs must be stored in their packing trays blunt end upwards, in a cool but not too dry place; a refrigerator of 0–5°C is ideal.
2 No strongly smelling foods such as cheese, onions and fish should be stored near the eggs because the eggshells are porous and the egg will absorb strong odours.
3 Eggs should not be washed before being stored as washing would remove the natural protective coating.
4 Eggs are stored point-end down.

Food value

Eggs contain most nutrients and are low in calories – two eggs containing 180 calories. Egg protein is complete and easily digestible, therefore it is useful to balance meals. Eggs may also be used as the main dish; they are a protective food and provide energy and material for growth and repair of the body.

Production

Hens' eggs are graded in seven sizes:

Size	Weight	Size	Weight	Size	Weight
Size 1	70 g	Size 3	60 g	Size 5	50 g
2	65 g	4	55 g	6	45 g
				7	under 45 g

The size of an egg does not affect the quality but does affect the price. The eggs are tested for quality, then weighed and graded.

Grade A – naturally clean, fresh eggs, internally perfect with intact shells and an air cell not exceeding 6 mm ($\frac{1}{4}$ in) in depth.

Grade B – eggs which have been down-graded because they have been cleaned or preserved, or because they are internally imperfect, cracked or have an air cell exceeding 6 mm but not more than 9 mm in depth.

Grade C – are eggs which are fit for breaking for manufacturing purposes but cannot be sold in their shells to the public.

They are then packed into boxes containing 30 dozen, 360 (3 long hundreds). The wholesale price of eggs is quoted per long hundred (120).

All egg-boxes leaving the packing station are dated.

Raw eggs and Salmonella

In the first half of 1988 there were 26 reported incidents of Salmonella infection, involving over 300 people, associated with the consumption of raw egg in uncooked foods. In September 1988, the Department of Health issued the following advice to all Chief Environmental Health Officers:

To advise food manufacturers and caterers that for all recipes currently needing raw shell eggs, which involve no cooking, pasteurised egg (frozen, liquid or dried) should be used instead.

Hens can pass Salmonella infection into their eggs and thus cause food poisoning. However, in terms of the United Kingdom's consumption of around 30 million eggs a day, the incidence of known infection is very small. Moreover, most infections cause only a mild stomach upset but the effects can be more serious in the very young or old or people weakened by other disease.

Preservation

Cold storage: Eggs are kept a little above freezing-point. The humidity of the air and the amount of carbon dioxide in the air are controlled. They will keep about 9 months under these conditions.

Frozen eggs: These are mainly used by bakers and confectioners, and are sold in large tins of various sizes. The eggs are washed, sanitised and then broken into sterilised containers. After combining the yolks and whites they are strained, pasteurised, packed and quick-frozen.

Egg yolks and whites are frozen separately.

Dried eggs: The eggs are broken, well mixed and then spray dried at a temperature of approximately 71°C. These are also used mainly by bakers and confectioners.

Grease method: A pure grease free from salt, water and other impurities must be used, such as Oteg, paraffin wax or lard. The eggs are dipped into the liquid grease and then allowed to dry. The grease fills up the porous shell, forms a skin and so excludes air. They may then be stored in the same way as fresh eggs.

Waterglass – sodium silicate: A solution is made up with sodium silicate and boiling water. When used it must be quite cold; the newlaid eggs are packed point downwards in an earthenware bowl or galvanised pail and covered with the solution. A lid is placed on the container to prevent evaporation.

Pasteurised eggs: The same procedure is followed as for frozen eggs. The liquid eggs are heated to 63°C (145°F) for one minute, then rapidly cooled (this does not affect their culinary quality).

Dried egg white is available and is suitable for meringues, royal icing etc.

Dried egg white substitute is also available and can be used for meringues, royal icing and similar albumen-based confections. Dried egg white and dried egg white substitute must be stored in cool, dry conditions.

Uses of eggs

Hors-d'œuvre: Hard-boiled egg for egg mayonnaise and for salads.

Soups: For the clarifying of consommé, in the preparation of royales for garnishing consommé, for thickening certain soups and veloutés.

Egg dishes: Scrambled, poached, soft-boiled, hard-boiled, en cocotte, sur le plat and omelets etc.

Farinaceous: Eggs are used in the making of various pastas eg ravioli, canneloni and noodles.

Fish: In the preparation of frying batters and for coating fish prior to crumbing.

Sauces: Mayonnaise, hollandaise, béarnaise, sabayon etc.

Meat and poultry: For binding mixtures such as Vienna steaks and coating cuts of meat and poultry prior to cooking.

Salads: Usually hard-boiled and included in many composed salads.

Sweets and pastries: Eggs are used in many ways for these items.

Savouries: Scotch woodcock, cheese soufflé, savoury flans etc.

The DHSS endorses the Code of Practice recommended by the egg industry itself in handling its product, ie:

Eggs should be stored in a cool place preferably under refrigeration;
Eggs should be stored away from possible contaminants like raw meat;
Stocks should be rotated: first in, first out.
Hands should be washed before and after handling eggs;
Cracked eggs should *not* be used;
Preparation surfaces, utensils and containers should be regularly cleaned and always cleaned between preparation of different dishes;
Egg dishes should be *consumed as soon as possible* after preparation or, if not for immediate use, refrigerated.

Other eggs

Turkeys' and guinea fowls' eggs may be used in place of hens' eggs.

The eggs of the goose or duck may be used only if they are thoroughly cooked.

Quails eggs are used in some establishments as a garnish, or as a hors-d'œuvre.

Further information

British Egg Information, Bury House, 126–128 Cromwell Road, London SW7 4ET.

10 Milk (*le lait*)

Milk is a white nutritious liquid produced by female mammals for feeding their young. The milk most used in this country is that obtained from cows. Goats' milk and ewes' milk can also be used.

Food value

Milk is almost a perfect food as it contains all the nutrients required for growth, repair, energy, protection and regulation of the body.

Storage

Milk keeps less well than almost any other food; it readily becomes dirty and unsafe; therefore it must be stored with care.

Milk is an excellent food for human beings; it is also, unfortunately, an excellent food for bacteria. Cows are subject to tuberculosis and other infections; precautions are therefore taken and herds are tested for TB.

As milk is so easily contaminated it can be dangerous. Contamination can occur before milking – cows may be diseased; during milking – by unclean cows, premises or milkers; after milking – at the dairy, in transit or in the kitchen.

Packaging

Bulk fresh milk can be supplied in six ways: Milkpak, Churnpak or Handipak, Portabag, Churnbox and Carrypak. All packs contain homogenised, pasteurised milk.

The Milkpak system provides a constant supply of milk from a refrigerated unit. Available in 3 or 5 gallon packs.

Churnpak or Handipak is a disposable plastic bag of 4 gallon capacity that fits into a tough returnable crate.

Portabag is a strong disposable plastic bag holding 3 gallons of milk with a tap for pouring.

Churnbox is similar to Churnpak, the 3 or 5 gallon plastic bag is fitted into a non-returnable corrugated case.

Carrypak is a modified form of 'bag in a box'. Available in 3 or 5 gallon capacity packs with taps or spouts.

Carton packs of fresh milk are available in ½, 1 and 2 pint sizes.

Fresh milk is also available in ½ and 1 gallon containers.

Storage points

1 Fresh milk should be kept in the container in which it is delivered.
2 Milk must be stored in the refrigerator.

3 Milk should be kept covered as it absorbs strong smells such as onion or fish.
4 Fresh milk and cream should be purchased daily.
5 Tinned milk is stored in a cool, dry ventilated room.
6 Dried milk is stored in air-tight tins and kept in a dry store.
7 Imitation cream is kept in the refrigerator.
8 Pasteurised milk will keep for up to five days under refrigeration.
9 Sterilised milk should keep for a minimum of seven days if *unopened*, but several weeks without refrigeration is usual.
10 UHT milk will keep unopened for several months. Before using, always check the date stamp which expires six months after processing, and make sure to rotate stocks. Once opened, store as for pasteurised milk.

Pasteurised: Milk is heated for 15 seconds at 72°C to kill harmful bacteria, followed by rapid cooling.

UHT (ultra heat treatment): Milk is given this treatment by heating to 132°C for one second. Whole, semi-skimmed and skimmed are available.

Homogenised: Milk is homogenised by forcing it through a fine aperture to break down the fat globules. These do not rise to the surface but remain distributed throughout the milk. It is then pasteurised.

Channel Island milk: This is produced by Jersey and Guernsey breeds of cow. The milk has a very distinct creamline and is pasteurised. It has a high (4 per cent) fat content.

Sterilised milk: This milk is homogenised, bottled, sealed and heated to at least 100°C for 20–30 minutes, then cooled. Semi-skimmed milk contains half the fat content of whole milk. The milk is homogenised and pasteurised. It keeps for 2–3 months under refrigeration in the unopened bottle, but has a different taste from fresh milk.

Preservation

Evaporated milk has had 60 per cent of the water removed by evaporation before canning.

Condensed milk is richer than evaporated because more water has been removed. It can be sweetened or unsweetened.

Dried milk is available as whole milk powder, skimmed milk powder and filled milk powder (skimmed milk powder to which vegetable fat has been added).

Uses of milk

1 Soups and sauces;
2 Cooking of fish, vegetables and gnocchi;
3 Making of puddings, cakes, sweet dishes;
4 Cold drinks – milk, milk shakes, malts;
5 Hot drinks – tea, coffee, cocoa, chocolate.

Cream (*la crème*)

This is the concentrated milk fat which is skimmed off the top of the milk and should contain at least 18 per cent butterfat. Cream for whipping must contain more than 30 per cent butterfat.

Cream: types, packaging, storage and uses

Type of cream	*Legal minimum fat %*	*Processing and packaging*	*Storage*	*Characteristics and uses*
Half cream	12	Homogenised and may be pasteurised or ultra-heat treated	2–3 days	Does not whip; used for pouring. Suitable for low fat diets
Cream or single cream	18	Homogenised and pasteurised by heating to about 79.5°C (175°F) for 15 seconds then cooled to 4.5°C (40°F). Automatically filled into bottles and cartons after processing. Sealed with foil caps. Bulk quantities according to local suppliers	2–3 days in summer 3–4 days in winter under refrigeration	A pouring cream suitable for coffee, cereals, soup or fruit. A valuable addition to cooked dishes. Makes delicious sauces. Does not whip
Soured cream	18	Pasteurised homogenised cream is soured by the addition of a starter culture of bacteria to produce a piquant acid flavour	2–3 days	Suitable for savoury dishes and salad dressing
Whipping cream	35	Not homogenised, but pasteurised and packaged as above	2–3 days in summer 3–4 days in winter under refrigeration	The ideal whipping cream. Suitable for piping, cake and dessert decoration, ice-cream, cake and pastry fillings
Double cream	48	Slightly homogenised, and pasteurised and packaged as above	2–3 days in summer 3–4 days in winter under refrigeration	A rich pouring cream which will also whip. The cream will float on coffee or soup
Double cream 'thick'	48	Heavily homogenised, then pasteurised and packaged. Usually only available in domestic quantities	2–3 days in summer 3–4 days in winter under refrigeration	A rich spoonable cream which will not whip
Clotted cream	55	Heated to 82°C (180°F) and cooled for about 4½ hours. The cream crust is then skimmed off. Usually packed in cartons by hand. Bulk quantities according to local suppliers	2–3 days in summer 3–4 days in winter under refrigeration	A very thick cream with its own special flavour and colour. Delicious with scones, fruit and fruit pies
Sterilised half cream	12	Homogenised, filled into cans and sealed. Heated to 115°C (240°F) for 20 minutes, then cooled rapidly	Up to 2 years if unopened	A pouring cream with a slight caramel flavour
Sterilised cream	23	Processed as above	Up to 2 years if unopened	A thicker, caramel-flavoured cream which can be spooned but not whipped

Type of cream	*Legal minimum fat %*	*Processing and packaging*	*Storage*	*Characteristics and uses*
Ultra-heat treated cream	12 18 35	Half (12%), single (18%) or whipping cream (35%) is homogenised and heated to 132°C (270°F) for one second and cooled immediately. Aseptically packed in polythene and foil lined containers. Available in bigger packs for catering purposes	6 weeks if unopened. Needs no refrigeration. Usually date stamped	A pouring cream
Aerosol cream		UHT cream in sterile aerosol canister. This cream starts to collapse almost immediately		Suitable for squeezing on milk shakes, iced coffee and items for immediate consumption

Commercially frozen cream is available in 2 and 10 kg (4 and 20 lb) slabs.

Non-dairy creams

There are several types and qualities available which are produced from an emulsion of oil, margarine or butter with milk powder and water. Non-dairy creams can be can be used for filling and decorating small and large cakes and making and finishing sweet dishes.

Use of cream

1 Fresh cream must be cold when required for whipping.
2 For preference it should be whipped in china or stainless steel bowls. If any other metal is used, the cream should be transferred to china bowls as soon as possible.
3 If fresh cream is whipped too much it turns to butter. This is more likely to happen in hot conditions. To prevent this, stand the bowl of cream in a bowl of ice while whisking.
4 When adding cream to hot liquids dilute the cream with some of the liquid before adding to the main bulk. This helps to prevent the cream from separating.

Yogurt

Yogurt is a curd-like food, prepared from milk fermented by the action of bacteria feeding on the lactose (milk sugar) and producing lactic acid. Species of lactobacillus bacteria are used. There are two distinct variations in the final processing: stir-type yogurts give a smooth cream-like consistency; set-type yogurts have a junket-like consistency. All yogurt is 'live yogurt' unless heat-treated after preparation and contains live bacteria which remains dormant when kept at low temperature. If stored at room temperature or above, the dormant bacteria become active and produce more acid. Too high an acidity kills the bacteria, impairs the flavour and causes yogurt to separate.

Types of yogurt

1 Fat free yogurt – contains less than 0.5 per cent milk fat.

2 Low fat yogurt – contains maximum 1.5 per cent milk fat.
3 Wholemilk yogurt – contains fat as in whole milk (3.8 per cent).
4 Whole or real fruit yogurt – contains whole fruit in sugar syrup.
5 Fruit flavoured yogurt – contains fruit juices or syrup.
6 Natural yogurt – should contain no colour, preservatives, stabilisers or thickeners and may be fortified with vitamins A and D. Natural yogurt may be flavoured with fruit juice, honey, chocolate, nuts, sugar or natural flavourings.

Storage: Keep all yogurt under refrigeration and check the date stamp has not expired.

Buttermilk is a by-product of butter manufacture. It is made commercially by adding a buttermilk culture to skim milk to give a refreshing drink with a slightly acid flavour.

Smetana is a low-fat product, a cross between soured cream and yogurt.

Further information
National Dairy Council, 5–7 John Prince's Street, London W1M 0AP; Milk Marketing Board, Thames Ditton, Surrey.

11 Fats and oils

Storage of all fats
Fats should be kept in a cold store, and in a refrigerator in warm weather.

Butter (*le beurre*)

Butter must be kept away from strong-smelling foods. Butter is produced by churning fresh cream. One litre of cream yields approximately one $\frac{1}{2}$ kg butter.

Food value
Butter is an energy food as it has a very high fat content.

Quality

1 The taste should be creamy and pleasant.
2 The texture should be soft and smooth.
3 It must smell fresh.
4 The colour of pure butter is almost white or very pale yellow.
5 Fresh butter should be used quickly, otherwise it goes rancid (acquires an unpleasant taste and smell).

Production
Butter consumed in this country is produced in England, New Zealand, Australia, France, Holland and Denmark. Butter is often blended and can be salted or unsalted, the salt acting as a preservative. Butter is also mixed with margarine and sold as a special blend.

Use
Butter is used for most kitchen purposes where expense does not have to be considered.

Butter can be used for: making roux for soups and sauces; finishing sauces such as sauce vin blanc for fish, sauce madère for meat; hard butter sauces (maître d'hôtel) and butter sauces (hollandaise); pot-roasting meat, poultry and game; finishing vegetables (petits pois au beurre); making of all pastes except suet, hot water and nouille paste; decorating cold dishes and cocktail savouries; making cakes and butter creams.

It can be clarified and used for shallow frying of all kinds of food. *Ghee* is clarified butter used in Indian cooking; *concentrated butter* has most of the water and salt removed, contains 96 per cent butterfat and is specially made for cooking and baking.

Further information

Butter Information Council, Tubs Hill House, London Road, Sevenoaks, Kent TN13 1BL.

Margarine (*la margarine*)

Margarine is produced from milk and a blend of vegetable oils emulsified with lecithin, flavouring, salt, colouring and vitamins A and D.

Food value

Margarine is an energy and protective food. With the exception of palm oil, the oils used in the manufacture of margarine do not contain vitamins A and D; these are added during production. Margarine is not inferior to butter from the nutritional point of view.

Quality

There are several grades of margarine: block (hard or semi-hard); soft (butter substitute); semi-hard for making pastry; and cake margarine which creams easily and absorbs egg. Some margarines are blended with butter. Taste is the best guide to quality.

Production

The vegetable oils are obtained from Commonwealth countries, West Africa and South-east Asia. Margarine is made first by extracting the oils and fats from the raw materials, and these are next refined, blended, flavoured and coloured, then mixed with fat-free pasteurised milk. The emulsion is then churned, cooled and packed. Cake and pastry margarines are blended in a different manner to table margarine to produce the texture suitable for mixing.

Use

Margarine can be used in place of butter. The difference being that the smell is not so pleasant, and nut brown (beurre noisette) or black butter (beurre noir) cannot satisfactorily be produced from margarine. The flavour of margarine when used in the kitchen is inferior to butter – it is therefore not so suitable for finishing sauces and dishes.

It should be remembered that it is equally nutritious and may be cheaper than butter.

Vegetable shortening and high-ratio fat are available. They are used extensively in bakery products.

Animal fats

Lard (*le saindoux*)
Lard is the rendered fat from the pig. Lard has almost 100 per cent fat content. It may be used in hot water paste and with margarine to make short paste. It can also be used for deep or shallow frying.

Suet
Suet is the hard solid fat deposits in the kidney region of animals. Beef suet is the best and it is used for suet paste and mince-meat.

Dripping
Dripping is obtained from clarified animal fats and it is used for deep or shallow frying.

Further information
Unilever Ltd, Unilever House, Blackfriars, London EC4.

Oil (*l'huile*)

Oils are fats which are liquid at room temperature.

Oil is obtained from sunflower seed, soya bean, walnut, grape seed, sesame, almond, wheatgerm, olives, maize, ground-nuts (peanuts), hazelnuts, pine kernels, palm and coleseed (rape).

Food value
As oil has a very high fat content it is useful as an energy food.

Storage

1 Oil should be kept in a cool place.
2 If refrigerated some oils congeal; they return to a fluid state in a warm temperature.
3 Oils keep for a fairly long time, but they do go rancid if not kept cool.

Quality
Olive oil is considered one of the best, owing to its flavour. Better grade oils are almost without flavour, odour and colour.

Production
Olive oil is extracted from olives grown in Mediterranean countries, particularly Spain, Italy, Greece and France.

Ground-nut oil is obtained from ground-nuts grown in West Africa.

Maize oil is obtained from maize grown in Europe and the USA.

The oil is extracted from the raw material, refined and stored in drums.

Use
Olive oil is used for making vinaigrette and mayonnaise and in the preparation of hors-d'œuvre dishes. Walnut and ground-nut oils may also be used. It is also used in making farinaceous pastes and for shallow frying.

Other oils are used for deep frying. Oil is used for lubricating utensils, trays and also marble slabs to prevent cooked sugar from sticking.

Oil may also be used to preserve foods by excluding air.

Oil temperatures

Type	*Approx flash-point*	*Smoke point*	*Recommended frying temp*
	(°C)	(°C)	(°C)
finest quality vegetable oils	324	220	180
finest vegetable fat	321	220	180
high-class vegetable oil	324	204	180
pure vegetable fat	318	215	170–182
pure vegetable oil	330	220	
finest quality maize oil	224	215	180
finest fat	321	202	180
finest quality dripping	300	165	170–180
finest natural olive oil	270–273	148–165	175

Points on the use of of all fats and oils

For frying purposes a fat or oil must, when heated, reach a high temperature without smoking. The food being fried will absorb the fat if the fat smokes at a low temperature.

Fats and oils should be free from moisture, otherwise they splutter.

As they are combustible, fats and oils can catch fire. In some fats the margin between smoking and flash point may be narrow.

A good frying temperature is 75°C–180°C.

Further information

British Edible Oils Ltd, Knights Road, London, E16; Proctor and Gamble, Headley House, St Nicholas Avenue, Gosforth, Newcastle upon Tyne NE99 1EE.

12 Cheese (*les fromages*)

Cheese is made worldwide from cows', ewes', or goats' milk and it takes approximately five litres of milk to produce $\frac{1}{2}$ kg of cheese.

There are many hundreds of varieties; most countries manufacture their own special cheeses.

Quality

1 The skin or rind of cheese should not show spots of mildew, as this is a sign of damp storage.
2 Cheese when cut should not give off an over-strong smell or any indication of ammonia.
3 Hard, semi-hard and blue-vein cheese when cut should not appear dry.
4 Soft cheese when cut should not appear runny, but should have a delicate creamy consistency.

Production

Rennet is the chief fermenting agent used in cheese-making and is a chemical substance found in the gastric juice of a calf or lamb.

A typical cheese-making process, briefly, is as follows:

1 One gallon of milk makes approximately one pound of cheese.
2 The milk is tested for acidity and then made sour by using a starter (bacteria which produce lactic acid).
3 Rennet is added, which causes the milk to curdle.
4 The curds are stirred, warmed and then allowed to settle.
5 The liquid (whey) is run off.
6 The curds are ground, salted and put into moulds. If a hard cheese is being made, then pressure is applied in order to squeeze out more of the whey.
7 The curds are now put into the special mould and a skin or rind is allowed to form.
8 When set, the cheese is removed from the mould and is then kept in special storage in order to mature and develop flavour.

Storage
All cheese should be kept in a cool, dry, well-ventilated store and whole cheeses should be turned occasionally if being kept for any length of time. Cheese should be kept away from other foods which may be spoilt by the smell.

Food value
Cheese is a highly concentrated form of food. Fat, protein, mineral salts and vitamins are all present. Therefore it is an excellent body-building, energy-producing, protective food.

Preservation
Certain cheeses may be further preserved by processing. A hard cheese is usually employed, ground to a fine powder, melted, mixed with pasteurised milk, poured into moulds then wrapped in lacquered tinfoil, eg processed Gruyère, Kraft, Primula.

Uses

Soups
Grated Parmesan cheese is served as an accompaniment to many soups, eg minestrone.

It is also used to form a crust on top of brown onion soup.

Farinaceous
A grated hard cheese, usually Parmesan, is mixed in with or is also served as an accompaniment to most farinaceous dishes, eg spaghetti italienne, ravioli.

Egg dishes
Cheese omelet
Oeuf dur Chimay

Fish dishes
Coquille Saint Jacques Mornay
Filets de sole florentine

Vegetables
Cauliflower cheese
Chou de mer Mornay

Savouries
Welsh rarebit
Quiche lorraine

A well-ordered restaurant should always be able to offer a good selection of assorted cheeses on a 'cheese board', and this should be available after lunch or dinner. At least six varieties should be presented, always in prime condition, eg

Cheddar	Gorgonzola
Gruyère	Edam
Camembert	Caerphilly

If demand for cheese is low, then it may be a good policy to offer one or two cheeses only, provided they are in excellent condition, eg Stilton, Brie.

English and Welsh cheese

Cheddar – golden colour with a close texture and a fresh mellow, nutty flavour. It is available in mild, medium mature and mature versions.

Cheshire – orange-red or white, loose crumbly texture and a mild mellow slightly salty flavour.

Double Gloucester – orange-red, a buttery open texture with a delicate creamy flavour.

Leicester – red in colour with a buttery open texture. It is a mellow medium-strength cheese famous for its use in Welsh rarebit.

Derby – honey-coloured, close and buttery texture with a mild fresh flavour which goes well with fruit.

Caerphilly – white in colour and flaky, with a fresh, mild, slightly salty flavour.

Lancashire – white in colour, soft and crumbly with a fresh mild flavour. Excellent for toasted cheese.

Wensleydale – white in colour, moderately close texture with a fresh, mild slightly salty flavour. Excellent with crisp apples or apple pie.

Stilton – white with blue veins, soft and close texture and a strong flavour. 'The King of Cheeses' traditionally accompanied by port.

Scotch cheese

Caboc – small full cream cheese coated in oatmeal, slightly sharp nutty taste.

Dunlop – similar to Cheddar and Double Gloucester, but paler, blander and more moist.

French cheese

Brie – white round cheese with close, soft, creamy texture and delicate flavour.

Camembert – white, round (approximately 10 cm, 4 in) with soft, close, creamy texture and full flavour.

Chèvre – a generic name for a wide range of goats' cheeses. Easily digestible with a sharp sweetness and crumbly texture.

Fourme d'Ambert – sometimes called a French stilton. Salty, full flavour.

Port Salut – round, cream-coloured, mild almost-bland, semi-hard.

Roquefort – blue cheese made from ewe's milk. Rich, sharp flavour with salty aftertaste.

Italian cheese

Bel Paese – round, firm, pearly-white texture and a fresh, creamy taste.

Gorgonzola – blue vein with a rich, sharp flavour. Dolcelatte is a milder version.

Mozzarella – originally made from buffalo milk. Pale and plastic looking, sweet flavour with a little bite.
Parmesan – hard, low fat cheese with a rich pithy flavour. Grated and used extensively in cooking.
Ricotta – fresh, white, crumbly and slightly sweet, similar to cottage cheese.

Other cheeses
Germany – Cambazola: creamy-white round cheese with blue veins and what is considered a good flavour.
Netherlands – Edam: round, full-flavoured with low fat content. Covered in red skin.
Switzerland – Gruyère: firm, creamy-white with a full fruity flavour.
Greece – Fetta: white, moist, crumbly with a refreshing salty-sour taste.

Soft curd cheeses
Curd cheese – made from pasteurised milk soured by the addition of a milk-souring culture and rennet. The milk separates into curds and whey. The whey is drained off, the curds are blended with a little salt and skimmed milk powder to produce a soft, mild flavoured low fat (11 per cent) cheese. Made from either skimmed or medium-fat milk.
Cottage cheese – is a low-fat, high protein product made from pasteurised skimmed milk. Also available are very low fat, sweet and savoury varieties.
Fromage frais – (fresh cheese) or fromage blanc is a fat-free soft curd cheese to which cream can be added to give richer varieties. Also available, low fat, medium-fat, savoury and fruit flavours.
Quark – is a salt free, fat-free soft cheese made from skimmed milk.

Low fat hard cheese
There is a range of hard cheese with half the fat of traditional cheese. These include 'Tendale' (available as Cheshire or Cheddar), 'Shape' (available as Cheshire or Cheddar) and 'Bodyline' available in 2½ kg, 5 lb packs.

Vegetarian cheese
Traditional hard cheeses made using a non-animal rennet of microbial origin are available.

Further information
English Country Cheese Council, 5–7 John Prince's Street, London W1M 0AP.

13 Cereals

Cereals are cultivated grasses, but the term is broadened to include sago, rice and arrowroot. All cereal products contain starch. The following are the important cereals used in catering: wheat, oats, rye, barley, maize, rice, tapioca, sago and arrowroot.

Wheat (*le blé*)

Source
Wheat is the most common cereal produced in the western world and is grown

in most temperate regions. Large quantities are home-grown and a great deal, particularly in the form of strong flour, is imported from Canada.

Food value

Cereals are one of the best energy foods. Whole grain cereals provide vitamin B and are therefore protective foods.

Storage

1 The store room must be dry and well ventilated.
2 Flour should be removed from the sacks and kept in wheeled bins with lids.
3 Flour bins should be of a type that can be easily cleaned.

Flour is probably the most common commodity in daily use. It forms the foundation of bread, pastry and cakes and is also used in soups, sauces, batters and other foods.

Production of flour

The endosperm of the wheat grain contains all the material used by the baker. It consists of numerous large cells of net-like form in which starch grains are tightly packed. In addition, the cells contain an insoluble gluten protein. When flour is mixed with water it is converted into a sticky dough. This characteristic is due to the gluten which becomes sticky when moistened. The relative proportion of starch and gluten varies in different wheats, and those with a low percentage of gluten are not suitable for bread-making, ie soft flour. For this reason, wheat is blended.

In milling, the whole grain is broken up, the parts separated, sifted, blended and ground into flour. Some of the outer coating of bran is removed as is also the wheatgerm which contains oil and is therefore likely to become rancid and so spoil the flour. For this reason wholemeal flour should not be stored for more than 14 days.

White flour contains 72 to 85 per cent of the whole grain (the endosperm only).

Wholemeal flour contains 100 per cent of the whole grain.

Wheatmeal flour contains 85 to 95 per cent of the whole grain.

Hovis flour contains 85 per cent of the whole grain.

High ratio or patent flour contains 40 per cent of the whole grain.

'Self-raising flour' is white flour with the addition of cream of tartar and bicarbonate of soda.

Uses of wheat products

Soft flour: Large and small cakes, biscuits, all pastes except puff and flaky, thickening soups and sauces, batters and coating various foods.

Strong flour: Bread, puff and flaky pastry, and Italian pastes.

Wholemeal flour: Wholemeal bread and rolls.

Further information

Flour Advisory Bureau, 21 Arlington Street, London SW1 1RN.

Semolina is granulated hard flour prepared from the central part of the wheat grain. White or wholemeal semolina is available.

Uses: Gnocchi, milk puddings, moulds and as a dusting for certain pastes such as noodle and ravioli.

Menu example: Gnocchi Romaine.

Macaroni and spaghetti: Soups, farinaceous dishes, garnishes.

Menu examples: Minestrone, Macaroni au gratin.

Noodles: Garnishing soups, farinaceous dishes, meat dishes.

Menu example: Bœuf braisé aux nouilles.

Oats (*l'avoine (f)*)

Oats are either rolled into flakes or ground into three grades of oatmeal: coarse, medium and fine.

Source

Oats are one of the hardiest cereals, and are grown in large quantities in Scotland and the north of England.

Food value

Oats have the highest food value of any of the cereals. They contain a good proportion of protein and fat.

Storage

Because of the fat content, the keeping quality of oat products needs extra care. They should be kept in containers with tight-fitting lids, and stored in a cool, well-ventilated store room.

Uses

Rolled oats: porridge.

Oatmeal: porridge, thickening soups, coating foods, cakes and biscuits, haggis.

Patent rolled oats nowadays largely displace oatmeal and have the advantage of being already heat treated and consequently more quickly and easily cooked.

Barley (*l'orge (f)*)

The whole grain of barley is known as pot or Scotch barley and requires soaking overnight. Pearl barley has most of the bran and germ removed, and it is then polished. These products are used for making barley water for thickening soups and certain stews.

Barley, when roasted, is changed into malt and as such is used extensively in the brewing and distilling of vinegar.

Barley needs the same care in storage as oats.

Buckwheat is the seed of the plant 'bran buckwheat'. The grain is usually roasted before cooking, and is also ground into a strong savoury flour for pancakes and baking.

Rye is a grain producing a dark flour used for rye bread and biscuits.

Maize (*le maïs*)

Maize is also known as corn, sweetcorn or corn-on-the-cob, and besides being served as a vegetable it is processed into cornflakes and cornflour. Maize yields a good oil suitable for cooking.

Cornflour
Cornflour is produced from maize and is the crushed endosperm of the grain which has the fat and protein washed out so that it is practically pure starch.

Cornflour is used for making custard and blancmange powders, because it thickens very easily with a liquid, and sets when cold into a smooth paste that cannot be made from other starches.

Custard powder consists of cornflour, colouring and flavouring.

Cornflour is used for thickening soups, sauces, custards and also in the making of certain small and large cakes.

Rice (*le riz*)

Rice needs a hot, wet atmosphere and is grown chiefly in India, the Far East, South America, Italy and the USA.

There are three main types used in this country:

(a) *Long grain:* a narrow, pointed grain, best suited for savoury dishes and plain boiled rice because of its firm structure, which helps to keep the rice grains separate, eg basmati, patna.
Menu examples: Curried beef and rice; Kedgeree.

(b) *Medium grain:* an all-purpose rice suitable for sweet and savoury dishes, eg carolina, arborio.

(c) *Short grain:* a short, rounded grain, best suited for milk puddings and sweet dishes because of its soft texture, eg arborio.
Menu examples: Baked rice pudding; Poire Condé.

Brown rice
Brown rice is any rice that has had the outer covering removed but retains its bran and as a result is more nutritious.

Whole grain rice
This is whole and unprocessed.

Wild rice
Wild rice is the seed of an aquatic plant related to the rice family.

Ground rice
Ground rice is used for milk puddings.

Rice flour (*la crème de riz*)
Rice flour is used for thickening certain soups, eg cream soups.

Rice paper
This is a thin edible paper produced from rice, used in the preparation of macaroons and nougat.

Storage
Rice should be kept in tight-fitting containers in a cool, well-ventilated store.
Pre-cooked instant rice, par-boiled, ready cooked and boil in the bag are also available.

Tapioca (*le tapioca*)

Tapioca is obtained from the roots of a tropical plant called cassava.

Types
Flake (rough); seed (fine).

Uses
Garnishing soups, milk puddings.

Menu examples: Tapioca pudding; Purée lamballe

Storage
Tapioca should be stored as for rice.

Sago (*le sagou*)

Sago is produced in small pellets from the pith of the sago palm. It is used for garnishing soups and for making milk puddings.

Menu example: Consommé au sagou.

Storage
Sago should be stored as for rice.

Arrowroot (*la marante*)

Arrowroot is obtained from the roots of a West Indian plant called maranta.
It is used for thickening sauces and is particularly suitable when a clear sauce is required as it becomes transparent when boiled. Arrowroot is also used in certain cakes and puddings, and is particularly useful for invalids as it is easily digested.

Storage
Arrowroot is easily contaminated by strong-smelling foods, therefore it must be stored in air-tight tins.

Potato flour (*le fécule de pomme de terre*)

Potato flour is a preparation from potatoes, suitable for thickening certain soups and sauces.

Breakfast cereal foods
A wide variety of cereals is processed into breakfast foods, eg barley, wheat, rice, bran, corn, etc.

14 Raising agents

The method of making mixtures light or aerated may be affected in several ways:

1 Sifting the flour. When sifting flour air is incorporated.
2 Rubbing fat into flour. During this process air can be incorporated.
3 Whisking or beating with:
(a) eggs – for sponges, genoise, Swiss rolls;
(b) egg whites for meringue;
(c) butter or margarine for puff or rough puff pastry;
(d) sugar and fat for creaming method of sponge puddings and rich cakes. In all cases the whisking, beating or rolling (as with puff pastry) encloses air in the mixture.
4 Using baking powder.
5 Using yeast.
6 Layering of fat in a puff paste (known as lamination).

During cooking, steam develops in between the layers of fat and paste in puff and flaky pastry, thus causing the pastry to rise.

1 Baking powder

Baking powder may be made from one part sodium bicarbonate to two parts of cream of tartar. In commercial baking the powdered cream of tartar may be replaced by another acid product eg acidulated calcium phosphate.

When used under the right conditions it produces carbon dioxide gas; to produce gas a liquid and heat are needed. As the acid has a delayed action, only a small amount being given off when the liquid is added, the majority of the gas is released when the mixture is heated. Therefore cakes and puddings when mixed do not lose the property of the baking powder if they are not cooked right away.

Hints on using baking powder

1 Mix the baking powder thoroughly with the flour.
2 Replace the lid tightly on the tin.
3 Measure accurately.
4 Do not slam oven doors in early stages of cooking.
5 Excess baking powder causes a cake to collapse in the middle and dumplings to break up.
6 Insufficient baking powder results in a close, heavy texture.
7 Use within one month of purchase.

Use: It is used in sponge puddings, cakes and scones and in suet puddings and dumplings.

2 Yeast (*la levure*)

Yeast is a fungus form of plant life.

Storage and quality points

1 Yeast should be wrapped and stored in a cold place.
2 It is ordered only as required.
3 It must be perfectly fresh and moist.
4 It should have a pleasant smell.
5 Yeast should crumble easily.
6 It is pale grey in colour.

Food value: Yeast is rich in protein and vitamin B. It is therefore a help towards building and repairing the body and provides protection.

Production: Yeast is a form of plant life consisting of minute cells; these grow and multiply at blood heat provided they are fed with sugar and liquid. The sugar causes fermentation – this is the production of gas (carbon dioxide) and alcohol in the form of small bubbles in the mixture or dough. When heat is applied to the mixture or dough it causes it to rise.

Dried yeast has been dehydrated and requires creaming with a little water before use. Its main advantage is that it will keep for several months in its dry state.

Use: To use yeast these points should be remembered:

1 The yeast should be removed from the refrigerator and used at room temperature.
2 Salt retards the working of yeast.
3 The more salt used the slower the action of yeast.
4 Best temperature for yeast action is 21°C–27°C.
5 The liquid for mixing the dough should be 36°C–37°C.
6 Temperatures over 52°C destroy yeast.
7 Yeast can withstand low temperatures without damage.

Hints on the use of yeast

1 *Warmth* – the flour, bowl and liquid should be warm.
2 *Kneading* – yeast doughs must be kneaded (worked) to make an elastic dough and to distribute the yeast evenly. An elastic dough is required to allow the gases to expand.
3 *Proving* – this term means that the dough is allowed to double its size. This should occur in a warm place, free from draughts. The dough must be covered. The quality of the dough is improved by 'knocking back'. This means the dough is pressed down to its original size and allowed to prove again. The dough is lightly kneaded, moulded and proved again before baking.

Overproving: The dough should not overprove, either in the bowl or in the moulded state. Excess or uneven heat or too long a proving time can cause overproving.

Uses

Bread doughs: rolls, white, brown, wholemeal loaves, etc.
Bun doughs: currant, Chelsea, Swiss, Bath, doughnuts.
Baba, savarin and marignans.

Croissants and brioche.
Danish pastry.
Frying batter.

15 Sugar (*le sucre*)

Sugar is produced from sugar cane grown in a number of tropical and sub-tropical countries and from sugar beet which is grown in Great Britain and Europe.

Food value
As sugar contains 99.9 per cent pure sugar, it is invaluable for producing energy.

Refined white sugars:
granulated
castor
cube
icing

Unrefined sugar:
brown sugar

Partially refined sugar:
Demerara

Storage
Sugar should be stored in a dry, cool place. When purchased by the sack, the sugar is stored in covered bins.

Production
The sugar is extracted from cane or beet, crystallised, refined and then sieved. The largest holed sieve produces granulated, the next size castor and fine linen sieves are used for icing sugar. Loaf or cube sugar is obtained by pressing the crystals while slightly wet, drying them in blocks and then cutting the blocks into squares.

Syrup and treacle are produced during the production of sugar. They are filtered and evaporated to the required colour and thickness.

Use
Sugar is chiefly used for pastry, confectionery and bakery work.

Pastry uses: for pies, puddings, sweet dishes, ice creams and pastries.

Confectionery uses: decorating gâteaux and celebration cakes (birthday, christening, wedding), sweets and petits fours. Sugar work (pulled, blown and spun).

Bakery uses: yeast doughs, large and small cakes.

In the kitchen it is used in certain sauces, such as mint and Robert. Sugar may be added to peas and carrots. It is used in some meat dishes, eg Carbonnade de bœuf, Baked sugar ham. Sugar is also added to the brine solution.

Sugar as well as being used to sweeten foods is also used to give colour, eg Crème caramel and the production of blackjack.

Glucose is a syrup made from potatoes, cane sugar and fruit, treated and refined to a liquid or powder form. Glucose is not as sweet as sugar, but it is an important energy producer. Glucose is used extensively in confectionery work.

Further information
British Sugar Refiners Association, Plantation House, Mincing Lane, London EC3.

16 Cocoa (*le cacao*)

Cocoa is a powder produced from the beans of the cacao tree. It is imported mainly from West Africa.

Food value

As cocoa contains some protein and a large proportion of starch it helps to provide the body with energy. Iron is also present in cocoa.

Storage

Cocoa should be kept in air-tight containers in a well-ventilated store.

Production

The cocoa beans grow in the pods of the cacao tree. The beans are dried, fermented, re-dried and roasted. The shells are cracked and removed; the nibs which are left are ground to a thick brown liquid called cococa mass. The mass is compressed, then crushed, ground and sifted, making cocoa. The cocoa butter has been removed, because it would make the drink greasy.

Uses

For hot drinks cocoa is mixed with milk, milk and water, or water. Hot liquid is needed to cook the starch and make it more digestible.

Cocoa can be used to flavour puddings, cakes, sauces, icing and ice cream.

To make cocoa:

1 Measure the amount of cocoa and liquid carefully (30 g cocoa; 60 g sugar; 1 litre milk or milk and water).
2 Mix the cocoa with a little of the cold liquid.
3 Bring the remaining liquid to the boil, add the cocoa, stirring all the time.
4 Return to the pan and bring to the boil, stirring until it boils, then add the sugar.

Chocolate (*le chocolat*)

Cocoa beans are used to produce chocolate, and over half of the cocoa bean consists of cocoa butter. To produce chocolate, cocoa butter is mixed with crushed cocoa beans and syrup. With baker's chocolate, the cocoa fat (butter) is replaced by vegetable fat thus giving a cheaper product which does not need tempering. For commercial purposes, chocolate is sold in blocks known as *couverture*. Pure chocolate couverture is made from cocoa mass, highly refined sugar and extracted cocoa butter. It is the additional cocoa butter which gives couverture its qualities for moulding, its flavour and therefore its higher price.

Uses: Chocolate or couverture is used for icings, butter creams, sauces, dipping chocolates and moulding into shapes.

Drinking chocolate

This is ground cocoa from which less fat has been extracted and to which sugar has been added. It can be obtained in flake or powder form.

17 Coffee (*le café*)

Coffee is produced from the beans of the coffee tree, and is grown and exported by 14 countries including Brazil, Columbia, Kenya, Indonesia, the Ivory Coast. The varieties of coffee are named after the areas where they are grown eg: Mysore, Kenya, Brazil, Mocha, Java.

Purchasing unit

Coffee beans (a) unroasted, (b) roasted, (c) ground, are sold by the pound and in 7 lb or 28 lb parcels or tins.

Coffee essence is obtained in 5½ oz, 10 oz, 25 oz and 1 gallon bottles.

Quality points for buying

1 Good quality coffee beans should be bought.
2 The beans should be freshly roasted and ground.
3 As water varies in different areas, sample brews with several kinds of coffee should be made to select the best result.

Storage

Coffee should be kept in air-tight containers in a well-ventilated store. The beans should be roasted and ground as they are required.

Food value

It is the milk and sugar served with coffee that have food value. Coffee has no value as a food by itself.

Production

The coffee tree or bush produces fruit called a cherry which contains seeds. The outer-side pulp is removed and the seeds or beans are cleaned, graded and packed into sacks. When required, the beans are blended and roasted to bring out the flavour and aroma.

French coffee usually contains chicory; the root is washed, dried, roasted and ground. The addition of chicory gives a particular flavour and appearance to the coffee.

Coffee essence is a concentrated form of liquid coffee which may contain chicory.

Instant coffee is liquid coffee which has been dried into powder form.

Decaffeinated coffee has most of the caffeine removed, and is therefore less of a stimulant.

Uses

Coffee is mainly used as a beverage which may be served with milk, cream or as a flavouring for cakes, icings, bavarois and ice cream.

The following are the rules for making good coffee:

1 Use good coffee which is freshly roasted and ground.
2 Use freshly drawn, freshly boiled water cooled to 92°–96°C.
3 Measure the quantity of coffee carefully, 300–360 g per 5 litres.
4 After the coffee has been made it should be strained off, otherwise it will acquire a bitter taste, if kept hot for more than 30 minutes.

5 Milk, if served with coffee, should be hot but not boiled.
6 All coffee-making equipment must be kept scrupulously clean, washed thoroughly after each use and rinsed with clean hot water (never use soda).

The various methods for making coffee are as follows:

Instant coffee: Boiling water is added to soluble coffee solids.

Jug or saucepan method: Boiling water is poured on to the coffee grounds in a jug or a saucepan, allowed to stand for a few minutes, then strained.

Plungerpot: This is designed to prevent pouring the coffee grounds.

Percolator: When the water boils it rises up through a tube and percolates through the coffee grounds.

Cona coffee: The water is boiled in a glass globe then it passes up a tube to a glass cup which contains the ground coffee. Here it infuses and as it cools it drops as liquid coffee into the bottom of the glass globe.

Still set: This consists of a container into which the ground coffee is placed. Boiling water is passed through the grounds and the coffee is piped into an urn at the side.

Espresso: This method involves passing steam through coffee grounds and infusing under pressure.

Filter method: Boiling water is poured into a container into which the ground coffee has been placed. The infusion takes place and the coffee drops into the cup below. Automatic drip machines and drip pots use filter papers.

Turkish or Greek coffee is very strong and is made in long-handled copper containers called *ibriks*.

Further information
London Coffee Information Centre, 21 Berners Street, London W1P 4DD.

18 Tea (*le thé*)

Tea is the name given to the young leaves and leaf buds of the tea plant after they have been specially treated and dried.

Tea is produced in India (Assam, Darjeeling), Pakistan, Sri Lanka, Indonesia, China, Uganda, Kenya, Tanzania and Malawi.

Teas show marked differences according to the country and district in which they are produced and it is usual to blend several types.

China teas have the most delicate flavour of any, but lack 'body'.

Types

There are a large number of teas on the market, and as water in different districts affects the flavour, the only sure way to select a tea for continual use is by trying out several blends, tasting them and then assessing the one that gives the most satisfactory flavour.

Buying

Tea may be obtained in packs from ½ oz to 100 lb so obviously many factors to do with the type of business must be considered when deciding how to buy.

The cheapest way of purchasing tea is in 100 lb chests which are lined with lead or aluminium paper. This is to prevent the tea from absorbing moisture and odours.

Storage
Tea should always be stored in dry, clean, air-tight containers in a well-ventilated store room.

Food value
Tea alone has no nutritional properties, but it is a most refreshing drink. Nutritional value is only supplied by the milk and sugar in the tea. Decaffeinated tea is also available

Use

1 Use a good tea – the ideal recipe is 60 g to 5 litres of boiling water; there should be no guesswork, and the tea should be weighed or measured for each brew.
2 Always use freshly drawn, freshly boiled water.
3 Heat the pot – unless this is done the water goes off the boil rapidly, thus preventing the correct infusion of the tea.
4 Take the pot to the boiling water – the water must be as near boiling point as possible to enable the leaves to infuse properly.
5 Allow the tea to brew for four or five minutes, and stir well before pouring.

Further information
The Tea Council, Sir John Lyon House, 5 High Timber Street, London EC4 3NJ.

19 Pulses

Pulses are the dried seeds of plants which form pods.

Types
Aduki beans – small, round, deep red, shiny beans.
Haricot beans – white smooth oval beans.
Soissons – the finest haricot beans.
Flageolets – pale-green kidney shaped beans.
Cannellini – Italian haricots, slightly fatter than the English.
Dutch brown beans – light brown in colour.
Butter beans – available large or small, also known as Lima beans.
Red kidney beans – used in Chilli con carne.
Black beans – glistening black skins and creamy flesh.
Borlotti beans – pink blotched mottled colour.
Pinto beans – pink blotched mottled colour.
Black-eyed beans – white beans with a black blotch.
Broad beans – strongly flavoured beans, sometimes known as fava beans.
Ful medames or Egyptian brown beans – small, brown knobbly beans, also known as the field bean in England.
Chick-peas – look like the kernel of a small hazel-nut.
Split peas – available in bright green or golden yellow.
Lentils – available in bright orange, brown or green.
Dhal – is the Hindi word for dried peas and beans.
Mung beans – chiefly used for bean sprouts.
Soya beans – the most nutritious of all beans.

Food value

Pulses are good sources of protein and carbohydrate and therefore help to provide the body with energy. With the exception of the soya bean, they are completely deficient in fat.

Storage

All pulses should be kept in clean containers in a dry, well-ventilated store.

Use

Pulses are used extensively for soups, stews, vegetables, salads and accompaniments to meat dishes and vegetarian cookery.

Menu examples: Haricot oxtail; boiled belly of pork; pease pudding; lentil soup; lentil and courgette flan; yellow-pea soup; green-pea soup; black-eyed peas with bacon.

20 Herbs (*les herbes*)

Of the thirty known types of herbs, approximately twelve are generally used in cookery. Herbs may be used fresh, but the majority are dried, so as to ensure a continuous supply throughout the year. The leaves of herbs contain an oil which gives the characteristic smell and flavour. They are simple to grow and where possible any well-ordered kitchen should endeavour to have its own fresh herb patch. Tubs or window-boxes can be used if no garden is available.

Herbs have no food value but are important from a nutritive point of view in aiding digestion because they stimulate the flow of gastric juices. These are the most commonly used herbs:

Basil (*le basilic*)

Basil is a small leaf with a pungent flavour and sweet aroma. Used in raw or cooked tomato dishes or sauces, salads and lamb dishes.

Bay-leaves (*le laurier*)

Bay-leaves are the leaves of the bay laurel or sweet bay trees or shrubs. They may be fresh or dried and are used for flavouring many soups, sauces, stews, fish and vegetable dishes, in which case they are usually included in a faggot of herbs (bouquet-garni).

Borage

This is a plant with furry leaves and blue flowers that produces a flavour similar to cucumber when added to vegetables and salads.

Celery seeds (*la graine de céleri*)

Celery seed is dried and used for flavouring soups, sauces, stews, eggs, fish and cheese dishes, when fresh celery is unobtainable. If used in a white soup or sauce it should be tied in a piece of muslin, otherwise it can cause discoloration. When celery seed and salt are ground together it is known as celery salt.

Chervil (*le cerfeuil*)

Chervil has small, neatly shaped leaves with a delicate aromatic flavour. It is best used fresh, but may also be obtained in dried form. Because of its neat shape it is employed a great deal for decorating chaud-froid work. It is also one of the 'fines-herbes', the mixture of herbs used in many culinary preparations.

Chive (***la ciboulette***)
Chive is a bright green member of the onion family resembling a coarse grass. It has a delicate onion flavour. It is invaluable for flavouring salads, hors-d'œuvre, fish, poultry and meat dishes, and chopped as a garnish for soups and cooked vegetables. It should be used fresh.

Dill (***aneth odorant***)
Dill has feathery green-grey leaves and is used in fish recipes and pickles.

Fennel (***la fenouil***)
Fennel has feathery bright green leaves, and a slight aniseed flavour and is used for fish sauces, meat dishes and salads.

Lovage (***la livèche***)
Lovage leaves have a strong celery-like flavour, when finely chopped they can be used in soups, stews sauces and salads.

Marjoram (***la marjolaine***)
Marjoram is a sweet herb which may be used fresh in salads and pork, fish, poultry, cheese, egg and vegetable dishes, and when dried can be used for flavouring soups, sauces, stews and certain stuffings.

Mint (***la menthe***)
There are many varieties of mint. Fresh sprigs of mint are used to flavour peas and new potatoes. Fresh or dried mint may be used to make mint sauce or mint jelly for serving with roast lamb. Another lesser known but excellent mint for the kitchen is apple mint. Chopped mint can be used in salads.

Oregano
Oregano has a flavour and aroma similar to marjoram but stronger. Used in Italian and Greek-style cooking in meats, salads, soups, stuffings, pasta, sauces, vegetable and egg dishes.

Parsley (***le persil***)
Parsley is probably the most common herb in Britain and has numerous uses for flavouring, garnishing and decorating a large variety of dishes. When garnishing deep fried fish it is customary to fry whole heads of fresh parsley till crisp.

Rosemary (***le romarin***)
Rosemary is a strong fragrant herb which should be used sparingly and may be used fresh or dried for flavouring sauces, stews, salads and for stuffings. Rosemary can also be sprinkled on roasts or grills of meat, poultry and fish during cooking and on roast potatoes.

Sage (***la sauge***)
Sage is a strong, bitter, pungent herb which aids the stomach to digest rich fatty meat and is therefore used in stuffings for duck, goose and pork.

Tarragon (*l'estragon (m)*)
This plant has a bright green attractive leaf. It is best used fresh, particularly when decorating chaud-froid dishes. Tarragon has a pleasant flavour and is used in sauces, one well-known example being sauce béarnaise. It is one of the 'fines-herbes' and as such is used for omelets, salads, fish and meat dishes.

Thyme (*le thym*)
Thyme is a popular herb in Great Britain and is used fresh or dried for flavouring soups, sauces, stews, stuffings, salads and vegetables.

Fine herbs (*fines-herbes*)
This is a mixture of fresh herbs, usually chervil, tarragon and parsley, which is referred to in many classical cookery recipes.

Balm, bergamot, borage, dill, fennel, savory, sorrel, tansy, lemon thyme
These and other herbs are used in cookery, but on a much smaller scale.

Harvesting and drying of herbs

1 The shoots and leaves should be collected from the plants just before they bloom.
2 They should be inspected to see that they are sound.
3 They are then tied in small bundles and hung up to dry in a warm but not sunny place.
4 After 24 hours paper bags should be tied over them to keep out dust and to help retain colour in the leaves.
5 When sufficiently dry they should break up easily if rubbed between forefinger and thumb.
6 The leaves have the middle vein removed and they are then passed through a sieve.
7 The sieved herbs must be kept in air-tight bottles or tins in order to conserve flavour.

21 Spices (*les épices*)

Spices are natural products obtained from the fruits, seeds, roots, flowers or the bark of a number of different trees or shrubs. They contain oils which aid digestion by stimulating the gastric juices. They also enhance the appearance of food and add a variety of flavours. As spices are dried, they are concentrated in flavour and should be used sparingly, otherwise they can make foods unpalatable. Most spices are grown in India, Africa, the West Indies and the Far East.

Allspice or pimento (*la toute épice*)
This is so called because the flavour is like a blend of cloves, cinnamon and nutmeg. It is the unripe fruit of the pimento tree which grows in the West Indies. Allspice is picked when still green, and dried when the colour turns to reddish brown. Allspice is ground and used as a flavouring in sauces, sausages, cakes, fruit pies and milk puddings. It is one of the spices blended for mixed spice.

Anise
This is also known as sweet cumin, and has a sweet aniseed flavour. It is used for fish, sweets, creams and cakes.

Anise (pepper)
A strong hot-flavoured red pepper.

Anise (star)
Stronger than anise, this has a slight liquorice flavour. Used in Chinese cookery with pork and duck.

Asafoetida
This is used in Indian cookery to add flavour to vegetarian dishes. Available in block or powder form.

Cardamom (*le cardomome*)
Cardamom is frequently used in curry, and has a warm, oily sharp taste.

Caraway (*le carvi*)
Caraway seeds come from a plant grown in Holland. The seeds are about $\frac{1}{2}$ cm long, shaped like a new moon and brown in colour. Caraway seeds are used in seed-cake and certain breads, sauerkraut, cheese and confectionery. Also for flavouring certain liqueurs such as Kümmel.

Cassia (*la canéfice*)
This comes in thicker rolls than cinnamon, and is less delicate and more expensive. Used in spiced meats and curries.

Celery seed
Slightly bitter, this should be used sparingly if celery or celery salt is not available.

Chillies and capsicums (*le piment*)
These are both from the same family and grow on shrubs. They are bright red and are used in pickles and for red pepper. The larger kind are called capsicums; they are not as hot and, when ground, are called paprika. This is used for a Hungarian type of stew known as goulash.

Chinese five spice powder
Usually consists of: powdered anise, fennel, cloves, cinnamon and anise pepper.

Cinnamon (*la cannelle*)
Cinnamon is the bark of the small branches of the cinnamon shrub which grows in China and Sri Lanka. The inner pulp and the outer layer of the bark are removed and the remaining pieces dried. It is a pale brown colour and is obtained and used in stick or powdered form, mainly by bakeries and for pastry work. When stewing pears, a stick of cinnamon improves the flavour. Doughnuts may be passed through a mixture of sugar and ground cinnamon, and slices of apple for fritters may be sprinkled with cinnamon before being passed through the frying batter. It is another of the spices blended for mixed spice.

Cloves (*le clou de girofle*)
Cloves are the unopened flower-buds of a tree which grows in Zanzibar, Penang and Madagascar. The buds are picked when green, and dried in the sun until they turn to a rich brown colour. They are used for flavouring stocks, sauces, studding roast ham joints and mulled wine.

The studded onion (oignon piqué or clouté) is an onion and a bay leaf studded with a clove.

When apples are cooked, cloves are, in most cases, used as a flavouring. Cloves may be obtained in ground form and as such they are used in mixed spice.

Coriander (*la coriandre*)
Coriander is a pleasant spice obtained from the seed of an annual plant grown chiefly in Morocco. It is a yellowish brown colour and tastes like a mixture of sage and lemon peel. It is used in sauces, curry powder and mixed spice.

Cumin
This is frequently used in curry and is powerful, warm, sweet and has a slightly oily taste.

Dill seeds
These are used for flavouring fish soups, stews and cakes.

Fennel seeds
Fennel seeds have a sweet aniseed flavour, used in fish dishes and soups.

Fenugreek
Fenugreek is roasted, ground and frequently used in curry; slightly bitter, with a smell of fresh hay.

Garam masala
This literally means 'hot spices' and is not a standardised recipe, but a typical mixture which could include: cardamom seeds, stick cinnamon, cumin seeds, cloves, black peppercorns, nutmeg.

Ginger (*le gingembre*)
Ginger is the rhizome or root of a reed-like plant grown in the Far East. The root is boiled in water and sugar syrup until soft. Ground ginger is used mainly for pastry and bakery work and for mixed spice. Whole root is used for curries, pickles, stir fry dishes and sauces.

Juniper berries
If these are added to game, red cabbage, pork, rabbit and beef dishes, they give an unusual background flavour.

Nutmegs and mace (*la muscade et la macis*)
The tropical nutmeg tree bears a large fruit like an apricot which, when ripe, splits. Inside is a dark brown nut with a bright red net-like covering which is the part that becomes mace. Inside the nut is the kernel or seed which is the nutmeg. Although the two spices come from the same fruit, the flavour is

different. Mace is more delicate and is used for flavouring sauces and certain meat and fish dishes. Nutmeg is used in sweet dishes (particularly milk puddings), sauces, soups, vegetable and cheese dishes. It is also used for mixed spice.

Poppy seeds
Poppy seeds are used as a topping for bread and cakes, etc.

Saffron (*le safran*)
The stigmas from a crocus known as the saffron crocus (grown chiefly in Spain) are dried and form saffron, which is a flavouring and colouring spice. It is used in soups, sauces and particularly in rice dishes, giving them a bright yellow colour and distinctive flavour. Saffron is very expensive as it takes the stigmas from approximately 4000 crocus flowers to yield 30 g.

Sesame seeds
These are used as a topping for bread, cakes and in Chinese and vegetarian cookery.

Surmac seeds
These are used in Middle Eastern cooking for their acidic lemon peppery flavour. Deep red-maroon colour.

Turmeric (*le curcuma*)
Turmeric grows in the same way as ginger and it is the rhizome which is used. It is without any pronounced flavour and its main use is for colouring curry powder. It is ground into a fine powder, which turns it yellow. Tumeric is also used in pickles, relishes and as a colouring in cakes and rice.

Ingredients for a typical curry powder

2 parts bay-leaves	2 parts garlic	4 parts cinnamon
3 parts ginger	3 parts caraway	4 parts mace
3 parts chillies	40 parts coriander	4 parts mustard
2 parts nutmeg	3 parts clove	4 parts pepper
3 parts saffron	3 parts allspice	20 parts turmeric

Ingredients for mixed spice

4 parts allspice	4 parts cloves	4 parts cinnamon
4 parts coriander	1 part nutmeg	1 part ginger

Further information
National Herb and Spice Information Bureau, Cavendish House, 51–55 Mortimer Street, London W1N 7TD.

22 Condiments

Salt (*le sel*)

Food value: Salt (sodium chloride) is essential for stabilising body fluids and preventing muscular cramp.

Storage: Salt must be stored in a cool, dry store as it readily absorbs moisture. It should be kept in air-tight packets, drums or bins.

Production: Salt occurs naturally in the form of rock salt in underground deposits, mainly in Cheshire. It may be mined or pumped out of the earth after water has been introduced into the rock salt. The salt is extracted from the brine by evaporation and it is then purified.

Use: Salt is used for curing fish such as herrings and haddocks and for cheese and butter making. Salt is also used for the pickling of foods, in the cooking of many dishes and as a condiment on the table.

Pepper (*le poivre*)

Pepper is obtained from black peppercorns, which are the berries of a tropical shrub. White peppercorns are obtained by removing the skin from the black peppercorn. White pepper is less pungent than black, and both may be obtained in ground form.

Peppercorns are used whole in stocks, court-bouillons, sauces and dishes where the liquid is passed. They are crushed for reductions for sauces and used in a pepper-mill for seasoning meats before frying or grilling. Green peppercorns are fresh unripe pepper berries, milder than dried peppercorns, available frozen or in tins. Pink peppercorns are softer and milder than green peppercorns, available preserved in vinegar.

Ground pepper is used for seasoning many dishes and as a condiment at the table.

Cayenne pepper (*le cayenne*)

Cayenne is a red pepper used on savoury dishes and cheese straws. It is a hot pepper which is obtained from grinding chillies and capsicums, both of which are tropical plants related to the tomato.

Paprika (*le paprika*)

Paprika is a bright red mild pepper used in goulash and for decorating hors-d'œuvre dishes such as egg mayonnaise.

It is produced from capsicums grown in Hungary.

Mustard (*le moutarde*)

Mustard is obtained from the seed of the mustard plant, which is grown mainly in East Anglia. It is sold in powder form and is diluted with water, milk or vinegar for table use.

Mustard is used in the kitchen for sauces (eg mustard, mayonnaise, vinaigrette) for devilled dishes such as grilled leg of chicken, and in Welsh Rarebit.

A large variety of continental mustards are sold as a paste in jars, having been mixed with herbs and wine vinegar.

Vinegar (*le vinaigre*)

Malt vinegar is made from malt, which is produced from barley. Yeast is added, which converts it to alcohol, and bacteria are then added to convert the alcohol into acetic acid. The resulting vinegar is stored for several months before being bottled or casked.

Artificial, non-brewed, pure or imitation vinegars are chemically produced solutions of acetic acid in water. They are cheaper and inferior to malt vinegar, having a pungent odour and a sharp flavour.

Spirit vinegars are produced from potatoes, grain or starchy vegetables, but they do not have the same flavour as malt vinegar.

Red or white wine vinegars are made from grapes and are more expensive and have a more delicate flavour than the other vinegars.

All vinegars can be distilled; this removes the colour. The colour of vinegar is no indication of its strength as burnt sugar is added to give colour.

To produce flavoured vinegar the required herbs, eg tarragon, are stored in a jar and covered with good quality vinegar and then stored for at least two weeks and used as required (eg sauce béarnaise).

Uses: Vinegar is used as a preservative for pickles, rollmops and cocktail onions; and as a condiment on its own or with oil as a salad dressing; it is used for flavouring sauces such as mayonnaise and in reductions for sharp sauces (sauce piquante, sauce à la diable).

23 Colourings, flavourings, essences

A number of food colourings are obtained in either powder or liquid form.

1 Natural colours

Cochineal
Cochineal is a red colour, produced from the cochineal beetle, used in pastry and confectionery work.

Green colouring
This can be made by mixing indigo and saffron, but chlorophyll, the natural green colouring of plants, eg spinach, may also be used. This is used in pastry, confectionery and in green sauce which is sometimes served with salmon.

Indigo
Indigo is the blue colour seldom used on its own, but which, when mixed with red, produces shades of mauve.

Yellow colouring
A deep yellow colour can be obtained from tumeric roots and is prepared in the form of a powder mainly used in curry and mustard pickles.

Yellow colour is also obtained by using egg yolks or saffron.

Brown sugar
This is used to give a deep brown colour in rich fruit cakes; it also adds to the flavour.

Blackjack or browning
Blackjack or commercial caramel is a dark brown, almost black liquid, and is

used for colouring soups, sauces, gravies, aspics and in pastry and confectionery.

Chocolate colour
This can be obtained in liquid or powder form, and is used in pastry and confectionery.

Coffee colour
This is usually made from coffee beans with the addition of chicory.

A large range of artificial colours are also obtainable; they are produced from coal tar and are harmless. Some mineral colours are also used in foodstuffs. All colourings must be pure and there is a list of those permitted for cookery and confectionery use.

2 Essences

Essences are generally produced from a solution of essential oils with alcohol, and are prepared for the use of cooks, bakers and confectioners.

Among the many types of essence obtainable are:

Almond	Lemon	Orange	Peppermint
Pineapple	Raspberry	Strawberry	Vanilla

Essences are available in many size bottles.

Flavouring essences are obtained in three categories. *Natural essences* are made from:

1 Fruit juices pressed out of soft fruits, eg raspberries or strawberries.
2 Citrus fruit peel, eg lemon, orange.
3 Spices, beans, herbs, roots, nuts, eg caraway seeds, cinnamon, celery, mint, sage, thyme, clove, ginger, coffee beans, nutmeg and vanilla pod.

Artificial essences such as vanilla, pineapple, rum, banana, coconut are produced from various chemicals blended to give a close imitation of the natural flavour.

Compound essences are made by blending natural products with artificial products.

The relative costs vary considerably and it is advisable to try all types of flavouring essence before deciding on which to use for specific purposes.

24 Grocery, delicatessen

Delicatessen literally means 'provision store', but the name is commonly used to cover the place where a wide range of table delicacies may be bought.

Agar agar
This is obtained from the dried purified stems of a seaweed (Gelidium algae); also known as vegetable gelatine.

Anchovy essence
This is a strong, highly seasoned commodity used for flavouring certain fish sauces and fish preparations such as anchovy sauce or fish cakes.

Angelica
This is not a herb, but can be found growing in herb gardens. It has a long bamboo-like stem, and grows to a height of about 1.5 metres. The stems are bleached, cut into 36 cm pieces, boiled in green syrup, cooled, then reboiled daily in syrup for five days.

Aspic
Aspic jelly is a clear savoury jelly which may be the flavour of meat, game or fish. It may be produced from fresh ingredients (*Practical Cookery*, page 77) or obtained in a dried form.

It is used for cold larder work, mainly for coating chaud-froid dishes, and may also be chopped or cut into neat shapes to decorate finished dishes.

Bombay duck
These are dried fillets of a fish found in southern Asia. They are lightly cooked, usually by grilling and served as an accompaniment to curry dishes of meat and poultry. Bombay duck are purchased in packets of 12 fillets.

Brawn
This is a preparation from the boiled, well-seasoned head of a pig. After being cooked the meat is picked off the bones, roughly chopped or minced, then set in a mould with some of the cooking liquor. When cold and set it is carved in thick slices and served as a cold meat.

Caviar
Caviar is the uncooked roe of the sturgeon which is prepared by carefully separating the eggs from the membranes of the roe and gently rubbing them through sieves of coarse hemp. It is then soaked in a brine solution, sieved and packed.

Sturgeon fishing takes place in the estuaries of rivers which run into the Caspian or Black Sea, therefore caviar is Russian, Persian or Romanian in origin. The types normally obtainable in Britain are Beluga, Osetrova and Sevruga. These names refer to the type of sturgeon from which the caviar is taken.

Caviar is extremely expensive and needs to be handled with great care and understanding. Caviar should be kept at a temperature of 0°C but no lower otherwise the extreme cold will break the eggs down. Caviar must never be deep frozen.

A red caviar (keta) is obtained from the roe of salmon. From the lumpfish a mock caviar is obtained. These are both considerably cheaper than genuine caviar.

Ceps (*les cèpes*)
A species of French mushroom obtainable as cèpes au naturel or cèpes à l'huile.

They are usually sold in tins or bottles or in dried form. They are used in many French-style dishes.

Chow-chow
(a) A Chinese or pidgin English word for a mixture. It is the name given to oriental fruits preserved in syrup which is served with curry.
(b) The name also of a fleshy fruit obtainable at Christmas time.

Continental sausages

A large variety of these are imported from European countries.

Salami: Salami is a popular sausage imported chiefly from Italy and Hungary. It is usually made from pork, beef and bacon; highly seasoned and coloured with red wine; it is then well dried and cured so as to keep for years.

It is thinly sliced and eaten cold; usually as part of an hors-d'œuvre.

Mortadella: This large, oval-shaped, cooked sausage is imported from Italy. Mortadella is made from pork and veal and has pieces of pork fat showing. It is thinly sliced and eaten in the same way as salami.

Cervelat beef or pork sausage: These sausages are chiefly imported from Germany; they are dried, smoked and eaten raw.

Frankfurt or Vienna sausage: There are several varieties of these small sausages which are made from ham or pork. They are dried, then smoked, and are boiled before being used. Frankfurters are obtainable in tins. They should be served as part of the garnish to sauerkraut, eg choucroûte garni.

Liver sausage: Liver sausage is produced in large quantities in this country and may be made from pigs' or calves' liver mixed with lean and fat pork and highly seasoned. It is sliced and served cold, usually as part of an hors-d'œuvre. Liver sausage is also used in sandwiches, and it may be served with other cold meats. This needs to be kept in a refrigerator.

Extracts (meat and vegetable)

Extracts are highly concentrated forms of flavouring used in some kitchens to strengthen stocks and sauces eg Bovril, Marmite, Maggi, Jardox, etc.

Foie gras

This expensive delicacy is obtained from the livers of specially fattened geese and is produced mainly in Strasbourg. It is obtainable either plain or with truffles in tins of various sizes, and at certain times of the year is also obtained in round pastry cases (foie gras en croûte) and in earthenware terrines. Foie gras is a classic first course for any lunch, dinner or supper menu. It is also used as a garnish, eg Tournedos Rossini, and is included in the rice stuffing for certain chicken dishes. A purée or mousse of foie gras is obtainable and is suitable for sandwiches and to help the flavour of certain stuffings.

Frogs' legs (*les cuisses de grenouilles (f)*)

The flesh of the hindquarters of a certain species of green frog are esteemed as a delicacy in certain continental restaurants. They are cooked in various ways, eg fried, braised, grilled.

Galantine

This is a cooked meat preparation made from well-seasoned finely minced chicken, veal or other white meat. A first-class galantine is stuffed with strips of fat pork, tongue, chicken or veal, truffles and pistachio nuts, then rolled in thin fat pork, tied in a cloth and boiled. When cold, galantines are coated with chaud-froid and masked with aspic and served on cold buffets (see p. 286 *Practical Cookery*).

Gelatine

Gelatine is obtained from the bones and connective tissue, collagen, of certain animals; it is manufactured in leaf or powdered form and used in varying sweets, eg bavarois. See also 'agar agar' on p. 170.

Haggis
This traditional Scottish dish is made from the heart, lungs and liver of the sheep, mixed with suet, onion and oatmeal and sewn up in a stomach bag. It is boiled and served with mashed potatoes.

Hams
A ham is the hind leg of a pig cured by a special process which varies according to the type of ham. One of the most famous English hams is the York ham (6–7 kg) which is cured by salting, drying and sometimes smoking. The Bradenham ham is of coal-black colour and is a sweet-cured ham from Chippenham in Wiltshire. Hams are also imported from Northern Ireland and Denmark.

All the above hams should be soaked in cold water for several hours before being boiled or braised. Ham may be eaten hot or cold in a variety of ways. Continental raw hams, Bayonne and Ardenne from France and Parma from Italy, are cut in thin slices and served raw, usually as an hors-d'œuvre.

Horseradish (*le raifort*)
Horseradish is a plant of which only the root is used. The root is washed, peeled, grated and used for horseradish sauce and horseradish cream. It is obtainable in sauce or cream form in jars or bottles; either may be served with hot or cold roast beef and smoked eel.

Pâté maison
Pâté is a well seasoned cooked mixture of various combinations of meat, poultry, game, fish or vegetables, usually served cold as a first course. There are numerous recipes; an example is on p. 83 of *Practical Cookery*.

Pickles
These are vegetables and/or fruits preserved in vinegar or sauce and include:

Red cabbage, which can be served as part of hors-d'œuvre and may also be offered as an accompaniment to Irish Stew.

Gherkins are a small, rough-skinned variety of cucumber, the size of which should not exceed that of the small finger. Gherkins are used for hors-d'œuvre, tartare sauce, charcutière sauce, certain salads and for garnishing some cold dishes, and as an accompaniment to Bœuf bouilli à la française.

Olives are the fruit of the olive tree and there are three main varieties:

(a) *Manzanilla* – the small green olive used for cocktail savouries, hors-d'œuvre and garnishing many dishes such as Escalope de veau viennoise. These olives may also be obtained stuffed with pimento.
(b) *Spanish queens* – the large green olives used for hors-d'œuvre and cocktail savouries.
(c) *Black olives* – used for hors-d'œuvre and certain salads.

Cocktail onions: These are the small queen or silver-skin onions used for cocktail savouries and hors-d'œuvre.

Walnuts are pickled when green and tender before the shell hardens. They are used for hors-d'œuvre, salads and garnishing certain dishes such as Canapé Ivanhoe.

Capers are the pickled flower buds of the caper plant. They are used in caper sauce, tartare sauce, piquant sauce and for garnishing many hot and cold dishes such as Trout grenobloise, Mayonnaise of lobster.

Mango chutney: This is a sweet chutney which is served as an accompaniment to curried dishes.

Poppadums

These are thin round biscuits prepared in India from a mixture of finely ground pigeon peas (dhal) and other ingredients. When lightly cooked, either by frying or grilling, they are also served as an accompaniment to curry dishes. Poppadums are obtainable in tins of 50 pieces.

Potted shrimps

These are the peeled tails of cooked shrimps, which are preserved in butter and are usually served as an hors-d'œuvre. They must be refrigerated.

Rollmops – Bismarck herrings

These are fillets of herring which are rolled, well spiced and pickled, then served cold, usually as an hors-d'œuvre.

Saltpetre

This is a natural product (nitrate of potash) which may also be produced artificially. It is used for pickling, and is one of the chief ingredients in a brine-tub for pickling meats.

Sauerkraut

Sauerkraut is a pickled product made by finely cutting white cabbage. Salt is added in a ratio of 1 kg salt to 40 kg cabbage, the mixture is packed tightly in containers and heavy weights placed on top. A liquid soon forms to cover the cabbage and fermentation begins. Sauerkraut can be kept in a cool place for 4–6 months.

Smoked herring fillets

These are preserved in oil and used as hors-d'œuvre.

Smoked salmon

London is a world-famous centre for this very popular food. British, Scandinavian or Canadian salmon weighing between 6–8 kg are used for smoking. The salmon are cleaned, split into two sides, salted, rinsed, dried, then smoked. A good quality side of smoked salmon should have a bright deep colour and be moist when lightly pressed with the finger tip at the thickest part of the flesh. A perfectly smoked side of salmon will remain in good condition for not more than seven days when stored at a temperature of 18°C. This versatile food is used for canapés, hors-d'œuvre, sandwiches, and as a first course for lunch, dinner or supper.

Snails (*les escargots (m)*)

These edible snails are raised on the foliage of the vine. They are obtainable in boxes which include the tinned snails and the cleaned shells. The snails are replaced in the shells with a mixture of butter, garlic, lemon juice and parsley, then heated in the oven and served in special dishes as a first course. Snails are now farmed in Britain.

Tomatoes
These are obtainable: (a) peeled whole in tins of various sizes; (b) as a purée in tins of various sizes and of different strengths; (c) in paste form in tubes and tins. Tomato pureé is produced from plum tomatoes.

All types are used a great deal in the preparation of many soups, sauces, egg, fish and farinaceous, meat and poultry dishes.

Truffles (*la truffe*)
The truffles chiefly used in this country are imported in tins of varying sizes. Truffles are a fungus and many varieties are found in many parts of the world. The black truffle found in the Périgord region of France is the most famous. White truffles are found in Italy.

Because of the jet black colour truffles are used a great deal in the decorating of cold buffet dishes, particularly on chaud-froid work. Slices of truffle are used in the garnishing of many classical dishes such as Sole Cubat, Tournedos Maréchale, Poulet Sauté Archiduc. Truffles are considered to be a delicacy and are extremely expensive.

A truffle substitute suitable for cold buffet decorative work is available at a much lower price.

Worcestershire sauce
This is a thin, highly seasoned, strong-flavoured sauce used as an accompaniment at table and in flavouring certain sauces, meat puddings and pies.

25 Confectionery and bakery goods

Cake covering
This is produced from hardened vegetable fat with the addition of chocolate flavouring and colour.

Cape gooseberries (physalis)
A tasty, yellow-berried fruit resembling a large cherry. Cape gooseberries are often dipped into fondant and served as a petit four.

Chocolate vermicelli
A ready-made preparation of small fine chocolate pieces used in the decorating of small and large cakes and some chocolate-flavoured sweets. Chocolate vermicelli is obtainable in 7 lb boxes.

Cocktail cherries
Bright red cherries preserved in a syrup often flavoured with a liqueur known as maraschino. They are obtainable in jars and bottles of various sizes. In addition to being used for cocktails they are also used to give colour to grapefruit and grapefruit cocktails.

Fondant
A soft white preparation of sugar. It is made by boiling sugar and glucose to a temperature of about 102°C, allowing it to cool slightly, then working it to a soft cream. Fondant has many uses in pastry and confectionery work, chiefly for coating petit fours, pastries and gâteaux. It may also be obtained as a ready-made preparation.

Gum tragacanth
A soluble gum used for stiffening pastillage; only a very clear white type of gum tragacanth should be used. It is obtained from the shrubs of the genus *Astragalus*.

Honey
A natural sugar produced by bees working upon the nectar of flowers. It is generally used in the form of a preserve and as such it may be offered on breakfast and tea menus. Honey is obtainable in 1 lb jars and 7 lb tins.

Ice cream (*la glace*)
A frozen preparation of a well-flavoured, sweetened mixture which can be made in many ways and in many flavours. Ice cream may be bought ready prepared, usually in 5 litre cans which are suitable for deep-freeze storage. The storage temperature for ice cream should not exceed −19°C. A large number of sweets can be prepared using ice cream as a base mixed with various fruits, nuts, sauces and cream. Many variations of semi-hot sweets of the baked Alaska type have ice cream as one of the chief ingredients. Other sweets are made from an enriched ice-cream mixture and frozen in specially shaped moulds which give their names to the sweets, eg a heart-shaped mould – cœur glacé; a bomb-shaped mould – bombe glacé. All caterers must comply with the Ice Cream Regulations which govern the production and labelling of ice cream; if in doubt, contact the local environmental health officer.

Jam
A preserve of fruit and sugar which is obtainable in 1 oz, 1 lb and 2 lb jars and 7 lb tins. Raspberry and apricot jams are those mostly used in the pastry.

Marmalade
A preserve of citrus fruits and sugar, which is used mainly for breakfast menus and for certain sweets.

Marrons glacés
Peeled and cooked chestnuts preserved in syrup. They are used in certain large and small cakes, sweet dishes and as a variety of petit fours.

Marzipan
A preparation of ground almonds, sugar and egg yolks used in the making of petits fours, pastries and large cakes. Marzipan is freshly made by pastry cooks; it is also obtained as a ready-prepared commodity.

Mincemeat
A mixture of dried fruit, fresh fruit, sugar, spices, nuts, etc, chiefly used for

mince-pies. A recipe for mincemeat is on page 43 in *Practical Cookery*. It can also be obtained in 1 lb and 2 lb jars and 6 lb tins.

Pastillage (gum paste)
A mixture of icing sugar and gum tragacanth which may be moulded into shapes for set pieces for cold buffets and also for making baskets, caskets, etc, for the serving of petits fours.

Piping jelly
A thick jelly of piping consistency obtainable in different colours and flavours. It is used for decorating pastries and gâteaux and cold sweets. Piping jelly is obtainable in large tins.

Redcurrant jelly
A clear preserve of redcurrants used as a jam and also in the preparation of savoury sweet sauces such as reforme and Cumberland sauce. Redcurrant jelly is also used as an accompaniment to roast saddle of mutton and jugged hare.

Rennet
A substance originally obtained from the stomach of calves, pigs and lambs, and can now be obtained in synthetic form. Rennet is prepared in powder, extract or essence form and is used in the production of cheese and for making junket. See p. 415 of *Practical Cookery*. Vegetable rennet, for vegetarians, is also available.

Vanilla
This is the dried pod of an orchid used for infusing mild sweet flavour into dishes. After use rinse the vanilla stick, dry and store in a sealed jar of castor sugar ready for reuse.

Wafers (*le gaufrette*)
Thin crisp biscuits of various shapes and sizes usually served with ice cream. They are obtainable in large tins of approximately 1000 and half-tins of approximately 500 wafers.

Further information
Food commodities, B Davis, Heinemann 1987. *The Book of Ingredients*, Dowell and Bailey, Michael Joseph 1988. *Delicatessen Cookbook*, Glynn Christian, Macdonald 1984.

Commodities list

Product	Unit Cost	Product	Unit Cost	Product	Unit Cost	Product	Unit Cost	Product	Unit Cost
Herbs		*Condiments*		*Cereals*		*Pulses*		*Oils*	
basil		salt:		flour:		aduki beans		olive	
bay-leaves		cooking		soft		haricot beans		maize	
borage		table		strong		soissons		ground-nut	
chervil		sea		wholemeal		flageolets		margarine	
chive		pepper:		semolina		cannelini		vegetable	
dill		white ground		macaroni		Dutch brown		shortening	
fennel		corns		spaghetti		beans		lard	
lovage		black ground		vermicelli		butter beans			
marjoram		corns		noodles		red kidney		*Cheese*	
mint		cayenne		oats:		beans		British:	
oregano		paprika		rolled		borlotti beans		Cheddar	
parsley		mustard:		coarse		pinto beans		Cheshire	
rosemary		English		oatmeal		black eyed		Double	
sage		vinegar		medium		beans		Gloucester	
tarragon		Worcester		oatmeal		broad or fava		Leicester	
thyme		sauce		fine oatmeal		beans		Derby	
				pearl barley		ful mesdames		Caerphilly	
Spices		*Gravy*		barley flour		chick peas		Lancashire	
allspice		browning		buckwheat		split peas:		Wensleydale	
anise		Bovril		cornflour		green		Stilton	
anise pepper		Jardox		custard powder		yellow		Caboc	
anise star				rice:		lentils:		Dunlop	
capsicum		*Delicatessen*		long grain		red		French:	
caraway		*items*		short grain		brown		Brie	
cardamom		anchovy		ground		green		Camembert	
cassia		essence		brown		dhals		Port Salut	
celery seed		aspic		rice flour		mung beans		Roquefort	
chillies		Bombay duck		rice paper		soya beans		Italian:	
cinnamon		caviar		tapioca				Bel Paese	
cloves		cèpes		sago		*Eggs*		Gorgonzola	
cumin		chow chow		arrowroot		hens		Mozzarella	
coriander		continental		potato flour		ducks		Parmesan	
dill seeds		sausage				quails			
fennel seeds		foie gras		*Raising agents*				*Confectionery*	
fenugreek		frogs' legs		baking powder		*Milk*		colourings	
ginger, ground		gelatine:		yeast:		pasteurised		cocktail cherries	
ginger, root		leaf		fresh		UHT		chocolate	

juniper berries
nutmeg
mace
poppy seeds
saffron
sesame seeds
turmeric

powdered
olives:
manzanilla
Spanish
queens
black
capers
poppadums
potted shrimps
truffles

dried

Sugar
granulated
castor
cube
icing
demerara
Barbados
syrup
treacle
cocoa
couverture (sweetened)
couverture (unsweetened)

coffee
tea

Channel Island
sterilised
homogenised
evaporated
condensed

Cream
double
whipping
single
clotted
UHT
(non-dairy creams)

yogurt
smetana
butter

vermicelli
Cape gooseberries
fondant
gum tragacanth
honey
jam
lemon curd
marron glacé
marmalade
mincemeat
redcurrant jelly
rennet
wafers

FRUIT & NUTS

Apples, Cooking		
Bramley	lb.	24p
Apples, Dessert		
Cox	lb.	35p-48p
Delicious, red	lb.	20p
Worcester	lb.	18p
Bananas	lb.	32p
Cherries	lb.	230p*
Chestnuts	lb.	50p-54p
Coconuts	each	25p
Dates	packet	50p
Figs, Slab	each	30p
Grapefruit, Large	each	20p
Grapefruit, Medium	each	12p
Grapefruit, Pink	each	25p
Grapes, White, Cape	lb.	85p
American, Italian	lb.	50p
Almeria/Spanish	lb.	120p
Grapes, White, seedless	lb.	55p
Grapes, Black, Spanish	lb.	125p
Grapes, Black, Cape	lb.	80p
Kiwifruit	each	20p
Lemons	each	7p-12p
Limes	each	20p
Lychees, Mauritius/Cape	lb	135p-145p*
Mandarins	lb.	50p
Mangoes	each	70p
Melons,		
Galias	each	160p
Honeydew, Large	each	180p
Honeydew, Small	each	80p
Ogen	each	200p
Mixed nuts	lb.	56p
Nectarines	lb.	25p
Oranges, Medium	each	12p
Oranges, Large	each	16p
Passion Fruit	each	15p
Paw Paws	each	70p
Peaches	each	25p
Pears, Comice	lb.	30p
Conference	lb.	24p
William	lb.	36p
Pineapples, Large	each	180p
Pineapples, Med	each	120p
Plums	lb.	120p
Rhubarb, early forced	lb.	42p-47p
Outdoor	lb.	40p*
Root Ginger	lb.	160p
Satsumas	lb.	25p
Strawberries	lb. punnet	130p
Dutch	lb. punnet	75p
Spanish	½lb. punnet	80p-90p

POTATOES

Jackets	56 lb.	480p
Whites	56 lb.	170p
Reds	56 lb.	190p
Prepared, Chipped	28 lb.	550p
Prepared, Whole, Large	28 lb.	520p
New, Egyptian	lb.	20p
English	lb.	25p*
Jersey Glasshouse Royals	14 lb	240p*
Cypria	lb.	35p

SALADSTUFFS

Beetroot, Cooked	lb.	20p
Beetroot, Raw	lb.	6p
Chicory	lb.	120p
Chinese Leaf	each	32p
Cucumbers, Spanish/Canary Islands	each	60p-65p
English	each	40p-55p*
Curly Endive	per head	120p-220p
Fennel	lb.	55p
Lettuce, flat	each	12p
Lettuce, Iceberg	each	30p-60p*
Lettuce, Round, English	each	26p
Lettuce, Oakleaf	each	55p
Mustard/Cress	punnet	10p
Radicchio	per head	60p
Radishes	pack	25p
Spring Onions, English	bunch	35p
Tomatoes, Beef	lb.	70p
English	lb.	50p
Spanish/Canary Islands	lb.	45p-50p*
Watercress	bunch	30p

Salad days are here

AS THE root vegetables come to an end the salad season starts, with good cucumbers and soft home-grown lettuce. Watercress, spring onions, radish and beetroot are all in superb condition, with imported celery full of flavour.

Strawberries from Spain and Portugal are well flavoured and reasonably priced. Star apple buys Golden Delicious and Dunns Seedlings from The Cape, home-produced Cox's and some huge Red Delicious from British Colombia.

Prices will fluctuate due to the Easter market closures, but will settle down again in a few days time.

VEGETABLES

Artichokes, Globe	lb.	50p-75p
Aubergines, Spanish/Canary Islands	lb.	120p
Avocados	each	60p
Beans, Fine	lb.	120p
Cabbage, January King	lb.	20p-25p
Cabbage, English Celtic	lb.	18p-23p
Cabbage, Green	lb.	14p
Cabbage, Red	lb.	16p
Cabbage, Savoy	lb.	14p
Cabbage, White	lb.	16p
Calabrese	lb.	60p
Capsicums, Spanish Green	lb.	70p
Red	lb.	80p
Carrots, main crop	lb.	6p
Dutch, finger	lb.	20p-25p
Cauliflowers, Jersey/English	each	67p-87p*
Celery	head	40p-65p*
Courgettes	lb.	100p
Garlic	lb.	160p
Greens, Spring	lb.	15p
Leeks	lb.	24p
Mange-tout	lb.	150p
Mushrooms, Caps/Buttons	lb.	80p-90p
Mushrooms, Flat	lb.	60p
Onions, Cooking	lb.	7p
Onions, Large, Spanish	lb.	14p
Onions, pickling	lb	28p
Parsley	bunch	60p
Parsnips	lb.	20p
Shallots, English	lb.	30p
Spinach	lb.	50p
Sprouts	lb.	20p-27p
Swedes	lb.	16p
Sweetcorn	lb.	20p-25p
Turnips	lb.	16p

FRESH FISH

Item	Size	Price
Cod		per lb.
Headless	5-10 lb.	126p
Codling Fillets	4-6 oz.	143p
Cod Fillets	¾-3 lb.	173p
Cod Fillet Smoked	¾-3 lb.	167p
Haddock/Whiting		
Haddock Fillets	4-6 oz.	171p
Haddock Fillets	6-8 oz.	182p
Haddock Fillets	8-16 oz.	182p
Haddock Finnans	12-16 oz.	140p
Whiting Fillets	lb.	133p
Salmon		
Farm Scotch (fresh)	lb.	310p
Norwegian and Scotch (frozen)	lb.	265p
Canadian (frozen)	lb.	225p
Dover Sole		
Dover Sole Whole	8-10 oz.	180p
Dover Sole Whole	10-12 oz.	340p
Dover Sole Whole	12-14 oz.	340p
Dover Sole Whole	14-16 oz.	370p
Dover Sole Whole	16-18 oz.	370p
Dover Sole Whole	Large	340p
Trout		
Trout Whole Rnd	lb.	126p
Trout Whole Gutted	lb.	140p
Halibut/Turbot		
Halibut Whole	lb	330p
Turbot Whole	2-8 lb.	350p
Turbot Whole	8-14 lb.	410p
Shellfish		
Crabmeat 50/50	lb.	320p
Lobster Boiled, Graded (frozen)	lb.	380p
Scampi Whole (frozen)	lb.	250p
Scampi Select (frozen)	lb.	440p
Scampi Tails (frozen)	lb.	410p
Herring/Mackerel		
Herring Whole	5-10 oz.	53p
Kippers Large	18-22 oz.	80p
Kipper Fillets	lb.	85p
Mackerel Whole	6-12 oz.	53p
Plaice		
Plaice Whole	8-16 oz.	72p
Plaice Whole	1-2 lb.	97p
Plaice Fillets	3-4 oz.	150p
Plaice Fillets	4-6 oz.	200p
Plaice Fillets	6-8 oz.	212p
Plaice Fillets	8-10 oz.	214p
Lemon Sole		
Lemon Sole Whole	8-16 oz.	236p
Lemon Sole Whole	16-24 oz.	250p
Lemon Sole Fillets	2-4 oz.	260p
Lemon Sole Fillets	4-6 oz.	360p
Lemon Sole Fillets	6-8 oz.	390p
Whitebait		
Whitebait	lb.	100p

MEAT

Beef Bone-in (per lb.)	**Scotch**	**English**
Foreribs	115p	110p
Rump & Loin	180p	170p
Rumps	185p	175p
Sirloins	220p	210p
Beef Boneless (per lb.)		
Chuck Steak	—	146p
Whole Fillets	495p	465p
Mince	—	108p
Rumps	230p	225p
Salt Silverside	—	188p
Striploins	—	315p
Topside, rolled	—	198p
Lamb (per lb.)	**English**	**NZ**
Whole	103p*	
Legs	118p	98p
Middle Neck	60p	50p
Saddles	110p	65p
Best End, short cut	130p	70p
Shoulders	70p	54p
Portion Control Red Meats		
Pork Chops, English	(per lb.)	120p
Lamb Chops, New Zealand	(per lb.)	92p
Lamb Cutlets, French Trimmed, English	(per lb.)	220p
Lamb Cutlets, French trimmed, English		198p
New Zealand	(per lb.)	120p
Steaks (per lb.)		**English**
Braising		165p
Entrecote		410p
Fillet		595p
Rump, English		235p
Scotch		240p
Offal	**English**	**NZ**
Calves Liver, Dutch	395p	
Lambs Hearts	48p	
Lambs Kidney		60p
Lambs Liver		54p
Ox Kidney	44p	
Ox Liver	38p	
Ox Tails	69p	
Ox Tongue, Salt	128p	
Pigs Kidney	42p	
Pigs Liver	34p	
Pork	**English**	
Fillets	245p	
Legs, Whole	80p	
Neck Ends, Boneless	80p	
Short Loins	94p	
Veal		
Escalopes	410p	
Best End	145p	
Legs	180p	
Loins	325p	
Shoulders	130p	
Bacon (Vacuum Packed)	**Smoked**	**Unsmoked**
Middle (per lb.)	120p	110p
Short Back (per lb.)	132p	126p
Streaky (per lb.)	72p	70p

GAME

Fallow deer	lb.	190p*
Wild pigeon	8 oz.	76p
Rabbits prepared	lb.	115p

POULTRY

	Clean Plucked per lb.	Oven Ready per lb.
Capon	70p	86p
Chicken Suprême 6 oz. (each)		85p
Fresh Chickens 1½-4½ lb. Eviscerated		59p
Fresh Turkey Cock (over 30 lb.)	68p	78p
Fresh Ducks, Eviscerated		98p
Oven Ready Chickens		53p
Oven Ready Turkey 20 lb. +		63p

THE ABOVE prices are estimated by our team of experts as those that should prevail during the current week. They are calculated on a national basis, but are obviously subject to regional variation according to seasonal conditions and the local supply situation. Prices are inclusive of wholesalers' current distribution charges. Quality quoted is for Grade One. Fruit and vegetable items marked with an asterisk are highly fluctuating commodities affected by changing weather conditions and the immediate import situation.

N/A—Not Available
MP—Market Price. DQ—Daily Quote. *Highly fluctuating commodities.

Fig. 5.14 Food prices index (printed weekly in *Caterer and Hotelkeeper* magazine)

6

Purchasing, costing, control and storekeeping

Having read the chapter these learning objectives, both general and specific, should be achieved.

General objectives Understand the principles of portion and cost control. Be aware of the factors affecting purchase of food and know how to cost dishes and menus.

Specific objectives Specify the factors to consider when purchasing each commodity. Identify and use portion control equipment and state the amounts of food required per portion. Accurately cost dishes and menus. Be able to apply cost control. State the principles of producing purchasing specifications and standardised recipes. Define and calculate gross profit, net profit and percentage discount.

The purchasing of commodities

The responsibility for the buying of commodities varies from company to company according to the size and the management policy. Buying may be the responsibility of the chef, manager, storekeeper, buyer or the buying department.

The following is a suggested list to assist efficient buying:

1 Acquire, and keep up to date, a sound knowledge of all commodities, both fresh and convenience, to be purchased.
2 Be aware of the different types and qualities of each commodity that is available.
3 When buying fresh commodities be aware of part-prepared and ready-prepared items available on the market.
4 Keep a sharp eye on price variations. Buy at the best price to ensure the required quality and also an economic yield. The cheapest item may prove to be the most expensive if waste is excessive. When possible order by number and weight, eg:

20 kg plaice could be $80 \times \frac{1}{4}$ kg plaice
$40 \times \frac{1}{2}$ kg plaice
20×1 kg plaice

It could also be 20 kg total weight of various sizes and this makes efficient portion control difficult.

5 Organise an efficient system of ordering with copies of all orders kept for cross checking, whether orders are given in writing, verbally or by telephone.
6 Compare purchasing by retail, wholesale and contract procedures to ensure the best method is selected for your own particular organisation.
7 Explore all possible suppliers: local or markets, town or country, small or large.
8 Keep the number of suppliers to a minimum. At the same time have at least two suppliers for every group of commodities, when possible. The principle of having competition for the caterer's business is sound.
9 Issue all orders to suppliers fairly, allowing sufficient time for the order to be implemented efficiently.
10 Request price lists as frequently as possible and compare prices continually to make sure that you buy at a good market price.
11 Buy perishable goods when they are in full season as this gives the best value at the cheapest price. To help with the purchasing of the correct quantities, it is useful to compile a purchasing chart for 100 covers from which items can be divided or multiplied according to requirement. Indication of quality standards can also be inserted in a chart of this kind.
12 Deliveries must all be checked against the orders given for quantity, quality and price. If any goods delivered are below an acceptable standard they must be returned either for replacement or credit.
13 Containers can account for large sums of money. Ensure that all the containers are correctly stored, returned to the suppliers and the proper credit given.
14 All invoices must be checked for quantities and prices.
15 All statements must be checked against invoices and passed swiftly to the office so that payment may be made in time to ensure maximum discount on the purchases.
16 Foster good relations with trade representatives because much useful up-to-date information can be gained from them.
17 Keep up-to-date trade catalogues, visit trade exhibitions, survey new equipment and continually review the space, services and systems in use in order to explore possible avenues of increased efficiency.
18 Organise a testing panel occasionally in order to keep up to date with new commodities and new products coming on to the market.
19 Consider whether computer application can assist the operation. See Chapter 16.

Portion control

Portion control means controlling the size or quantity of food to be served to each customer. The amount of food allowed depends on the three following considerations:

1 The type of customer or establishment

There will obviously be a difference in the size of portions served, for example, to those working in heavy industry and female clerical workers. In a restaurant offering a three-course table d'hôte menu for £x including salmon, the size of the portion would naturally be smaller than in a luxury restaurant charging £x for the salmon on an à la carte menu.

2 The quality of the food

Better quality food usually yields a greater number of portions than poor quality food, eg low quality stewing beef often needs so much trimming that it is difficult to get six portions to the kilo, and the time and labour involved also loses money. On the other hand, good quality stewing beef will often give eight portions to the kilogramme with much less time and labour required for preparation.

3 The buying price of the food

This should correspond to the quality of the food if the person responsible for buying has bought wisely. A good buyer will ensure that the price paid for any item of food is equivalent to the quality – in other words a good price should mean good quality, which should mean a good yield, and so help to establish a sound portion control. If, on the other hand, an inefficient buyer has paid a high price for indifferent quality food then it will be difficult to get a fair number of portions, and the selling price necessary to make the required profit will be too high.

Portion control should be closely linked with the buying of the food; without a good knowledge of the food bought it is difficult to state fairly how many portions should be obtained from it. To evolve a sound system of portion control each establishment (or type of establishment) needs individual consideration. A golden rule should be 'a fair portion for a fair price'.

Convenient portioned items are available, eg individual sachets of sugar, sauce, salt, pepper; individual cartons of milk, cream and individual butter and margarine portions.

Portion control equipment

There are certain items of equipment which can assist in maintaining control of the size of the portions. For example:

Scoops – for ice cream or mashed potatoes.
Ladles – for soups and sauces.
Butter pat machines – butter pats can be regulated from 7 g onwards.
Fruit juice glasses – 75–150 g.
Soup plates – 14, 16, 17, 18 cm.
Milk dispensers and tea-measuring machines.
Individual pie dishes, pudding basins, moulds and coupes.

As examples of how portion control can save a great deal of money the following instances are true:

1 It was found that 0.007 litre of milk was being lost per cup by spilling it from a jug. 32 000 cups = 224 litres of milk lost daily; this resulted in a loss of hundreds of pounds per year.
2 When an extra pennyworth of meat is served on each plate it means a loss of £1000 over the year when 1000 meals are served daily.

The following list is of the approximate number of portions that are obtainable from various foods:

Soup: 2–3 portions to the ½ litre.
Hors-d'œuvre: 120–180 g per portion.
Smoked salmon: 16–20 portions to the kg when bought by the side; 20–24 portions to the kg when bought sliced.
Shellfish cocktail: 16–20 portions per kg.
Melon: 2–8 portions per melon, depending on the type of melon.
Foie gras: 15–30 g per portion.
Caviar: 15–30 g per portion.

Fish

Plaice, cod, haddock fillet	8 portions to the kg
Cod and haddock on the bone	6 portions to the kg
Plaice, turbot, brill, halibut, on the bone	4 portions to the kg
Herring and trout	1 per portion (180g–¼ kg fish)
Mackerel and whiting	¼ kg–360 g fish
Sole for main dish	300–360 g fish
Sole for filleting	½–¾ kg best size
Whitebait	8–10 portions to the kg
Salmon (gutted, but including head and bone)	4–6 portions to the kg
Crab or lobster	¼ kg–360 g per portion

(A ½ kg lobster yields approx. 150 g meat; a 1 kg lobster yields approx. 360 g meat).

Sauces

8–12 portions to ½ litre

Hollandaise	Custard
Béarnaise	Apricot
Tomato	Jam
Any demi-glace sauce	Chocolate

10–14 portions to ½ litre	**15–20 portions to ½ litre**
Apple	Tartare
Cranberry	Vinaigrette
Bread	Mayonnaise

Meats

Beef:

Roast on the bone	4–6 portions per kg
Roast boneless	6–8 portions per kg
Boiled or braised	6–8 portions per kg
Stews, puddings and pies	8–10 portions per kg

Steaks – Rump	120 g–¼ kg per one portion
Sirloin	120 g–¼ kg per one portion
Tournedos	90–120 g per one portion
Fillet	120–180 g per one portion
Offal:	
Ox-liver	8 portions to the kg
Sweetbreads	6–8 portions to the kg
Sheep's kidneys	2 per portion
Oxtail	4 portions per kg
Ox-tongue	4–6 portions per kg
Lamb:	
Leg	6–8 portions to the kg
Shoulder boned and stuffed	6–8 portions to the kg
Loin and best-end	6 portions to the kg
Stewing lamb	4–6 portions to the kg
Cutlet	90–120 g
Chop	120–180 g
Pork:	
Leg	8 portions to the kg
Shoulder	6–8 portions to the kg
Loin on the bone	6–8 portions to the kg
Pork chop	180 g–¼ kg
Ham:	
Hot	8–10 portions to the kg
Cold	10–12 portions to the kg

Sausages are obtainable 12, 16 or 20 to the kg
Chipolatas yield approximately 32 or 48 to the kg

Cold meat	16 portions to the kg
Streaky bacon	32–40 rashers to the kg
Back bacon	24–32 rashers to the kg
Poultry:	
Poussin	1 portion 360 g (1 bird) 2 portions ¾ kg (1 bird)
Ducks and chickens	360 g per portion
Geese and boiling fowl	360 g per portion
Turkey	¼ kilo per portion

Vegetables

New potatoes	8 portions to the kg
Old potatoes Cabbage	4–6 portions to the kg
Turnips Parsnips	6–8 portions to the kg

Swedes Brussels sprouts Tomatoes French beans Cauliflower	6–8 portions to the kg
Spinach Peas Runner beans	4–6 portions to the kg

Methods of purchasing

There are three main methods for buying, each depending on the size and volume of the business.

1 The primary market

Raw materials may be purchased at the source of supply, the grower, producer or manufacturer, or from central markets such as Smithfield, Covent Garden, Nine Elms, or Isle of Dogs in London. Some establishments or large organisations will have a buyer who will buy directly from the primary markets. Also, a number of smaller establishments may adopt this method for some of their needs, ie the chef patron may buy his fish, meat and vegetables directly from the market.

2 The secondary market

Goods are bought wholesale from a distributor or middle man; the catering establishment will pay wholesale prices and obtain possible discounts.

3 The tertiary market

The retail or cash and carry warehouse is a method suitable for smaller companies. A current pass obtained from the warehouse is required in order to gain access. This method also requires the user to have his or her own transport. Some cash and carry organisations require a VAT number before they will issue an authorised card. It is important to remember that there are added costs:

(a) running the vehicle and petrol used;
(b) the person's time for going to the warehouse.

Cash and carry is often an impersonal way of buying as there are no staff to discuss quality and prices.

Standard purchasing specifications

Standard purchasing specifications are documents which are drawn up for every commodity describing exactly what is required for the establishment. These standard purchasing specifications will assist with the formulation of standardised recipes. A water-tight specification is drawn up which, once approved, will be referred to every time the item is delivered. It is a statement of various criteria related to quality, grade, weight, size and method of preparation (if required, ie washed and selected potatoes for baking). Other information given may be variety, maturity, age, colour, shape etc. A copy of standard specification is often given to the supplier and the storekeeper who are left in no doubt as to what is needed. These specifications assist in the costing and control procedures.

Example – purchasing specification for rib of beef
(Source: Scotch – Aberdeen Angus)

1 Cut from a T-bone rib, weighing preferably 38–40 lbs, to measure on the flank no more than $1\frac{1}{2}$ in. from the meat of the main muscle (eye) on the loin end, and no more than 4 in. from inside of the chine bone on the chuck end. The rib is cut straight between these points.
2 The chine bone is removed squarely to where the meat splits.
3 The ribs should not show heavy fat layers on chuck end or along flank, nor should the back have heavy fat covering.
4 Ribs are aged not less than 10 days and not more than 21 days from date of slaughter.
5 The cap (back) is removed from the entire length of the rib and the lean meat trimmed from the cap.
6 The back strap, blade bone and blade bone cartilage is removed and the cap securely tied back again to its natural position.
7 The fabricated rib will weigh not less than 17 lbs, nor more than 21 lbs.
8 The rib should not show heavy layers of fat along the flank or on the chuck end, nor should the back have heavy fat covering.
9 Ribs with hooks holes and knife cuts are not acceptable.

Quality in ribs is evidenced by meat which looks rich, fine grained and smooth, and is firm but elastic to the touch.

The rib has an even distortion of fat all around, while the lean or muscular positions (eye or rib) are ingrained (marbled) with fine dots and streaks of fat.

The standard recipe

Standard recipes are a written formula for producing a food item of a specified quality and quantity for use in a particular establishment. It should show the precise quantities and qualities of the ingredients together with the sequence of preparation and service. It enables the establishment to have a greater control over cost and quantity.

Objective
To predetermine the following:

(a) the quantities and qualities of ingredients to be used stating the purchase specification;
(b) the yield obtainable from a recipe;
(c) the food cost per portion;
(d) the nutritional value of a particular dish;

And to facilitate:

(e) menu planning;
(f) purchasing and internal requisitioning;
(g) food preparation and production;
(h) portion control.

Also the standard recipe will assist new staff in preparation and production of standard products – which can be facilitated by photographs or drawings illustrating the finished product.

Cost control

It is important to know the exact cost of each process and every item produced, so a system of cost analysis and cost information is essential.

The advantages of an efficient costing system are:

1 It discloses the net profit made by each section of the organisation and shows the cost of each meal produced.
2 It will reveal possible sources of economy and can result in a more effective use of stores, labour, materials, etc.
3 Costing provides information necessary for the formation of a sound price policy.
4 Cost records provide and facilitate the speedy quotations for all special functions, eg special parties, wedding receptions, etc.
5 It enables the caterer to keep to a budget.

No *one* costing system will automatically suit every catering business, but the following guide-lines may be helpful.

(a) The co-operation of all departments is essential.
(b) The costing system should be adapted to the business and not vice versa. If the accepted procedure in an establishment is altered to fit a costing system then there is danger of causing resentment among the staff and as a result losing their co-operation.
(c) Clear instructions in writing must be given to staff who are required to keep records. The system must be made as simple as possible so that the amount of clerical labour required is kept to a minimum. An efficient mechanical calculator or computer should be provided to save time and labour.

To calculate the total cost of any one item or meal provided it is necessary to analyse the total expenditure under several headings. Basically the total cost of each item consists of three main elements:

1 Food or materials cost.
2 Labour.
3 Overheads (rent, rates, heating, lighting, equipment, repairs and maintenance).

(a) Food or materials costs are known as variable costs because the level will vary according to the volume of business. In an operation that uses part-time or extra staff for special occasions, the money paid to these staff also comes under variable costs. By comparison salaries and wages paid regularly to permanent staff are fixed costs.
(b) All cost of labour and overheads which are regular charges come under the heading of fixed costs.
(c) Labour costs in the majority of operations fall into two categories: direct labour cost, which is salaries and wages paid to staff such as chefs, waiters, barstaff, housekeepers, chambermaids and where the cost can be allocated to income from food, drink and accommodation sales; and indirect labour cost.

Indirect labour cost would include salaries and wages paid, for example, to managers, office staff and maintenance men who work *for all* departments and so their labour cost should be charged *to all* departments.

Cleaning materials

An important group of essential items that is often overlooked when costing are cleaning materials. There are over 60 different items that come under this heading, and approximately 24 of these may be required for an average catering establishment. These may include: brooms, brushes, buckets, cloths, drain rods, dusters, mops, sponges, squeegees, scrubbing/polishing machines, suction/vacuum cleaners, wet and wet/dry suction cleaners, scouring pads, detergents, disinfectants, dustbin powder, washing-up liquids, fly sprays, sacks, scourers, steel wool, soap, soda etc.

It is important to understand the cost of these materials and to ensure that an allowance is made for them under the heading of overheads.

Profit

It is usual to express each element of cost as a percentage of the selling price. This enables the caterer to control his profits.

Gross profit or kitchen profit is the difference between the cost of the food and the selling price of the food.

Net profit is the difference between the selling price of the food (sales) and total cost (cost of food, labour and overheads).

Sales − Food cost = Gross profit (kitchen profit)
Sales − Total cost = Net profit
Food cost + Gross profit = Sales

Example:		
	If food sales for 1 week	= £4000
	and food cost for 1 week	= £1760
	labour and overheads for 1 week	= £1720
	then total costs for 1 week	= £3480
	Gross profit (kitchen profit)	= £2240
	Net profit	= £ 520

Food sales − food cost	£4000 − £1760 = £2240 (gross profit)
Food sales − net profit	£4000 − £ 520 = £3480 (total costs)
Food cost + gross profit	£1760 + £2240 = £4000 (food sales)

Profit is always expressed as a percentage of the selling price.

∴ the percentage profit for the week was

$$\frac{\text{Net profit}}{\text{Sales}} \times 100 = £\frac{520 \times 100}{4000} = 13 \text{ per cent}$$

A breakdown shows:

		Percentage of sales
Food cost	£1760	44 per cent
Labour	£1000	25 per cent
Overheads	£ 720	18 per cent
	£3480	
Net profit	£ 520	13 per cent
Sales	£4000	

If the restaurant served 1000 meals then the average spent by each customer would be

$$\frac{\text{Total sales £4000}}{\text{No. of customers 1000}} = \text{£4.00}$$

As the percentage composition of sales for a month is now known, the average price of a meal for that period can be further analysed.

Average price of a meal = £4.00 = 100 per cent
4p = 1 per cent

which means that the customer's contribution towards:

Food cost	= 4p × 44 =	176p
Labour	= 4p × 25 =	100p
Overheads	= 4p × 18 =	72p
Net profit	= 4p × 13 =	52p
Average price of meal	=	£4.00

A rule that can be applied to calculate the food cost price of a dish is: let the dish equal 40 per cent and *fix the selling price* at 100 per cent.

eg Cost of dish = 80p = 40 per cent

$$\therefore \text{ Selling price} = \frac{80 \times 100}{40} = \text{£2.00}$$

Selling the dish at £2, making 60 per cent gross profit above the cost price, would be known as 40 per cent food cost. For example:

Sirloin steak (8 oz)
½ lb entrecote steak at £8.00 a pound = £4.00

$$\text{To fix the selling price at 40 per cent food cost} = \frac{4.00 \times 100}{40} = \text{£10.00}$$

The following will help you with various food costings:

Food costings

Food cost	*To find the selling price multiply the cost price of the food by*	*If the cost price of food is £2 the selling price is*	*If cost price is 60p the selling price is*	*Gross profit*
60%	1⅔	£3.32	£0.96	40%
55%	1¾	£3.50	£1.02	45%
50%	2	£4.00	£1.20	50%
45%	2²⁄₉	£4.44	£1.32	55%
40%	2½	£5.00	£1.44	60%
33⅓%	3	£6.00	£1.80	66⅔%

If food costing is controlled accurately the food cost of particular items on the menu and the total expenditure on food over a given period are worked out. Finding the food costs helps to control costs, prices and profits.

An efficient food cost system will disclose bad buying and inefficient storing and should tend to prevent waste and pilfering. This can help the caterer to run an efficient business and enable him to give the customer adequate value for money.

The caterer who gives the customer value for money together with the desired type of food is well on the way to being successful.

Food cost and operational control

As food is expensive, efficient stock control levels are essential to help the profitability of the business.

The main difficulties of controlling food are as follows:

1 Food prices fluctuate frequently because of inflation and falls in the demand and supply – through poor harvests, bad weather conditions etc.
2 Transport costs, which rise due to wage demands and cost of petrol.
3 Fuel costs rise, which affects food companies' and producers' costs.
4 Removal of food subsidies to bring the UK into line with the EEC.
5 Changes in the amount demanded by the customer; increased advertising increases demand. Changes in taste and fashion influence demand from one product to another.
6 Media focus on certain products which are labelled healthy or unhealthy will affect demand, eg butter being high in saturated fats. Sunflower margarine is high in polyunsaturates.

Each establishment should devise its own control system to suit the needs of that establishment.

Factors which affect a control system are:

(a) Regular changes in the menu.
(b) Menus with a large number of dishes.
(c) Dishes with a large number of ingredients.
(d) Problems in assessing customer demand.
(e) Difficulties in not adhering to or operating standardised recipes.
(f) Raw materials purchased incorrectly.

Factors assisting a control system:

(a) The menu remains constant eg McDonald's, Berni Inns.
(b) Standardised recipes and purchasing specifications are used.
(c) The menu has a limited number of dishes.

Stocktaking is therefore easier and costing more accurate.

In order to carry out a control system, food stocks must be secure, refrigerators and deep freezers should be kept locked. Portion control must be accurate. A book-keeping system must be developed to monitor the daily operation.

The control cycle of daily operation

Purchasing
Receiving
Storing and issuing
Preparing
Selling

1 Purchasing

It is important to determine yields from the range of commodities in use which will determine the unit costs. Yield testing indicates the number of items or portions obtained and helps to provide the information required for producing, purchasing and specification. Yield testing should not be confused with product testing which is concerned with the physical properties of the food – texture, flavour, quality. Although in reality tests are frequently carried out which combine these objectives.

2 Receiving

Goods must be checked on delivery to make sure they meet the purchase specifications.

3 Storing and issuing

Raw materials should be stored correctly under the right conditions, temperature etc. A method of pricing the materials must be decided, and one of the following should be adopted for charging the food to the various departments. The cost of items does not remain fixed over a period of time; over a period of one year a stores item may well have several prices. The establishment must decide which price to use:

(a) actual purchase price;
(b) simple average price;
(c) weighted average price;
(d) inflated price (price goes up after purchase);
(e) standard price (fixed price).

4 Weighted average price example (of beans)

= 10 lbs × 15p = 150p
20 lbs × 20p = 400p

Total 550p

∴ 550 ÷ 30 lbs = 18.3p per lb = weighted average price.

5 Preparing

This is an important stage of the control cycle. The cost of the food consumed depends on two factors:

(a) the number of meals produced;
(b) the cost per meal.

In order to control food costs we must be able to:

(a) control the number to be catered for;

(b) control the food cost per meal in advance of production and service by using a system of pre-costing, using standardised recipes, indicating portion control.

Sales and volume forecasting

This is a method of predicting the volume of sales for a future period. In order to be of practical value the forecast must:

1 Predict the total number of covers.
2 Predict the choice of menu items.

Therefore it is important to:

(a) keep a record of the numbers of each dish sold from a menu;
(b) work out the average spent per customer;
(c) calculate the proportion, expressed as a percentage, of each dish sold in relation to total sales.

Forecasting is in two stages:

(a) Initial forecasting – this is done once a week in respect of each day of the following week. It is based on sales histories, information related to advance bookings and current trends, and when this has been completed, the predicted sales are converted into the food/ingredients requirements.
Purchase orders are then prepared and sent to suppliers.
(b) The final forecast – this normally takes place the day before the actual preparation and service of the food. This forecast must take into account the latest developments, eg the weather and any food that needs to be used up; if necessary suppliers' orders may need to be adjusted.

Sales forecasting is not a perfect method of prediction, but does help with production planning. Sales forecasting, however, is important when used in conjunction with cyclical menu planning.

Pre-costing of dishes

This method of costing is associated with standardised recipes which give the total cost of the dish per portion and often with a selling price.

Summary of factors which will affect the profitability of the establishment

1 Over-cooking food resulting in portion loss.
2 Inefficient preparation of raw materials.
3 Poor portion control.
4 Too much wastage, insufficient use of raw materials. Left-over food not being utilised.
5 Theft.
6 Inaccurate ordering procedures.
7 Inadequate checking procedures.
8 No reference mark to standardised recipes and yield factors.

9 Insufficient research into suppliers.
10 Inaccurate forecasting.
11 Bad menu planning.

Further information

Peter Odgers, *Purchasing, Costing and Control*; Grace Paige, *Catering Cost and Control* (Cassell); Michael Riley, *Understanding Food Cost Control* (Arnold); Hughes and Ireland, *Costing and Calculations for Caterers* (Stanley Thornes).

Storekeeping

Having read this section, these learning objectives, both general and specific, should be achieved.

General objective Understand the principles of storekeeping and know why stores control is essential.

Specific objective Explain why efficient storekeeping is necessary. List the features which make a well-planned store. Specify how each commodity is stored. Explain the correct use of cold room, chill room and refrigerator. Identify the responsibilities of the storekeeper. Accurately use bin cards, stores ledger, requisition book, order book and stock sheets. Operate a control system using delivery notes, invoices, credit notes and statements.

A clean, orderly food store, run efficiently, is essential in any catering establishment for the following reasons:

1 Stocks of food can be kept at a suitable level, so eliminating the risk of running out of any commodity.
2 All food entering and leaving the stores can be properly checked; this helps to prevent wastage.
3 A check can be kept on the percentage profit of each department of the establishment.

This control may be assisted by computer application, see Chapter 16, p. 417.

A well-planned store should include the following features:

(a) It should be cool and face the north so that it does not have the sun shining into it.
(b) It must be well ventilated, vermin proof and free from dampness (dampness in a dry store makes it musty, and encourages bacteria to grow and tins to rust).
(c) It should be in a convenient position to receive goods being delivered by suppliers and also in a suitable position to issue goods to the various departments.
(d) A wash hand basin, soaps, nail brush and hand drier must be provided for staff; also a first aid box.
(e) A good standard of hygiene is essential, therefore the walls and ceilings should be free from cracks, and either painted or tiled so as to be easily cleaned. The floor should be free from cracks and easy to wash. The junction between the wall and floor should be rounded to prevent the accumulation of dirt. A cleaning rota should clearly show daily, monthly and weekly cleaning tasks.
(f) Shelves should be easy to clean.
(g) Good lighting, both natural and artificial, is very necessary.
(h) A counter should be provided to keep out unauthorised persons, thus reducing the risk of pilfering.
(i) The storekeeper should be provided with a suitable desk.
(j) There should be ample well-arranged storage space, with shelves of varying depths and separate sections for each type of food. These sections may

include deep-freeze cabinets, cold rooms, refrigerators, chill rooms, vegetable bins and container stores. Space should also be provided for empty containers.

(k) Efficient, easy-to-clean weighing machines for large and small-scale work should be supplied.

(l) Stores staff must wear clean overalls at all times, and suitable shoes to help prevent injury if a heavy item is dropped on the feet.

(m) Steps to help staff reach goods on high shelves and an appropriate trolley should be provided.

Store containers

Foods delivered in flimsy bags or containers should be transferred to suitable store containers. These should be easy to wash and have tight-fitting lids. Glass or plastic containers are suitable for many foods, such as spices and herbs, as they have the advantage of being transparent; therefore it is easy to see at a glance how much of the commodity is in stock.

Bulk dry goods (pulses, sugar, salt, etc) should be stored in suitable bins with tight-fitting lids. These bins should have wheels so that they can be easily moved for cleaning. All bins should be clearly labelled or numbered.

Sacks or cases of commodities should not be stored on the floor; they should be raised on duck boards so as to permit a free circulation of air.

Some goods are delivered in containers suitable for storage and these need not be transferred. Heavy cases and jars should be stored at a convenient height to prevent any strain in lifting.

Special storage points

1 All old stock should be brought forward with each new delivery.

2 Commodities with strong smells or flavours should be stored as far away as possible from those foods which readily absorb flavour. For example, strong-smelling cheese should not be stored near eggs.

3 Bread should be kept in a well-ventilated container with a lid. Lack of ventilation causes condensation and encourages moulds. Cakes and biscuits should be stored in airtight tins.

4 Stock must be inspected regularly, particularly cereals and cereal products, to check for signs of mice or weevils.

5 Tinned goods should be unpacked, inspected and stacked on shelves. When inspecting tins, these points should be looked for:

(a) Blown tins – this is where the ends of the tins bulge owing to the formation of gases either by bacteria growing on the food or by the food attacking the tin-plate. All blown tins should be thrown away as the contents are dangerous and the use of the contents may cause food-poisoning.

(b) Dented tins – these should be used as soon as possible, not because the dent is an indication of inferior quality but because dented tins, if left, will rust and a rusty tin will eventually puncture.

(c) Storage life of tins varies considerably and depends mainly on how the contents attack the internal coating of the tin which may corrode and lay bare the steel.

(d) Due to fewer additives, many bottled foods now need to be refrigerated once they are opened.
(e) Cleaning materials often have a strong smell; therefore they should be kept in a separate store. Cleaning powders should never be stored near food.

Storage accommodation
Foods are divided into two groups for the purpose of storage: dry foods and perishable foods.

(a) *Dry stores* include: cereals, pulses, sugar, flour, etc; bread, cakes; jams, pickles and other bottled foods; canned foods; cleaning materials.
(b) *Perishable foods* include: meat, poultry, game, fish; dairy produce and fats; vegetables and fruit.

Frozen foods

When frozen foods are delivered they must immediately be placed into a deep freeze at a temperature of −2°C.

The cold room (see also *Refrigeration*, p. 227)

A large catering establishment may have a cold room for meat, with possibly a deep-freeze compartment where supplies can be kept frozen for long periods. The best temperature for storing fresh meat and poultry (short term) is between 4°C and 6°C with a controlled humidity (poultry is stored in a cold room). Fish should have a cold room of its own so that it does not affect other foods. Game, when plucked, is also kept in a cold room.

Chill room

A chill room keeps food cold without freezing, and is particularly suitable for those foods requiring a consistent, not too cold, temperature, such as dessert fruits, salads, cheese, etc. Fresh fruit, salads and vegetables are best stored at a temperature of 4°–6°C with a humidity that will not result in loss of water from the leaves causing them to go limp. Green vegetables should be stored in a dark area to prevent leaves turning yellow. Certain fruits such as peaches and avocados are best stored at 10°C, while bananas must not be stored below 13°C. Dairy products (milk, cream, yogurt and butter) are best stored at 2°C. Cheese requires differing storage temperatures according to the type of cheese and degree of ripeness. Fats and oils are best stored at 4°–7°C otherwise they are liable to go rancid.

Refrigerator

The refrigerator gives cold-room and chill-room conditions and is ideal for storing fats.

Use of refrigeration

1 All refrigerators, cold rooms, chill rooms and deep-freeze units should be regularly inspected and maintained by qualified refrigeration engineers.

2 Defrosting should take place regularly, according to the instructions issued from the manufacturers. Refrigerators usually need to be defrosted weekly; if this is not done, then the efficiency of the refrigerator is lessened.
3 While a cold unit is being defrosted it should be thoroughly cleaned, including all the shelves.
4 Hot foods should never be placed in a refrigerator or cold room because the steam given off can affect nearby foods.
5 Peeled onions should never be kept in a cold room because the smell can taint other foods.

Vegetable store

This should be designed to store all vegetables in a cool, dry, well-ventilated room with bins for root vegetables and racking for others. Care should be taken to see that old stocks of vegetables are used before the new ones; this is important as fresh vegetables and fruits deteriorate quickly. If it is not convenient to empty root vegetables into bins they should be kept in the sack on racks off the ground.

Ordering of goods within the establishment

In a large catering establishment the stores carry a stock which for variety and quantity often equals a large grocery store. Its operation is similar in many respects, the main difference being that requisitions take the place of cash. The system of internal and external accountancy must be simple but precise.

The storekeeper

The essentials which go to making a good storekeeper are, not necessarily in this order:

1 Experience.
2 Knowledge of how to handle, care for and organise the stock in his or her charge.
3 A tidy mind and sense of detail.
4 A quick grasp of figures.
5 Clear handwriting.
6 A liking for his or her job.
7 Honesty.

There are many departments which draw supplies from these stores – kitchen, still room, restaurant, grill room, banqueting, floor service. A list of these departments should be given to the storekeeper, together with the signatures of the heads of departments or those who have the right to sign the requisition forms.

All requisitions must be handed to the storekeeper in time to allow the ordering and delivery of the goods on the appropriate day. Different coloured requisitions may be used for the various departments if desired.

Types of records used in stores control

(a) *Bin card:* There should be an individual bin card for each item held in stock. The following details are found on the bin card:

BIN CARD		PRICE		
UNIT (lbs, Tins, etc)		MAX STOCK		
COMMODITY		MIN STOCK		
DATE	RECEIVED	ISSUED	STOCK IN HAND	

Fig. 6.1 Example of a bin card

1 Name of the commodity.
2 Issuing unit.
3 Date goods are received or issued.
4 From whom they are received and to whom issued.
5 Maximum stock.
6 Minimum stock.
7 The quantity received.
8 The quantity issued.
9 The balance held in stock.

(b) *Stores ledger:* This is usually found in the form of a loose-leaf file giving one ledger sheet to each item held in stock. The following details are found on a stores ledger sheet:

1 Name of commodity.
2 Classification.
3 Unit.
4 Maximum stock.
5 Minimum stock.
6 Date of goods received or issued.
7 From whom they are received and to whom issued.
8 Invoice or requisition number.
9 The quantity received or issued and the remaining balance held in stock.
10 Unit price.
11 The cash value of goods received and issued and the balancing cash total of goods held in stock.

BIN No DESCRIPTION CLASSIFICATION CODE UNIT MAXIMUM MINIMUM

Date	DETAIL	Invoice or Req No	QUANTITY			UNIT PRICE	VALUE		
			Received	Balance	Issued		Received	Balance	Issued

Fig. 6.2 Example of a stores ledger sheet

Every time goods are received or issued the appropriate entries should be made on the necessary stores ledger sheets and bin cards. In this way the balance on the bin card should always be the same as the balance shown on the stores ledger sheet.

(c) *Departmental requisition book:* One of these books should be issued to each department in the catering establishment which needs to draw goods from the store. These books can either be of different colours or have departmental serial numbers. Every time goods are drawn from the store a requisition must be filled out and signed by the necessary head of department – this applies whether one item or twenty items are needed from the store. When the storekeeper issues the goods he will check them against the requisition and tick them off; at the same time he fills in the cost of each item. In this way the total expenditure over a period for a certain department can be quickly found. The following details are found on the requisition sheet:

1 Serial number.
2 Name of department.
3 Date.
4 Description of goods required.
5 Quantity of goods required.
6 Unit.
7 Price per unit.
8 Issue, if different.
9 Quantity of goods issued.
10 Unit.
11 Price per unit.
12 Cash column.
13 Signature.

DEPARTMENTAL REQUISITION BOOK 267

Date ______ Class ______

Description	Quan	Unit	Price per Unit	Issued if Different	Quan	Unit	Price per Unit	Code	£	

Fig. 6.3 Example of a stores requisition sheet

(d) *Order book:* This is in duplicate and has to be filled in by the storekeeper every time he or she wishes to have goods delivered. Whenever goods are ordered, an order sheet must be filled in and sent to the supplier, and on receipt of the goods they should be checked against both delivery note and duplicate order sheet. All order sheets must be signed by the storekeeper. Details found on an order sheet are as follows:

1 Name and address of catering establishment.
2 Name and address of supplier.
3 Serial number of order sheet.
4 Quantity of goods.
5 Description of goods to be ordered.
6 Date.
7 Signature.
8 Date of delivery, if specific day required.

(e) *Stock sheets:* Stock should be taken at regular intervals of either one week or one month. Spot checks are advisable about every three months. The stock check should be taken where possible by an independent person, thus preventing the chance of 'pilfering' and 'fiddling' taking place. The details found on the stock sheets are as follows:

1 Description of goods.
2 Quantity received and issued, and balance.
3 Price per unit.
4 Cash columns.

The stock sheets will normally be printed in alphabetical order.

All fresh foodstuffs such as meat, fish, vegetables, etc, will be entered in the stock sheet in the normal manner, but as they are purchased and used up daily a NIL stock will always be shown on their respective ledger sheets.

Commercial documents

Essential parts of a control system of any catering establishment are delivery notes, invoices, credit notes and statements.

Delivery notes are sent with goods supplied as a means of checking that everything ordered has been delivered. The delivery note should also be checked against the duplicate order sheet.

Invoices are bills sent to clients, setting out the cost of goods supplied or services rendered. An invoice should be sent on the day the goods are despatched or the services are rendered or as soon as possible afterwards. At least one copy of each invoice is made and used for posting up the books of accounts, stock records and so on. (See invoice and statement on p. 204.)

Invoices contain the following information:

(a) The name, address, telephone numbers, etc (as a printed heading), of the firm supplying the goods or services.
(b) The name and address of the firm to whom the goods or services have been supplied.
(c) The word INVOICE.
(d) The date on which the goods or services were supplied.
(e) Particulars of the goods or services supplied together with the prices.
(f) A note concerning the terms of settlement, eg 'Terms 5 per cent one month', which means that if the person receiving the invoice settles his account within one month he may deduct 5 five per cent as discount.

Credit notes are advices to clients, setting out allowances made for goods returned or adjustments made through errors of overcharging on invoices. They should also be issued when chargeable containers such as crates, boxes or sacks are returned. Credit notes are exactly the same in form as invoices except that the word CREDIT NOTE appears in place of the word INVOICE. To make them more easily distinguishable they are usually printed in red, whereas invoices are always printed in black. A credit note should be sent as soon as it is known that a client is entitled to the credit of a sum with which he has been previously charged by invoice.

Statements are summaries of all invoices and credit notes sent to clients during the previous accounting period, usually one month. They also show any sums owing or paid from previous accounting periods and the total amount due. A statement is usually a copy of a client's ledger account and does not contain more information than is necessary to check invoices and credit notes.

When a client makes payment he usually sends a cheque, together with the statement he has received. The cheque is paid into the bank and the statement may be returned to the client duly receipted.

Cash discount is a discount allowed in consideration of prompt payment.

At the end of any length of time chosen as an accounting period (eg one month) there will be some outstanding debts. In order to encourage customers to pay within a stipulated time, sellers of goods frequently offer a discount. This is called cash discount. By offering cash discount, the seller may induce his customer to pay more quickly, so turning debts into ready money. Cash discount varies from 1¼ per cent to 10 per cent, depending on the seller and the time, eg 2½ per cent if paid in 10 days; 1¼ per cent if paid in 28 days.

Discount table

Percentage	*Part of £1*
2½	2½ p
5	5 p
10	10 p
12½	12½ p
15	15 p
20	20 p
25	25 p

Trade discount is discount allowed by one trader to another. This is a deduction from the catalogue price of goods made before arriving at the invoice price. The amount of trade discount does not therefore appear in the accounts. For example, in a catalogue of kitchen equipment a machine listed at £250 less 20 per cent trade discount shows:

Catalogue price	£250
Less 20 per cent trade discount	50
Invoice price	£200

The £200 is the amount entered in the appropriate accounts.

In the case of purchase tax on articles, discount is taken off *after* the tax has been deducted from list price.

Gross price is the price of an article before discount has been deducted.

Net price is the price after discount has been deducted; in some cases a price on which no discount will be allowed.

Stores control

In conclusion, the following list gives the duties of a storekeeper.

Duties of a storekeeper

1 To keep a good standard of tidiness and cleanliness.
2 To arrange proper storage space for all incoming foodstuffs.
3 To keep up-to-date price-lists of all commodities.
4 To ensure that an ample supply of all important foodstuffs is always available.

5 To check that all orders are correctly made out, and dispatched in good time.
6 To check all incoming stores – quantity, quality and price.
7 To keep all delivery notes, invoices, credit notes, receipts and statements efficiently filed.
8 To keep a daily stores issue sheet.
9 To keep a set of bin cards.
10 To issue nothing without receiving a signed chit in exchange.
11 To check all stock at frequent intervals.
12 To see that all chargeable containers are properly kept, returned and credited – that is, all money charged for sacks, boxes, etc, is deducted from the account.
13 To obtain the best value at the lowest buying price.
14 To know when foods are in or out of season.

Daily Stores Issues Sheet

Commodity	Unit	Stock in hand	Monday In	Monday Out	Tuesday In	Tuesday Out	Wednesday In	Wednesday Out	Thursday In	Thursday Out	Friday In	Friday Out	Total pur- chases	Total issues	Total stock
Butter	kg	27		2						3				5	22
Flour	Sacks	2		1			1						1	1	2
Olive oil	Litres	8		1						½				1½	6½
Spices	30g packs	8		4			8						8	4	12
Peas, tin	A10	30		6						3				9	21

.... CANTEEN Week ending .... No. meals served .... Cost per meal ....

Commodity	hand B/F	Stock received during week						Stock used during week									in hand C/F
		M.	Tu.	W.	Th	F.	Total	M.	Tu.	W.	Th.	F.	S.	Total	@*	Cost*	
Apples, canned																	
Apples, dried																	
Apricots, etc – dried																	
Baking powder																	
Baked beans																	

* The cost of stock used can also be checked by using two extra columns

Fig. 6.4 Example of a daily stores issue sheet

Cash account

The following are the essentials for the keeping of a simple cash account:

1 All entries must be dated.
2 All monies received must be clearly named and entered on the left-hand or debit side of the book.
3 All monies paid out must also be clearly shown and entered on the right-hand or credit side of the book.
4 At the end of a given period – either a day, week or month or at the end of each page – the book must be balanced: that is, both sides are totalled and the difference between the two is known as the balance. If, for example, the debit side (money received) is greater than the credit side (money paid out), then a credit or right-hand side balance is shown, so that the two totals are then equal. A credit balance then means cash in hand.

5 A debit balance cannot occur because it is impossible to pay out more than is received.

Invoice and statement

INVOICE

Phone: 574 1133 Telegrams: SOUT Messrs. L. Moriarty & Co., 597 High Street, Ealing, London, W5	No. 03957 Vegetable Suppliers Ltd., 5 Warwick Road, Southall, Middlesex Terms: 5% One month
Your order No. 67 Dated 3rd September, 19 . . .	£
Sept 26th 56 lbs Potatoes at 12p per lb	6.72
7 lbs Sprouts at 15p per lb	1.05
	7.77

STATEMENT

Phone: 574 1133 Telegrams: SOUT Messrs. L. Moriarty & Co., 597 High Street, Ealing, London, W5		Vegetable Suppliers Ltd., 5 Warwick Road, Southall, Middlesex Terms: 5% One month
19 . . .		£
Sept 10th	Goods	45.90
17th	Goods	32.41
20th	Goods	41.30
26th	Goods	16.15
		135.76
28th	Returns credited	4.80
		130.96

General rule
Debit monies coming in
Credit monies going out

Cash account

Dr.		*First week*			Cr.
Date	*Receipts*	£	*Date*	*Payment*	£
Oct 3	To Lunches	222.00	Oct 1	By Repairs	54.50
4	,, Teas	76.15	2	,, Grocer	74.40
5	,, Tax Rebate	48.92	6	,, Butcher	48.64
				,, Balance c/fwd	169.53
		347.07			347.07

Dr.		*Second week*			Cr.
Date	*Receipts*	£	*Date*	*Payment*	£
Oct	To Balance b/fwd	169.53	Oct 8	By Fishmonger	36.30
9	,, Sale of Pastries	56.45	10	,, Fuel	40.00
11	,, Goods	175.64	11	,, Tax	30.00
			12	,, Greengrocer	56.16
				,, Balance c/fwd	239.16
		401.62			401.62

Dr.		*Third week*			Cr.
Date	*Receipts*	£	*Date*	*Payment*	£
Oct	To Balance b/fwd	239.16	Oct 19	By Butcher	38.42
15	,, Teas	60.10	21	,, Grocer	40.65
17	,, Pastries	75.00		,, Balance c/fwd	469.11
24	,, Goods	57.40			
26	,, Goods	64.32			
29	,, Goods	52.20			
		548.18			548.18

Example
Make out a cash account and enter the following transactions:

Oct.	1	Paid for repair to stove	£54.50
	2	Paid to grocer	74.40
	3	Received for lunches	220.00
	4	Received for teas	76.15
	5	Received tax rebate	48.92
	6	Paid to butcher	48.64
Oct.	8	Paid to fishmonger	36.30
	9	Received for sale of pastries	56.45
	10	Paid for fuel	40.00
	11	Paid tax	30.00
	11	Received for goods	175.64
	12	Paid to greengrocer	56.16

Oct.	15	Received for teas	60.10
	17	Received for pastries	75.00
	19	Paid to butcher	38.42
	21	Paid to grocer	40.65
	24	Received for goods	57.40
	26	Received for goods	64.32
	29	Received for goods	52.20

Fig. 6.5 An example of a well laid-out store

7

Kitchen equipment

Having read the chapter these learning objectives, both general and specific, should be achieved.

General objectives Know the various pieces of equipment and understand their purpose in the establishment so that they can be used in the practical situation.

Specific objectives Identify each piece of equipment and specify the materials it may be made from. Explain the function and state the cleaning and maintenance of each piece of equipment.

Kitchen equipment is expensive so initial selection is important, and the following points should be considered before each item is purchased or hired:

Overall dimensions – in relation to available space.
Weight – can the floor support the weight?
Fuel supply – is the existing fuel supply sufficient to take the increase?
Drainage – where necessary, are there adequate facilities?
Water – where necessary, is it to hand?
Use – does the food to be produced justify good use?
Capacity – can it cook the quantities of food required efficiently?
Time – can it cook the given quantities of food in the time available?
Ease – is it easy for staff to handle, control and use properly?
Maintenance – is it easy for staff to clean and maintain?
Attachments – is it necessary to use additional equipment or attachments?
Extraction – does it require extraction facilities for fumes or steam?
Noise – does it have an acceptable noise level?
Construction – is it well made and are all handles, knobs and switches sturdy and heat resistant?
Spare parts – are they and replacement parts easily obtainable?

Kitchen equipment may be divided into three categories:

1 Large equipment – ranges, steamers, boiling pans, fish-fryers, sinks, tables, etc. (see Fig. 7.31, p. 241).
2 Mechanical equipment – peelers, mincers, mixers, refrigerators, dishwashers, etc.
3 Utensils and small equipment – pots, pans, whisks, bowls, spoons, etc.

Manufacturers of large and mechanical kitchen equipment issue instructions on

Fig. 7.1 Kitchen equipment at the Royal Lancaster Hotel

how to keep their apparatus in efficient working order, and it is the responsibility of everyone using the equipment to follow these instructions (which should be displayed in a prominent place near the machines).

Arrangements should be made with the local gas board for regular checks and servicing of gas-operated equipment; similar arrangements should be made with the electricity board. It is a good plan to keep a log-book of all equipment, showing where each item is located when servicing takes place, noting any defects that arise, and instructing the fitter to sign the log-book and to indicate exactly what has been done.

Large equipment

Stoves

A large variety of stoves is available operated by gas, electricity, solid fuel, oil, microwave or microwave plus convection.

Solid tops should be washed or wiped clean with a pad of sacking. When cool the stove tops can be more thoroughly cleaned by washing and using an abrasive. After any kind of cleaning a solid top should always be lightly greased.

On the open type of stove all the bars and racks should be removed, immersed in hot water with a detergent, scrubbed clean, dried and put back in place on the stove. The gas jets should then be lit to check that none are blocked. All enamel parts of stoves should be cleaned while warm with hot detergent water, rinsed and dried.

The insides of ovens and oven racks should be cleaned while slightly warm, using detergent water and a mild abrasive if necessary. In cases of extreme dirt or grease being baked on to the stove or oven a caustic jelly may be used, but thorough rinsing must take place afterwards.

Oven doors should not be slammed as this is liable to cause damage.

The unnecessary or premature lighting of ovens can cause wastage of fuel, which is needless expense. This is a bad habit common in many kitchens.

When a solid-top gas range is lit, the centre ring should be removed, but it should be replaced after approximately five minutes, otherwise unnecessary heat is lost (see p. 316 – *Explosions*).

Convection ovens

These are ovens in which a circulating current of hot air is rapidly forced around the inside of the oven by a motorised fan or blower. As a result, a more even and constant temperature is created which allows food to be cooked successfully in any part of the oven. This means that the heat is used more efficiently, cooking temperatures can be lower, cooking times shortened and overall fuel economy achieved.

Forced air convection can be described as fast conventional cooking; conventional in that heat is applied to the surface of the food, but fast since moving air transfers its heat more rapidly than does static air. In a sealed oven, fast hot air circulation reduces evaporation loss, keeping shrinkage to a minimum, and gives the rapid change of surface texture and colour which are traditionally associated with certain cooking processes.

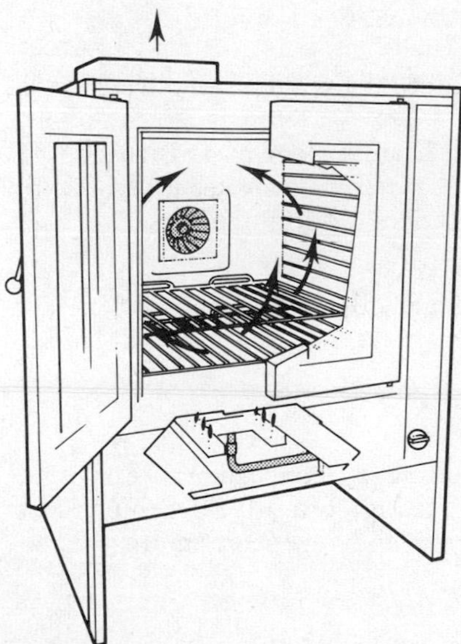

Fig. 7.2 Forced air convection oven

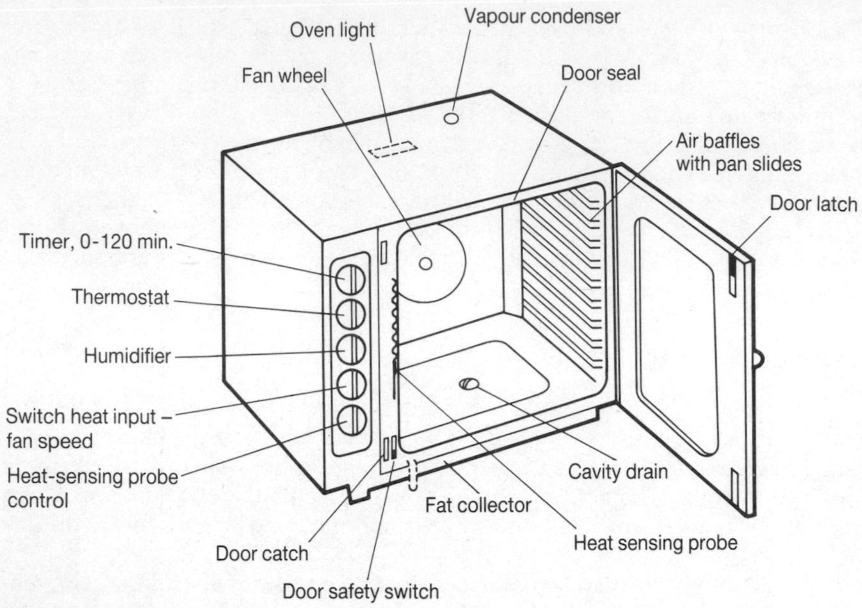

Fig. 7.3 Hot air convection oven

These are four types of convection oven:

1 Where forced air circulation within the oven is accomplished by means of a motor-driven fan, the rapid air circulation ensures even temperature distribution to all parts of the oven.
2 Where low velocity, high volume air movement is provided by a power blower and duct system.
3 A combination of a standard oven and a forced convection oven designed to operate as either by the flick of a switch.
4 A single roll-in rack convection oven with heating element and fan housed outside the cooking area. An 18-shelf mobile oven rack makes it possible to roll the filled rack directly from the preparation area into the oven.

Further information
Forced Air Convection Ovens (Cornwell, Greene, Belfield, Smith & Co.), 20 Kingsway, London WC1.

Convection and steaming oven

This combination oven can be used for cooking by convection, steam or a combination of both. It can be used for roasting, braising, poaching, fast steaming, baking, grilling, toasting, defrosting and regenerating frozen and cook-chill foods.

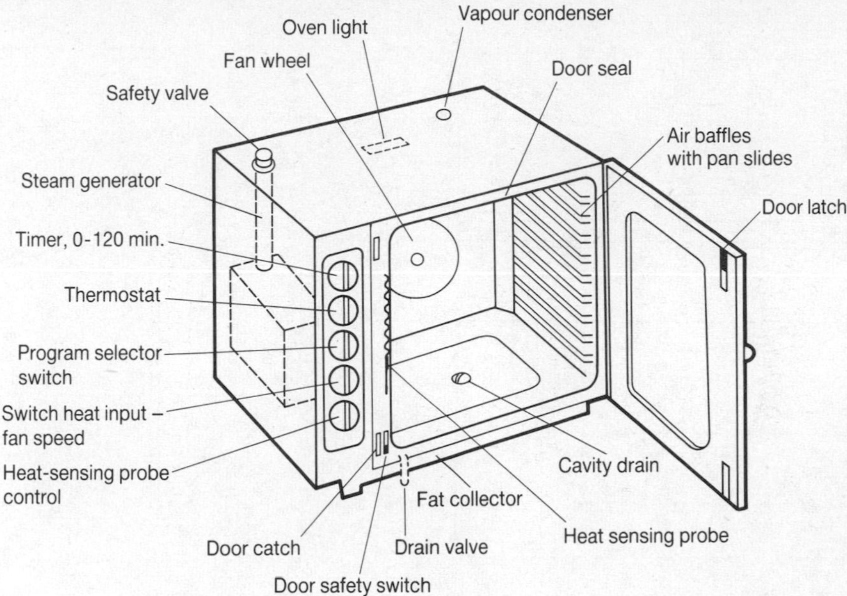

Fig. 7.4 Hot air steamer oven

Microwave ovens (see also *Practical Cookery*, pp. 39–42)

Microwave is a method of cooking and heating food by using high frequency power. The energy used is the same as that which carries television from the transmitter to the receiver, but is at a higher frequency.

The waves disturb the molecules or particles of food and agitate them, thus causing friction which has the effect of cooking the whole of the food. In the conventional method of cooking, heat penetrates the food only by conduction from the outside. Food being cooked by microwave needs no fat or water, and is placed in a glass, earthenware, plastic or paper container before being put in the oven. Metal is not used as the microwaves are reflected by it.

All microwave ovens consist of a basic unit of various sizes with varying levels of power. Some feature additions to the standard model, such as automatic defrosting systems, browning elements, 'stay-hot' controls and revolving turntables.

The oven cavity has metallic walls, ceiling and floor which reflect the microwaves. The oven door is fitted with special seals to ensure that there is minimum microwave leakage. A cut-out device automatically switches off the microwave energy when the door is opened.

When cleaning, do not allow the cleaning agent to soil or accumulate around the door seal as this could prevent a tight seal when the door is closed. Never use an abrasive cleaner to clean the interior of the oven as it can scratch the metallic walls; do not use aerosols either as they may penetrate the internal parts of the oven. Follow the manufacturer's instructions carefully for cleaning.

Further information

The Microwave Oven Association, 16a The Broadway, London SW19.

(a)

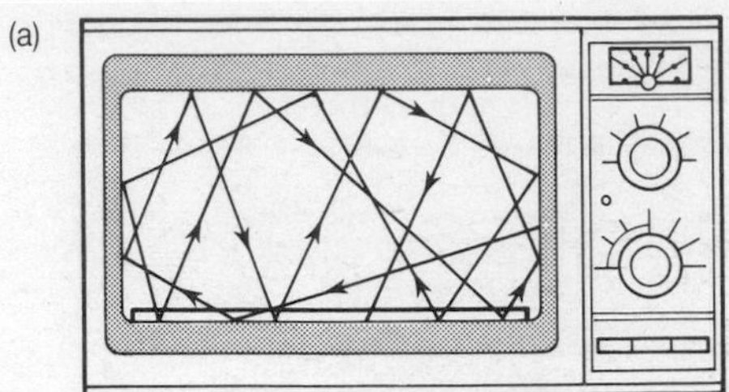

(b)

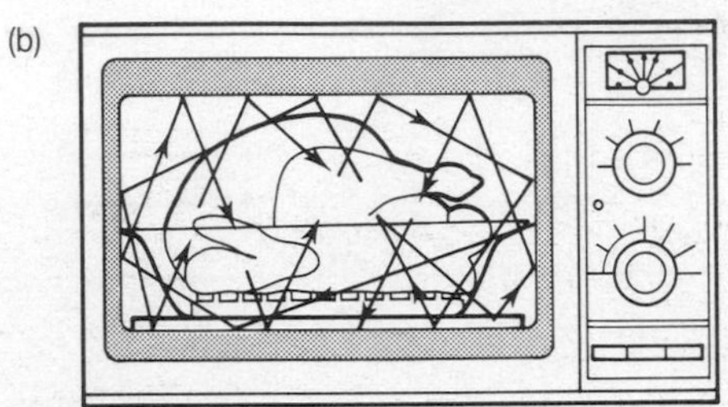

(c)

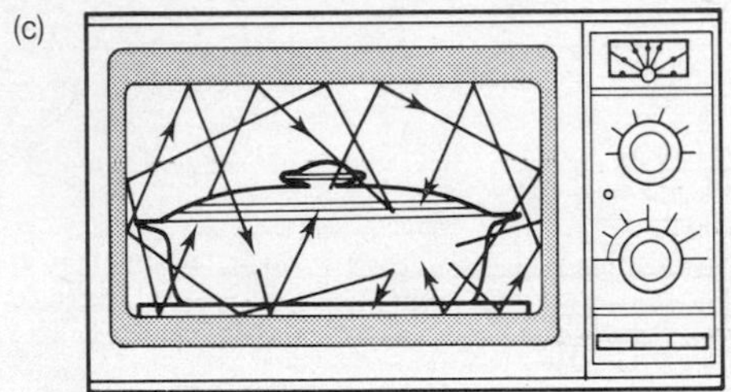

Fig. 7.5 (a) Microwave energy being reflected off cooking cavity walls (b) Microwave energy being absorbed by food (c) Microwave energy passing through cooking container material

Combination convection and microwave cooker

This cooker combines forces air convection and microwave, either of which can be used separately but which are normally used simultaneously, thereby giving the advantages of both systems: speed, coloration and texture of food. Traditional metal cooking pans may also be used without fear of damage to the cooker.

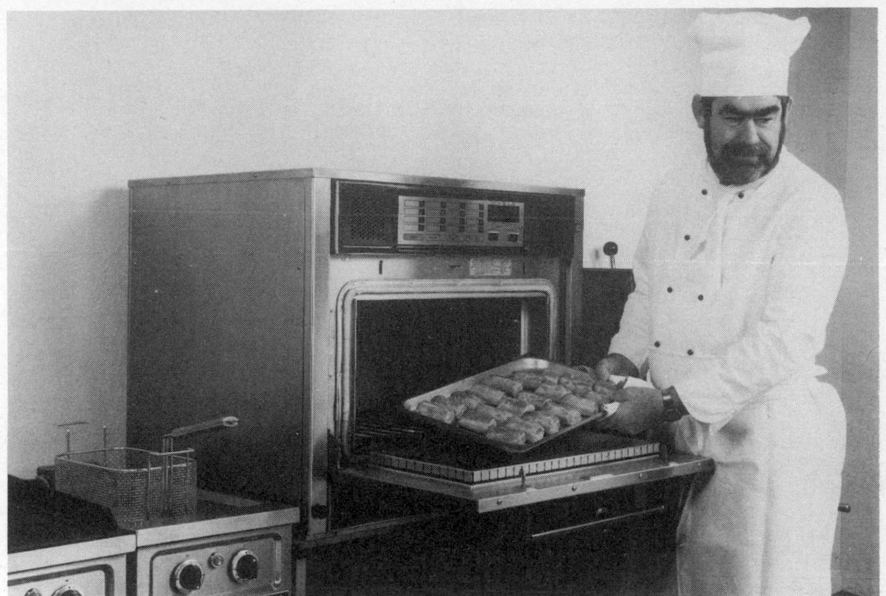

Fig. 7.6 A convection microwave oven

Induction cookers

These are solid top plates made of vitroceramic material which provide heat only when pans are put on them and which stop the heat immediately the pans are removed.

A generator creates a two-way magnetic field at the top level. When a utensil with a magnetic base is placed on the top a current passes directly to the pan, meaning that a far more efficient use is made of the energy than with conventional cooking equipment. Since the ceramic top is not magnetic but merely a tray to stand the pots and pans on, it never heats up. Tests indicate more than 50 per cent energy saving. If a pan of water is to be brought to the boil there is no delay waiting for the top to heat up; the transmission of energy through the pan is immediate. When shallow frying, cold oil and the food can be put into the pan together without affecting the quality of the food as the speed of heating is so rapid.

Induction tops have a number of advantages over ranges using conventional sources:

energy saving
flexible
faster cooking time
easy maintenance
hygienic
safe
improved working environment (less heat in the kitchen)

However, induction tops are expensive and special cooking utensils are

Fig. 7.7 An induction hob

required. Any non-magnetic material does not work and aluminium and copper are unsuitable. Stainless steel, steel enamelled ware, iron and specially adapted copper pans are suitable.

Further information
Stangard Metal Workers Ltd, Herringham Road, Charlton, London SE7 8NW.

The halogen hob

This runs on electricity, and comprises five individually controlled heat zones, each of which has four tungsten halogen lamps located under a smooth ceramic glass surface. The heat source glows red, when switched on, getting brighter as the temperature increases.

When the hob is switched on, 70 per cent of the heat is transmitted as infra red light directly into the base of the cooking pan, the rest is from conducted heat via the ceramic glass. Ordinary pots and pans may be used on the halogen hob.

The halogen range includes a convection oven, and the halogen hob unit is also available mounted on a stand.

Fig. 7.8 A halogen hob

Steamers

There are basically three types of steaming ovens:

(a) atmospheric (see Fig. 7.9), (b) pressure, (c) pressureless (see Fig. 7.10).

There are also combination steaming ovens, eg pressure/convection steam; pressureless/fully pressurised; steaming/hot air cooking; combination of hot air and steam; combination of hot air and steam with two settings.

In addition, dual pressure steamers, switchable between low pressure and high pressure, and two pressure settings plus zero are available. Steaming ovens continue to develop, improve and become more versatile. The modern combination steamer can be selected for steaming, stewing, poaching, braising, roasting, grilling, baking, vacuum cooking, gratinating, toasting, reconstituting, blanching and defrosting.

With such a wide range of models available it is increasingly important to consider carefully which model is best suited to a particular kitchen's requirements.

Cleanliness of steamers is essential, and trays and runners should be washed in hot detergent water and then rinsed. Any water generating chamber should be drained, cleaned and refilled and the inside of the steamer cleaned. Grease door controls occasionally, and when steamer is not in use, leave door slightly open to let air circulate.

Further information
Catering Equipment Manufacturers Association of Great Britain, 15 Pall Mall, London SW1Y 5LZ.

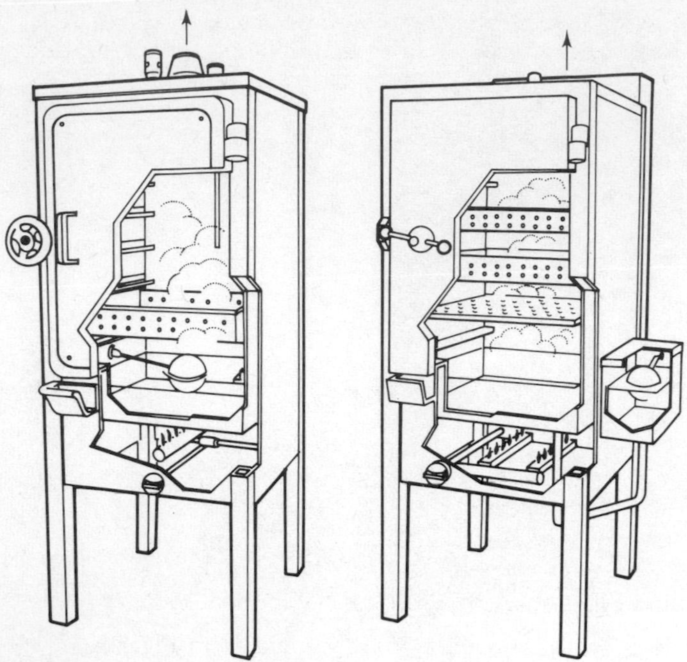

Fig. 7.9 Atmospheric steamers

Fig. 7.10 A pressureless steamer

Bratt pan

The bratt pan is one of the most versatile pieces of cooking equipment in the kitchen because it is possible to use it for shallow frying, deep frying, stewing, braising and boiling. A bratt pan can cook many items of food at one time because of its large surface area. A further advantage is that it can be tilted so that the contents can be quickly and efficiently poured out on completion of the cooking process. Bratt pans are heated by gas or electricity and several models are available incorporating various features to meet differing catering requirements (see Fig. 7.11).

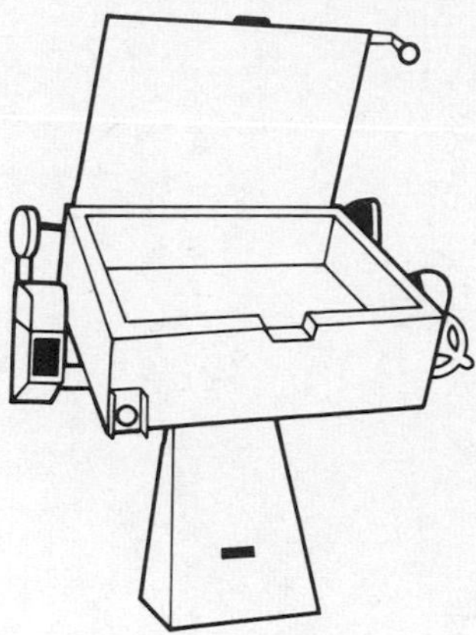

Fig. 7.11 A bratt pan

Boiling pans

Many types are available in different metals – aluminium, stainless steel, etc, in various sizes (10, 15, 20, 30 and 40 litre capacity) and they may be heated by gas or electricity or from the mains supply. As they are used for boiling or stewing large quantities of food it is important that they do not allow the food to burn; for this reason the steam-jacket type boiler is the most suitable. Many of these are fitted with a tilting device to facilitate the emptying of the contents.

After use, the boiling pan and lid should be thoroughly washed with mild detergent solution and then well rinsed. The tilting apparatus should be greased occasionally and checked to see that it tilts easily. If gas fired, the gas jets and pilot should be inspected to ensure correct working. If a pressure gauge and safety valve are fitted these should also be checked. (See Fig. 7.32, p. 242.)

Deep fat-fryers

These are one of the most extensively used items of equipment in many catering establishments. The careless worker who misuses a deep fat-fryer and spills food or fat can waste money.

Fryers are heated by gas or electricity and incorporate a thermostatic control in order to save fuel and prevent overheating. There is a cool zone below the source of heat into which food particles can sink without burning, thus preventing spoiling of other foods being cooked. This form of heating also saves fat (see overleaf).

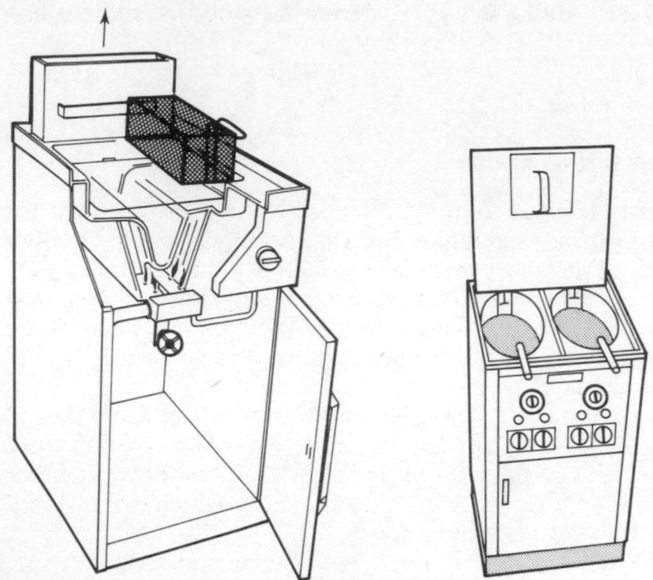

Fig. 7.12 Two examples of deep fat fryers

Pressure fryers

Food is cooked in an air-tight frying vat thus enabling food to be fried a lot faster and at a lower oil temperature.

Hot air rotary fryers

These are designed to cook batches of frozen blanched chips or battered foods without any oil in 4–6 minutes.

Computerised fryers are available which may be programmed to automatically control cooking temperatures and times, on and off switches, basket lifting and product holding times. Operational information is fed from a super-sensitive probe, which is immersed in the frying medium and passes information about temperature and rates of temperature change which may be caused by: the initial fat temperature, amount of food being fried, fryer efficiency and capacity, fryer recovery rate, quantity and condition of fat, product temperature and water content.

With all the above information the fryer computes exact cooking times and an automatic signalling device indicates the end of a cooking period.

Deep fat-fryers should be cleaned daily after use by:

1. Turning off the heat and allowing the fat to cool.
2. Draining off and straining the fat.
3. Closing the stopcock, filling the fryer with hot water containing detergent and boiling for 10–15 minutes.
4. Draining off the detergent water, refilling with clean water plus $\frac{1}{8}$ litre of vinegar per 5 litres of water and reboiling for 10–15 minutes.

5 Draining off the water, drying the fryer, closing the stopcock and refilling with clean fat.

Hot-cupboards and bains-marie

Hot-cupboards (commonly referred to in the trade as the hotplate) are used for heating plates and serving dishes and for keeping food hot. Care should be taken to see that the amount of heat fed into the hot-cupboard is controlled at a reasonable temperature. This is important, otherwise the plates and food will either be too hot or too cold and this could obviously affect the efficiency of the service. A temperature of 60°C–76°C is suitable for hot-cupboards and a thermostat is a help in maintaining this.

Hot-cupboards may be heated by steam, gas or electricity. The doors should slide easily, and occasional greasing may be necessary. The tops of most hot-cupboards are used as serving counters and should be heated to a higher temperature than the inside. These tops are usually made of stainless steel and should be cleaned thoroughly after each service.

Bains-marie are open wells of water used for keeping foods hot, and are available in many designs, some of which are incorporated into hot-cupboards, some in serving counters, and there is a type which is fitted at the end of a cooking range. They may be heated by steam, gas or electricity and sufficient heat to boil the water in the bain-marie should be available. Care should be taken to see that a bain-marie is never allowed to burn dry when the heat is turned on. After use the heat should be turned off, the water drained and the bain-marie cleaned inside and outside with hot detergent water, rinsed and dried. Any drain-off tap should then be closed.

Fig. 7.13 Hot plate area of a central kitchen

Grills and salamanders

The salamander or grill heated from above by gas or electricity probably causes more wastage of fuel than any other item of kitchen equipment through being allowed to burn unnecessarily for long unused periods. Most salamanders have more than one set of heating elements or jets and it is not always necessary to have them all turned on full.

Salamander bars and draining trays should be cleaned regularly with hot water containing a grease solvent such as soda. After rinsing they should be replaced and the salamander lit for a few minutes to dry the bars.

For under-fired grills to work efficiently they must be capable of cooking food quickly and should reach a high temperature 15–20 minutes after lighting, and the heat should be turned off immediately after use. When the bars are cool they should be removed and washed in hot water containing a grease solvent, rinsed, dried and replaced on the grill. Care should be taken with the fire bricks if they are used for lining the grill as they are easily broken.

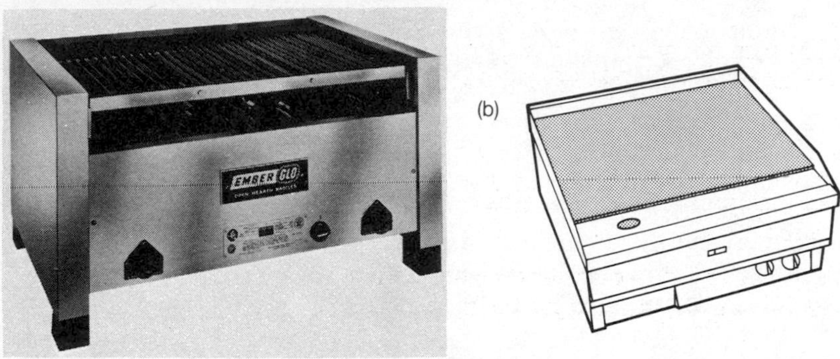

Fig. 7.14 (a) Under-fired grill (b) Griddle

Contact grills

These are sometimes referred to as double-sided or infra-grills and have two heating surfaces arranged facing each other. The food to be cooked is placed on one surface and is then covered by the second. These grills are electrically heated and are capable of cooking certain foods very quickly, so extra care is needed, particularly when cooks are using this type of grill for the first time.

Fry plates, griddle plates

These are solid metal plates heated from below, and are used for cooking individual portions of meat, hamburgers, eggs, bacon, etc. They can be heated quickly to a high temperature and are suitable for rapid and continuous cooking. Before cooking on griddle plates a light film of oil should be applied to the food and the griddle plate to prevent sticking. To clean griddle plates, warm them and scrape off loose food particles; rub the metal with pumice stone or griddle stone, following the grain of the metal; clean with hot detergent water,

Fig. 7.15 Continuous output roller toaster for bread

rinse with clean hot water and wipe dry. Finally reseason (prove) the surface by lightly oiling with vegetable oil.

Sinks

Different materials are used for sinks according to the purpose for which they are intended:

(a) heavy galvanised iron for heavy pot wash;
(b) stainless steel for general purposes.

Tables

Wooden tables should be scrubbed clean with hot soda water, rinsed and wiped as dry as possible to avoid warping.

Formica or stainless steel topped tables should be washed with hot detergent water, rinsed with hot water and dried.

Marble slabs should be scrubbed with hot water and rinsed. All excess moisture should be removed with a clean dry cloth.

No cutting or chopping should be allowed on table tops; cutting boards should be used.

Hot pans should not be put on tables; triangles must be used to protect the table surface.

The legs and racks or shelves of tables are cleaned with hot detergent water and then dried. Wooden table legs require scrubbing.

Butcher's or chopping block

A scraper should be used to keep the block clean. After scraping, the block should be sprinkled with a few handfuls of common salt in order to absorb any moisture which may have penetrated during the day.

Do not use water or liquids for cleaning unless absolutely necessary as water will be absorbed into the wood and cause swelling.

Storage racks
All type of racks should be emptied and scrubbed or washed periodically.

Mechanical equipment

If a piece of mechanical equipment can save time and physical effort and still produce a good end result then it should be considered for purchase or hire. The performance of most machines can be closely controlled and is not subject to human variations, so it should be easier to obtain uniformity of production over a period of time.

The caterer is faced with two considerations:

1 The cost of the machine: installation, maintenance, depreciation and running cost.
2 The possibility of increased production and a saving of labour cost.

The mechanical performance must be carefully assessed and all the manufacturer's claims as to the machine's efficiency thoroughly checked. The design should be fool-proof, easy to clean and operated with minimum effort.

When a new item of equipment is installed it should be tested by a qualified fitter before being used by catering staff. The manufacturer's instructions must be displayed in a prominent place near the machine. The manufacturer's advice regarding servicing should be followed and a record book kept showing what kind of maintenance the machine is receiving, and when. The following list includes machines typically found in catering premises which are classified as dangerous under the Prescribed Dangerous Machines Order, 1964.

I Power-driven machines of the following type:

1 Worm-type mincing machines.
2 Rotary knife bowl-type chopping machines.
3 Dough mixers.
4 Food mixing machines when used with attachments for mincing, slicing, chipping and any other cutting operation, or for crumbling.
5 Pie and tart making machines.
6 Vegetable slicing machines.

II The following machines whether power-driven or not:

7 Circular knife slicing machines used for cutting bacon and other foods (whether similar to bacon or not).
8 Potato chipping machines.

Before cleaning, the machine should be switched off and the plug removed from the socket.

Potato-peelers

1 Potatoes should be free of earth and stones before loading into the machine.
2 Before any potatoes are loaded the water spray should be turned on and the abrasive plate set in motion.

3 The interior should be cleaned out daily and the abrasive plate removed to ensure that small particles are not lodged below.
4 The peel trap should be emptied as frequently as required.
5 The waste outlet should be kept free from obstruction.

Food processing equipment

Food-mixer

This is an important labour-saving, electrically operated piece of equipment used for many purposes, for example mixing pastry, cakes, mashing potatoes, beating egg whites, mayonnaise, cream, mincing or chopping meat and vegetables.

1 It should be lubricated frequently in accordance with manufacturer's instructions.
2 The motor should not be overloaded, which can be caused by obstruction to the rotary components. For example, if dried bread is being passed through the mincer attachment without sufficient care the rotary cog can become so clogged with bread that it is unable to move. If the motor is allowed to run, damage can be caused to the machine.
3 All components as well as the main machine should be thoroughly washed and dried. Care should be taken to see that no rust occurs on any part. The mincer attachment knife and plates will rust if not given sufficient care.

Vertical high speed cuttermixer or bowl cutter

These are fast, versatile labour-saving machines which can deal with a great

Fig. 7.16 Vertical high speed cuttermixer

amount of the repetitive time-consuming work which takes place in some kitchen operations.

They are used mainly for cutting and mixing and some models have attachments for kneading dough and other mixes or for mincing meat.

Food processing machines

Food processors are generally similar to vertical high speed cutters except that they tend to be smaller and to have a larger range of attachments. They can be used for a large number of mixing and chopping jobs but they cannot whisk or incorporate air to mixes.

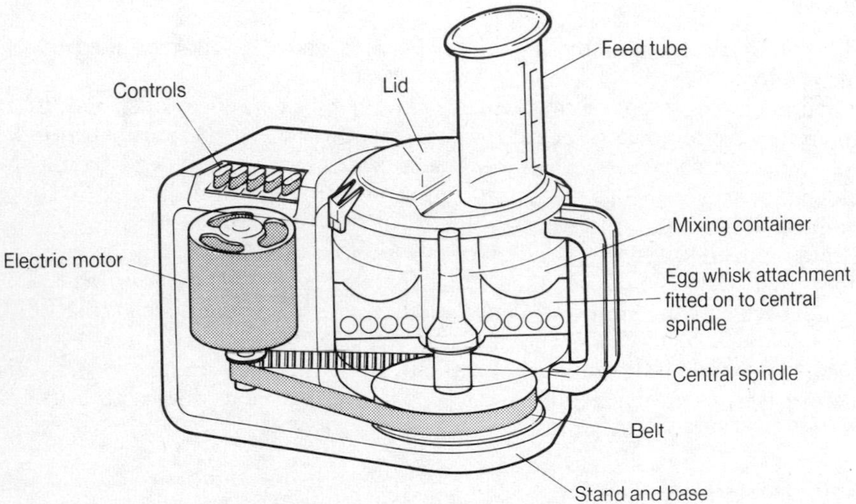

Fig. 7.17 Belt driven food processor

Liquidiser or blender

This is a versatile, labour saving piece of kitchen machinery which uses a high speed motor to drive specially designed stainless steel blades to chop, purée or blend foods efficiently and very quickly. They are also useful for making breadcrumbs. As a safety precaution food must be cooled before being liquidised.

Food-slicers

Food-slicers are obtainable both manually and electrically operated. They are labour-saving devices, but can be dangerous if not used with care so working instructions should be placed in a prominent position near the machine.

1 Care should be taken that no material likely to damage the blades is included in the food to be sliced. It is easy for a careless worker to overlook a piece of bone which, if allowed to come into contact with the cutting blade, could cause severe damage.
2 Each section in contact with food should be cleaned and carefully dried after use.

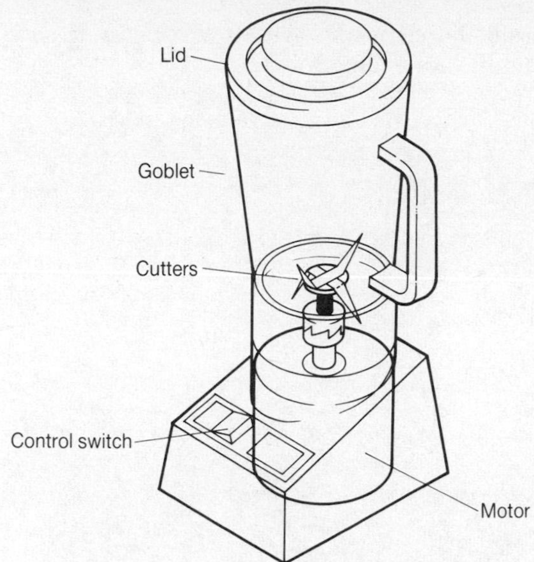

Fig. 7.18 Example of a blender machine

3 The blade or blades should be sharpened regularly.
4 Moving parts should be lubricated, but oil must not come into contact with the food.
5 Extra care must be taken when blades are exposed.

Chipper (hand or electric)
The manual type should be washed and dried after use. Care should be taken with the interior of the blades, and they should be cleaned with a folded cloth. When chipping potatoes, pressure should be applied gradually to prevent damage to the cutting blades which can be caused by violent jerking.

The electric chipper should be thoroughly cleaned and dried after use, particular attention being paid to those parts which come into contact with food. Care should be taken that no obstruction prevents the motor from operating at its normal speed. Moving parts should be lubricated according to the maker's instructions.

Masher (hand or electric)
The hand type should be washed immediately after use, then rinsed and dried.

The electric masher should have the removal sections and the main machine washed and dried after use, extra care being taken over those parts which come into contact with food. The same care should be taken as with electric chippers regarding obstruction and lubrication.

Boilers

Water boiling appliances for tea- and coffee-making
There are two main groups of water boilers: bulk boilers from which boiling

water can only be drawn when all the contents have boiled, and automatic boilers which provide a continuous flow of boiling water.

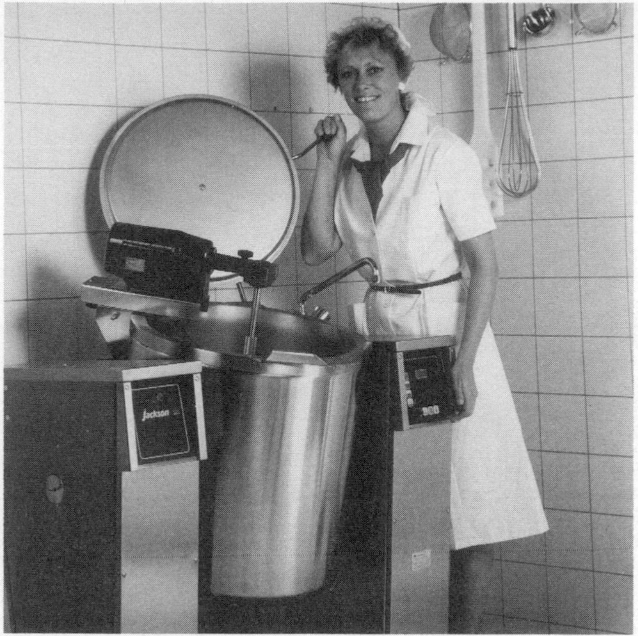

Fig. 7.19 A tilting kettle

Bulk boilers

These are generally used when large quantities of boiling water are required at a given time. They should be kept scrupulously clean, covered with the correct lid to prevent anything falling in, and when not used for some time they should be left filled with clean cold water.

Automatic boilers

These boilers have automatic waterfeeds and can give freshly boiled water at intervals. It is important that the water supply is efficiently maintained, otherwise there is a danger of the boiler burning dry and being damaged.

Pressure boilers

This is the type that operates many still sets, consisting of steam heating milk boilers and a pressure boiler providing boiling water. Care should be taken with the pilot light to see that it is working efficiently. As with all gas-fired equipment it is essential that regular inspection and maintenance is carried out by gas company fitters (see Fig. 7.20).

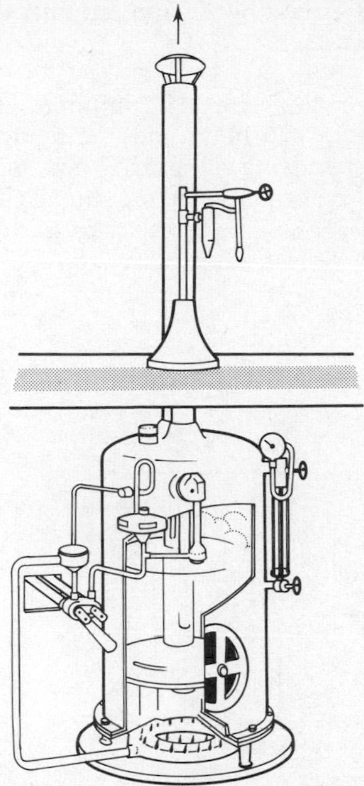

Fig. 7.20 A pressure boiler

Coffee and milk heaters
Water-jacket boilers are made for the storage of hot coffee and hot milk with draw-off taps from the storage chamber. Inner linings may be of glazed earthenware, stainless steel or heat-resistant glass. It is very important that the storage chambers are thoroughly cleaned with hot water after each use and then left full of clean cold water. The draw-off taps should be cleaned regularly with a special brush.

Refrigeration

How refrigeration works

Cold is the absence of heat, and to make things cold it is necessary to remove the heat that items have absorbed. This is the function of a refrigerator. To raise water to boiling point (100°C) from tap water temperature (10°C), heat must be added; add further heat and the boiling water turns to water vapour or steam. A substance such as ammonia which boils at −30°C would absorb heat at even lower temperatures. Ammonia is one of a number of liquids called 'refrigerants' which are used to absorb heat from the interior of well-insulated containers or cabinets known as refrigerators. Water, from which heat is removed, cools down and forms ice. Ice blocks can be used to cool a refrigerator interior. The heat from the food stored in the refrigerator is absorbed by the ice and turned back into water as the interior cools down. Further ice blocks are then required to prolong the cooling process.

By using a refrigerant like liquid ammonia circulating through the pipes in the refrigerated compartment, heat is taken out of the food and the liquid ammonia boils, becoming a vapour or 'gas'. By removing or sucking out this vapour and replacing it with more liquid, the cooling process can be maintained as long as required. In practice the vapour is not lost but compressed back into a liquid, cooled by giving up its heat to the air outside the refrigerator, and then pumped back into the refrigerator cooling units for re-use.

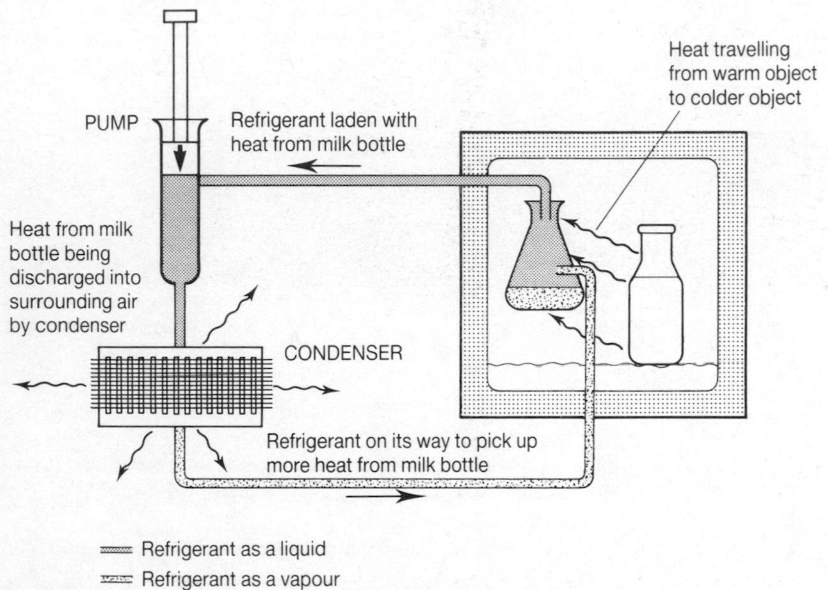

Fig. 7.21 How refrigeration works

Compression-type refrigerator

The compression-type refrigerator works on the principle described. The three main parts are:

1 *The evaporator* inside the cabinet where the refrigerant boils and changes into a vapour and absorbs the heat.
2 *The compressor* which puts pressure on the refrigerant so that it can get rid of its heat. To enable the compressor to work, it is necessary to have an electric motor to operate the compressor or pump.
3 *The condenser* which helps to discharge the heat.

Absorption-type refrigerator

This type of refrigerator does not have any moving parts as no compressor is used. A solution of ammonia gas in water is the refrigerant, and the gas is given

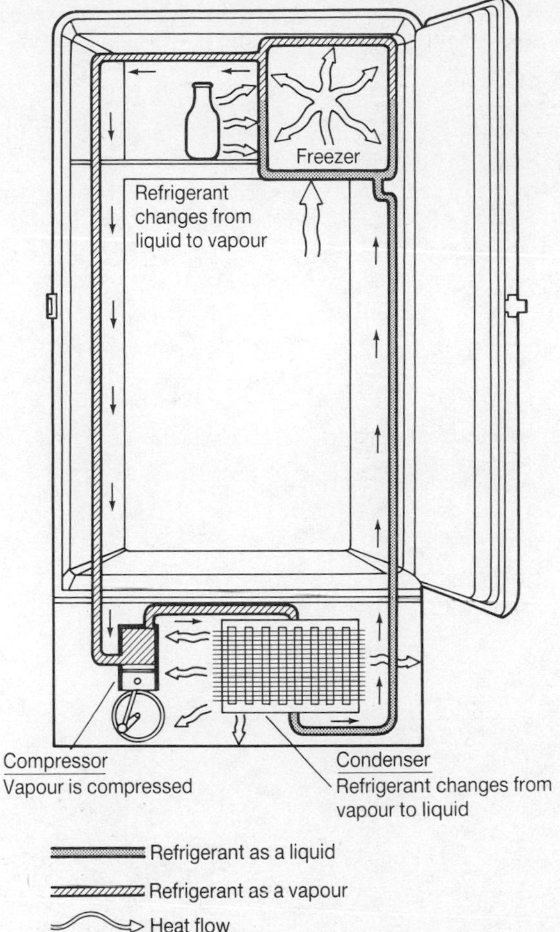

Fig. 7.22 Compression-type refrigeration

off from the solution when it is heated by an electrical element or gas flame. The ammonia gas passes to the condenser where it is liquefied; the liquefied ammonia then passes to the evaporator with some hydrogen, where it expands and draws the heat from the cabinet. The gases produced pass to the absorber, where they mix with water and become a solution again. The solution returns to be heated again while the hydrogen goes to the evaporator. (See Fig. 7.23 overleaf.)

Refrigerants

A refrigerant must have a boiling-point below the temperature at which ice forms and it should be non-corrosive and non-explosive. Substances such as sulphur dioxide, methyl chloride and dichloro-difluoromethane are used as refrigerants.

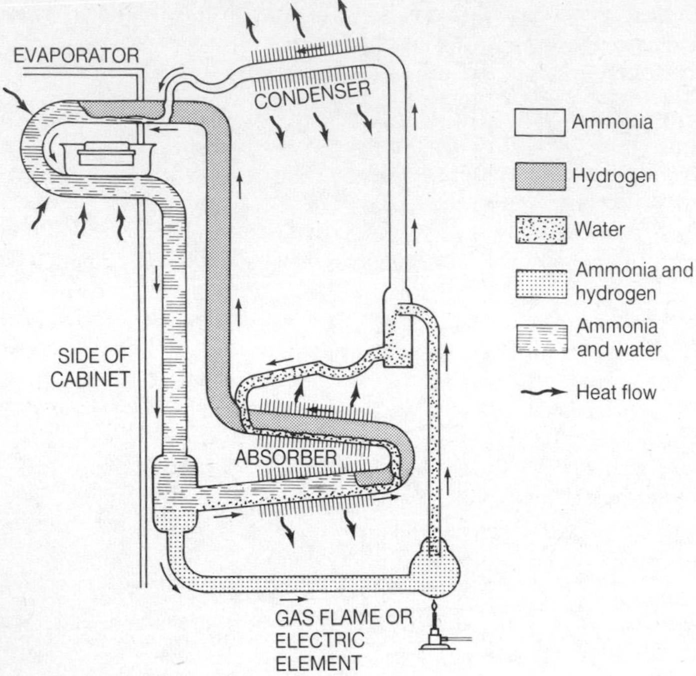

Fig. 7.23 Absorption-type refrigeration

The cabinet

This must be well insulated to prevent entry of heat from outside. In modern refrigerators, insulations such as expanded polystyrene and foamed polyurethane are used extensively.

Cold rooms, chill rooms, deep-freeze cabinets and compartments

In large establishments it is necessary to have refrigerated space at different temperatures. The cold rooms may be divided into separate rooms: one at a chill temperature for storing salads, fruits, certain cheeses; one for meats, poultry, game and tinned food which have to be refrigerated; one for deep-frozen foods. Frequently, the cold room storage is designed so that the chill room, the cold room and the deep-freeze compartment lead on from each other. Refrigerated cabinets, thermostatically controlled to various desired temperatures, are also used in large larders. Deep-freeze cabinets are used where a walk-in deep-freeze section is not required and they maintain a temperature of −18°C. Deep-freeze cabinets require defrosting twice a year.

Hygiene precautions

Refrigeration equipment is only designed to retard the natural process of deterioration. At best it can only preserve food in similar conditions as when it was put in the refrigerator.

For maximum storage life of food and minimum health risk:

1 Select the appropriate refrigerator equipment for the temperature and humidity requirement of the food.
2 Always ensure refrigerators maintain correct temperature for food stored.
3 Keep unwrapped foods, vulnerable to contamination and flavour and odour transfer, in separate refrigerators and away from products such as cream, other dairy products, partly cooked pastry, cooked meat and delicatessen foods.
4 Do not store foods for long periods in a good general-purpose refrigerator because a single temperature is not suitable for keeping all types of food safely and at peak condition.
5 Never keep uncooked meat, poultry or fish in the same refrigerator, or any other food which is not in its own sealed air-tight container.
6 Never re-freeze foods that have been thawed out from frozen.
7 Always rotate stock in refrigerator space.
8 Clean equipment regularly and thoroughly, inside and out.

Location

As adequate ventilation is vital, locate refrigeration equipment in a well-ventilated room away from:

(a) Sources of intense heat – cookers, ovens, radiators, boilers etc.
(b) Direct sunlight – from window or sky lights.
(c) Barriers to adequate air circulation.

Loading

(a) Ensure there is adequate capacity for maximum stock.
(b) Check that perishable goods are delivered in a refrigerated vehicle.
(c) Only fill frozen food storage cabinets with pre-frozen food.
(d) Never put hot or warm food in a refrigerator unless it is specially designed for rapid chilling.
(e) Ensure no damage is caused to inner linings and insulation by staples, nails etc in packaging.
(f) Air must be allowed to circulate within a refrigerator to maintain the cooling effect – do not obstruct any airways.

Cleaning

Clean thoroughly inside and out at least every two months as blocked drain lines, drip trays and air ducts will eventually lead to a breakdown.

1 Switch off power.
2 If possible transfer stock to available alternative storage.
3 Clean interior surfaces with lukewarm water and a mild detergent. Do not use abrasives and strongly scented cleaning agents.
4 Clean exterior and dry all surfaces inside and out.
5 Clear away any external dirt, dust or rubbish which might restrict circulation of air around the condenser.

6 Switch on power, check when correct working temperature is reached, refill with stock.

Defrosting

This is important as it helps equipment perform efficiently and prevents a potentially damaging build up of ice. Pressure of ice on the evaporator or internal surfaces indicates the need for urgent defrosting; if the equipment is designed to defrost automatically this also indicates a fault.

Automatic defrosting may lead to a temporary rise in air temperature; this is normal and will not put food at risk.

For manual defrosting always follow suppliers' instructions to obtain optimum performance. Never use a hammer or any sharp instrument which could perforate cabinet linings – a plastic spatula can be used to remove stubborn ice.

Emergency measures

Signs of imminent breakdown include: unusual noises, fluctuating temperatures, frequent stopping and starting of condenser, excessive frost build up.

Prepare to call a competent refrigeration service engineer, but first check that:

1 The power supply has not been accidentally switched off.
2 The electrical circuit has not been broken by a blown fuse or the triggering of an automatic circuit breaker.
3 There has been no unauthorised tampering with the user temperature control device.
4 Any temperature higher than recommended is not due solely to routine automatic defrosting or to overloading the equipment or to any blockage of internal passage of air.
5 Check there is no blockage of air to the condenser by rubbish, crates, cartons, etc. If you still suspect a fault, call the engineer and be prepared to give brief details of the equipment and the fault. Keep the door of the defective cold cabinet closed as much as possible to retain cold air. Destroy any spoilt food.

Further information

Refrigeration and Unit Air-Conditioning Group, 34 Palace Court, London W2 4JG.

Dishwashing machines

For hygienic washing up the generally recognised requirements are a good supply of hot water at a temperature of 60°C for general cleansing followed by a sterilising rinse at a temperature of 82°C for at least one minute. Alternatively low-temperature equipment is available which sterilises by means of a chemical, sodium hypochlorite (bleach).

Further information

Lever Industrial, Lever House, St James Road, Kingston-upon-Thames, Surrey KT1 2BA.

Dishwashing machines take over an arduous job and save a lot of time and labour, ensuring that a good supply of clean, sterilised crockery is available.

There are three main types:

1. *Spray types* in which the dishes are placed in racks which slide into the machines where they are subjected to a spray of hot detergent water at 48°C–60°C from above and below.

   The racks move on to the next section where they are rinsed by a fresh hot shower at 82°C. At this temperature they are sterilised, and on passing out into the air they dry off quickly.
2. *Brush-type machines* use revolving brushes for the scrubbing of each article in hot detergent water; the articles are then rinsed and sterilised in another compartment.
3. *Agitator water machines* in which baskets of dishes are immersed in deep tanks and the cleaning is performed by the mechanical agitation of the hot detergent water. The loaded baskets are then given a sterilising rinse in another compartment.

Dishwashing machines are costly and it is essential that the manufacturer's instructions with regard to use and maintenance are followed at all times.

Food waste disposers

Food waste disposers are operated by electricity and take all manner of rubbish, including bones, fat, scraps and vegetable refuse. Almost every type of rubbish and swill, with the exception of rags and tins, is finely ground, then rinsed down the drain. It is the most modern and hygienic method of waste disposal. Care should be taken by handlers not to push waste into the machine with a metal object as this can cause damage.

Small equipment and utensils

Small equipment and utensils are made from a variety of materials such as non-stick coated metal, iron, steel, copper, aluminium, wood, etc.

Iron

Items of equipment used for frying, such as movable fritures and frying-pans of all types, are usually made of heavy, black wrought iron.

Fritures should be washed in a strong grease-solvent solution, then thoroughly rinsed and dried; or they can be thoroughly cleaned with a clean cloth.

Frying-pans (poêles). When new they should be 'proved'; they are coated with a layer of oil and placed on a hot stove or in a hot oven for 15–20 minutes, then wiped firmly with a clean cloth. A little fat or oil is added and they are wiped with another clean cloth. If an abrasive is necessary to clean the pan, salt may be used; if not, a good firm rub with dry cloth or paper and a final light greasing are sufficient. Always keep lightly oiled.

Frying-pans are available in several shapes and many sizes; for example:

Omelet pans	Frying-pans
Oval fish frying-pans	Pancake pans

Baking sheets are made in various sizes of black wrought steel. The less they are washed the less likely they are to cause food to stick. New baking sheets should be well heated in a hot oven, thoroughly wiped with a clean cloth and then lightly oiled. Before being used baking trays should be lightly greased with a pure fat or oil. Immediately after use and while still warm they should be cleaned by scraping and dry-wiping. When washing, hot soda or detergent water should be used.

Tartlet and barquette moulds and cake tins should be cared for in the same way as for baking sheets.

Tinned steel

A number of items are made from this metal, for example:

Conical strainer (*chinois*), used for passing sauces and gravies.
Fine conical strainer (*chinois fin*), used for passing sauces and gravies.
Colander, used for draining vegetables.
Vegetable reheating container (*passoir*), used for reheating vegetables.
Soup machine and mouli strainer, used for passing thick soups, sauces and potatoes for mash.
Sieves (*tamis*).

Fig. 7.24 Examples of equipment which are hard to clean: 1 Jelly Bag 2 Mouli 3 and 4 Mouli attachments 5 Muslin 6 Sieve 7 Colander 8 Conical strainer – coarse 9 Conical strainer – fine 10 Potato ricer 11 Twelve inch ruler

All the above items should be thoroughly washed immediately after each use and dried; if this is done, washing is simple and quick. If the food or liquid clogs and dries in the mesh it is difficult to clean. The easiest way to wash a sieve is to hold it upside down under running water and tap vigorously with the bristles of a stiff scrubbing brush. If the sieve is moved up and down quickly in water, clogged food will be loosened.

Care should be taken when using sieves: they should be the right way up when food is passed through; the food should be stroked through with a wooden mushroom, not banged, as this can damage the mesh. Only foodstuffs such as flour should be passed through the sieve upside down.

Copper

Pans of copper, lined with tin, are made in various shapes, sizes and capacities and are used to cook practically every kind of food.

Shallow saucepan with sloping sides	*sauteuse*
Shallow flat round pan with vertical sides	*plat à sauter*
Saucepan	*russe*
Stockpot	*marmite*
Large round deep pan	*rondeau*
Rectangular braising-pan	*braisière*
Roasting tray	*plaque à rôtir*
Turbot kettle	*turbotière*
Salmon kettle	*saumonière*
Gravy, soup, sauce storage pans	*bain-marie*
Moulds of various sizes and shapes	*dariole, charlotte, savarin, bombe, timbale*

Fig. 7.25 Examples of copper equipment: 1 Salmon kettle 2 Saucepan 3 Sauteuse 4 Sauté pan 5 Sugar boiler 6 Pomme Anna mould 7 Bowl 8 Braising pan 9 Dariole mould 10 Savarin mould 11 Twelve inch ruler

Copper equipment is expensive, but it is first-class for cooking as copper is a good conductor of heat; also, food burns less easily in copper pans than in pans of many other metals.

The disadvantages of copper are that it tarnishes easily and looks dirty. The tin lining of copper pans can be damaged by misuse, for example excessive dry heat can soften the tin and spoil the lining. Putting a pan on a fierce fire without liquid or fat is bad practice and can damage the tin lining. Retinning is expensive.

Copper equipment should be inspected periodically to see if the tin is being worn away; if so, it should be collected by a tinsmith and retinned.

Certain items of copper equipment, for example large vegetable boilers, sugar boilers, mixing bowls and egg white bowls, are not lined with tin but made wholly of copper.

The cleaning of copper equipment

To keep large quantities of copper equipment clean the following points should be observed:

1 Two large sinks, into which the pots may be completely immersed, should be available. The water in one sink should be capable of being raised to boiling-point.
2 All dirty pans should be well soaked for a few minutes in boiling water to which a little soda has been added.
3 They should be well scoured, using either a brush or wire wool or similar agent with a scouring powder.
4 The pans are then rinsed in clean hot water and placed upside down to dry.
5 The copper surfaces, if tarnished, may be cleaned with a paste made from equal quantities of silver sand, salt and flour mixed with vinegar; the pans are then thoroughly rinsed and dried. Alternatively, a commercial cleaner may be used.

Aluminium

Saucepans, stockpots, sauteuses, sauté pans, braising pans, fish kettles and large round deep pans and dishes of all sizes are made in cast aluminium. They are expensive, but one advantage is that the pans do not tarnish; also, because of their strong, heavy construction they are suitable for many cooking processes.

A disadvantage is that in the manufacture of aluminium, which is a soft metal, other metals are added to make pans stronger. As a result certain foods can become discoloured; for example, care should be taken when making white sauces and white soups. A wooden spoon should be used for mixing, then there should be no discoloration. The use of metal whisks or spoons must be avoided.

Water boiled in aluminium pans is unsuitable for tea-making as it gives the tea an unpleasant colour. Red cabbage and artichokes should not be cooked in aluminium pans as they will take on a dark colour, caused by chemical reaction.

Cleaning of cast aluminium pans

1 All pans should be well soaked in hot detergent water; soda should not be used.
2 After a good soaking, pans should be scoured with a hard bristle brush or rough cloth with an abrasive powder if necessary. Harsh abrasives should be avoided if possible.
3 After scouring, the pans are rinsed in clean hot water and thoroughly dried.

Stainless steel

Specially manufactured stainless steel pots and pans are now being extensively used in place of copper. Copper is considered inappropriate in terms of initial cost, re-tinning and cleanliness. The vast majority of new establishments buy stainless steel.

Stainless steel is also used for many small items of equipment.

Fig. 7.26 Examples of stainless steel equipment: 1 Saucepan 2 Mixing bowl 3 Tray 4 Stockpot 5 Bowl 6 Basin 7 Mandolin 8 Twelve inch ruler

Non-stick metal

An ever-increasing variety of kitchen utensils eg saucepans, frying pans, baking and roasting tins are available and are suitable for certain types of kitchen operation, such as small scale or à la carte. Particular attention should be paid to the following otherwise the non-stick properties of the equipment will be affected:

(a) excessive heat should be avoided;
(b) use plastic or wooden spatulas or spoons when using non-stick pans so that contact is not made to the surface with metal;
(c) extra care is needed when cleaning non-stick surfaces, the use of cloth or paper is most suitable.

Wood and compound materials

Cutting boards are an important item of kitchen equipment which should be kept in use on all table surfaces to protect the table and the edges of cutting knives.

Fig. 7.27 Examples of metal equipment: 1 Frying basket 2 Friture and draining wire 3 Baking tray 4 Double grill wires 5 Cooling wire 6 Raised pie mould 7 Frying pan 8 Omelet pan 9 Water 10 Pancake pan 11 Flan ring 12 Deep tartlet mould 13 Shallow tartlet ring 14 Boat-shaped mould 15 Twelve inch ruler

Wooden chopping boards

To comply with current regulations, wooden boards should not splinter or leak preservatives. They should be of close-grained hard wood either in a thick solid slab or separate pieces with close fitting joints.

1 Before using a new board, wash to remove wood dust.
2 After use scrub with hot detergent water, rinse with clean water, dry as much as possible and stand on its longest end to prevent warping.
3 Do not use for heavy chopping – use a chopping block instead.

Disadvantages of wooden chopping boards

(a) They are porous and can retain taste, smell, bacteria, grease and dirt.
(b) They may expand and contract when washed, trapping small particles of food.
(c) Cut and scored surfaces may trap food particles and bacteria.

Cutting boards of compound materials

There are several types available, one of which is made of polyethylene and offers six boards marked in different colours along one edge. These can be kept in a special rack after washing and when not in use. This system is designed to cut down on cross-contamination by using one board exclusively for one type of food, eg raw meat, raw poultry, cooked meats, vegetables, raw fish and dairy products. When selecting compound cutting boards it is essential to have a non-slip surface.

Rubber: Cutting boards are also made of hard rubber and rubber compounds,

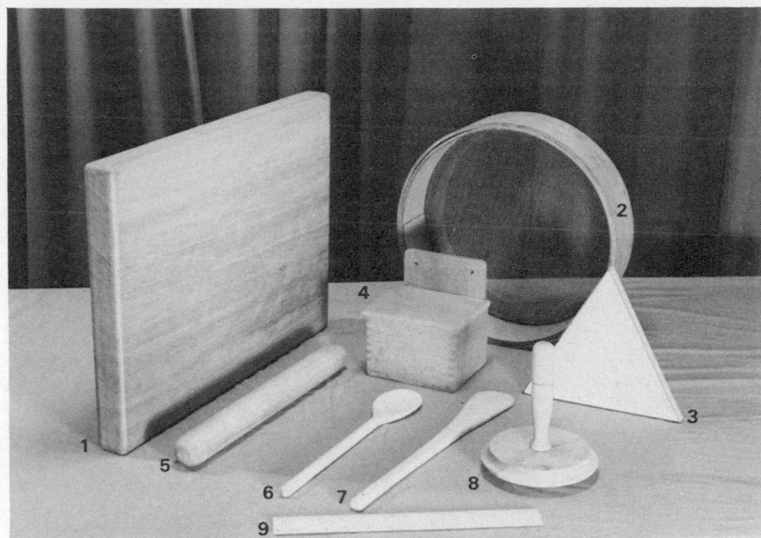

Fig. 7.28 Examples of wooden equipment: 1 Chopping board 2 Sieve 3 Triangle 4 Salt box 5 Rolling pin 6 Spoon 7 Spatula 8 Mushroom 9 Twelve inch ruler

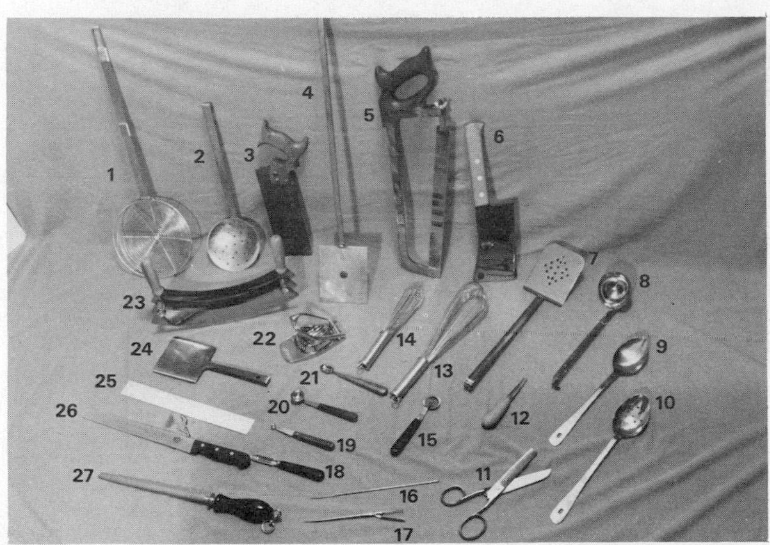

Fig. 7.29 Examples of small equipment: 1 Spider 2 Skimmer 3 Tenon saw 4 Iron spatule 5 Butcher's saw 6 Chopper 7 Fish slice 8 Ladle 9 Metal spoon 10 Perforated spoon 11 Fish scissors 12 Oyster knife 13 Balloon whisk 14 Small whisk 15 Ravioli wheel 16 Trussing needle 17 Larding needle 18 Vegetable peeler 19 Solferino cutter 20 Parisienne cutter 21 Olivette cutter 22 Egg slicer 23 Four bladed chopper 24 Meat bat 25 Twelve inch ruler 26 Carving knife 27 Steel

eg rubber, polystyrene and clay. These are hygienic because they are solid, in one piece and should not warp, crack or absorb flavours. They are cleaned by scrubbing with hot water and then drying.

Rolling pins, wooden spoons and spatulas: These items should be scrubbed in hot detergent water, rinsed in clean water and dried. Rolling-pins should not be scraped with a knife as this can cause the wood to splinter. Adhering paste can be removed with a cloth. Wooden spoons and spatulas will soon be replaced by a high density plastic capable of withstanding very high temperatures. Wooden spoons/spatulas are considered unhygienic unless washed in a sodium hypochloride solution (bleach). Metal piping tubes are being replaced by plastic. These can be boiled and do not rust.

Wooden sieves and mandolins: When cleaning, care of the wooden frame should be considered taking into account the previous remarks. The blades of the mandolin should be kept lightly greased to prevent rust (stainless steel mandolins are available).

Fig. 7.30 Examples of china and other earthenware: 1 Casserole 2 Oval dish 3 Ravier 4 Bowl 5 Soufflé dish 6 Egg cocotte 7 Twelve inch ruler 8 Pie dish 9 Sole dish 10 and 11 Egg dishes 12 Basin

Materials

Muslin (la mousseline): *tammy cloth (l'étamine)* which is made from calico. Both muslin and tammy cloth are used for straining soups and sauces.

The jelly bag made from thick flannel or nylon for straining jellies.

Piping bags (les poches) are made from linen, nylon or plastic and are used for piping preparations of all kinds.

All materials should be washed immediately after use in hot detergent water, rinsed in hot clean water and then dried. Tammy cloths, muslins and linen piping bags must be boiled periodically in detergent water.

Kitchen cloths, papers and foils etc

Kitchen cloths

(a) General purpose – for washing up and cleaning surfaces.
(b) Tea towel (teacloth) – for drying up and general purpose hand cloths.
(c) Bactericide wiping cloths – are impregnated with bactericide to disinfect work surfaces. The cloths have a coloured pattern which fades and disappears when the bactericide is no longer effective; the cloth should then be discarded.
(d) Oven cloths – thick cloths designed to protect the hands when removing hot items from the oven. Oven cloths must only be used dry, never damp or wet otherwise the user is likely to be burned.

It is essential that all kitchen cloths are washed or changed frequently, otherwise accumulating dirt and food stains may cause cross contamination of harmful bacteria/germs on to clean food.

Papers

(a) Greaseproof or silicone – for lining cake-tins, making piping bags and wrapping greasy items of food.
(b) Kitchen – white absorbent paper for absorbing grease from deep-fried foods and for lining trays on which cold foods are kept.
(c) General purpose – thick absorbent paper for wiping and drying equipment, surfaces, food etc.
(d) Towels – disposable, for drying of hands.

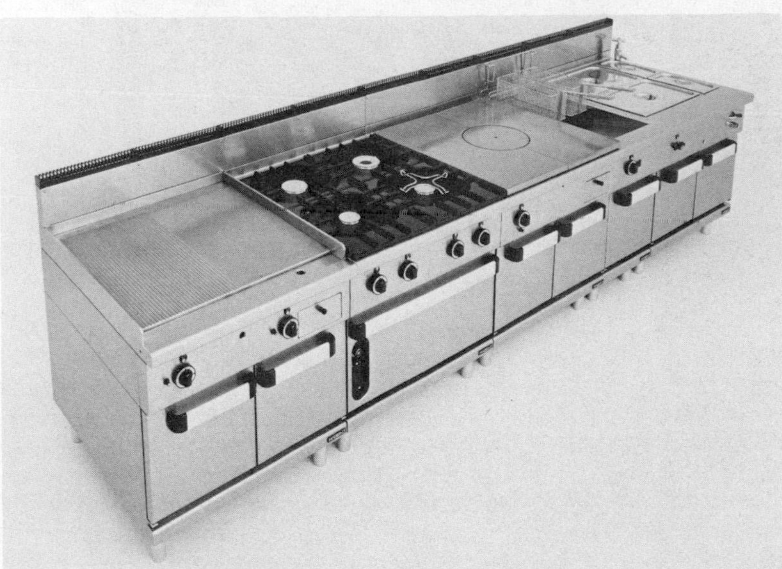

Fig. 7.31 Compact griddle, open top, solid top, deep fryer and oven range

Foils

(a) Clingwrap – thin transparent material for wrapping sandwiches, snacks, hot and cold foods. Clingwrap has the advantage of being very flexible and easy to handle and seal. Due to risk of contamination, it is advisable to use a clingwrap that does not contain PVC, or is plasticiser-free.
(b) Metal – thin pliable silver coloured material for wrapping and covering foods and for protecting oven roasted joints during cooking.

Fig. 7.32 Tilting boiling pans

8

Gas, electricity and water

The studies of gas, electricity and water are highly technical. A simple study can be made, however, which is a help to the student in understanding how important a part all three play in the catering industry.

Gas

Having read this part of the chapter these learning objectives, both general and specific, should be achieved.

General objectives Know the part played by gas in the industry, and understand how gas is used for cooking, heating and hot water. Be aware of how to use gas safely.

Specific objectives State the basic principles of conduction, radiation and convection and give an example of each. Demonstrate how to read a gas meter and calculate gas bills. Explain the principles of thermostats, pressure governors and flame-failure devices.

Transference of heat

This is carried out by one of three methods illustrated below: radiation, conduction and convection.

Radiation: heat passes from the salamander directly on to the food being grilled (see Fig. 8.1).

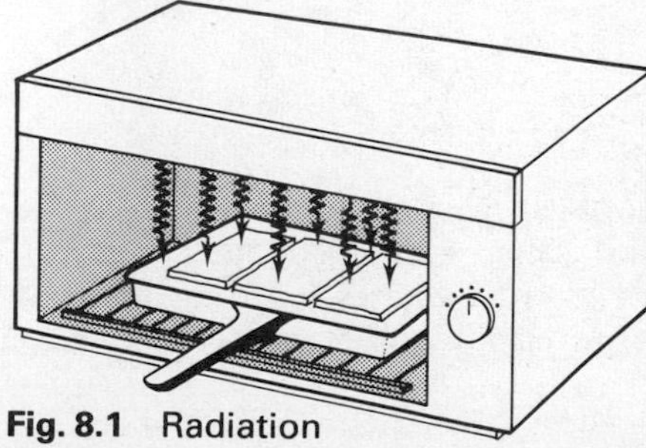

Fig. 8.1 Radiation

Conduction: heat is conducted from the range top through the solid base of the pan (see Fig. 8.2).

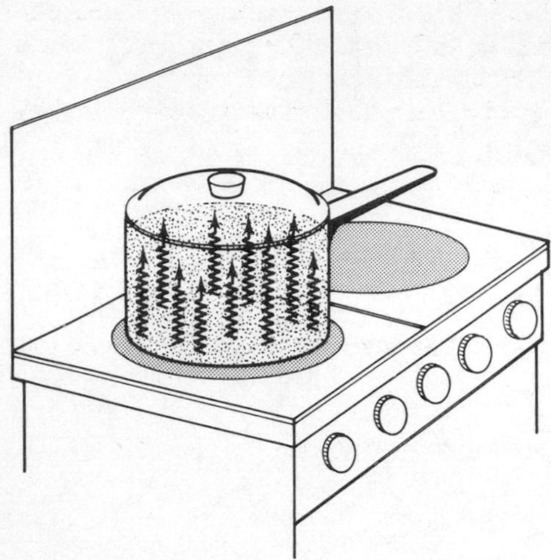

Fig. 8.2 Conduction

Convection: heated air is convected around the oven (see Fig. 8.3).

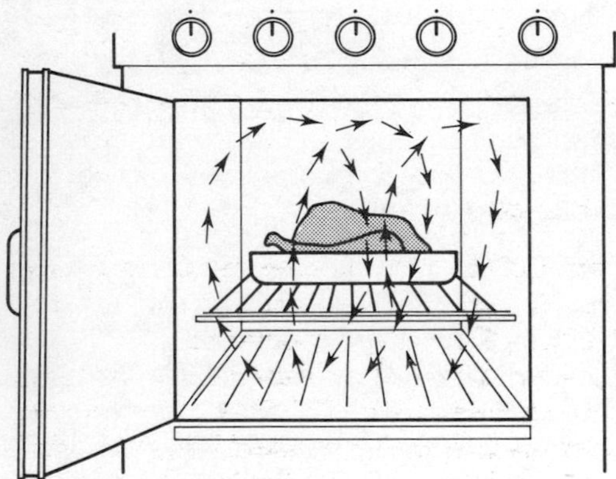

Fig. 8.3 Convection

Modern gas

The gas used today is almost entirely natural gas from underground sources in the seas around the British Isles. Although it is non-toxic and odourless, a scent is introduced to give a characteristic smell in order that escapes can be easily detected. To make gas burn it needs to be mixed with approximately ten times as much air.

If a gas escape is suspected the main gas supply must be turned off at the tap next to the meter. The gas service must be called immediately (the telephone number is under 'Gas' in the directory).

In those areas where British Gas is unable to supply the workplace or home with gas through underground pipes, gas in liquid form can be stored adjacent to the place of use in containers or tanks, eg Calor gas. These gases will have a different calorific value to that supplied by British Gas.

The heat contained by given quantities of a fuel is known as the *calorific value*, eg

natural gas	– 950–1200 Btu/ft^3
propane gas (Calor)	– 2500 Btu/ft^3
methane gas	– 3200 Btu/ft^3
light fuel oil	– 19 900 Btu/lb

Ideally, supply pipes are colour coded for easy identification. The following are the colours that should be used:

gas	– yellow ochre
air	– light blue
electricity	– orange
water	– green
steam	– silver grey

Measuring gas consumption

Gas passes along mains into houses and other establishments through a gas meter which records the amount in cubic feet but charges for it in therms. Future changes in legislation might require gas to be charged in megajoules per cubic metre, so for this reason the heating power of gas used is shown on all gas bills in both ways (see Figs. 8.4 and 8.5).

British Standards and gas catering equipment

Standard specifications are laid down for the manufacture of gas catering equipment. Quality assurance is covered by BS 5750 and the Catering Equipment Manufacturers' Associations' (CEMA) 'CEMARK' guarantee.

Under their 'Tested for Safety' scheme British Gas lists all gas catering appliances which have met the safety requirements of BS 5314. The scheme itself has been developed in order to be in line with proposed European and international safety standards which are projected for the future. It has been adopted by CEMA and by the National Association of Restaurant Engineers in their continuing efforts to upgrade and improve the quality of their products.

Care and servicing of gas equipment

In order to be sure of getting the best performance from catering equipment it should be regularly serviced. But the general efficiency of appliances can be sustained by careful use plus regular cleaning and checks. Every local branch of British Gas can arrange to service all gas catering, water heating and space heating equipment, either as a 'one-off' or on a regular basis.

When having gas equipment installed it is best always to have either British

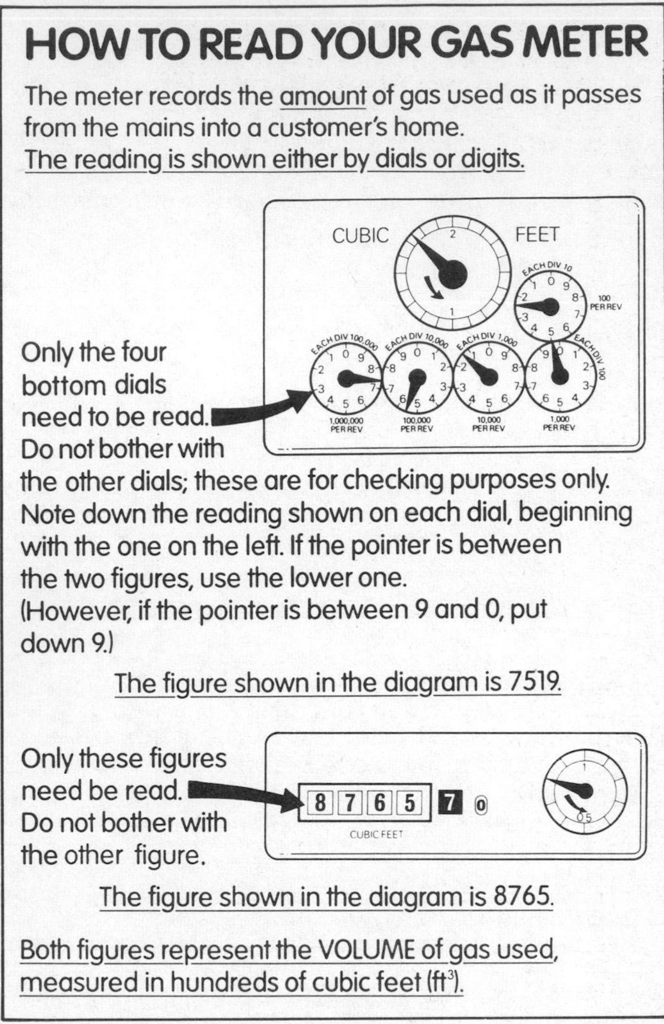

HOW TO READ YOUR GAS METER
The meter records the amount of gas used as it passes from the mains into a customer's home.
The reading is shown either by dials or digits.
CUBIC
FEET
EACH DIV 10
100 PER REV
EACH DIV 100,000
EACH DIV 10,000
EACH DIV 1,000
EACH DIV 100
1,000,000 PER REV
100,000 PER REV
10,000 PER REV
1,000 PER REV
Only the four bottom dials need to be read. Do not bother with the other dials; these are for checking purposes only.
Note down the reading shown on each dial, beginning with the one on the left. If the pointer is between the two figures, use the lower one.
(However, if the pointer is between 9 and 0, put down 9.)
The figure shown in the diagram is 7519.
Only these figures need be read. Do not bother with the other figure.
8 7 6 5 7 0
CUBIC FEET
The figure shown in the diagram is 8765.
Both figures represent the VOLUME of gas used, measured in hundreds of cubic feet (ft³).

Fig. 8.4 How to read your gas meter

Gas or an approved CORGI (Confederation for the Registration of Gas Installers) installer carry out the work.

Control equipment

Thermostats

Thermostats maintain specific temperatures within the appliances to which they are fitted by controlling the heat output of a burner. There are two types:

(a) rod type, the action of which depends upon the fact that some metals expand more than others when heated;

(b) mercury vapour or liquid type, the action of which depends upon the fact that a vapour expands when heated.

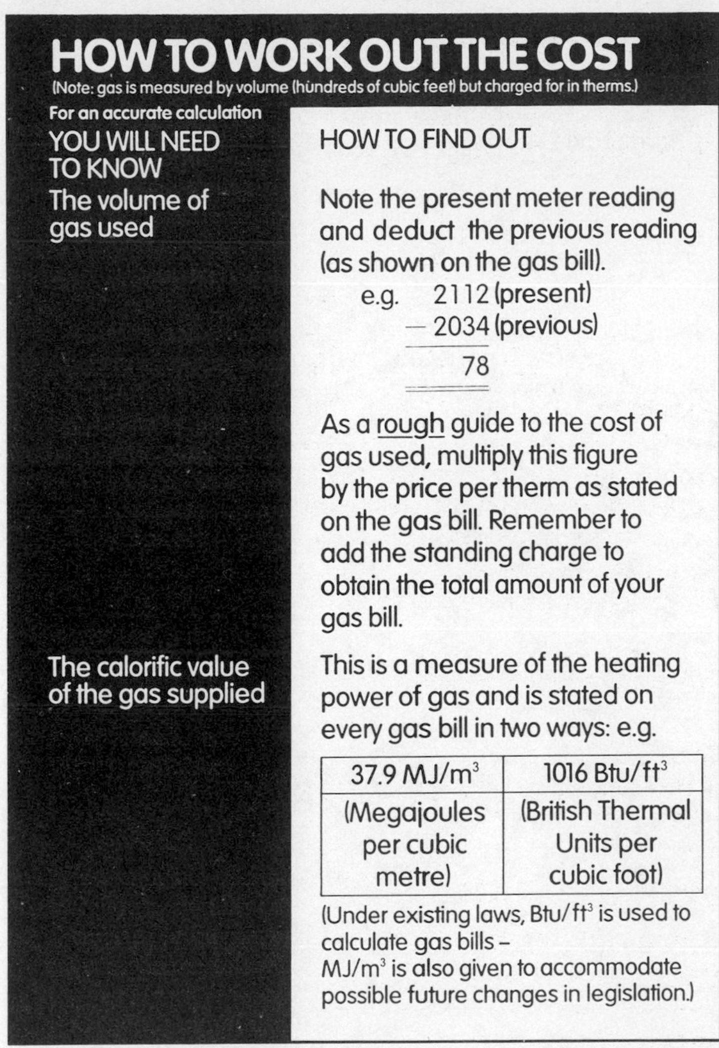

HOW TO WORK OUT THE COST

(Note: gas is measured by volume (hundreds of cubic feet) but charged for in therms.)

For an accurate calculation

YOU WILL NEED TO KNOW	HOW TO FIND OUT
The volume of gas used	Note the present meter reading and deduct the previous reading (as shown on the gas bill). e.g. 2112 (present) − 2034 (previous) 78 As a rough guide to the cost of gas used, multiply this figure by the price per therm as stated on the gas bill. Remember to add the standing charge to obtain the total amount of your gas bill.
The calorific value of the gas supplied	This is a measure of the heating power of gas and is stated on every gas bill in two ways: e.g.

$37.9 MJ/m^3$	$1016 Btu/ft^3$
(Megajoules per cubic metre)	(British Thermal Units per cubic foot)

(Under existing laws, Btu/ft^3 is used to calculate gas bills – MJ/m^3 is also given to accommodate possible future changes in legislation.)

Fig. 8.5 How to work out the cost

Pressure governors

These are fitted to appliances to compensate for any inequalities in the pressure of the gas supply. They are usually set at a pressure that will ensure the best performance from the appliance. By setting the pressure of the gas the maximum gas rate of the appliance is fixed, guesswork is removed and the regulation of the burners and temperature control by the thermostat is made positive and more accurate.

Flame-failure devices

In order to safeguard against a burner failing to light, a device can be fitted so that if the pilot light fails the main gas supply is sealed off until the pilot is relit and the control returned to the open position. The system is suitable for controlling burners where access is difficult and ignition can only be properly effected by means of pilot or electrical ignition.

Flame-failure devices vary from simple bi-metal operation and use of mercury vapour expansion, to thermodynamic or electric controls which include ignition as part of the operation.

Gas catering equipment

Open top range

The open top range (see Fig. 8.6) can be either medium or heavy-duty but is more frequently the former. It can have either four or six rings on the hob. The one in Fig. 8.6 has a directly fired oven which gives a heat gradient, being hotter at the top. This allows different dishes to be cooked at the same time.

Fig. 8.6 Open top range with direct heated oven

Solid top range

Usually heavy-duty rather than medium-duty, this range will have either a directly or semi-externally heated oven. It is frequently the most important piece of equipment in a large conventional kitchen (see Fig. 8.7).

Convection oven

Convection ovens may be externally or semi-externally heated; the one illustrated in Fig. 8.8 is externally heated. They are suitable for all normal roasting and baking. Because of the built-in circulation fan and the even temperature distribution, the full oven capacity may be used and cooking time reduced. This

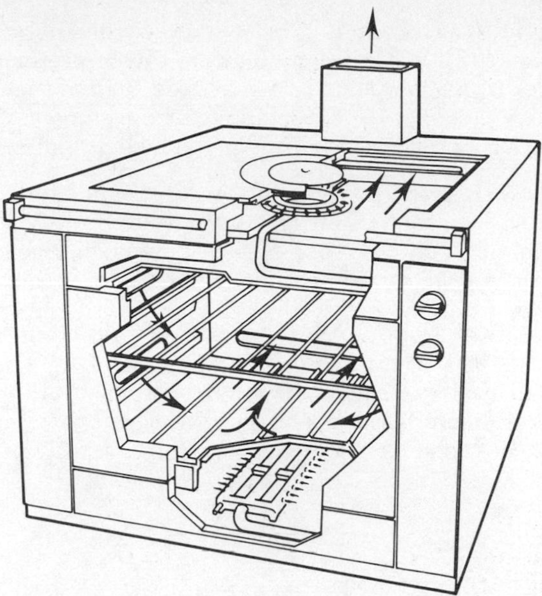

Fig. 8.7 Solid top range with semi-externally heated oven

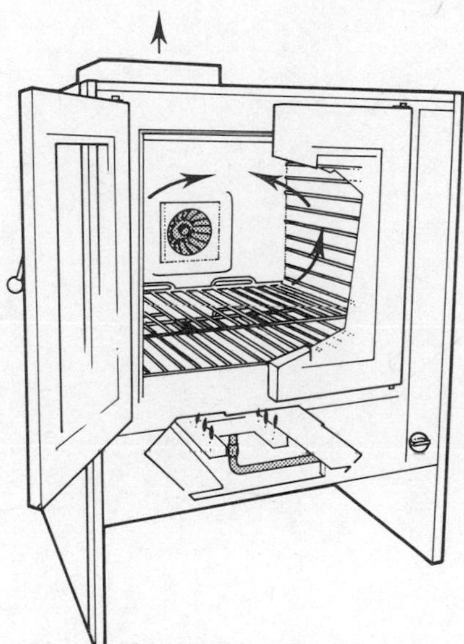

Fig. 8.8 Convection oven

type of oven is extremely suitable for the rapid reheating and end-cooking of frozen foods.

Atmospheric steaming oven
The atmospheric steaming oven is suitable for cooking all root vegetables, sweet and savoury puddings and some fish dishes. See Fig.7.9 on p. 216.

Bratt pan
This is capable of handling up to 200 average portions an hour. The bratt pan is mainly used as a multi-purpose appliance for shallow and deep frying and boiling. See Fig. 7.11 on p. 217.

Deep fat fryer
There are two main types of deep fat fryer: the 'V' pan type where the heating burners are external; and models with immersion tube heaters. In both types there is a zone of relatively cool oil below the source of heat into which food particles can sink without charring. They can be used for cooking all fried foods that are immersed in a heating medium, ie the oil or fat. See Fig. 7.12 on p. 218.

Over-fired grill (salamander)
The source of heat, either from refractory bricks or a metal fret, is above the food. The salamander is used to cook food by radiant heat, eg chops, steak, toast and for the quick heating of dishes before service (see Fig. 8.9.)

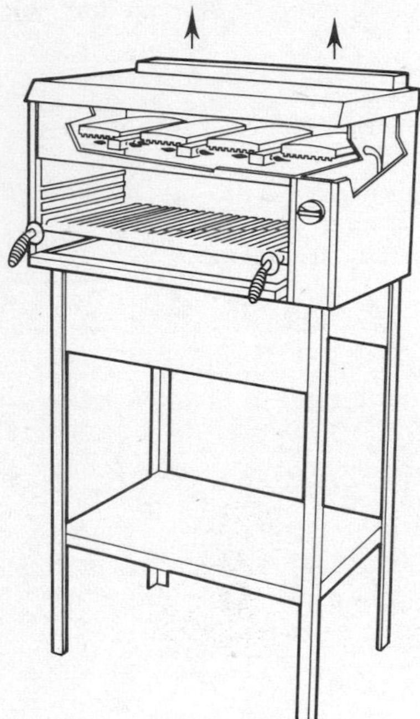

Fig. 8.9 Over-fired grill (salamander)

Expansion water boiler
Operating on the principle that water expands when heated, expansion water boilers can cater for boiling water demands in excess of 170 litres (300 pints) an hour.

Further information
Commercial Gas Centre, 139 Tottenham Court Road, London W1P 9LN, 01–242 0789.

At these premises there is a comprehensive display of gas catering, heating and hot water appliances, at which student visits are welcome.

Calor gas

Calor gas is liquefied petroleum gas, often abbreviated to LPG. The particular gas used by the catering industry is propane, which is as powerful and efficient as mains gas. Calor gas is used by thousands of establishments of varying sizes that are situated beyond the reach of mains gas. It is supplied by being piped into storage tanks or in cylinders, depending on the number of appliances required to be operated.

Leading equipment manufacturers make all types of equipment using Calor gas for cooking, water heating and central heating. The gas is also invaluable in outdoor catering, where it is used extensively.

Charcoal

This is the black porous residue of burnt wood. Traditionally, charcoal was the fuel used most often for grilling and was considered the best because of the flavour it gave to the meat being grilled. The most popular alternative is a gas-fired grill (see Fig. 8.10). From the economic point of view the following considerations have to be borne in mind:

(a) comparative costs of charcoal and gas;
(b) lack of flexibility in use of charcoal;
(c) ease of flexibility in use of gas;
(d) labour requirements for charcoal grill (lighting, refuelling, cleaning);
(e) no labour requirement for gas grill;
(f) comparison of flavour of meats grilled by charcoal and gas;
(g) customer likes and dislikes.

Fig. 8.10 Charcoal flavour grill. Gas heated with refractory stones, fitted with flame-failure device and pilot assembly, produces same taste effect as charcoal and is suitable for all types of gas

Electricity

Having read this part of the chapter these learning objectives, both general and specific, should be achieved.

General objectives Know the part played by electricity in the catering industry and how it is used for cooking, heating and refrigerating. Appreciate the need to handle wires, plugs, appliances etc with care.

Specific objectives Make a comparison between gas and electricity. Read an electricity meter and calculate electricity bills. Explain the terms watt, volt, ampere and ohm. Identify which fuses to use with which applicance. Specify the safety measures necessary when dealing with electricity. Compare the costs of the various fuels available and evaluate them.

Electricity cannot be seen, heard, tasted or smelt; nevertheless, electricity can kill or cause serious injury. It is therefore important that any electrical installation is undertaken by qualified engineers in accordance with the current Institution of Electrical Engineers' Regulations for the Electrical Equipment of Buildings (IEE Regs). All installations should be carried out by registered contractors of the National Inspection Council for Electrical Contracting (NICEIC).

As electricity cannot be stored (except in batteries) it has to be produced as required by the consumers, in a power station. Over 80 per cent of electricity in the UK is produced from coal, about 4 per cent from oil and about 10 per cent from nuclear fuel. The remainder is produced from hydro-electric schemes and other renewable sources. Whether fossil or nuclear fuel is used, the principle of generation is the same. Heat is used to produce steam, which in turn drives the turbines to 'make' electricity. In a hydro-electric power station, water flows down shafts which turn the turbines.

Once electricity is generated it is distributed to the consumers via the National Grid. All electricity supplied to the UK is Alternating Current (AC) and must form a complete circuit from the source of supply, through the load, eg an appliance, and back to the source. Some substances are conductors of electricity and some are insulators. All substances can allow electricity to pass through them but those that allow this to happen most easily are known as conductors, eg metal, water, damp earth and the human body. Those which resist are known as insulators, eg porcelain, wood, rubber.

Electrical terms

Watts measure power, that is, the rate at which any electrical appliance is using electric current for given pressure (voltage).

Volts measure pressure of flow. Comparing electricity to water, 'voltage' corresponds to pounds per square inch of water supply. Before electricity can flow through a wire the electrical pressure at one end of the wire must be greater than at the other end. 240 volts is a common measure in domestic use. Knowledge of the voltage is essential.

Amperes measure the rate of flow of a current, and can be obtained by dividing the watts by the volts.

Ohms measure the resistance of the wires to the passage of electricity. This resistance is comparable with the friction offered by a water pipe to water flowing through it.

'Ohm's Law', on which the science of electricity is founded, can be stated as:

$$\text{Amperes} = \frac{\text{Volts}}{\text{Ohms}} \quad \text{Volts} = \text{Amperes} \times \text{Ohms} \quad \text{Ohms} = \frac{\text{Volts}}{\text{Amperes}}$$

Electrical installation

As stated earlier, all electrical installation work must meet the requirements of the current IEE Regulations and these will be met if members of the NICEIC (National Inspection Council for Electrical Contracting) are used for such work. *Any worn or frayed wiring or damaged plugs or sockets should be replaced as soon as noticed.*

Consumer unit is the term used to describe the fuse box. It may contain fuses, miniature circuit breakers (mcb's), main switches and residual current devices (rcd's). An mcb is an electrical device that switches off a circuit automatically when a certain current is exceeded. Such devices can be reconnected by manual means by activating a switch lever or push button. In modern installations an mcb is used as an alternative to a fuse.

Sometimes known as an elcb or rccb, an rcd detects a faulty current passing to earth and switches off the supply in micro-seconds. These devices are not a replacement for fuses, as mcb's, but they do provide additional protection from death by electricity shock. *Note* There are circumstances where they do not protect, so they should never be considered as a substitute for sound wiring practices and maintenance.

Industrial plugs and sockets

Modern installations frequently use industrial plugs and sockets made to International Standard IEC 309, British Standard BS 4343. They are easily recognised by the colour coding for both the plug and sockets or socket lid (see Fig. 8.11).

Yellow is for 110 v–130 v (not normally seen in a kitchen but common on building sites etc).
Red is 380 v–415 v, usually three-phase supply in the UK.
Blue is 220 v–240 v, the single phase supply.

The sockets when marked 'IP44' are 'splashproof' and when marked 'IP67' are 'watertight' (either with the plug fitted or less plug and the socket lid closed).

There are various sizes from 16 A to 125 A, configured so that a plug will only fit its equivalent socket and no other.

All electric catering equipment should be installed using plug and socket connections. Equipment must not be fixed (hard wired) into a isolator or switch box.

Plug and socket connections allow the equipment to be easily disconnected for cleaning and mechanical servicing, which is especially important in maintaining hygiene standards.

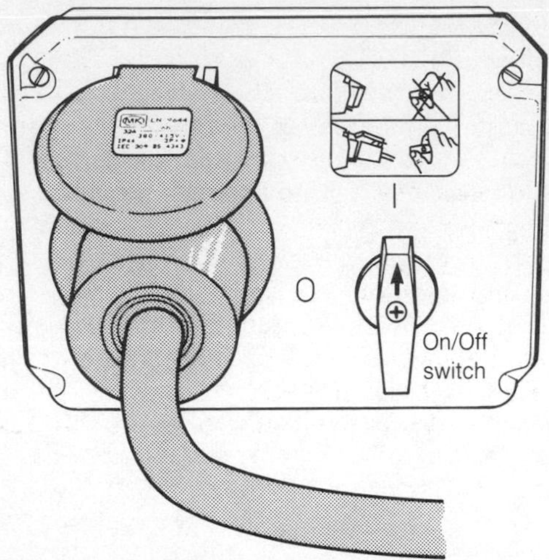

Fig. 8.11 Plug and socket connection

Where light switches are provided and are fitted in a kitchen or storeroom, waterproof types should be selected. This will enable wet washing of walls, ducting etc to be carried out safely.

Fuses

The fuse in an electrical circuit acts as a safety device. Fuse wire is obtainable in varying thicknesses, usually 5, 10, 15 and 30 amperes, and for general purposes should be used as follows:

lighting circuits – maximum of 5 amperes
radial circuits – maximum of 15 or 20 amperes
cookers or ring circuits – 30 amperes

See Fig. 8.12 below.

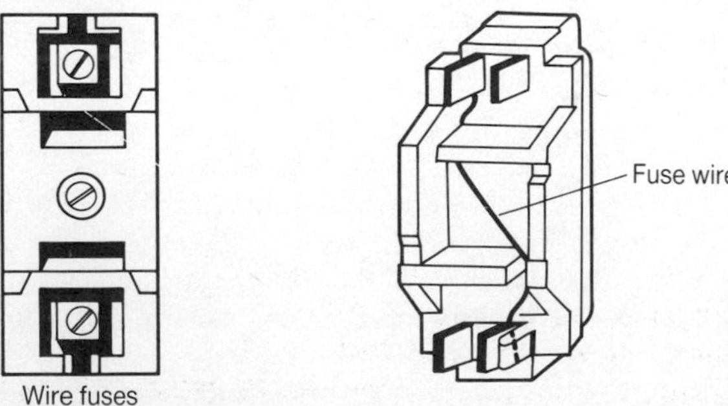

Fig. 8.12 Fuses

Cartridge fuses and miniature circuit breakers

Always fit fuses of the correct rating for the circuit. *Never* use a larger cartridge fuse or a thicker wire in a rewireable fuse, even as a temporary measure. Do not rely on the blown fuse as a guide, it may have been the wrong one in the first place. Instead of fuses you may have miniature circuit breakers. Once the fault has been fixed, you simply press the button or switch on to restore power.

Remember: always *switch off* before changing fuses.

If more than the maximum safe current passes through the circuit the wires will get hot, the insulation may burn, and there may be a fire.

The fuse consists of a short length of wire within the circuit and is of such a thickness that it will melt if more than the maximum safe current flows through it, so breaking the circuit. This is known as a blown fuse.

The fuse should always be connected in the live side of the supply. No fuse should ever be connected in the neutral side.

See Figs. 8.13 and 8.14 below.

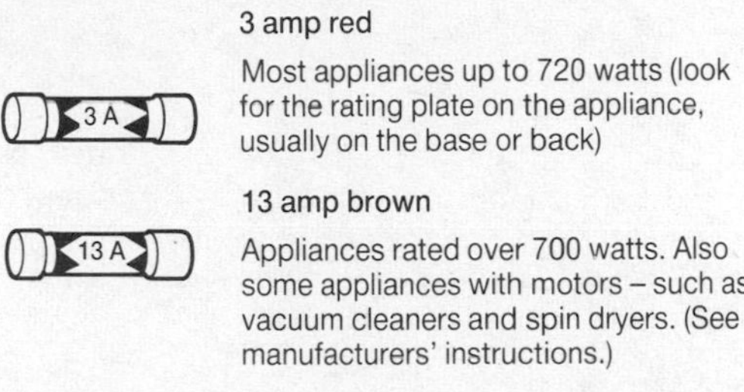

3 A
3 amp red
Most appliances up to 720 watts (look for the rating plate on the appliance, usually on the base or back)
13 A
13 amp brown
Appliances rated over 700 watts. Also some appliances with motors – such as vacuum cleaners and spin dryers. (See manufacturers' instructions.)

Fig. 8.13 Plug fuses (usually two sizes as above)

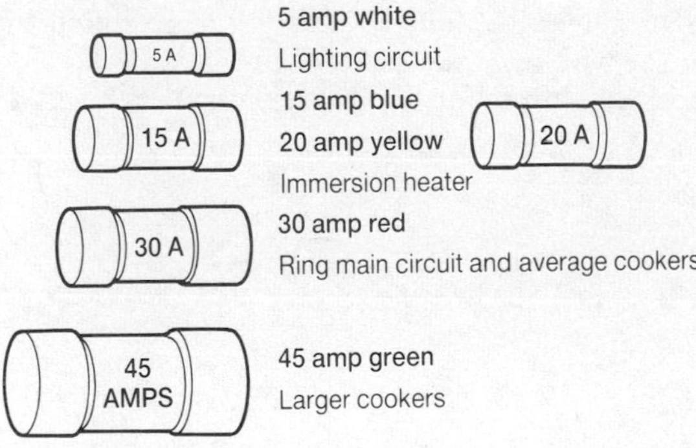

Fig. 8.14 Main fuses

Causes of a blown fuse

(a) too many appliances plugged into a circuit;
(b) plugging a power appliance into a lighting circuit;
(c) short circuit due to insulation failure, ie lead and return wires touch and therefore current does not reach the appliance; often due to wear of wire insulation (see Fig. 8.15 over page).

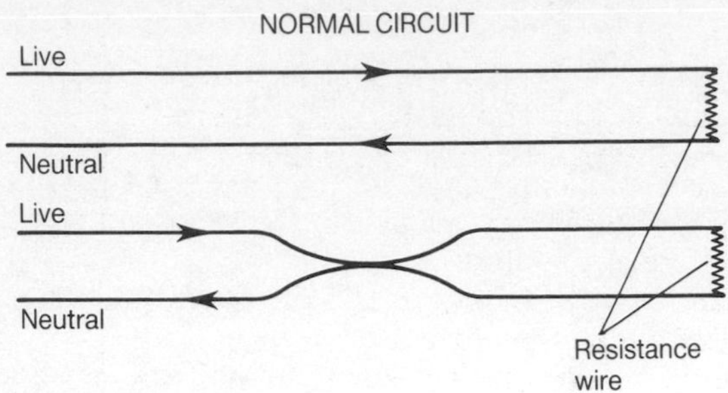

Fig. 8.15 Short circuit

Repair of fuses

1 Turn off the main switch.
2 Find the fuse that has blown – this may be known beforehand; if not, try each one in turn.
3 Remove broken fuse wire.
4 Replace with appropriate cartridge fuse or –
5 Replace with new fuse wire of the correct size (5, 10, 15 or 30 amperes).
6 Before replacing the repaired fuse and before switching on, endeavour to trace fault and repair.

The wiring of plugs

1 Remove the outer sheath for about 3.8 cm–5 cm, thus leaving three coloured wires exposed.
2 If the plug has a bridge, clamp the flex sheath lightly under the cord grip.
3 Measure each wire; cut it off at a length which will allow it to go round the terminal. The last portion of the wire only is cleared of insulation.
4 Wind uncovered wire in clockwise direction around terminal or insert in terminal and tighten screw.
5 Replace the casing of the plug.

See Fig. 8.16 below.

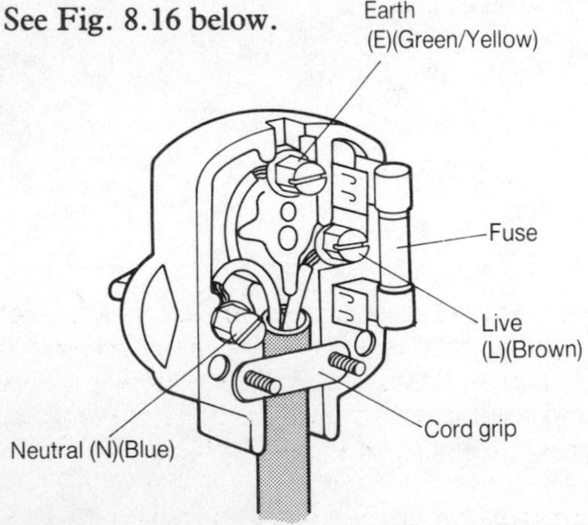

Fig. 8.16 3 pin cartridge fused plug

Reading an electricity meter

The readings are taken from left to right. The numbers are those that the pointer has just passed, or the number which the pointer is at. When the pointer is between 0 and 9, record the 9; between 0 and 1, record the 0.

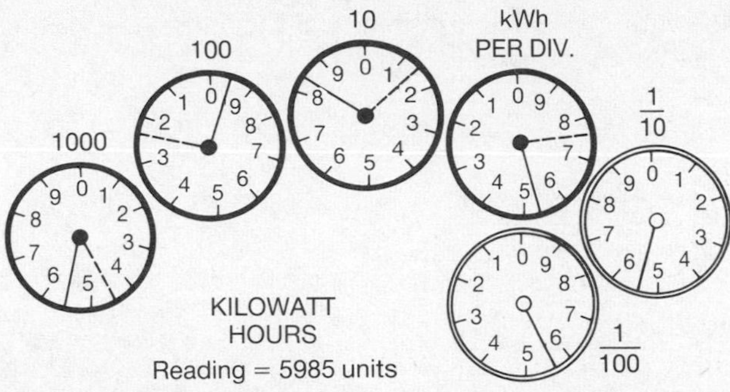

Calculating an electricity bill

To calculate the amount of power used, record the present meter reading and subtract the previous reading. To calculate the cost, multiply the number of units used by the cost per unit.

The dials read as follows:

——— Current reading	5985
- - - - Previous reading	− 4217
Units used	1768
Cost per unit	5.5 pence

Cost of electricity used 1768 × 5.5 pence = 9724.0 pence
= £97.40

Fig. 8.17 How to read your electricity meter

Further information

Electricity Council, 30 Millbank, London SW1P 4RD.

Comparison of fuels

Many factors need to be taken into consideration when comparing different types of fuels. For example, the cheapest fuel to buy may not be the cheapest to burn. When comparing electricity with coal, the initial cost of electricity will be much higher; but when considering coal, one has to think of the storage space required, the cost of labour to move it, the cost of labour to clean the dirt it causes, etc.

A list of advantages and disadvantages of each fuel helps to make comparisons.

Gas cooking

Advantages

1 Convenient, labour saving.
2 Free from smoke and dirt.
3 Easily controlled with immediate full heat and the flames are visible.
4 Special utensils are not required.
5 No fuel storage required.

Disadvantages

1 Some heat is lost into the kitchen.
2 Regular cleaning is necessary for efficiency.

Electric cooking

Advantages

1 Clean to use and maintain.
2 Easily controlled and labour saving.
3 A good working atmosphere for kitchen staff as no oxygen is required to burn electricity.
4 Little heat is lost.
5 No fuel storage is required.

Disadvantages

1 Time is taken to heat up.
2 Initial cost of equipment and maintenance costs.
3 Special utensils are required.

Steam cooking

Advantages

1 Good heat for boiling liquids.
2 Low maintenance costs.

Disadvantages

1 Methods of cooking are limited.
2 High initial cost of installation.

Solid fuel cooking

Advantage

Low maintenance costs.

Disadvantages

1 Cannot meet all cooking requirements.
2 Storage of fuel.
3 Dirt and dust from fuel.

4 Labour costs to move fuel.
5 Difficulty of control of heat.

Oil cooking

Advantages

1 Clean and convenient.
2 Labour saving

Disadvantages

1 Need for large storage tanks.
2 Sources of supply may be affected.

Storage space required by various fuels (metric)

The table below shows the storage space needed by various fuels.

Fuel	*Storage space per tonne*
Oil	11 m^3
Anthracite	13 m^3
Coal	14 m^3
Coke	26 m^3

Note Gas and electricity do not require storage space; this advantage is paid for by higher initial cost.

Comparative fuel costs

Comparative fuel costs can be calculated by using the formulae below, inserting current prices of all four fuels and arriving at the cost of a 'useful therm' in each case.

1 therm = 100 000 British thermal units (Btu's).

A Btu is a measure of heat, the amount of heat required to raise the temperature of 1 lb of water by 1°F.

Coke

If coke cost £x per ton (insert the current price of coke for x)
Divide £. . . by 20 = cost per cwt.
Divide cost per cwt by 112 = cost per lb.
Coke produces 12 000 Btu's per lb.

$$\text{Therefore 1 therm costs } \frac{\text{cost per lb} \times 100\,000}{12\,000} = \ldots \text{p}$$

A useful therm is the amount of heat put to good use. Coke is calculated to be 60 per cent efficient.

$$\text{Therefore a useful therm costs } \frac{\text{cost per therm} \times 100}{60} = \ldots \text{p}$$

Gas

An average cost could be *x*p per therm (substitute current price for *x*).
Gas is calculated to be 80 per cent efficient.

$$\text{Therefore a useful therm costs } \frac{\text{cost per therm} \times 100}{80} = \ldots \text{p}$$

Electricity

1 unit of electricity produces 3412 Btu's.
1 unit of electricity costs *x*p (substitute current price for *x*).
Electricity is calculated to be 100 per cent efficient.

$$\text{Therefore 1 therm costs } \frac{\text{cost per unit} \times 100\,000}{3412} = \ldots \text{p}$$

Oil

If oil costs *x*p per gallon (substitute current price for *x*). (There are approximately 250 gallons to 1 ton.)
1 gallon produces 165 000 Btu's.
Oil is calculated to be 75 per cent efficient.

$$\text{Therefore 1 therm costs } \frac{\text{cost per gallon} \times 100\,000}{165\,000} = \ldots \text{p}$$

$$\text{1 useful therm } \frac{\text{cost per therm} \times 100}{75} = \ldots \text{p}$$

Energy conservation

The Energy Efficiency Office estimates that the total energy consumption of the British catering industry is in excess of 77 770 million megajoules (21 600 million KWh) per year. As a whole, the catering industry accounts for over 1.3 per cent of the total energy used in the United Kingdom.

Overall average energy costs per cooked meal are: 4p in snack bars, over 7p in coffee shops, 18p in steakhouses, 19p in traditional restaurants and almost 36p in hotel restaurants. In non-commercial catering, average energy costs are between 9p and 11p per meal.

With moderate improvements in efficiency, and some rationalisation in the use of equipment, savings in excess of 20 per cent are achievable which, overall, could save the industry over £87.8 million per year; this would also assist the national interest by reducing energy consumption by over 16 000 million mejajoules per year.

Around 40 per cent of energy is expended in preparing, cooking and serving food. The greatest proportion of this energy is used in the cooking equipment and much of it is wasted by excess use and poor utilisation, eg salamanders and all stoves and ovens being turned fully on as soon as chefs appear in the kitchen, regardless of whether they are required immediately or not. This type of practice inevitably causes maximum heat to be expended in a short space of time which requires further energy to be expended for mechanical ventilation.

Saving energy

In the interest of energy conservation be aware of the following:

Cookers, ranges, grills: keep clean and regularly maintained; check thermostats and heating controls regularly; turn off after use.

Hot cabinets and bains-marie: keep clean, especially door runners; check temperature controls; switch off after use. Do not use for reheating food, maintain lower temperature in plate-warming cabinets.

Refrigeration equipment: keep doors closed; check door seals and temperatures; defrost regularly; do not overload but utilise space sensibly. Do not place hot food in refrigerator.

Dishwashers: maintain in good working order; de-scale regularly; check water and rinse temperatures; consider water softening.

Ventilation extracts: maintain regularly; check fan efficiency and suitability. Clean filters, ducting, fan blades, and fan motors regularly to free them from grease and dust.

Energy-saving equipment

Hot cupboards: with a double skin of metal, the space between is filled with an insulating material.

Microwave ovens: require a low degree of energy compared to traditional cooking methods.

High pressure steamers: can be used in place of boiling pans and steaming ovens.

Induction cookers: on average use 49 per cent less energy than a traditional electric hob; à la carte kitchens can save up to 64 per cent. Further savings can be made because ventilation and extraction are only needed a little or not at all.

Steamers: steaming foods is an energy-efficient process and has the added advantage of retaining a larger proportion of nutrients in food than boiling.

Combination ovens: ie forced-air/convection, steaming/convection, microwave/convection can result in savings of energy when used correctly.

Further information

Energy Efficiency Office, Energy Technical Support Group, Building 156 AERE, Harwell, Didcot, Oxon OX11 0RA.

Water

Having read this part of the chapter these learning objectives, both general and specific, should be achieved.

General objective Have an appreciation of the types of water supply available to catering establishments and be aware of the maintenance requirements.

Specific objectives Describe the storage, treatment and distribution of public water supply from storage reservoirs to the consumer. State the legal requirements for cold water supply installations in buildings. Describe the difference between direct and indirect systems of cold water supply. State the advantages and disadvantages of the direct and indirect systems of cold water supply. Indicate situations where point-of-use water treatment is required and describe common methods of treatment. State the methods of providing frost protection for water supply systems.

From collection to consumption

Water authorities are required, by law, to provide a supply of clean, wholesome water, ie water free from: suspended matter, odour and taste; all bacteria which are likely to cause disease; and mineral matter injurious to health.

Water is obtained from the residue of rainfall and is collected from a number of sources, dependent on the geography of the country. The collection points may include natural lakes, rivers, springs, artificial reservoirs, underground lakes and wells. The source may affect the nature and quality of the water. Water is normally collected and held in storage reservoirs in order to provide a constant supply of water and is passed through a number of cleansing processes prior to distribution to the consumer.

Primary filtration

Water collected from open sources such as rivers will be passed through a filter in order to remove large solid matter such as twigs and leaves.

The water is stored in reservoirs where suspended matter settles to the bottom.

Secondary filtration

The water is drawn from the reservoir as required and passed through a sand or micromesh filter to remove any particles still in suspension.

Chlorination

Water is treated with chlorine to kill any bacteria remaining in the water. (In some parts of the country fluoride may be added.)

Testing

The water is regularly tested to ensure that it is fit for consumption.

Distribution and consumption
Water is pumped into the distribution system of trunk and street mains for delivery to the consumer.

The consumer is required to comply with the local water by-laws made by the local water authority under Section 17 of the Water Act 1945 (England and Wales) or Section 70 of the Water (Scotland) Act 1980. These are designed to prevent waste, undue consumption, misuse or contamination of the water supply provided by the water authority.

Any persons contravening any of these by-laws may be liable for fines not exceeding £400 in respect of each offence.

The by-laws state the materials, methods of jointing and the types of installations which may be used, and also state that all new systems or alterations or additions to existing systems must conform.

Consumer's cold water supply

The water authority will provide a supply to the boundary of the premises and at this point a stopcock will be fitted. The consumer is responsible for the supply from the boundary onwards and a stopcock should be fitted just inside the boundary to enable the consumer to turn off the water in an emergency.

Water costs
Commercial premises will normally have a meter and will be charged for the amount of water used.

Domestic premises may have a meter or, more commonly, are charged a water rate related to the general building rate.

Types of systems of supply

On entering the building the water supply should be fitted with a stopcock and a facility for draining down for maintenance. There will normally be other stopcocks throughout the premises enabling water supplies to be cut off at different points.

The local water authority by-laws will indicate the type of system to be used in new and renovated systems.

New and existing systems fall into two categories: direct and indirect.

Direct system of cold water supply
This type of system provides water to all taps and items of equipment at mains pressure (see Fig. 8.18 over the page).

Water for the hot water system may be stored in a cistern.

Indirect system of cold water supply
Most modern systems are of this type, especially in commercial premises. The indirect system uses a cistern for storage of water which means that in the event of failure or heavy usage of the mains supply there is still a supply of water available until the mains supply is restored.

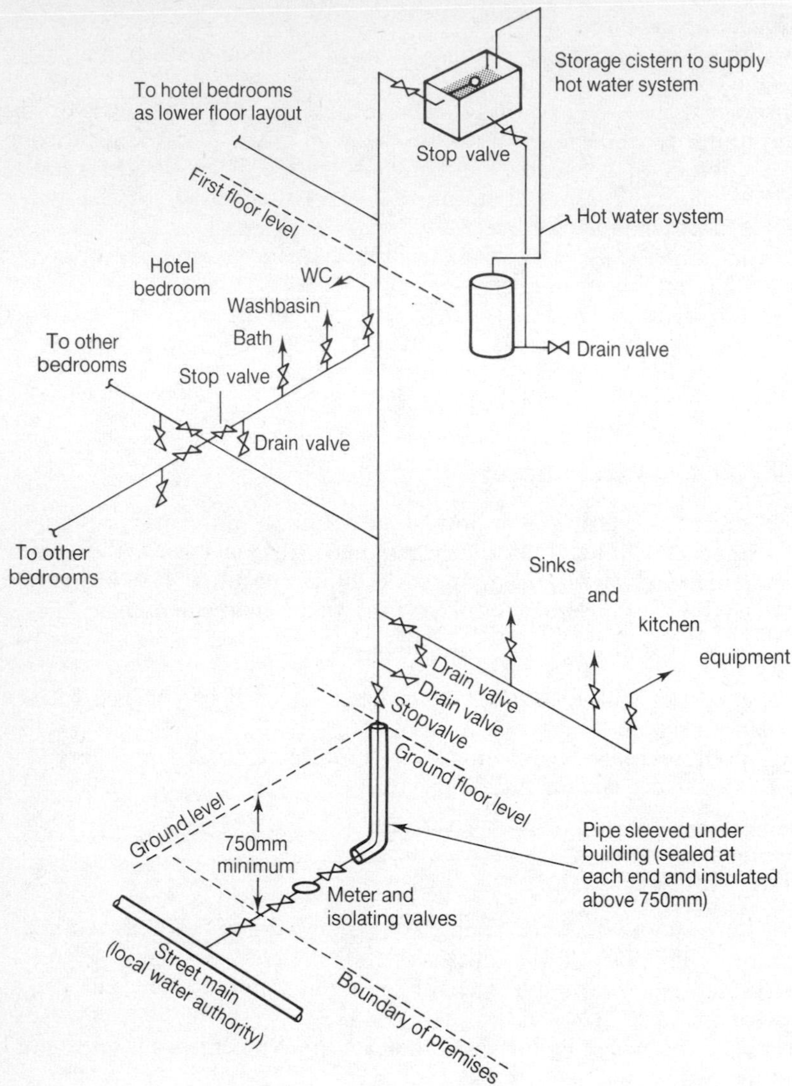

Fig. 8.18 Direct cold water supply to small hotel

Water for the hot and cold water systems will normally be supplied from this storage (see Fig. 8.19 opposite).

The indirect system will always have drinking water, or water used in food preparation, taken directly from the mains supply to ensure that it is uncontaminated. In large buildings, for example multi-storey blocks, the mains pressure may be insufficient to supply all drinking water direct from the main, in this case special drinking water cisterns are installed and the water is circulated after pumping.

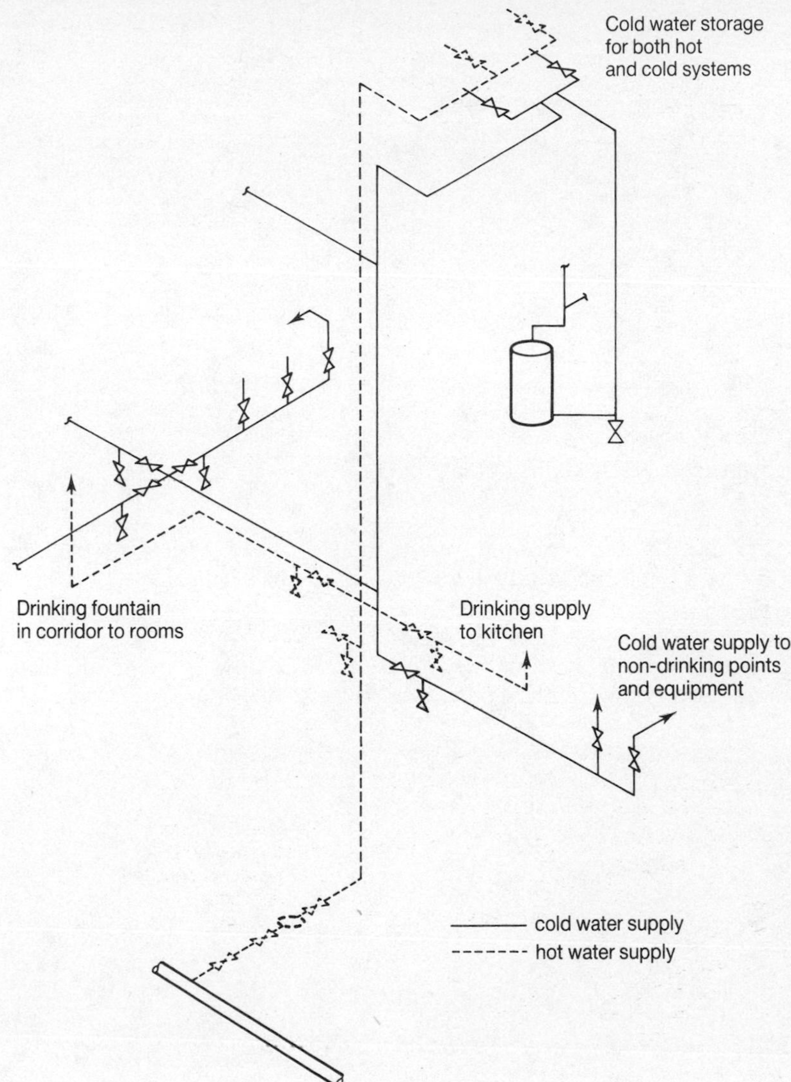

Fig. 8.19 Indirect cold water supply to small hotel

Types of equipment in cold water systems

Stopcock

This is a valve installed in a pipe to control the flow of water to a system or item of equipment (see Fig. 8.20 over the page).

The valve should be turned off and on during routine maintenance to ensure that it will operate in an emergency.

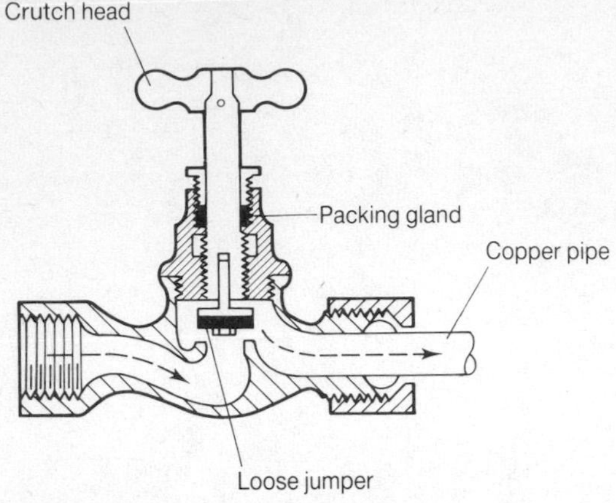

Fig. 8.20 Stop valve (section through a stopcock)

The washer may require replacing during maintenance, as may the packing gland or 'O' ring around the spindle connected to the handwheel.

Gate valve

This is an alternative type of valve used to control the flow of water in a pipe where the pressure is low or the water is at high temperature (see Fig. 8.21 below).

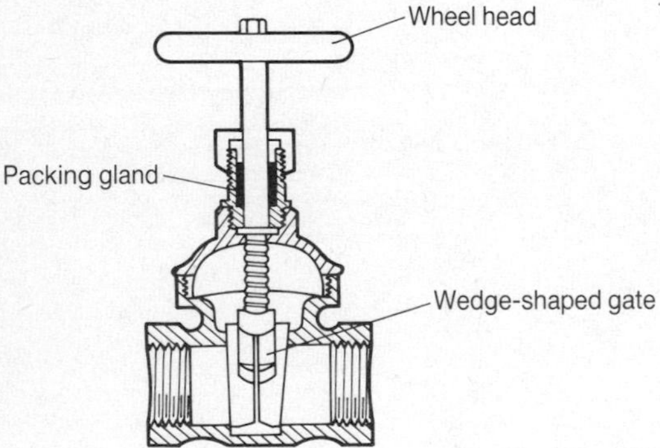

Fig. 8.21 Gate valve (section through)

The valve should be turned off and on during routine maintenance to ensure that it will operate in an emergency. The packing gland may require repacking during maintenance.

Tap or mixer fitting

Tap or mixer fittings are used to draw water from the pipe and may vary greatly in appearance but all use a similar principle of operation. See Figs. 8.22 and 8.23 opposite.

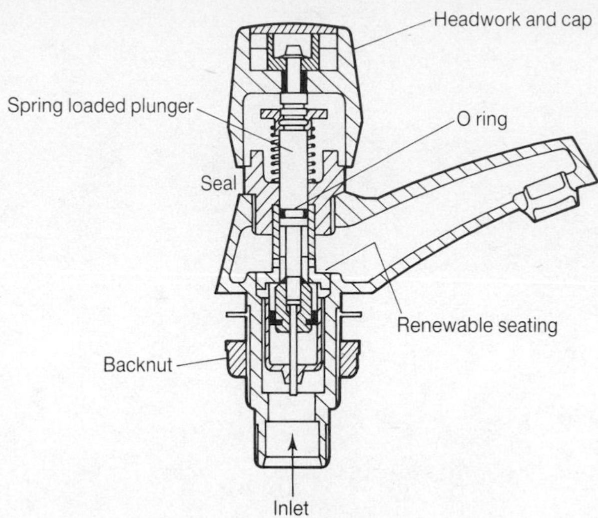

Fig. 8.22 Section through a tap

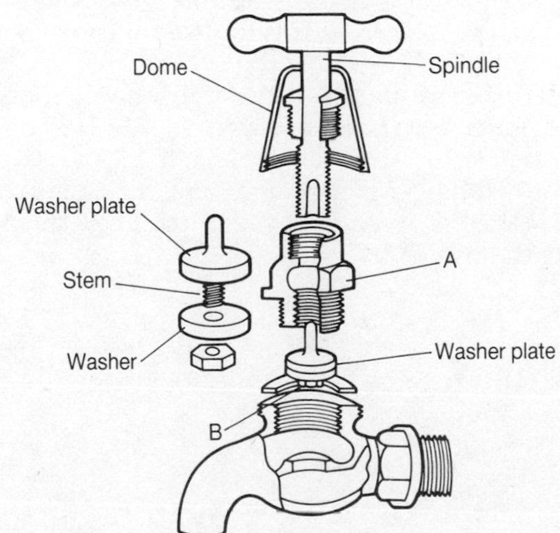

Fig. 8.23 Tap components

The tap or mixer should be regularly maintained for efficient operation. During maintenance the washer may require replacement, or the seating onto which it closes may require regrinding. The packing gland may also require repacking or replacement.

As taps and mixers in catering establishments are in constant use it is essential that adequate planned maintenance is provided.

Ball-valve

Ball-valves are float-operated valves used to control the flow of water into cisterns (see Fig. 8.24 over the page).

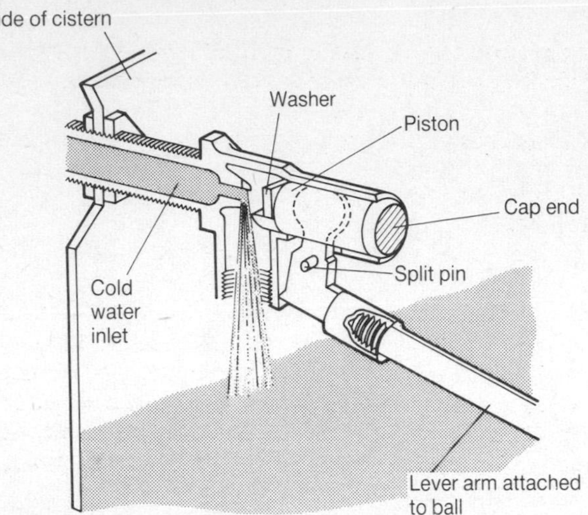

Fig. 8.24 Operation of the ball valve

The latest type of ball-valve is designed to prevent any possible contamination of the water supply in the cistern.

The ball-valve should be adjusted to make it close at the required water level in the cistern and should be fixed securely to the cistern.

The ball-valve should undergo regular maintenance because, like taps, it will be in constant use. The washer or diaphragm may require replacing; the float should be checked for buoyancy and the point at which it closes should correspond with the water level in the cistern.

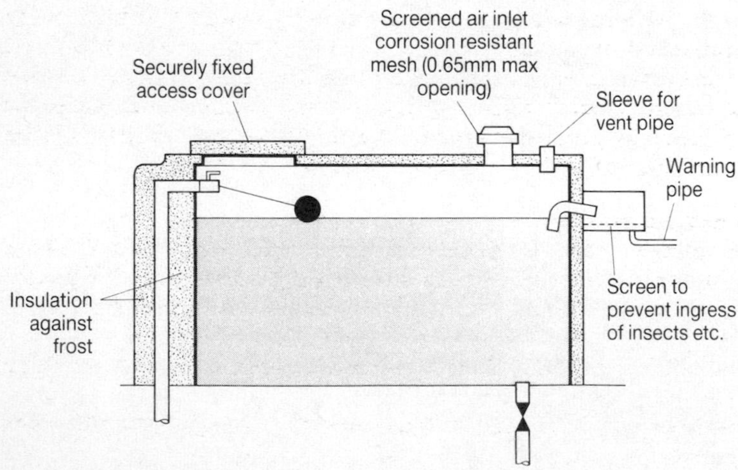

Fig. 8.25 Example of a cistern

Storage cistern
Modern cisterns are made of galvanised steel, plastic or GRP (glass-reinforced plastic) and should comply with the local water by-laws related to construction, material and installation (see Fig. 8.25).

Special provision is made for cisterns which are designed to supply drinking water.

Water fittings: general requirements
Each of the items mentioned above should be of a suitable design, approved by the local water authority.

Generally, compliance with the water by-laws will occur if: (a) all fittings chosen are listed in the *Water fittings and materials directory* and may be marked with a BSI kitemark or UK Water Fittings By-laws Scheme mark; (b) fittings are installed and maintained to operate correctly without risk of contamination or waste of water. Plumbers who are registered with the Institute of Plumbing will be qualified to confirm that an installation complies with the water by-laws.

Comparisons of types of systems of cold water supply

Advantages of direct system
The direct or non-storage system contains less pipework, has no cistern (or only a small one for the hot water system), and is therefore easier and cheaper to install and maintain.

As all the water passes direct to the taps, all taps will have drinking water which has not been subjected to possible risk of contamination during storage.

Disadvantages of direct system
In the event of damage to the mains supply, or during major maintenance, the premises may be completely without water. In many towns and cities the mains supply is subject to fluctuation of pressure at peak times (eg breakfast, lunch, and dinner) due to the demand, and the pressure and efficiency of the supply will be affected.

Catering and other items of equipment may cause contamination of the water supply, both in the building and to the water authority's supply, if incorrectly installed or unprotected by suitable devices. Items of equipment such as food and vegetable processors, bottle-washing and dishwashing machines, some water softeners, water-cooled refrigerators and certain types of drink vending or dispensing machines may cause this type of contamination, and they should be connected in accordance with the local water by-laws.

Advantages of indirect system
The indirect or storage system is provided with a large capacity cistern which will ensure that water is still available if the main supply is interrupted. Because the system is largely supplied from the cistern, the demand on the water main is reduced.

Equipment supplied from the cistern will not contaminate the drinking water supply.

Equipment which requires hot and cold supplies will be supplied with water at the same pressure.

The system will have a lower pressure and will be quieter in operation and this minimises wear on taps.

Disadvantages of indirect system

All stored water should be considered potentially contaminated, even though the cistern should have a tight-fitting lid, because the water will have come into contact with the air.

The system requires a storage cistern and has more and larger pipes than a direct system. This means it will be more expensive to install and may require more maintenance.

Physical characteristics of water

Soft water

Generally, water is soft; a practical test is that it will produce lather easily when soap is dissolved in the water. Soft water is mildly acidic and can dissolve salt, sugar and other substances used in catering processes.

The nature of water may be affected by the ground it has filtered through before collection and treatment by the water authority. Soft water which has passed through ground containing organic material will have had its acidity increased; this will not harm anyone who drinks the water but it may lead to some dissolving of utensils if they contain materials such as lead or copper or lead-based solder. The dissolved material may then contaminate the water to a state of toxicity above safe health levels.

Hard water

Water which has passed through ground containing limestone (chalk) is known as hard water. There are two types of hardness – temporary and permanent – and hard water will normally contain a percentage of both.

Temporary hardness is due to the natural presence of calcium or magnesium bicarbonates dissolved in the water. The hardness can be removed by heating, or boiling the water, but in a kettle or water boiler it can produce fur or scale which will coat the internal surface. Although this scale is harmless it can cause discoloured water and reduce the efficiency of heaters and, in extreme cases, it may cause complete blockages in pipes, resulting in steam generation and the explosion of tea or coffee makers.

Permanent hardness is created by chlorides of calcium and magnesium dissolved in the water and is much more difficult to remove.

Water treatments

In catering establishments a number of on-site processes are used to treat water.

Manual method

For general cleansing the most common types of treatment to soften water are:

(a) Soap added to water: the first amount softens the water and any more added will form a lather. But there are disadvantages: it is uneconomical; and scum forms, making it unsuitable for washing.

(b) Soda: which is cheap and quite effective. The correct amount should be added, eg London water with 16 degrees of hardness requires 28.39 g soda to 45.4 litres of water. When using soda and soap together the soda should be added first and allowed to dissolve so that it softens the water before the addition of soap.

(c) Ammonia solution. This works in the same way as soda.

These methods will remove temporary hardness as well as permanent hardness.

Automatic methods

(a) Water softeners: many establishments use an automatic water softening plant which will remove both temporary and permanent hardness. The size of softener is dependent on the volume of water to be passed through it. Manufacturers will give guidance on the choice of the correct unit.

Drinking water should not be softened as hard water is more 'healthy' and so the drinking supplies should be drawn off the system before being connected to a water softener.

Water softeners use a base exchange method. They remove the hardness by a chemical action but, dependent on the quality of the water, and the size of water softener, the chemical action with the agent slows as it becomes clogged and will need cleaning with a brine solution. This cleaning is carried out automatically in many modern machines but the salt tank must be kept topped up.

Where it is uneconomical or undesirable to soften water, for example when water is fed to a single tea or coffee maker, ion magnetic units may be used. In these situations, in hard water areas, the unit may 'fur' up quickly due to the removal of temporary hardness. The fitting of an ion magnetic unit on the supply to the coffee maker will reduce the amount of descaling required and lengthen the efficient operational life of the machine.

Owing to the small diameter of the water supplies of some tea and coffee making machines, the manufacturers may recommend the fitting of a filter on the supply to the unit. This is done to ensure the quality and, when used in conjunction with the scale reducer, will increase the working life.

(b) Descaling: where hard water has created scale in pipes or catering equipment the efficiency and useful lifetime will be reduced unless descaling is done. Descaling and flushing is carried out using a strong acid which is pumped through the equipment and then thoroughly flushed out. This work should be carried out by a plumber or specialist.

Small amounts of scale can be removed from utensils and kettles by commercial products or by boiling vinegar in the utensil and then boiling with clean water.

Freezing of pipes

All pipes and equipment installed inside or outside a building should be protected against frost and the risk of freezing.

External

Pipes below ground should be installed at a depth below the normal effect of frost, not less than 750 mm below the ground. Where pipes rise above this level then suitable insulation material should be applied.

A modern addition to insulation is the use of trace heating where a strip containing an electric element is spirally wrapped around the pipe and is controlled automatically by a thermostat to prevent the pipe from freezing. (See Fig. 8.26 over the page.)

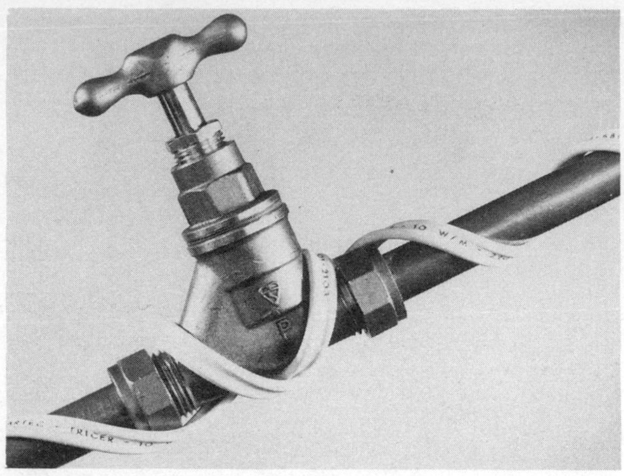

Fig. 8.26 Coping with frozen pipes

Internal

The water pipes should be located to prevent heat loss such as may occur in roof spaces and under ground floors. A suitable insulation material should be applied to pipes and storage cisterns.

Drinking water supplies are also subject to heat gain and condensation in hot places such as kitchens and centrally heated buildings; insulation should be used to prevent this.

Precautions

1 Lag all pipes.
2 Keep temperatures above 0°C.

Methods of thawing pipes

1 Wrap a cloth around the part, and pour hot water over it.
2 A blow lamp should only be used by a plumber or experienced person.
3 A heater placed near the frozen part to raise the temperature of the air.
4 If a waste pipe is frozen, pour hot water down it.

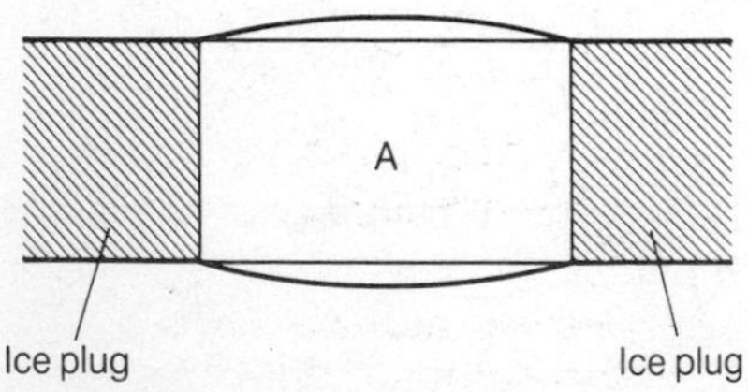

Fig. 8.27 Effect of water freezing in pipe causes bulge 'A'

For burst pipes

1 Turn off the main tap.
2 Turn off the stopcock between cistern and main pipe.
3 Open all taps, allow the water to escape.
4 Send for a plumber.

Drainage of water

Traps

Traps should be provided at each item of sanitaryware or equipment to prevent the penetration of foul smells and air-borne bacteria in the sanitation system into the room in which the equipment is placed.

The trap will contain a quantity of water (seal), which should be contained at all times in sufficient volume to prevent loss whilst the system is in operation or at rest.

The types of traps and depth of seal will vary (see Fig. 8.28), but most

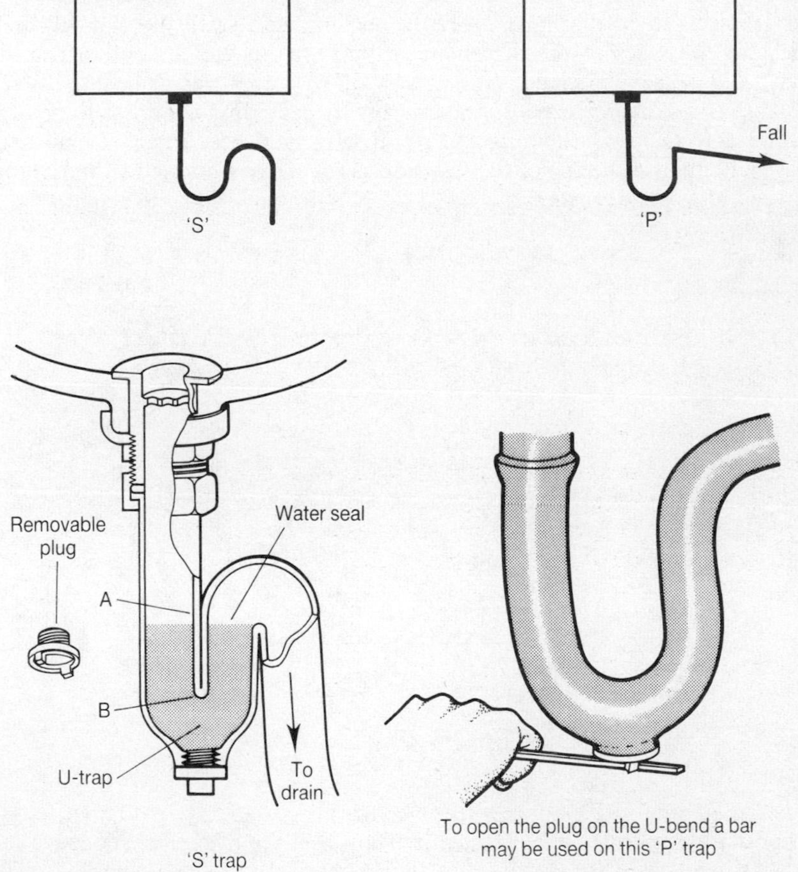

Fig. 8.28 'P' and 'S' traps

modern systems will have a trap seal of 75 mm except in the case of WCs where, because of the volume of water the seal would be more difficult to lose, it measures 50 mm.

Traps are normally fitted to the outlet of a fitting or item of equipment and will be no smaller in diameter than the outlet size of the fitting. The pipe connected should also be no smaller than the outlet size.

Tubular traps are the best design for hotel and catering establishments as they are less liable to blockages and scaling up. Traps made of plastic are smooth and are generally not affected by effluent from these types of establishments.

All traps in hotel and catering establishments should either include a cleaning eye or be of the sectional type which allows for disconnection for cleaning.

Minor blockages will be obviated by regular maintenance and may often be cleared by the use of a rubber plunger or a kinetic gun. (Care must be taken if water contains bleach or similar substances and protective gloves, clothing and eye protection should be worn.)

Grease trap

During the preparation of many foods and the cleaning of cooking utensils, grease and fat of different types may be discharged into the sanitation system. The grease will, in many cases, be in an emulsion state (hot liquid) and will adhere to the sides of pipes, causing a build-up to which solid particles may adhere and cause a blockage.

Grease traps may be used to prevent this by providing a large volume of water within a trap to act as a cooling and solidifying agent (see Fig. 8.29 below). The grease will float to the top of the trap and is regularly skimmed from the top and disposed of as solid waste.

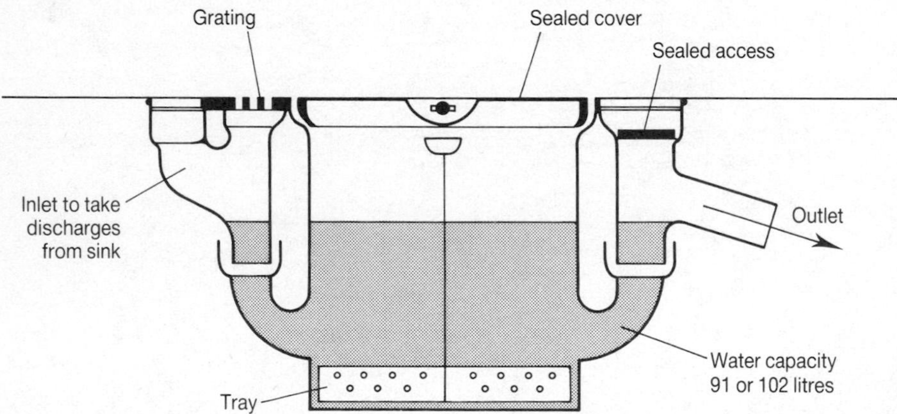

Dimensions: 600mm × 450mm × 135mm and 915mm × 450mm × 135mm

Fig. 8.29 Detail of grease trap

The frequency of cleaning will relate to the size of kitchen and the type of food preparation undertaken. It is important that regular maintenance is carried out as grease traps may easily cause blockages and unhygienic spillage into the food preparation area.

Some local authorities discourage the use of grease traps because they are often poorly maintained.

Inspection chambers

All drainage systems include inspection chambers at junctions of pipes, changes in direction or size, and in long drain runs so that in the event of a blockage no section is more than 45 metres from the access point provided by the inspection chamber. This dimension is used as it would be physically difficult to use drain rods longer than 45 metres to clear a blockage.

Inspection chambers will differ in design according to the material used for the drain pipes but may include brick, cast iron, and plastic. Minimum sizes of inspection chambers are indicated in the building regulations related to the position, type of material and depth.

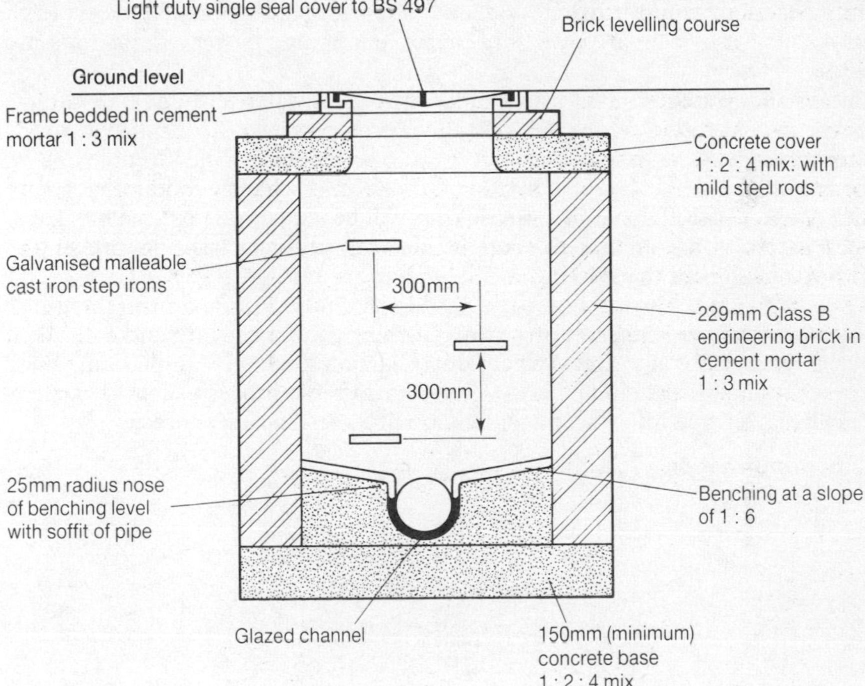

Fig. 8.30 Section through shallow brick inspection chamber

Clearing obstructions

Regular maintenance will assist in the efficient operation of sanitation systems but obstructions may still occur, normally due to misuse.

Preventative maintenance

Preventative maintenance of the sanitation systems in hotel and catering establishments is important in the hygienic and efficient running of the establishment. Many plumbing companies offer maintenance facilities as well as commercial cleaning specialists.

Registered plumbers will have a wide knowledge of the operation of the sanitation system whilst specialist cleaners may only have a limited knowledge of systems although a detailed knowledge of the cleaning process.

Descaling

Waste pipes which may be subject to heavy usage and scaling-up, such as urinal wastes, should be regularly treated with a suitable commercial de-scaling agent.

Drain and waste pipe rodding

This is the traditional method of clearing a blockage and preventing the build-up of solids during maintenance.

On waste pipes a thin, spirally bound wire rod is used, whilst in larger drainpipes modern polyethylene rods, scrapers and augers may be used. Each method may use manual power or, more commonly, power-driven rods are used.

Some specialist equipment uses a mix of rods and water jetting.

Water jetting

Drains which receive large volumes of catering discharge containing grease which has not passed through a grease trap will be subject to possible blockage. Water jetting is a common method of clearing obstructions and preventing build-up of solids in the system.

In each of the above processes protective clothing should be worn and care taken to clear and wash any areas where food is prepared on completion. Food processing should cease in any area where one of these processes has to occur as bacteria may escape into the atmosphere during the clearing process.

Further information

Local water board.

9

Kitchen organisation and supervision

Having read the chapter these learning objectives, both general and specific, should be achieved.

General objectives Know how kitchens operate and understand how they are organised, thus enabling the theories of organisation and supervision to be applied.

Specific objectives Define the personnel structure and the function of individuals in establishments of various sizes. Explain how the system enables the customer to receive the food that is ordered. Specify the aspects of supervision and explain their application in catering.

Kitchen organisation

The purpose of kitchen organisation is to produce the right quantity of food of the highest standard, for the required number of people, on time, by the most effective use of staff, equipment and materials. Regardless of whether the organisation is simple or complex, the factors which have the greatest effect on the organisation will be the menu and the system used to prepare and present the menu items. For example, a very extensive menu can be offered if much of the *mise-en-place* (preparation prior to service) is prepared throughout the day and kept refrigerated until required at service time. If an establishment has a finishing kitchen for the final preparation and presentation by a small number of skilled cooks, then, with adequate *mise-en-place*, fish, meat, vegetables, potatoes, pastas, eggs, etc, cooked by sautéing, grilling, deep frying and so on, can be completed quickly and efficiently to the benefit of the customer. This system, which has been operated very effectively in some establishments for many years, means that all staff are fully used. The design of the finishing kitchen is important here and needs to include refrigerated cabinets for holding perishable foods, adequate cooking facilities and bain-marie space for holding sauces, etc.

Restaurants which provide a limited menu, eg steak houses, are able to organise very few staff to cope with large numbers of customers to quite a high degree of skill. The required standard can be produced because few skills are needed. Nevertheless an employee producing grilled steaks, pancakes or whatever has to be organised in a systematic way and the flow of the work should be smooth.

Other kinds of establishments which are required to produce large amounts of food to be served at the same time include schools, hospitals, industrial establishments, airlines and departmental stores. Staff have to be well organised and supplied with large-scale preparation and production equipment and the means of finishing dishes quickly. To enable this to happen satisfactorily the preparation–production–freezing or chilling–reheat cycle (p. 293) has been developed, enabling staff to be involved in simply reheating or finishing the foods. Obviously very high standards of hygiene must be practised in situations using a system of deep freezing or chilling and reheating.

As costs of space, equipment, fuel, maintenance and labour are continually increasing, considerable time, thought and planning have had to be given to the organisation and layout systems of kitchens. The requirements of the kitchen have to be clearly identified with regard to the type of food that is to be prepared, cooked and served. All areas of space and the different types of equipment available must be fully justified and the organisation of the kitchen personnel must also be planned at the same time.

In the late nineteenth century, when labour was relatively cheap, skilled and plentiful, public demand was for elaborate and extensive menus; and in response to this, Auguste Escoffier, one of the most respected chefs of the past era, devised what is known as the *partie* system. The number of parties required and the number of staff in each will depend on the size of the establishment. Figure 9.1 (below) is an example of a large hotel's traditional kitchen brigade.

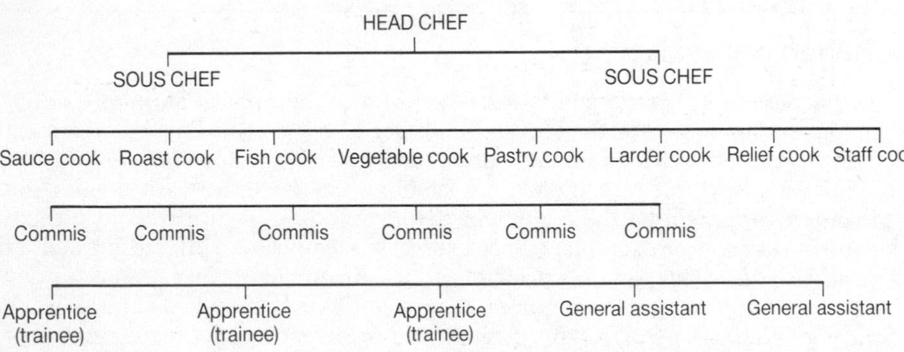

Fig. 9.1 Example of a traditional kitchen brigade in a large hotel

With a sound knowledge of fresh part-prepared and ready prepared foods, together with an understanding of kitchen equipment and planning (see Fig. 9.2 opposite), the organisation of a kitchen can be economically and efficiently implemented. Even with two similar kitchens the internal organisation is liable to vary as each person in charge will have their own way of running the kitchen. However, everyone working in the system should know what he or she has to do, and how and when to do it.

The kitchen organisation will vary mainly due to the size and type of establishment. Obviously where a kitchen has 100 chefs preparing banquets for up to 1000 people, a lunch and dinner service for 300 customers with an *à la carte* menu, and floor service, the organisation will be quite different to a small restaurant serving 30 *table d'hôte* lunches, or a full-view coffee shop, a speciality restaurant with a busy turnover, or a hospital kitchen.

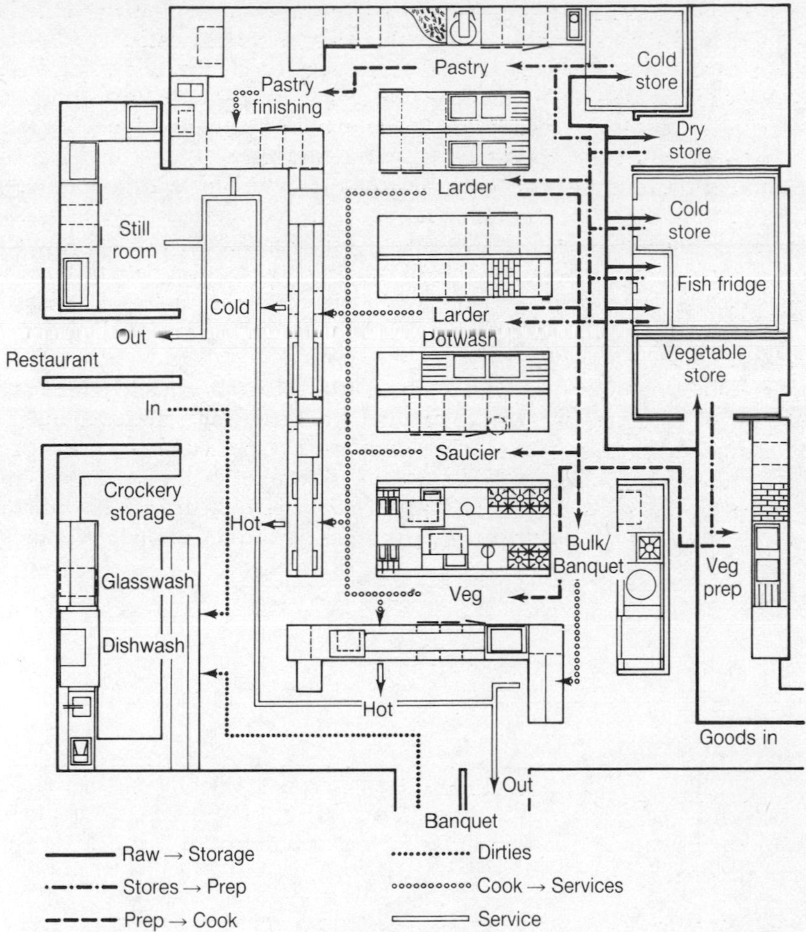

Fig. 9.2 Design for a well-planned kitchen

Role and function of personnel of a traditional kitchen as implemented by Escoffier

In many establishments it is necessary for staff to be working to provide meals throughout the day and in some places during the night. To meet this need staff will work straight shifts or, in some cases, split shifts. The split shift system is operated so that most staff are available for both lunch and dinner. With this system the working hours will be, for example, from 9.30 am to 2.30 pm and 6 pm to 10 pm. Some establishments operate two shifts to cover the lunch and dinner service, with one shift working from 8 am to 4 pm and the other from 4 pm to 11 pm.

Under the two shift system the *partie* will have a *chef de partie* in charge of one shift and a *demi chef de partie* responsible for the other shift.

Fig. 9.3 Working in a well-organised kitchen

Head chef (*le chef de cuisine*)
In large establishments the duties of the Executive Chef, Chef de cuisine, Head Chef or person in charge, are mainly administrative; only in small establishments would it be necessary for the chef to be engaged in handling the food. The function of the chef is to:

organise the kitchen,
compile the menus,
order the foodstuffs,
show the required profit,
engage the staff,
supervise the kitchen (particularly at service time),
advise on purchase of equipment,
be responsible, in many cases, either wholly or partially, for the stores, still room and the washing up of silver, crockery, etc.

Second chef (*le sous-chef*)
The Second Chef relieves the Head Chef when the latter is off duty and is the Chef's 'right hand', whose main function is to supervise the work in the kitchen so that it runs smoothly and according to the chef's wishes. In large kitchens there may be several sous-chefs with specific responsibility for separate services such as banquets, grill room, etc.

Chef de partie
The Chefs de partie are each in charge of a section of the work in the kitchen.

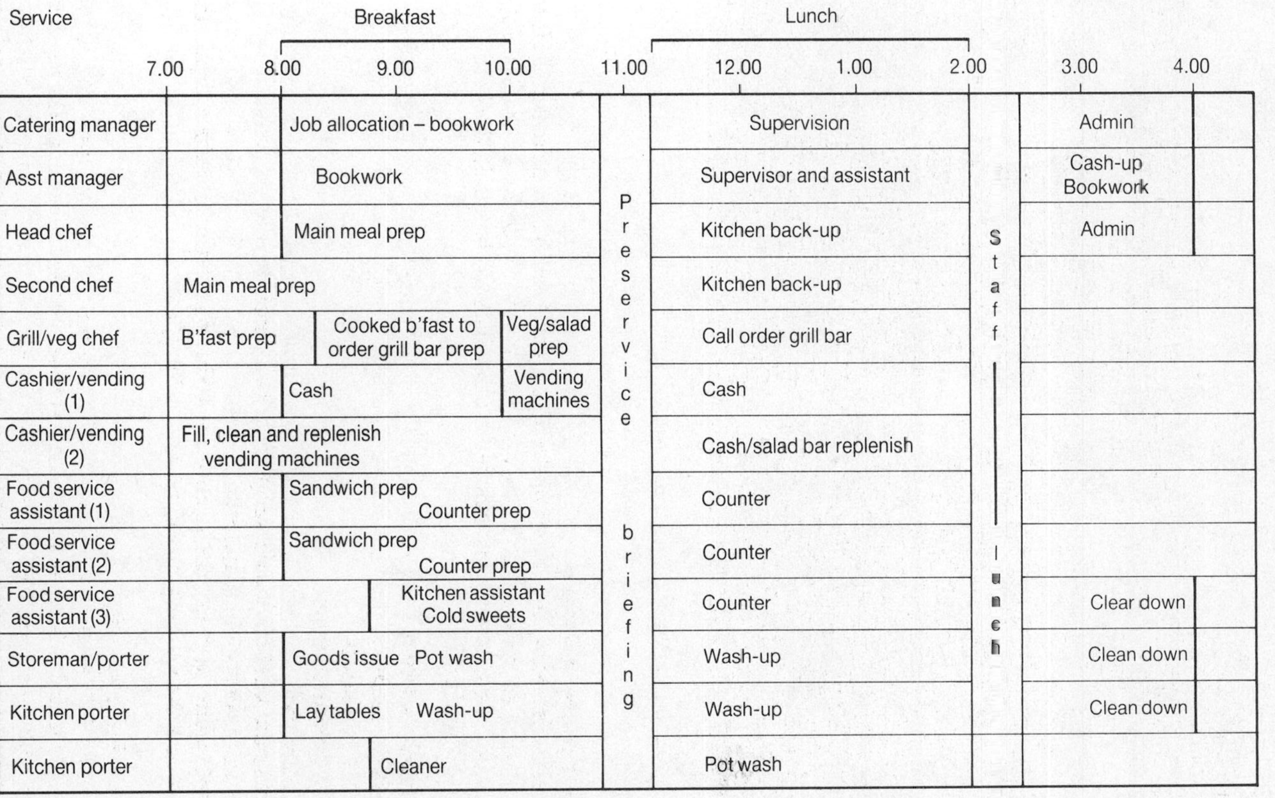

Service	7.00–8.00	8.00–11.00 (Breakfast 8.00–10.00)	11.00	11.00–2.00 (Lunch)	2.00	3.00–4.00
Catering manager		Job allocation – bookwork	Pre-service briefing	Supervision	Staff lunch	Admin
Asst manager		Bookwork		Supervisor and assistant		Cash-up Bookwork
Head chef		Main meal prep		Kitchen back-up		Admin
Second chef	Main meal prep	Main meal prep		Kitchen back-up		
Grill/veg chef	B'fast prep	Cooked b'fast to order grill bar prep; Veg/salad prep		Call order grill bar		
Cashier/vending (1)		Cash; Vending machines		Cash		
Cashier/vending (2)	Fill, clean and replenish vending machines	Fill, clean and replenish vending machines		Cash/salad bar replenish		
Food service assistant (1)		Sandwich prep; Counter prep		Counter		
Food service assistant (2)		Sandwich prep; Counter prep		Counter		
Food service assistant (3)		Kitchen assistant Cold sweets		Counter		Clear down
Storeman/porter		Goods issue; Pot wash		Wash-up		Clean down
Kitchen porter		Lay tables; Wash-up		Wash-up		Clean down
Kitchen porter		Cleaner		Pot wash		

Fig. 9.4 Example of staff hours in an industrial kichen

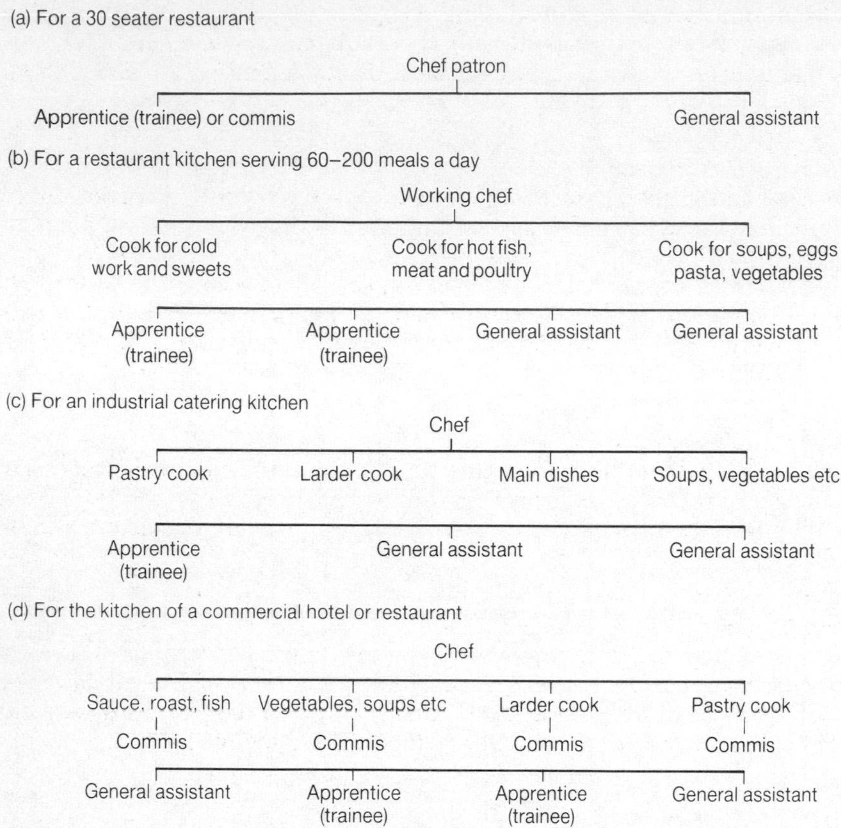

Fig. 9.5 Example of some types of kitchen organisation

This is the job of the specialist. The Chefs de partie organise their own sections, delegate the work to assistants and are, in fact, the 'backbone' of the kitchen.

Assistant cooks (*les commis chefs*)
The Chefs de partie are assisted by commis or assistants, the number varying with the amount of work done by the party; for example, the vegetable party is larger than the fish party, due to the quantity of work to be prepared, so there are more assistants on that party. The first commis is usually capable of taking over a great deal of the responsibility, and in some cases will take charge of the party when the chef is off duty.

Apprentice (*l'apprenti*)
The apprentice is learning the trade and is moved to each of the parties to gain knowledge of all the sections in the kitchen.

The work of the chefs and their parties

Sauce party (*le saucier*)
The sauce cook prepares the entrées, ie all the meat, poultry and game dishes

which are not roasted or grilled. This includes all made-up dishes, such as vol-au-vents, stews, and braised, boiled, poêled and sautéd dishes. The sauce cook will prepare certain garnishes for these dishes and make the meat, poultry and game sauces.

Roast party (*le rôtisseur*)

All roasted and grilled meat, poultry and game are cooked by the roast cooks. All grilled and deep-fried fish and other deep-fried foods, including potatoes, are also cooked by this party, as well as many savouries. The only deep-fried foods which may not be cooked by the roast party are cooked in the pastry. The work of the *rôtisseur* includes the garnishing of the grills and roasts; the roast cook therefore grills the mushrooms and tomatoes and makes the Yorkshire pudding and roast gravy.

Fish party (*le poissonnier*)

Except for grilled and deep-fried fish, all the fish dishes and fish sauces and garnishes are cooked by this party, as well as béchamel, sauce hollandaise and melted butter. The preparation of the fish is usually done by a fishmonger in the larder.

Vegetable party (*l'entremettier*)

All the vegetables and potatoes, other than those which are deep fried, and the egg and farinaceous dishes are the responsibility of the vegetable party as well as the vegetable garnishes to the main dishes. Such things as soups, savoury soufflés and, in some places, pancakes will be cooked by this party.

Soup party (*le potager*)

In large establishments there was a separate party to make the soups and their garnishes. In some brigades, the eggs and farinaceous dishes were the responsibility of this party.

Larder party (*le garde-manger*)

The larder is mainly concerned with the preparation of food which is cooked by the other parties. This includes the preparation of poultry and game and, in smaller establishments, the preparation of meat. The fish is prepared by a fishmonger in the larder by cleaning, filleting and portioning, although most establishments now order ready prepared fillets of fish.

All the cold soup, egg, fish, meat, poultry and game dishes are decorated and served by this party. Cold sauces, sandwiches and certain work for cocktail parties, such as canapés and the filling to bouchées, are done here.

The hors-d'œuvre and salads are made up by the *hors-d'œuvrier* in his or her own place, which is near to the larder.

The oysters, cheeses and dessert fruits may also be served from the larder.

Butcher (*le boucher*)

Usually the butcher worked under the direct control of the chef or sous-chef and dissected the carcasses and prepared all the joints and cuts ready for cooking. Many establishments now order meat pre-jointed or pre-cut.

Pastry party (*le pâtissier*)
All the sweets and pastries are made by the pastry cooks, as well as items required by other parties, such as vol-au-vents, bouchées, noodles, etc and also the covering for meat and poultry dishes.

Ice cream and petits fours are made here. Formerly, a *glacier* was employed to make all the ice creams, but most ice cream is now produced in factories.

The bakery goods, such as croissants, brioche etc, may be made by the pastry cook when there is no separate bakery.

Baker (*le boulanger*)
The baker would make all the bread, rolls, croissants, etc, but few hotels today employ their own bakers.

Relief cook (*le chef tournant*)
The *chef tournant* usually relieves the chefs of the sauce, roast, fish, and vegetable parties on their day off. The first commis in the larder and pastry usually relieves his own chef. In some places a commis tournant will also be employed.

Duty cook (*le chef de garde*)
The duty cook was employed where split duty was involved. This chef was on guard to do any orders in the kitchen during that time when most of the staff were off duty and also for the late period when the other staff had gone home. Split duty hours involved a break from approximately 2.30 pm to 5.30 pm. Usually a commis would be on guard in the larder and pastry.

Night cook (*le chef de nuit*)
A night cook was employed to be on duty part of the night and all night if necessary to provide late meals.

Breakfast cook (*le chef de petit déjeuner*)
The breakfast cook will prepare all the breakfasts and in smaller establishments will often do additional duties, sometimes working until after lunch.

Staff cook (*le communard*)
The staff cook provides the meals for the employees who use the staff room; these are the wage-earning staff and include uniformed and maintenance staff, room maids, etc. This applies in large hotels.

Grill cook (*le grillardin*) and carver (*le trancheur*)
In places where there is a call for a large number of grills and roast joints a grill cook and a carver will be employed, in many cases operating in front of the customers in the dining room or grill room.

Kitchen clerk and barker (*le contrôler/l'aboyeur*)
These two duties are usually performed by one person.

The kitchen clerk is responsible for much of the chef's routine clerical work and is, in fact, secretary to the chef.

During service time the clerk will often call out the orders from the hot plate.

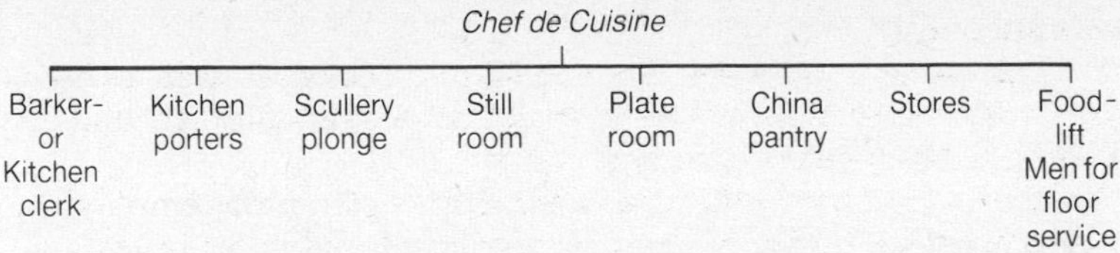

Fig. 9.6 Subsidiary departments under the control of the chef

Aboyeur means barker, caller or announcer. Today, in some establishments, computers would be used for ordering dishes.

Kitchen porters (*les garçons de cuisine*)

Kitchen porters are responsible for general cleaning duties.

Larger parties such as the pastry, larder and vegetable parties may have one or more porters to assist the chefs. They may prepare breadcrumbs, chop parsley, peel vegetables and carry food from one section to another.

When several porters are employed one is usually appointed head porter and he may be responsible for extra duties, eg changing laundry, etc.

Scullery (*le plongeur de batterie*)

The sculleryman or 'plongeur' is responsible for collecting and washing all the pots and pans and then returning them to the appropriate place in the kitchen.

In many establishments the work of the kitchen porter and the sculleryman is combined.

Stillroom (*le garçon/la fille d'office*)

The stillroom is used for the preparation and service of all the beverages, eg tea, coffee, chocolate, etc, as well as the bread and butter, rolls and toast. Simple afternoon teas are also served from the stillroom.

Plate room/silver (*l'argentier*)

All silver dishes and cutlery are cleaned and polished in the plate room. The kitchen is supplied from here with clean silver ready for service.

China pantry (*le vaisselier*)

Here the used crockery and glass are returned, washed and stored ready for service.

Food-lift men (*le room service*)

Where food is served to customers in their rooms, lift men are employed to send it to the floors by a food lift.

Stores (*l'economat*)

The storekeeper is in charge of the stores and is responsible for checking all inward delivery of goods. In some places the storekeeper will not be responsible for checking perishable foodstuffs; these will go direct to the kitchen and be checked by the chef or sous-chef.

The storekeeper will be responsible for the issuing of food to the separate parties.

More details of the stores and the duties of the storekeepers will be found in Chapter 6, p. 195.

Kitchen supervision

Introduction

The organisation within different industries varies according to their specific requirements and the names given to people doing similar jobs may also vary. Some firms will require operatives, technicians, technologists; others need craftsmen, supervisors, managers. The supervisory function of the charge hand, foreman, chef de partie or supervisor may be similar.

The catering industry is made up of: (a) people with craft skills, the craftsmen who are involved with production; (b) the supervisors, such as chefs de partie; (c) those who use managerial skills and determine policy. It is those who have a supervisory function that we are concerned with here.

A useful definition of good supervision is that it is the effective deployment of money, material and manpower.

Supervisory function

Certain leadership qualities are needed to enable the supervisor to carry out his or her role effectively. These qualities include the ability to:

communicate	mediate
co-ordinate	inspire
motivate	make decisions
initiate	organise

Those under supervision should expect from the supervisor:

consideration	understanding
respect	consistency

and in return the supervisor can expect:

loyalty
respect
co-operation

The good supervisor is able to obtain the best from those for whom he or she has responsibility and can also completely satisfy the management of the establishment that a good job is being done.

The job of the supervisor is essentially to be an overseer. In the catering industry the name given to the supervisor may vary, for example, sous-chef, chef de partie, kitchen supervisor or corner chef. In hospital catering the name would be sous-chef, chef de partie or kitchen supervisor. The kitchen supervisor will be responsible to the catering manager, while in hotels and restaurants the chef de partie will be responsible to the chef de cuisine. The exact details of the job will vary according to the different areas of the industry and the size of the various units, but generally the supervisory role involves three functions:

(a) technical
(b) administrative
(c) social

We will consider each of these in turn.

Technical function

Culinary skills and the ability to use kitchen equipment are essential for the kitchen supervisor. Most kitchen supervisors will have worked their way up through the section or sections before reaching supervisory responsibility. The supervisor needs to be able 'to do' as well as knowing 'what to do' and 'how to do it'. It is also necessary to be able to do it well and to be able to impart some of these skills to others.

Administrative function

The supervisor or chef de partie will, in many kitchens, be involved with the menu planning, sometimes with complete responsibility for the whole menu but more usually for part of the menu, as happens with the larder chef and pastry chef. This includes the ordering of foodstuffs (which is an important aspect of the supervisor's job in a catering establishment) and, of course, accounting for and recording materials used. The administrative function includes the allocation of duties and, in all instances, basic work-study knowledge is needed to

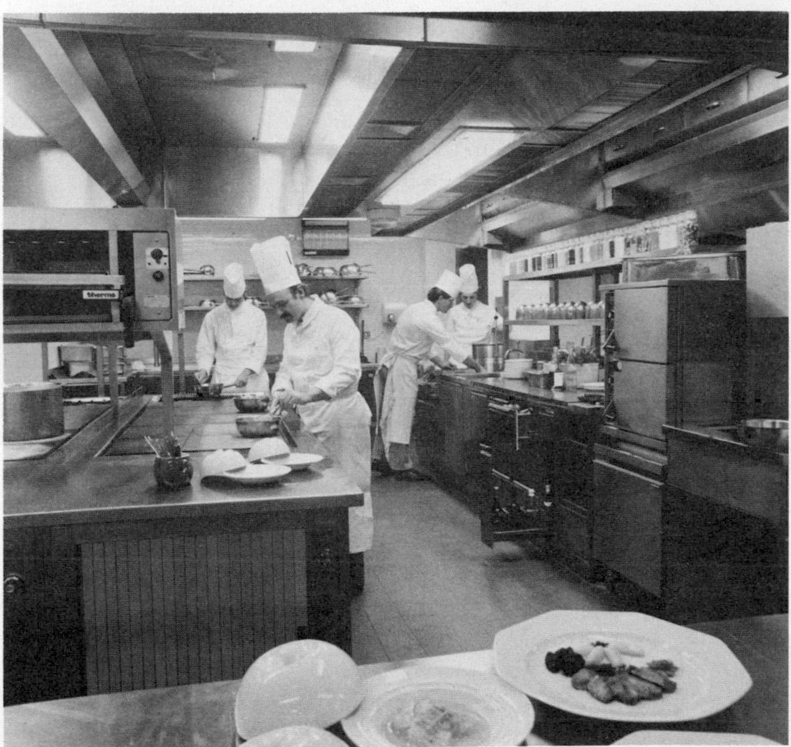

Fig. 9.7 A well-planned kitchen

enable the supervisor to operate effectively. The supervisor's job may also include the writing of reports, particularly in situations where it is necessary to make comparisons and when new developments are being tried.

Social function

The role of the supervisor is perhaps most clearly seen in staff relationships because the supervisor has to motivate the staff under his or her responsibility. 'To motivate' could be described as the initiation of movement and action; and having got the staff moving the supervisor needs to exert control. Then in order to achieve the required result the staff need to be organised.

Thus the supervisor has a threefold function regarding the handling of staff, namely: to organise, to motivate, to control; this is the essence of staff supervision.

Elements of supervision

The accepted areas of supervision include:

forecasting and planning
organising
commanding
co-ordinating
controlling

Each of these will be considered within the sphere of catering.

Forecasting

Before making plans it is necessary to look ahead, to foresee possible and probable outcomes and to allow for them. For example: the chef de partie knows that the following day is his assistant's day off, he looks ahead and plans accordingly; when the catering supervisor in the hospital knows that there is a 'flu epidemic and two of his cooks are feeling below par he plans for their possible absence; if there is a spell of fine hot weather and the cook in charge of the larder foresees a continued demand for cold foods, or when an end to the hot spell is anticipated, then the plans are modified. For the supervisor forecasting is the good use of judgement acquired from previous knowledge and experience. For example: because many people are on holiday in August fewer meals will be needed in the office restaurant; no students are in residence at the college hostel, but a conference is being held and 60 meals are required. The Motor Show, bank holidays, the effects of a rail strike or a wet day, as well as less predictable situations, such as the number of customers anticipated on the opening day of a new restaurant: all need to be anticipated and planned for.

Planning

From the forecasting comes the planning: how many meals to prepare; how much to have in stock (should the forecast not have been completely accurate); how many staff will be needed; which staff and when. Are the staff capable of what is required of them? If not, the supervisor needs to plan some training. This, of course, is particularly important if new equipment is installed. Imagine an expensive item, such as a new type of oven, ruined on the day it is installed because the staff have not been instructed in its proper use; or, more likely, equipment lying idle because the supervisor may not like it, may consider it is sited wrongly, does not train staff to use it, or for some similar reason.

As can be seen from these examples it is necessary for forecasting to precede planning, and from planning we now move to organising.

Organising

In the catering industry organisational skills are applied to food, to equipment and to staff. Organising in this context consists of ensuring that *what* is wanted is *where* it is wanted, *when* it is wanted, in the right amount and at the right time.

Such organisation involves the supervisor in the production of duty rotas, maybe training programmes and also cleaning schedules. Consider the supervisor's part in organising an outdoor function where a wedding reception is to be held in a church hall: 250 guests require a hot meal to be served at 2 pm and in the evening a dance will be held for the guests, during which a buffet will be provided at 9 pm. The supervisor would need to organise the staff to be available when required, to have their own meals and maybe to see that they have got their transport home. Calor gas stoves may be needed, and the supervisor would have to arrange for the stoves to be serviced and for the equipment used to be cleaned after the function. The food would need to be ordered so that it arrived in time to be prepared. If decorated hams were to be used on the buffet then they would need to be ordered in time so that they could be prepared, cooked and decorated over the required period of time. If the staff have never carved hams before, instruction would need to be given; this entails organising training. Needless to say, the correct quantities of food, equipment and cleaning materials would also have to be at the right place when wanted; and if all the details of the situation were not organised properly problems could occur.

Commanding

The supervisor has to give instructions to staff on *how*, *what*, *when* and *where*; this means that orders have to be given and a certain degree of order and discipline maintained. The successful supervisor is able to do this effectively, having made certain decisions and, usually, having established the basic priorities. Explanations of *why* a food is prepared in a certain manner, *why* this amount of time is needed to dress up food, say for a buffet, *why* this decision is taken and not that decision, and *how* these explanations and orders are given, determine the effectiveness of the supervisor.

Co-ordinating

Co-ordinating is the skill required to get staff to co-operate and work together. To achieve this, the supervisor has to be interested in the staff, to deal with their queries, to listen to their problems and to be helpful. Particular attention should be paid to new staff, easing them into the work situation so that they quickly become part of the team or *partie*. The other area of co-ordination for which the supervisor has particular responsibility is in maintaining good relations with other departments. However, the important persons to consider will always be the customers, the patients, the school children etc, who are to receive the service, and good service is dependent on co-operation between waiters and

Fig. 9.8 The Ganymede system

cooks, nurses and catering staff, stores staff, caretakers, teachers, suppliers and so on. The supervisor has a crucial role to play here.

Controlling

This includes the controlling of people and products, preventing pilfering as well as improving performance; checking that staff arrive on time, do not leave before time and do not misuse time in between; checking that the product, in this case the food, is of the right standard, that is to say, the correct quantity and quality; checking to prevent waste, and also to ensure that staff operate the portion control system correctly.

This aspect of the supervisor's function involves inspecting and requires tact; controlling may include the inspecting of the swill-bin to observe the amount of waste, checking the disappearance of a quantity of food, supervising the cooking of the meat so that shrinkage is minimised and reprimanding an unpunctual member of the team.

The standards of any catering establishment are dependent on the supervisor doing his job efficiently, and standards are set and maintained by effective control, which is the function of the supervisor.

Responsibilities of the supervisor

Delegation

It is recognised that delegation is the root of successful supervision; in other words, by giving a certain amount of responsibility to others the supervisor can be more effective.

The supervisor needs to be able to judge the person capable of responsibility before any delegation can take place. But then, having recognised the abilities of an employee, the supervisor who wants to develop the potential of those under his or her control must allow the person entrusted with the job to get on with it.

Motivation

Since not everyone is capable of, or wants, responsibility, the supervisor still needs to motivate those less ambitious. Most people are prepared to work so as to improve their standard of living, but there is also another very important motivating factor: most people desire to get *satisfaction* from the work they do. The supervisor must be aware of why people work and how different people achieve job satisfaction and then be able to act upon this knowledge.

Welfare

People always work best in good working conditions and these include freedom from fear: fear of becoming unemployed, fear of failure at work, fear of discrimination. Job security and incentives, such as opportunities for promotion, bonuses, profit sharing and time for further study etc, encourage a good attitude to work; but as well as these tangible factors people need to feel wanted and to feel that what they do is important. The supervisor is in an excellent position to ensure that this happens. Personal worries affect individuals' performance and can have a very strong influence on how well or how badly they work. The physical environment will naturally cause problems if, for example, the atmosphere is humid, the working situation ill-lit, too hot or too noisy, and there is constant rush and tear, and frequent major problems to be overcome. In these circumstances staff are more liable to be quick-tempered, angry and aggressive, and the supervisor needs to consider how these factors might be dealt with.

Understanding

The supervisor needs to try to understand both men and women (and to deal with both sexes fairly), to anticipate problems and build up a team spirit so as to overcome the problems. This entails always being fair when dealing with staff and giving them encouragement. It also means that work needs to be allocated according to each individual's ability; everyone should be kept fully occupied and the working environment must be conducive to producing their best work.

Communication

Finally, and most important of all, the supervisor must be able to communicate effectively. To convey orders, instructions, information and manual skills requires the supervisor to possess the right attitude to those with whom he or she needs to communicate. The ability to convey orders and instructions in a manner which is acceptable to the one receiving the orders is dependent not only on the words but on the emphasis given to the words, the tone of voice, the time selected to give them and on who is present when they are given. This is a skill which supervisors need to develop. Instructions and orders can be given with authority *without* being authoritative.

Thus the supervisor needs technical knowledge and the ability to direct staff and to carry responsibility so as to achieve the specified targets and standards required by the organisation; this he or she is able to do by organising,

Fig. 9.9 Job satisfaction

co-ordinating, controlling and planning but, most of all, through effective communication.

Further information

Julia Reay, *The Supervisor's Handbook* (Northwood Publications, 1981).

10

Food production systems

General objectives Understand the difference between traditional and centralised production systems. Comprehend how and when production systems can be effectively implemented.

Specific objectives Identify the different types of production systems available to the caterer. List a set of procedures common to the various operations.

Food production systems, such as cook-chill, cook-freeze and sous-vide, have been introduced into certain areas of catering in order to increase efficiency and productivity; changes have been made to maximise utilisation of equipment and to maintain high levels of output and viability.

The problems of the catering industry are as follows:

1 Staff
   - unattractive work conditions
   - limited skilled staff
   - mobility of labour
2 Food
   - high cost
   - wastage
3 Equipment
   - high cost of replacement and maintenance
   - under-usage
4 Energy
   - high-cost traditional systems are wasteful
   - availability
5 Overheads
   - wage increases
   - payments to National Insurance
6 Space
   - most kitchens and services are too large in relation to output
   - space is very costly

The solution to these problems comes in the form of centralisation of production, using the skilled staff available to prepare and cook in bulk and then to distribute to finishing kitchens, which are smaller in size, employing semi-skilled and unskilled labour.

Cook-freeze and cook-chill systems have been developed to meet these requirements, each system having advantages over the other depending on the size and nature of the overall operation. For example, cook-freeze is not adaptable to very small units or to haute cuisine. Cook-chill can be adapted to any type of unit but cannot take advantage of seasonal, cheaper commodities.

Sous-vide, which is a method of working under vacuum-sealing, ice-water bath chilling and chilled storage, has also been developed as a production system.

Many catering operations face problems because of the growing shortage of skilled catering staff and the ever-increasing turnover of employees. Therefore:

(a) It is essential that skilled staff are more fully utilised and given improved working conditions.
(b) Certain catering tasks require de-skilling so as to be carried out by a greater proportion of unskilled staff.
(c) Better benefits and conditions of employment must be provided for fewer key staff in order to reduce levels of staff turnover and enhance job satisfaction.

Standards of hygiene

To ensure safe hygienic standards in any system the following points are crucial:

Refrigeration

Efficient refrigeration and temperature control are essential otherwise there is

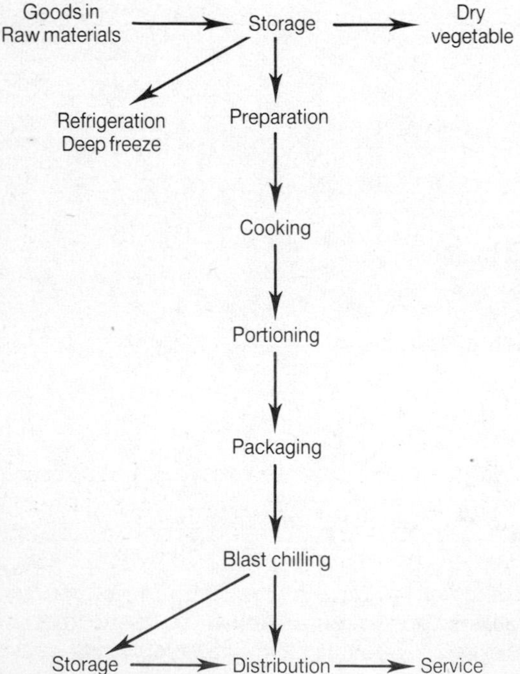

Fig. 10.1 Work flow model

the danger of deterioration in structure, quality, appearance and nutritional value. Any rise in temperature will encourage the growth of micro-organisms and lead to poor quality food which may need to be destroyed.

It is vital that accurate temperature control and monitoring are carried out throughout the cook-freeze, blast-freeze, storage and regeneration process to ensure that food is always held at acceptable and safe temperatures.

Devices used to measure temperature include:

Hand-held probes, which provide a digital read-out for random checking at all stages;
Audible alarms, fitted inside cold stores to warn of rises in temperature;
Temperature gauges, which give a visible reading of the temperature.

Production

In order to ensure that high quality, palatable food is produced at all times it is essential that working conditions are maintained to the highest possible standards, as laid down in the HMSO publication *Clean Catering*, such as:

1. Stringent personal hygiene precautions against infection of the food.
2. All working surfaces and utensils thoroughly cleaned to minimise spread of bacteria.
3. Clean equipment and utensils separated from used items awaiting cleaning.
4. Separation of raw and cooked foods at all times.
5. Strict control of cooking times and temperatures.
6. Staff training in food hygiene.
7. Consultation with medical and Public Health Officers when planning food production systems.

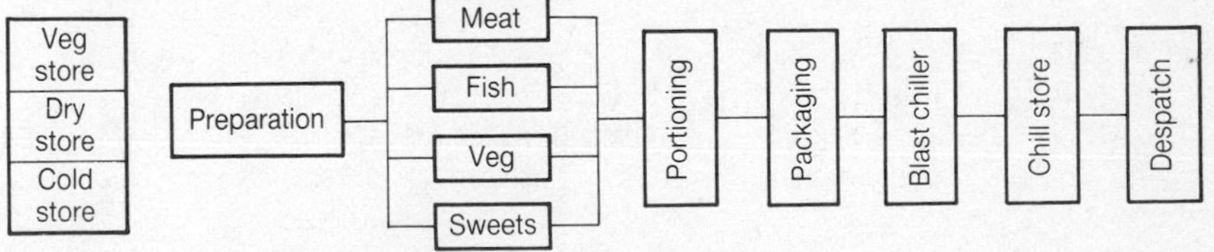

Fig. 10.2 Production unit: planning for cook-chill

Equipment

The equipment used will vary according to the size of the operation but if food is batch-cooked then convection ovens, steaming ovens, bratt pans, jacketed boiling pans, tilting kettles, etc may be used. Certain oven models are available into which a set of racks can be assembled with food and wheeled in for cooking.

The main difference between cook-freeze and cook-chill is the degree of refrigeration and the length of storage life. Other than these differences the information given in this chapter relates to both systems. (For details of cook-freeze see p. 301.)

Cook-chill system

Cook-chill is a catering system based on normal preparation and cooking of food followed by rapid chilling, storage in controlled low-temperature conditions above freezing point, 0°C to 3°C (32°F to 37°F), and subsequently reheating immediately before consumption. The chilled food is regenerated in finishing kitchens which require low capital investment and minimum staff.

The purpose of chilling food

The purpose of chilling food is to prolong its storage life. Under normal temperature conditions, food deteriorates rapidly through the action of micro-organisms and enzymic and chemical reactions. Reduction in the storage temperature inhibits the multiplication of bacteria and other micro-organisms and slows down the chemical and enzymic reactions. At normal refrigeration temperatures reactions are still taking place but at a much slower rate, and at frozen food storage temperatures (−20°C approx.) all reactions nearly cease. A temperature of 0°C to 3°C does not give a storage life comparable to frozen food but it does produce a good product.

It is generally accepted that, even where high standards of fast chilling practice are used and consistent refrigerated storage is maintained, product quality may be acceptable for only a few days (including day of production and consumption). The storage temperature of 0°C to 3°C is of extreme importance to ensure both full protection of the food from microbiological growth and the maintenance of maximum nutritional values in the food. It is generally accepted that a temperature of 10°C should be regarded as the critical safety limit for the storage of refrigerated food. Above that temperature, growth of micro-organisms may render the food dangerous to health.

In a properly designed and operated cook-chill system, cooked and prepared food will be rapidly cooled down to 0°C to 3°C as soon as possible after cooking and portioning and then stored between these temperatures throughout storage and distribution until required for reheating and service. Food prepared through the cook-chill system should be portioned and transferred to a blast chiller unit within 30 minutes. This will reduce the risk of the food remaining at warm incubation temperatures and prevent the risk of contamination and loss of food quality.

The cook-chill process

1 The food should be cooked sufficiently to ensure destruction of any pathogenic micro-organisms.
2 The chilling process must begin as soon as possible after completion of the cooking and portioning processes, within 30 minutes of leaving the cooker. The food should be chilled to 3°C (37°F) within a period of 1½ hours. Most pathogenic organisms will not grow below 7°C (45°F), while a temperature below 3°C (37°F) is required to reduce growth of spoilage organisms and to achieve the required storage life. However, slow growth of spoilage organisms does take place at these temperatures and for this reason storage life cannot be greater than five days.

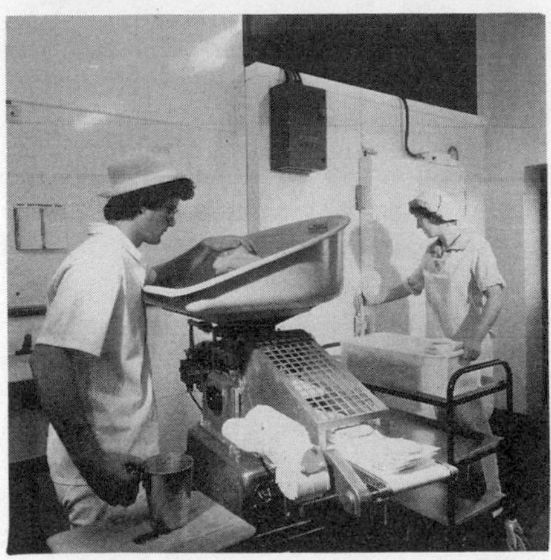

Fig. 10.3 Cook-chill process

3 The food should be stored at a temperature between 0°C and 3°C (32°F to 37°F).
4 The chilled food should be distributed under such controlled conditions that any rise in temperature of the food during distribution is kept to a minimum.
5 For both safety and palatability the reheating (regeneration) of the food should follow immediately upon the removal of the food from chilled conditions and should raise the temperature to a level of at least 70°C (158°F).
6 The food should be consumed as soon as possible and not more than two hours after reheating. Food not intended for reheating should be consumed as soon as convenient and within two hours of removal from storage. It is essential that unconsumed reheated food is discarded.
7 A temperature of 10°C (50°F) should be regarded as the critical safety limit for chilled food. Should the temperature of the chilled food rise above this level during storage or distribution the food concerned should be discarded.

Cook-chill is generally planned within a purpose-designed, comprehensive new central production unit to give small, medium or large-scale production along pre-defined flow lines, incorporating traditional catering/chilling/post-chilling packaging and storage for delivery to finishing kitchens. Within an existing kitchen, where existing equipment is retained with possible minor additions and modifications, chilling/post-chilling packaging and additional storage for cooked chilled food are added.

Finishing kitchens

These can consist of purpose-built regeneration equipment plus refrigerated storage. Additional equipment, such as a chip fryer, boiling table and pressure steamer for chips, sauces, custard, vegetables, etc can be added if required to give greater flexibility.

Where chilled food is produced to supply a service on the same premises, it is recommended that the meals should be supplied, stored and regenerated by exactly the same method as used for operations where the production unit and finishing kitchens are separated by some distance. Failure to adhere to just one procedure could result in disorganised production and reduced productivity. Once a decision is taken to sever production from service this method should be followed throughout the system.

Distribution of cook-chill

Distribution of the chilled food is an important part of the cook-chill operation. Fluctuations in storage temperature can affect the palatability and texture of food and lead to microbiological dangers requiring the food to be discarded. The distribution method chosen must ensure that the required temperature of below 3°C (37°F) is maintained throughout the period of transport. Should the temperature of the food exceed 5°C (41°F) during distribution the food ought to be consumed within 12 hours; if the temperature exceeds 10°C (50°F) it should be discarded (Department of Health guidelines). Because of this, refrigeration during distribution is to be encouraged in many circumstances.

In some cases the cook-chill production unit can also act as a centralised kitchen and distribution point. Food is regenerated in an area adjacent to the cook-chill production area and heat retention or insulated boxes are used for distribution. During transportation and service the food must not be allowed to fall below 62.8°C (145°F) as laid down in the Food Hygiene (General) Regulations 1970.

Containers

Food which is to be placed in the blast chiller can either be placed in re-usable containers made of metal or ceramic, or some other durable substance, or in disposable containers. With disposable containers the food is normally portioned out after cooking, chilled in the blast chiller and then transferred to the store. The food would then be distributed to the finishing kitchens and may be reheated in the disposable containers.

Ceramic containers possess great advantages in terms of heat retention whilst stainless steel or aluminium are widely used in self-service bulk operations.

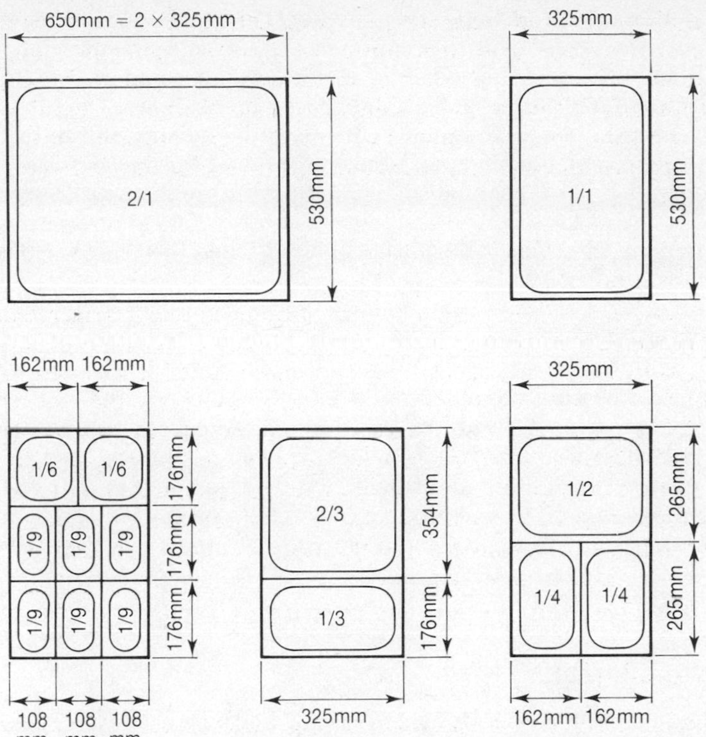

Fig. 10.4 Module sizes for gastronorm containers

The size and type of container used should relate to requirements of how the food is to be served. If the food is to be frozen and regenerated in an acceptable time, the containers should not exceed 50 mm (2 inches) in depth.

Cook-chill containers are based on the gastro-norm system, see Fig. 10.4. To ensure even and complete heating in the finishing cycle, and short chilling times in the air blast chiller, the depth of food in the containers must be carefully controlled. The food should be placed in the chiller as rapidly as possible after completing the cooking cycle.

Cooking hints for cook-chill

Chilling techniques can be applied to all pre-cooked dishes without any reformulation of recipes or ingredients. Sauce stability does not constitute any real problem with cook-chill and there is no need for special additives. However, cooking does thicken sauces and care should be taken to ensure that the viscosity of the sauce after cooking is slightly thinner than normal. Care should also be taken to avoid excessive contact between delicate sauces and the base of the containers to prevent overcooking during reheating, for example a concassée or croûte base may be used to insulate the sauce from the hot container.

Dishes can be assembled from individual components after chilling. The chilled ingredients are placed from bulk into individual containers prior to being covered with pre-chilled sauce. This procedure eradicates sauce skinning and ensures the retention of a traditional glazed sauce for the completed dish. Post-chill assembly is utilised for hospitals and banquet preparations.

The cooking process should be designed to maintain the nutritional value of the food as well as the production of a palatable end-product for the consumer. The time and temperature of the cooking should be sufficient to ensure that heat penetration to the centre of the food will result in the destruction of non-sporing pathogenic micro-organisms. This is normally achieved when the centre of the food reaches a temperature of 70°C (158°F).

Quality control

All staff working in a cook-chill production unit must be trained to the highest standard and must work under skilled supervision. Adequate control of bacterial contamination and multiplication, which are hazards in any kitchen, can be achieved by a survey of the initial installation by a qualified analyst and batch checks thereafter. In a very large production kitchen, producing 10 000 to 15 000 meals, a full-time microbiologist would normally be employed.

Regeneration food service system for hospitals

In hospitals the system utilises specially designed porcelain or stainless steel dishes with stainless steel covers. Centrally produced meals are chilled in a purpose-built chilling unit. The chilled meal packs are distributed for ward level regeneration to service temperature in a purpose-designed trolley/oven unit. The thermal heating system is based on quartz radiant heaters, proportionally spaced to ensure even and simultaneous heat distribution on both the porcelain dish and the stainless steel cover.

Alternatively, regeneration may be carried out in convection ovens with steam injection then a humidifier oven will prevent the food drying out and counteract any loss of moisture that may have occurred during the chilling process.

Employee self-service

This system utilises bulk stainless steel dishes into which cooked food is portioned prior to chilling and storage. At service time the food is batch regenerated behind service counters for self-help or self-service. One central kitchen can supply chilled meals to numerous satellite services where cooking operations are virtually eliminated.

Banqueting

This system utilises ceramic banquet dishes, divided into 10 to 12 portions, into which the cooked food is normally placed after chilling. Banquet meals are stored in cold rooms prior to regeneration which can take place in portable thermal units; this is particularly suitable for hotels where banquets and seminars occur in different venues or on different floors.

Production

1 Skilled staff are employed in the production operation.
2 It is largely unskilled staff, under strict supervision, who carry out packaging, chilling, storing and regeneration.

Maximum efficiency should follow if the production area is set up in a new location but, depending on circumstances, a simple layout can be established in an existing kitchen for possible use in room service, banqueting, small-scale staff catering (night shifts) and as a pilot scheme for a potentially larger operation.

Cook-freeze system

Blast freezers have increasingly been introduced with success into catering operations. The ability to freeze cooked dishes and prepared foods, as distinct from the storage of chilled foods in a refrigerator or already frozen commodities in a deep-freeze, allows a caterer to make more productive use of kitchen staff. It also enables economies to be introduced into the staffing of dining rooms and restaurants.

The cook-freeze process

Cook-freeze uses a production system similar to that used in cook-chill. The recipes used have to be modified, enabling products to be freezer-stable, and modified starches are used in sauces so that on reheating and regeneration the sauce does not separate. Blast freezers are used in place of blast chillers. The freezing must be carried out very rapidly to retain freshness and to accelerate temperature loss through the latent heat barrier, thus preventing the formation of large ice crystals and rupturing of the cells.

Blast freezing takes place when low temperature air is passed over food at high speed, reducing food in batches to a temperature of at least −20°C within 90 minutes. Blast freezers can hold from 20 to 400 kg (40 to 800 lb) per batch, the larger models being designed for trolley operation.

(a) Preparation of food

The production menu for a month is drawn up and the total quantities of different foods required calculated. Supplies are then ordered, with special attention given to their being:

1 of high quality;
2 delivered so that they can immediately be prepared and cooked without any possibility of deteriorating during an enforced period of storage before being processed.

The dishes included in the menu must be cooked to the highest standards with rigid attention to quality control and to hygiene. It will be remembered that deep-freeze temperatures prevent the multiplication of micro-organisms but do not destroy them. If, therefore, a dish were contaminated before being frozen, consumers would be put at risk months later when the food was prepared for consumption. The exact adjustment of recipes to produce the best result when the food is subsequently thawed and reheated is still in process of being worked out by chefs, using numerous variations of the basic system. The single change needed in cookery recipes involving sauces is the selection of an appropriate type of starch capable of resisting the effect of freezing. Normal starches will produce a curdled effect when subsequently thawed and reheated.

In order to achieve rapid freezing with a quick reduction of temperature to −18°C (0°F) or below, the cooked food must be carefully portioned (close attention being paid to the attainment of uniform portion size). Portions, each placed into a disposable aluminium foil container, may conveniently be placed into aluminium foil trays holding from 6 to 10 portions each, sealed and carefully labelled with their description and date of preparation.

(b) Freezing

The food thus divided into portions and arranged in trays is immediately frozen. An effective procedure is to place the trays on racks in a blast-freezing tunnel and expose them to a vigorous flow of cold air until the cooked items are frozen solid and the temperature reduced to at least −5°C (23°F). The quality of the final product is to a significant degree dependent on the rapidity with which the temperature of hot cooked food at say 80°C (178°F) is reduced to below freezing. The capacity of the blast freezer should be designed to achieve this reduction in temperature within a period of 1 to 1¼ hours.

(c) Storage of frozen items

Once the food items are frozen they must at once be put into a deep freeze store maintained at −18°C (0°F). For a catering operation involving several dining rooms and cafeterias, some of which may be situated at some distance from the kitchen and frozen store, a four weeks' supply of cooked dishes held at low temperature allows full use to be made of the facilities.

(d) Transport of frozen items to the point of service

If satisfactory quality is to be maintained, it is important to keep food frozen in the cooked state frozen until immediately prior to its being served. It should therefore be transported in insulated containers to *peripheral* kitchens, if such are to be used, where it will be reheated.

If frozen dishes are to be used in outside catering, provision should be available for transporting them in refrigerated transport and, if necessary, a subsidiary deep-freeze store should be provided for them on arrival.

(e) The reheating of frozen cooked portions

In any catering system in which a blast-freezing tunnel has been installed to freeze pre-cooked food, previously portioned and packed in metal foil or other individual containers, it is obviously rational to install equipment that is particularly designed for the purpose of reheating the items ready to be served. The blast freezing system is effective because it is, in design, a specially powerful form of forced convection heat exchanger arranged to extract heat. It follows that an equally appropriate system for replacing heat is the use of a forced convection oven, specially for the reception of the trays of frozen portions. Where such an oven is equipped with an efficient thermostat and adequate control of the air circulation system, standardised setting times for the controls can be laid down for the regeneration of the various types of dishes that need to be reheated.

Quality control

Adequate control of bacterial contamination and growth, which are hazards in any kitchen, can be achieved by a survey of the initial installation by a qualified analyst, and regular checks taken on every batch of food cooked. Very large kitchens employ a full-time food technologist/bacteriologist. In smaller operations the occasional services of a microbiologist from the public health authority should be used.

Overall benefits of cook-chill/cook-freeze

To the employer:

1 Portion control and reduced waste.
2 No over-production.
3 Central purchasing – bulk buying discounts.
4 Full utilisation of equipment.
5 Full utilisation of staff time.
6 Overall savings in staff.
7 Savings on equipment, space and fuel.
8 Fewer staff with better conditions – no unsociable hours, no week-end work, no overtime.
9 Simplified delivery to units – less frequent.
10 Solves problem of moving hot foods – hospital wards etc. (EC regulations forbid movement of hot foods unless the temperature is maintained over 65°C. Maintaining 65°C is regarded as very difficult to achieve and high temperatures inevitably will be harmful to foods.)

To the customer:

1 Increased variety and selection.
2 Improved quality, with standards maintained.
3 More nutritious foods.
4 Services can be maintained at all times, regardless of staff absences.

Advantages of cook-freeze over cook-chill

1 Seasonal purchasing provides considerable savings.
2 Delivery to units will be far less frequent.
3 Long-term planning of production and menus becomes possible.
4 Less dependence on price fluctuations.
5 More suitable for vending machines incorporating microwave.

Advantages of cook-chill over cook-freeze

1 Regeneration systems are simpler – infra-red and steam convection ovens are mostly used and only 12 minutes is required to reheat all foods perfectly.
2 Thawing time is eliminated.

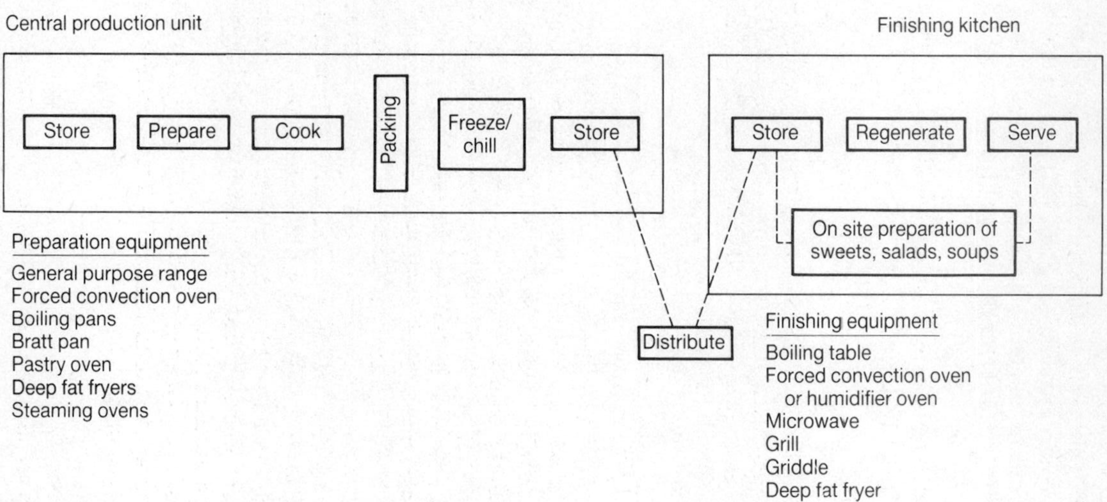

Fig. 10.5 Central production unit to finishing kitchen

3 Smaller capacity storage is required: three to four days supply as opposed to up to 120 days.
4 Chiller storage is cheaper to install and run than freezer storage.
5 Blast chillers are cheaper to install and run than blast freezers.
6 Cooking techniques are unaltered (additives and revised recipes are needed for freezing).
7 All foods can be chilled so the range of dishes is wider (some foods cannot be frozen). Cooked eggs, steaks and sauces such as Hollandaise can be chilled (after some recipe modification where necessary).
8 No system is too small to adapt to cook-chill.

Further information
Electricity Council, 30 Millbank, London SW1P 4RD; Department of Health.

Sous-vide

This is a form of cook-chill: a combination of vacuum sealing in plastic pouches, cooking by steam and then rapidly cooling and chilling. The objective is to rationalise kitchen procedures without having a detrimental effect on the quality of individual dishes.

The sous-vide process

1 Individual portions of prepared food are first placed in special plastic pouches. The food can be fish, poultry, meats, vegetables, etc to which seasoning, a garnish, sauce, stock, wine, flavouring, vegetables, herbs and/or spices can be added.
2 The pouches of food are then placed in a vacuum packaging machine which evacuates all the air and tightly seals the pouch.
3 The pouches are next cooked by steam. This is usually in a special oven equipped with a steam control programme, which controls the injection of steam into the oven, to give steam cooking at an oven temperature below 100°C. Each food item has its own ideal cooking time and temperature.
4 When cooked, the pouches are rapidly cooled down to 3°C – usually in an iced water chiller or an air blast chiller for larger operations.
5 The pouches are then labelled and stored in a holding refrigerator at an optimum temperature of 3°C.
6 When required for service the pouches are regenerated in boiling water or a steam combination oven until the required temperature is reached, cut open and the food presented.

Some points to note
Vacuum pressures are as important as the cooking temperatures with regard to weight loss and heat absorption. The highest temperature used in *sous-vide* cooking is 100°C and 1000 millibars is the minimum amount of vacuum pressure used.

As there is no oxidation or discoloration it is ideal for conserving fruits, such as apples and pears, for example pears in red wine, fruits in syrup. When preparing meats in sauces the meat is pre-blanched then added to the completed sauce.

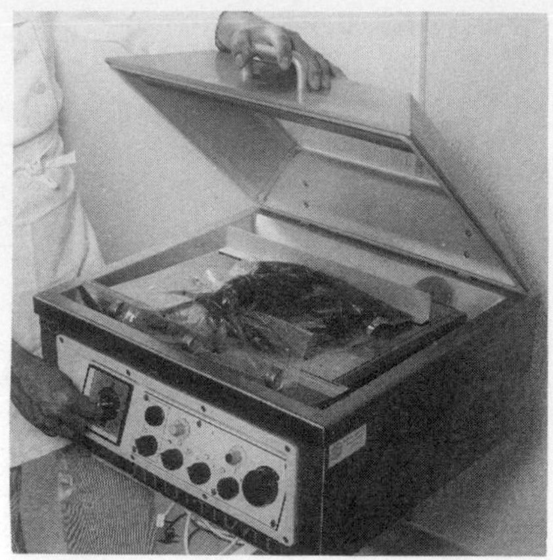

Fig. 10.6 Sous-vide cookery:
1 Place prepared raw product in pouch
2 Pouch evacuated and sealed
3 Cook in combination oven
4 Cool quickly to 3°C (not shown here)
5 Pouches labelled and refrigerated at optimum temperature of 3°C

Sous-vide is a combination of vacuum sealing, tightly controlled *en papillotte* cooking and rapid chilling. Potential users are brasseries, wine bars, airlines, private hospitals and function caterers seeking to provide top quality with portion convenience.

Advantages

1 Long shelf-life, up to 21 days – refrigerated.
2 Ability to produce meals in advance means better deployment of staff and skills.

3 Vac-packed foods can be mixed in cold store without the risk of cross-contamination.
4 Reduced labour costs at point of service.
5 Beneficial cooking effects on certain foods, especially moulded items and pâtés. Reduces weight loss on meat joints.
6 Full flavour and texture is retained as food cooks in its own juices.
7 Economises on ingredients (less butter, marinades etc).
8 Makes pre-cooking a possibility for *à la carte* menus.
9 Inexpensive regeneration.
10 Allows a small operation to set up bulk production.
11 Facilitates portion control and uniformity of standard.
12 Has a tenderising effect on tougher cuts of meat and matures game without dehydration.

Disadvantages

1 Extra cost of vacuum pouches and vacuum-packing machine.
2 Unsuitable for meats (eg fillet steak) and vegetables which absorb colour.
3 All portions in a batch must be identically sized to ensure even results.
4 Most dishes require twice the conventional cooking time.
5 Unsuitable for large joints as chilling time exceeds 90 minutes.
6 Complete meals (eg meat and two vegetables) not feasible; meat component needs to be cooked and stored in separate bags.
7 Extremely tight management and hygienic controls are imperative.
8 Potentially adverse customer reaction ('boil-in-the-bag' syndrome).

Further information
This can be found in an introductory handbook, available from the Department of Catering and Hotel Administration, Dorset Institute of Higher Education.

Centralised production – an introduction

1 Reasons for consideration

Reasons for considering centralised production units are as follows:

(a) Labour: reduction of kitchen preparation staff in end units.
(b) Food cost: greater control over waste and portion sizes; competitive purchasing through bulk buying.
(c) Equipment: intensive central use of heavy equipment reduces commitment in individual units.
(d) Product: more control on product quality.
(e) Labour strategy: staff are employed at regular times (eg 9–5) which can eliminate or lessen the difficulty of obtaining staff who will work shifts.

When considering a centralised production system it is essential that a detailed financial appraisal is produced and then looked at carefully, as each establishment has its own considerations. No general rule can be given as the profitability depends on the product, the size of each unit, the number of units and the method of preserving food.

2 Design

Centralised production systems can be designed in two ways:

(a) Using existing catering (operations) unit and modifying etc.
(b) Purpose-built.

3 Type of units

Centralised production units are grouped into four types:

(a) Units preparing fresh cooked foods which are then despatched.
(b) Cook-freeze: food is partly prepared or cooked, then frozen and regenerated when required.
(c) Cook-chill: food is cooked, then chilled and regenerated when required.
(d) Sous-vide: food is sealed in a special casing, vacuum-sealed, cooked and chilled.

4 Food production and preparation

The profitability of the production system depends largely upon contents of the end-unit menus.

Meat
Careful purchasing is essential and the menu must be planned carefully:

(a) The cut of meat required must be clearly specified in order to produce the exact dishes.
(b) Strict portion control.
(c) Trimmings/by-products must be fully utilised, eg meat trimming for cottage/shepherds pie, bones for stock, etc.

Vegetable preparation
Because of increasing labour costs and difficulty in obtaining staff, a number of establishments now purchase: prepared potatoes, that are washed, peeled and in some cases shaped; prepared root vegetables; topped and tailed French beans; and ready prepared salads.

5 Reception and delivery

It is desirable to have two loading bays, one for receiving and one for delivery. They should be adjacent to the relevant store to facilitate loading. The receiving bay should be adjacent to the prime goods store, ie purchased meat, vegetables etc, and the delivery bay near to the finished goods stores which contain items ready to go out to their end units.

6 Staff

Apart from a butcher some of the staff may not be highly skilled. The various processes involved in meat production can be divided as follows and staff trained for each procedure:

(a) Machine operators: staff operating dicing machines, mincing machines, hamburger machines, to a strict procedure.
(b) Trimmers: staff who are taught to trim carcasses and prime cuts.
(c) Packers: who pack goods into foil cans, operate vacuum packing machines, and label or pack finished goods into containers. Caterers will have to consider if it is economically viable to have a butchery or whether to buy in prepared meats (this very much depends upon the range of menu).

Frequently staff who are employed to carry out specific functions within a centralised kitchen may not have catering qualifications but will be trained by the organisation.

7 Method of operation

There are two types of operations:

(a) weekly production;
(b) daily total run.

Forecasts obtained from the end unit determine the quantity of the production run. This prepares items of a particular type on one occasion only. As soon as the run is completed the next run is then scheduled. The main advantage of this type of production is in the comparative ease with which a control system may be installed and operated.

A disadvantage is that, in the event of an error in production scheduling, it is wasteful and costly to organise a further production run of small volume. Another disadvantage is that the method leads to the building-up of stocks, both finished and unfinished, thereby affecting the profitability of the operation.

Method (b) (daily total run) is based upon the needs of items required by the end-unit. A disadvantage is that the forecast gap is shorter, so the end units are not able to provide accurate requisitions.

8 Purchasing

Any organisation depending for its existence on the economics of bulk purchasing must pay particular attention to the process of buying.

The following are the main objectives of the buyer:

(a) Quality and price of goods must be equalled with the size of purchase order.
(b) All purchase specifications must be met.
(c) Buying practice must supplement a policy of minimum stock holding.

9 Transport

The distribution of goods, routing and the maintenance of vehicles are very important to a centralised production operation. The usual practice is for transport to be under the control of a senior manager, who also has the complicated job of batching-up deliveries (normally weekly or bi-weekly). It is important that the senior manager has considerable administrative skill in order to prevent errors occurring.

Small centralised operations

There are some very good examples of smaller centralised operations to be seen now in the catering industry. The purpose of installation is to provide ready prepared goods which may be served to banquets or supplied to grills/coffee shops.

The preparation of the food takes place during the kitchen 'slack' period, principally after the luncheon service. The made-up items are put into polythene bags which contain from one to six portions. The packed items are marked with the date of packing, and the name of the item, and then blast frozen preparatory to storage. They are kept in store from three to six months and moved to a first-in, first-out basis. Some items have limited storage time so careful checking of dates is an important factor to consider. Refrigerators in the outlets are stocked up daily from the central cold store.

When an item is ordered it is reheated by a simple boiling process which is operated by a timer. The cooked items are placed on the plate, with the garnish and vegetables being added separately. There are also, of course, many other refinements, eg carefully calculated production schedules and coloured photographs of the dishes to guide presentation.

11

Health and safety

Having read the chapter these learning objectives, both general and specific, should be achieved.

General objectives Be aware of the main points of the Health and Safety at Work Act. Know of the accidents which may occur in catering establishments and understand why there is a need for care to be taken by people in working situations. Create a favourable attitude to safety so that in practice it is second nature.

Specific objectives Explain the responsibilities of the employee and employer and the function of the Environmental Health Officer. Specify the rules to be observed when handling all tools and equipment, both large and small. Explain how to prevent burns, scalds, and cuts. Specify the correct procedure for basic first aid and be able to apply first aid. Distinguish the correct equipment for dealing with fires and be able to use the appropriate appliance correctly.

Legislation

Every year in the UK a thousand people are killed at work; a million people suffer injuries; and 23 million working days are lost annually because of industrial injury and disease. As catering is one of the largest employers of labour the catering industry is substantially affected by accidents at work.

In 1974 the *Health and Safety at Work Act* was passed with two main aims:

1 To extend the coverage and protection of the law to all employers and employees.
2 To increase awareness of safety amongst those at work, both employers and employees.

The law imposes a general duty on an employer, 'to ensure so far as is reasonably practicable, the health, safety and welfare at work of all his employees'. The law also imposes a duty on every employee while at work to:

(a) Take reasonable care for the health and safety of himself or herself and of other persons who may be affected by his or her acts or omissions at work.
(b) To co-operate with his or her employer so far as is necessary to meet or comply with any requirement concerning health and safety.
(c) Not to interfere with, or misuse, anything provided in the interests of health, safety or welfare.

It can be clearly seen that both health and safety at work is everybody's responsibility.

Furthermore the Act protects the members of the public who may be affected by the activities of those at work.

Penalties are provided by the Act which include improvement notices, prohibition notices and criminal prosecution. The Health and Safety Executive has been set up to enforce the law and the Health and Safety Commission will issue codes of conduct and act as advisers.

Responsibilities of the employer

The employer's responsibilities are to:

1 Provide and maintain premises and equipment that are safe and without risk to health.
2 Provide supervision, information and training.
3 Issue a written statement of 'safety policy' to employees to include:
   (a) general policy with respect to health and safety at work of employees;
   (b) the organisation, to ensure the policy is carried out;
   (c) how the policy will be made effective.
4 Consult with the employees' safety representative and to establish a Safety Committee.

Responsibilities of the employee

Employees, for their part, should:

1 Take reasonable care to avoid injury to themselves or to others by their work activities.
2 Co-operate with their employer and others so as to comply with the law.
3 Refrain from misusing or interfering with anything provided for health and safety.

Enforcement of the Act

Health and safety inspectors and local authority inspectors (environmental health officers) have the authority to enforce the requirements of the Act. They are empowered to:

1 Issue a *prohibition notice* which immediately prevents further business until remedial action has been taken.
2 Issue an *improvement notice* whereby action must be taken within a stated time, to an employee, employer or supplier.
3 *Prosecute* any person breaking the Act. This can be instead of or in addition to serving a notice and may lead to a substantial fine or prison.
4 Seize, render harmless or destroy anything that the inspector considers to be the cause of imminent danger.

Environmental health officer

The environmental health officer has two main functions: one is to enforce the law; the other aspect of the job is to act as an adviser and educator in the areas of food hygiene and catering premises. Here their function is to improve the existing standard of hygiene and to advise how this may be achieved. Frequently health education programmes are organised by environmental health officers which may include talks and free literature. If in doubt about any matter concerning food hygiene, pests, premises or legal aspects of the Act the environmental health officer is there to be consulted.

Accidents

It is essential that people working in the kitchen are capable of using the tools and equipment in a manner which will neither harm themselves nor those with

<table>
<tr><td colspan="4">Full name of injured person:</td></tr>
<tr><td colspan="2">Occupation:</td><td colspan="2">Supervisor:</td></tr>
<tr><td>Time of accident:</td><td>Date of accident:</td><td>Time of report:</td><td>Date of report:</td></tr>
<tr><td colspan="4">Nature of injury or condition:</td></tr>
<tr><td colspan="4">Details of hospitalisation:</td></tr>
<tr><td colspan="4">Extent of injury (after medical attention):</td></tr>
<tr><td colspan="4">Place of accident or dangerous occurrence:</td></tr>
<tr><td colspan="4">Injured person's evidence of what happened (include equipment/items/or other persons):
Use separate sheets if necessary</td></tr>
<tr><td colspan="2">Witness evidence (1):</td><td colspan="2">Witness evidence (2):</td></tr>
<tr><td colspan="4">Supervisor's recommendations:</td></tr>
<tr><td colspan="2">Date:</td><td colspan="2">Supervisor's signature:</td></tr>
<tr><td colspan="4">This form must be sent to the company health and safety officer</td></tr>
</table>

Fig. 11.1 Sample in-house record of accidents and dangerous occurrences

whom they work. Moreover, they should be aware of the causes of accidents and be able to deal with any which occur.

Accidents may be caused in various ways:

(a) excessive haste;
(b) distraction;
(c) failure to apply safety rules.

It should be remembered that most accidents could be prevented. For example:

(a) Excessive haste – the golden rule of the kitchen is 'never run'. This may be difficult to observe during a very busy service but excessive haste causes people to take chances which inevitably lead to mishaps.
(b) Distraction – accidents may be caused by not concentrating on the job in hand, through lack of interest, personal worry or distraction by someone else. The mind must always be kept on the work so as to reduce the number of accidents.

Reporting accidents

Any accident occurring on the premises where the employee works must be reported to the employer and a record of the accident must be entered in the Accident Book.

Any accident causing death or major injury to an employee or member of the public must be reported by the employer to the Environmental Health Department. Also, accidents involving dangerous equipment must be reported even if no one is injured (see Fig. 11.1).

Accident prevention

It is the responsibility of everyone to observe the safety rules; in this way a great deal of pain and loss of time can be avoided.

Prevention of cuts and scratches

Knives

These should never be misused and the following rules should always be observed:

1 The correct knife should be used for the appropriate job.
2 Knives must always be sharp and clean; a blunt knife is more likely to cause a cut because excessive pressure has to be used.
3 Handles should be free from grease.
4 When carrying knives, the points must be held downwards.
5 Knives should be placed flat on the board or table so that the blade is not exposed upwards.
6 Knives should be wiped clean with the edge away from the hands.
7 Do not put knives in a washing-up sink.

Choppers

These should be kept sharp and clean. When in use care should be taken that no other knives, saws, hooks, etc, can be struck by the chopper, which could cause them to fly into the air. This also applies when using a large knife for chopping.

Cutting blades on machines
Guards should always be in place when the machine is in use; they should not be tampered with nor should hands or fingers be inserted past the guards. Before the guards are removed for cleaning, the blade or blades must have stopped revolving.

When the guard is removed for cleaning, the blade should not be left unattended, in case someone should put a hand on it by accident. If the machine is electrically operated the plug should, when possible, be removed.

Cuts from meat and fish bones
Jagged bones can cause cuts which may turn septic, particularly fish bones and the bones of a calf's head which has been opened to remove the brain. Cuts of this nature, however slight, should never be neglected. Frozen meat should not be boned out until it is completely thawed out because it is difficult to handle, the hands become very cold and the knife slips easily.

Prevention of burns and scalds

A burn is caused by dry heat and a scald by wet heat. Both burns and scalds can be very painful and have serious effects, so certain precautions should be taken to prevent them:

1 Sleeves of jackets and overalls should be rolled down and aprons worn at a sensible length so as to give adequate protection.
2 A good thick dry cloth is most important for handling hot utensils. It should never be used wet on hot objects and is best folded to give greater protection. It should not be used if thin, torn or with holes.
3 Trays containing hot liquid, for example roast gravy, should be handled carefully, one hand on the side and the other on the end of the tray so as to balance it.
4 Hot pans brought out of the oven should have something white, eg a little flour, placed on the handle and lid as a warning that it is hot. This should be done as soon as the pan is taken out of the oven.
5 Handles of pans should not protrude over the edge of the stove as the pan may be knocked off the stove.
6 Large full pans should be carried correctly, ie when there is only one handle the forearm should run along the full length of the handle and the other hand should be used to balance the pan where the handle joins the pan. This should prevent the contents from spilling.
7 Certain foods require extra care when heat is applied to them, as for example when a cold liquid is added to a hot roux or when adding cold water to boiling sugar for making caramel. Extra care should always be taken when boiling sugar.
8 Frying, especially deep frying, needs careful attention. When shallow or deep frying fish, for example, the fish should be put into the pan away from the person so that any splashes will do no harm. With deep frying, fritures should be moved with care and if possible only when the fat is cool.

Fritures should not be more than two-thirds full. Wet foods should be drained and dried before being placed in the fat, and when foods are tipped out of the frying basket a spider should be at hand. Should the fat in the friture bubble over on to a gas stove then the gas taps should be turned off immediately. Fire blankets and fire extinguishers should be provided in every kitchen, conveniently sited ready for use.

9 Steam causes scalds just as hot liquids do. It is important to be certain that before opening steamers the steam is turned off and that when the steamer door is opened no one is in the way of the escaping steam. The steamer should be in proper working condition; the drain hole should always be clear. The door should not be opened immediately the steam is turned off; it is better to wait for about half a minute before doing so.

10 Scalds can also be caused by splashing when passing liquids through conical strainers; it is wise to keep the face well back so as to avoid getting splashed. This also applies when hot liquids are poured into containers.

Machinery

Accidents are easily caused by misuse of machines (refer to p. 222 for further information). The following rules should always be put into practice:

1 The machine should be in correct running order before use.
2 The controls of the machine should be operated by the person using the machine. If two people are involved there is the danger that a misunderstanding can occur and the machine be switched on when the other person does not expect it.
3 Machine attachments should be correctly assembled and only the correct tools used to force food through mincers.
4 When using mixing machines the hands should not be placed inside the bowl until the blades, whisk or hook have stopped revolving. Failure to observe this rule may result in a broken arm.
5 Plugs should be removed from electric machines when they are being cleaned so they cannot be accidentally switched on.

Explosions

The risk of explosion from gas is considerable. To avoid this occurring it is necessary to ensure that the gas is properly lit. On ranges with a pilot on the oven it is important to see that the main jet has ignited from the pilot. If the regulo is low sometimes the gas does not light at once, the gas collects and an explosion occurs. When lighting the tops of solid-top ranges it is wise to place the centre ring back for a few minutes after the stove is lit as the gas may go out, gas then collects and an explosion can occur.

Floors

Accidents are also caused by grease and water being spilled on floors and not being cleaned up. It is most important that floors are always kept clean and clear; pots and pans, etc, should never be left on the floor, nor should oven doors be left open, because anyone carrying something large may not see the door, or anything on the floor, and trip over.

Many people strain themselves by incorrectly lifting or attempting to lift items which are too heavy. Large stock pots, rondeaus, forequarters and hindquarters of beef, for example, should be lifted with care. Particular attention should be paid to the hooks in meat so that they do not injure anyone.

On no account should liquids be placed in containers on shelves above eye-level, especially when hot. They may be pulled down by someone else.

Safe kitchens are those which are well lit and well ventilated and where the staff take precautions to prevent accidents happening. But when accidents do happen it is necessary to know something of first aid.

Further information
Royal Society for the Prevention of Accidents, Cannon House, Priory Queensway, Birmingham B4 6BS.
Health and Safety Executive, Baynards House, 1 Chepstow Place, Westbourne Grove, London W2 4TF.

First aid

As the term implies this is the immediate treatment on the spot to a person who has been injured or is ill. Since 1982 it has been a legal requirement that adequate first aid equipment, facilities and personnel to give first aid are provided at work. If the injury is serious the injured person should be treated by a doctor or nurse as soon as possible.

First aid equipment

A first aid box, as a minimum, should contain:

a card giving general first aid guidance
20 individually wrapped, sterile, adhesive, waterproof dressings of various sizes
4 × 25 g (1 oz) cotton wool packs
1 dozen safety pins
2 triangular bandages
2 sterile eye pads, with attachment
4 medium-sized sterile unmedicated dressings
2 large sterile unmedicated dressings
2 extra large sterile unmedicated dressings
tweezers
scissors
and a report book to record all injuries

First aid boxes must be easily identifiable (see Fig. 11.2 over the page) and accessible in the work area. They should be in the charge of a responsible person, checked regularly and refilled when necessary.

All establishments must have first aid equipment and employees qualified in first aid. Large establishments usually have medical staff such as a nurse and a first aid room. The room should include a bed or couch, blankets, chairs, a table, sink with hot and cold water, towels, tissues and a first aid box. Hooks for clothing and a mirror should be provided. Small establishments should have members of staff trained in first aid and in possession of a certificate. After a

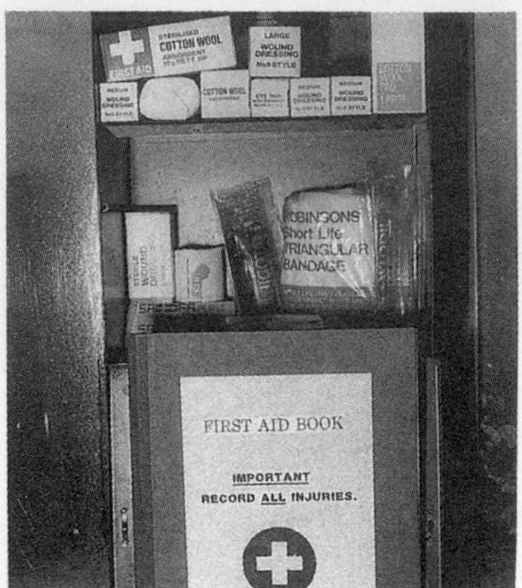

Fig. 11.2 First-aid kit and book

period of three years trained first aid staff must update their training to remain certificated.

All catering workers and students are recommended to attend a first aid course run by the St John Ambulance, St Andrew's Ambulance Association or British Red Cross Society.

Shock

The signs of shock are faintness, sickness, clammy skin and a pale face. Shock should be treated by keeping the person comfortable, lying down and warm. Cover the person with a blanket or clothing, but do not apply hot water bottles.

Fainting

Fainting may occur after a long period of standing in a hot, badly ventilated kitchen. The signs of an impending faint are whiteness, giddiness and sweating. A faint should be treated by raising the legs slightly above the level of the head and, when the person recovers consciousness, putting the person in the fresh air for a while and making sure that the person has not incurred any injury in fainting.

Cuts

All cuts should be covered immediately with a waterproof dressing, after the skin round the cut has been washed. When there is considerable bleeding it should be stopped as soon as possible. Bleeding may be controlled by direct pressure, by bandaging firmly on the cut. It may be possible to stop bleeding from a cut artery by pressing the artery with the thumb against the underlying bone; such pressure may be applied while a dressing or bandage is being prepared for application but not for more than 15 minutes.

Nose bleeds

Sit the person down with the head forward, and loosen clothing round the neck and chest. Ask them to breathe through the mouth and to pinch the soft part of the nose. After ten minutes release the pressure. Warn the person not to blow the nose for several hours. If the bleeding has not stopped continue for a further ten minutes. If the bleeding has not stopped then, or recurs in 30 minutes, obtain medical assistance.

Fractures

A person suffering from broken bones should not be moved until the injured part has been secured so that it cannot move. Medical assistance should be obtained.

Burns and scalds

Place the injured part gently under slowly running water or immerse in cool water, keeping it there for at least 10 minutes or until the pain ceases. If serious, the burn or scald should then be covered with a clean cloth or dressing (preferably sterile) and the person sent immediately to hospital.

Do *not* use adhesive dressings, apply lotions or ointments or break blisters.

Electric shock

Switch off the current. If this is not possible, free the person by using a dry insulating material such as cloth, wood or rubber, taking care not to use the bare hands otherwise the electric shock may be transmitted. If breathing has stopped, give artificial respiration and send for a doctor. Treat any burns as above.

Gassing

Do not let the gassed person walk, but carry them into the fresh air. If breathing has stopped apply artificial respiration and send for a doctor.

Artificial respiration

There are several methods of artificial respiration. The most effective is mouth-to-mouth (mouth-to-nose) and this method can be used by almost all age groups and in almost all circumstances.

Again it is stressed that we would recommend all students to complete a first aid course.

Further information
St John Ambulance Association, 1 Grosvenor Crescent, London SW1X 7EF.

Fire precautions

Fires in hotel and catering establishments are fairly common and all too often

Fig. 11.3 Staff watch as rescue from fire takes place

can result in injury to the employee and, in serious cases, either injury or loss of life to employees and customers.

Fire prevention

A basic knowledge regarding fire should assist in preventing fires and handling them if they do occur. Three components are necessary for a fire to start, if one of the three is not present, or is removed, then the fire does not happen or it is extinguished. The three parts are:

(a) fuel – something to burn;
(b) air – oxygen to sustain combustion (to keep the fire going);
(c) heat – gas, electricity etc.

Methods of extinguishing a fire

To extinguish a fire the three principal methods are:

(a) starving – removing the fuel;
(b) smothering – removing the air (oxygen);
(c) cooling – removing the heat.

Therefore one of the sides of the 'fire triangle' (see Fig. 11.4 page opposite) is removed.

The fuel is that which burns, heat is that which sets the fuel alight and oxygen is needed for fire to burn. Eliminate one of these and the fire is put out. Oxygen is present in air, so if air is excluded from the fuel and the heat then the fire goes out. For example, should the clothes of someone working in the kitchen catch alight then the action to be taken is quickly to wrap a fire blanket round the person and place them on the floor. In so doing the flames have been cut off

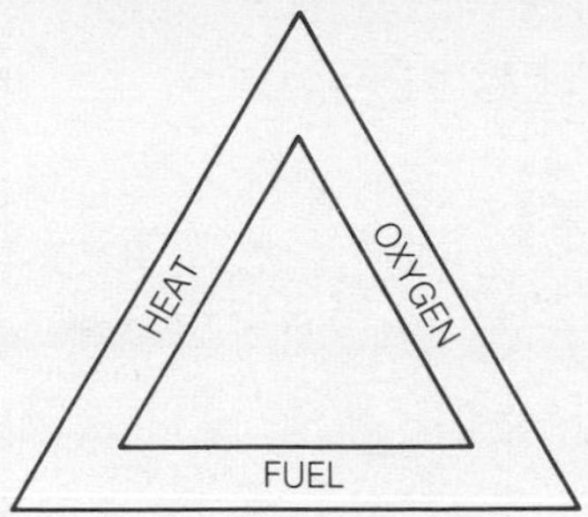

Fig. 11.4 The fire triangle

from the source of air. (The oxygen has been taken from the triangle.) In the event of a fire, windows and doors are to be closed so as to restrict the amount of air getting to the fire. Foam extinguishers work on the principle that the foam forms a 'blanket' thus excluding air from coming into contact with the fuel.

Should fat or oil in a pan ignite, then the pan should be quickly covered with a lid, or other item, or fire blanket so as to exclude air. It is also essential to turn off the source of heat, gas or electricity etc so that the heat is taken from the triangle.

Water extinguishes by dousing the flames, thus taking the heat out of the triangle provided the fuel is material such as wood, paper etc. If fat or oil is alight water must *not* be used as it causes the ignited fat to spread, thus increasing the heat. Water extinguishers must *not* be used on live electrical equipment because water is a conductor of electricity.

In the event of a small fire in a store it may be possible to remove items in the

Fig. 11.5 Fire blanket

Local hotel owner fined after fire

The owner of the Country Square Hotel has been fined under the Fire Prevention Act for 20 offences following investigations into a fire at the hotel in April last year.

He was prosecuted by the Fire Brigade and fined £3,550 after pleading guilty to all offences before magistrates.

The fire spread throughout the hotel following a chip-pan blaze in the basement kitchen.

The Fire Brigade told the court it had discovered obstructions in four exit routes while it was attempting to douse the flames at the five-storey hotel.

The court heard that doors protecting the staircase and exits had been left propped open or were missing. The same applied to doors at basement level and on upper floors, allowing the whole premises to become saturated with smoke, the court was told.

Corridors and exits in the basement were obstructed by builders' materials and gas cylinders and the door from the kitchen had been left open, allowing flames to travel unimpeded into the corridor to both staircases of the hotel, said the Fire Brigade report.

A nightly security check had not been carried out the night of the fire, while the overall effect of the 20 offences committed was "to place all the means of escape in jeopardy", the court heard.

A man was rescued from a second-floor window and a woman from an internal staircase.

store to prevent the fire from spreading; windows and doors are to be closed, if it is safe to do so. Evacuation should not be delayed if the fire is already well developed. Fighting a small fire in a store should normally take priority over removing items from it unless the store is large enough for both activities to be carried out.

Fire doors are installed for the purpose of restricting an area so that in the event of a fire the fuel is limited.

Procedure in the event of a fire

1 The fire brigade must be called immediately a fire is discovered.
2 Do not panic.
3 Warn other people in the vicinity.
4 Do not jeopardise your own safety or that of others.
5 Follow the fire instructions of the establishment.
6 If a small fire, use appropriate fire extinguisher.
7 Do close doors and windows, turn of gas, electricity and fans.
8 Do not wait for the fire to get out of control before calling the fire brigade.

It is important that in all catering establishments passageways are kept clear and that doors open outwards. Fire escape doors and windows should be clearly marked and fire fighting equipment must be readily available and in working order. Periodic fire drills should occur and be taken seriously since lives may be endangered if a fire should start. Fire alarm bells must be tested at least four times a year and staff should be instructed in the use of fire fighting equipment. All extinguishers should be refilled immediately after use.

All fire extinguishers should be manufactured in accordance with British Standard specifications; they should be coloured, with a code to indicate the type and with operating instructions on them.

Red – water
Cream – foam
Black – carbon dioxide

Blue – dry powder
Green – halon (vapourising liquid)

Fire blankets must also conform to British Standards specifications.

Use of portable fire extinguishers

1 Water (red)

Water is used for fire in ordinary combustible materials such as wood, paper etc. Water has better cooling properties than most other agents, therefore it is especially suitable for fires that may start up again if they are not cooled sufficiently. Most water extinguishers contain carbon dioxide gas which expels the water.

Disadvantages

(a) Because water is a conductor of electricity it must never be used on live electrical equipment.
(b) Water must never be used on fat fires because it may cause ignited fat to spread.

FIRE CLASS ACCORDING TO BS 4547, 1970	EXTINGUISHING PRINCIPLES	A.B.C. ALL PURPOSE POWDER (Blue)	CO_2 gas Black	FOAM Cream	WATER Red	B.C.F. (halons) Green
CLASS A Fires involving solid materials usually of organic nature in which combustion normally takes place with the formation of glowing embers. Wood, paper, textiles etc.	Water cooling or combustion inhibition	YES Excellent	NO	YES	YES Excellent	YES
CLASS B Fires involving liquids or liquefiable solids. Burning liquids, oil, fat, paint etc.	Flame inhibiting or surface blanketing and cooling	YES Excellent	YES	YES Excellent	NO	YES
CLASS C Fires involving gases		YES	YES	YES	NO	YES
FIRES INVOLVING ELECTRICAL HAZARDS	Flame inhibiting	YES	YES Excellent	NO	NO	YES

Fig. 11.6 Portable fire extinguishers

2 Foam (cream)

Foam puts out fires by forming a blanket of foam over the top of the fire and smothering it. It is particularly good for putting out fat fires because the foam stays in position and so stops the fire re-igniting. Foam can also be used on fires on natural materials.

Disadvantages

(a) Foam is a conductor of electricity and must not be used on live electrical equipment.
(b) Foam is not effective on free flowing liquids.

3 Carbon dioxide (CO_2) (black)

Carbon dioxide gas is used on fires of inflammable liquids and has the advantage that it does not conduct electricity.

Disadvantage
Carbon dioxide gas has limited cooling properties and therefore is not the most efficient way of putting out a fat fire.

Fig. 11.7 Examples of fire extinguishers

4 Dry powder (blue)

Dry powder is commonly used for fat fires. It does not conduct electricity and some all-purpose powders can be used on fires in natural materials. Powders based on bicarbonate of soda are used in most extinguishers.

Disadvantage
Dry powders usually have limited cooling properties.

5 Halon (green)

The halon used is known as BCF which is short for bromochlorodifluoromethane. This is a gas which does not conduct electricity.

Disadvantage
If used in an enclosed situation halon gives off a thick cloud which can irritate the user's throat and it should not be inhaled.

Choice of fire extinguisher

Type of fire risk	*Type of extinguisher*
1 Fires involving wood, paper, fabrics or similar materials requiring cooling or quenching.	*Water CO_2* (carbon dioxide) Operated by piercing a gas cylinder, the gas then forces the water out. When *hoses* are used for fighting a fire the hose should be connected to the mains water supply. *Soda-acid*
2 Fire involving flammable liquids, petrols, oils, greases, fats requiring rapid action.	*Foam* Contains a small canister within a large one, both containing different chemicals which when mixed form foam. This is forced out of the canister and forms a blanket, so preventing air reaching the fire and thus causing it to go out. *Dry powder* *CO_2 (gas)*
3 Fires involving live electrical apparatus.	A non-conducting extinguishing agent must be used, eg *halon*.

Each extinguisher should be fixed on a suitable bracket, be properly maintained and always available for use, and immediately refilled after use. It is important that staff learn how to use them.

Other extinguishers

Fire hoses
Fire hoses are used for similar fires to those classified under water fire extinguishers. It is necessary to be familiar with the instructions displayed by the fire hose before using it.

Water sprinkler systems
A sprinkler system consists of an array of sprinkler heads at ceiling level connected to a mains water supply. The distances between sprinkler heads and the water pressure required is laid down for each occupancy in the Rules of the Fire Office's Committee for Automatic Sprinkler Installations, 29th Edition. In the event of a fire the nearest sprinkler head above the fire operates when the

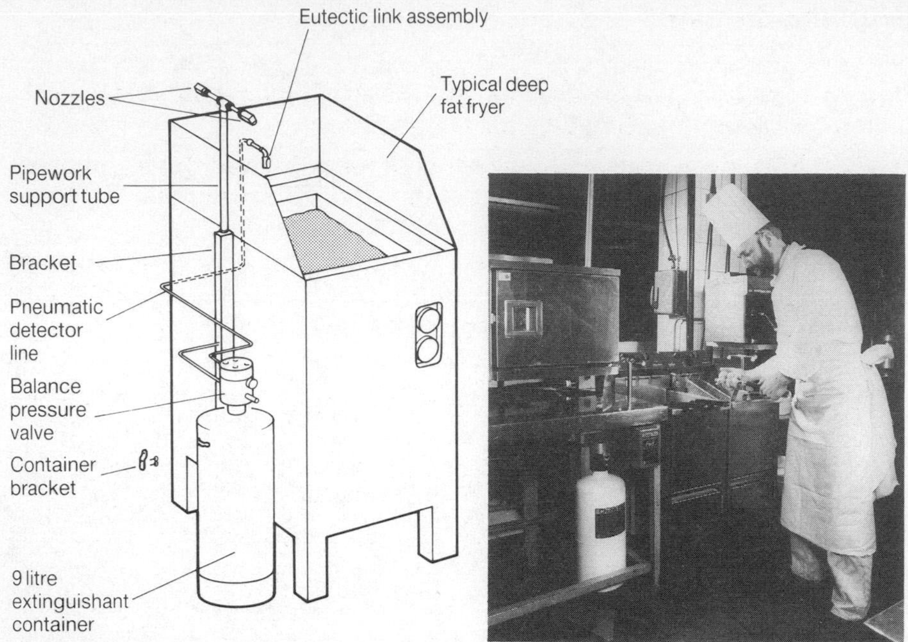

Fig. 11.8 Foam fire extinguishing systems for deep fat fryers

temperature at ceiling level rises above a pre-set level, eg 68°C (154°F) and sprays an area of 12 to 20 sq m. Additional heads operate later if necessary to control the fire.

Research and development by the manufacturers of fire-fighting equipment inevitably leads to changes and increased efficiency in the various appliances; as it is important that the best fire extinguishers are always available, always consult the Fire Prevention Branch of the Fire Brigade, and for a list of approved extinguishers apply to the Fire Officers' Committee.

Further information

Fire Protection Association, 140 Aldersgate Street, London EC1A 4HX.

Working methods

Having read this part of the chapter these learning objectives, both general and specific, should be achieved.

General objectives Be aware of the need for economy of time, energy and materials in the working situation. Develop an attitude to work which conserves energy and saves time and materials.

Specific objectives State examples of smooth work flow in catering situations. Relate the principles of work study so as to implement them by efficient practical application in the working environment.

A skilled craftsman or craftswoman is one who, among other things, completes the skill in the minimal time, to the highest standard and with the *least* effort. Effort requires expenditure of energy, and energy is the commodity which needs to be conserved, not wasted, in the kitchen. Any person working in a hot environment, with the stress of working against the clock, needs to get into the habit of working in such a way that energy is not wasted. To achieve this it is necessary to use common sense and to acquire some knowledge, to practise thinking about how to save energy so that the habit of working methodically and economically becomes second nature. This state of mind can be developed by students producing 12 items even though the real effects will only be evident when producing, say, 100 or 500 items.

The objective is to make work easier and this can be achieved by simplifying the operation, eliminating unnecessary movements, combining two operations into one or improving old methods. For example, if you are peeling potatoes and you allow the peelings to drop into the container in the first place, the action of moving the peelings into the bowl and the need to clean the table could have been eliminated. This operation is simplified if instead of a blunt knife a good hand potato peeler is used, because it is simple and safe to use, requires less effort, can be used more quickly and requires less skill to produce a better result. If the quantity of potatoes is sufficient, then a mechanical peeler could be used, but it would be necessary to remember that the electricity used would add to the cost and that the time needed to clean a mechanical aid may lessen its work-saving value. If it takes 25 minutes to clean a potato mashing machine which has been used to mash potatoes for 500 meals, it could be time well spent in view of the time and energy saved mashing the potatoes. It may not be considered worthwhile using the machine to mash potatoes for 20 meals. Factors such as this need to be taken into account.

Working methods may be observed in catering at many different levels, from the experienced methodical chef wiping the knife after cutting a lemon, to the complexity of the Ganymede system in a large hospital or the carefully planned

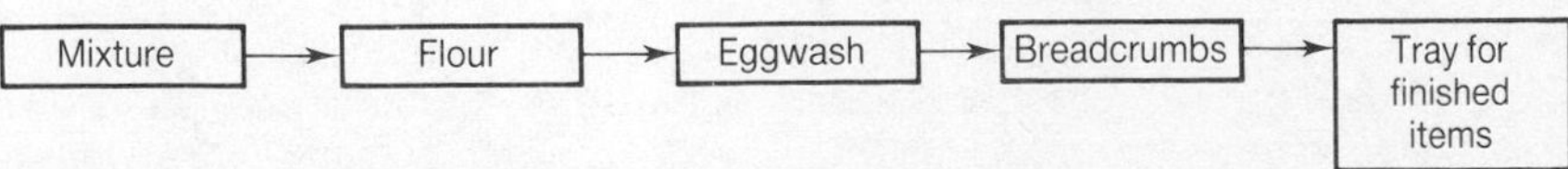

Fig. 11.9 Example to show correct sequence for working methods

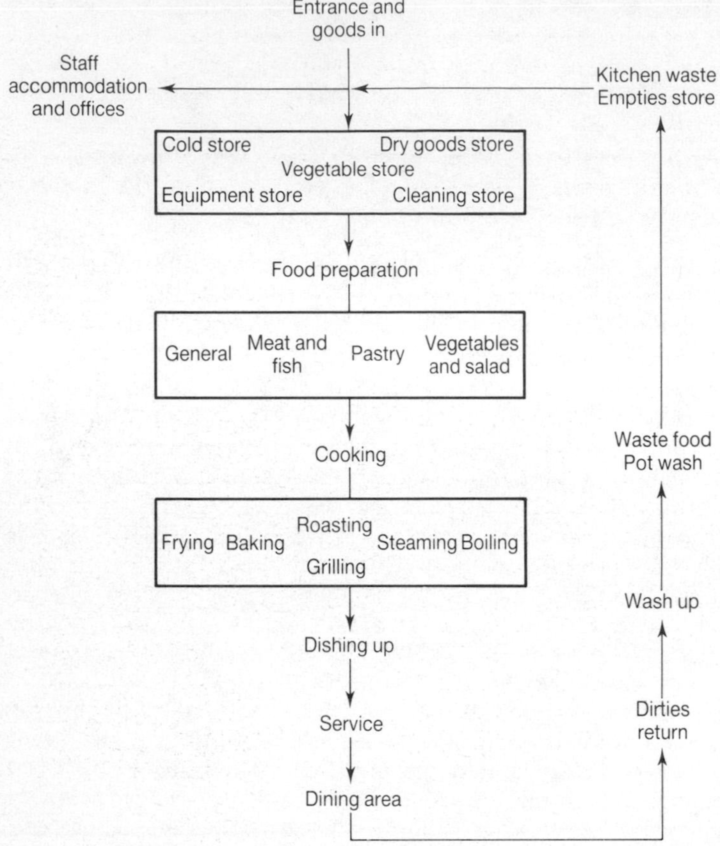

Fig. 11.10 Work flow, incorporating: delivery – storage – preparation – cooking – service

call-order unit in a fast food operation where, because of careful thought and study, wastage of time, money and materials is reduced to a minimum. But even with the aid of mechanical devices, labour-saving equipment and the extensive use of foods which have been partially or totally prepared, people at work still become fatigued. It is most important to stand correctly, well balanced with the weight of the body divided on to both legs with the feet sensibly spaced and the back reasonably straight when working for long periods in one place. Particular care is needed when lifting: it is desirable to stand with legs apart and bend the knees (not the back) and use the leg muscles to assist lifting. The object to be raised should be held close to the body.

It is possible to cultivate the right attitude to work as well as good working habits. Certain jobs are repetitive, some require considerable concentration, while others cause physical strain; not all work provides equal job satisfaction, therefore students need to develop the kind of attitude which is helpful. If 500 fish cakes have to be shaped it is worthwhile setting targets to complete a certain number in a certain time. Such simple things as not counting the completed items but counting those still to be done motivates some people to greater effort.

Some circumstances do not lend themselves to overcoming the physical pressures; for example, if 150 people require 150 omelets then, provided the eggs are broken and seasoned and kept in bulk with the correct size ladle for portioning, the attitude to adopt may be to try to do each omelet better and quicker than the last.

If careful thought and study are given to all practical jobs wastage of time, labour and materials can often be eliminated.

Properly planned layouts with adequate equipment, tools and materials to do the job are essential if practical work is to be carried out efficiently. If equipment is correctly placed then work will proceed smoothly in proper sequence without back-tracking or criss-crossing. Work tables, sinks and stores and refrigerators should be within easy reach in order to eliminate unnecessary walking. Equipment should be easily available during all working times.

Fig. 11.11 Systematic working

The storage, handling of foods, tools and utensils and the movement of food in various stages of production needs careful study. Many people carry out practical work by instinct and often evolve the most efficient method instinctively. Nevertheless careful observation of numerous practical workers will show a great deal of time and effort wasted through bad working methods. It is necessary to arrange work so that the shortest possible distance exists between storage and the place where the items are to be used.

When arranging storage see that the most frequently used items are nearest to hand. Place heavy items where the minimum of body strain is required to move them. Keep all items in established places so that time is not lost in hunting and searching. Adjustable shelving can be a help in organising different storage requirements.

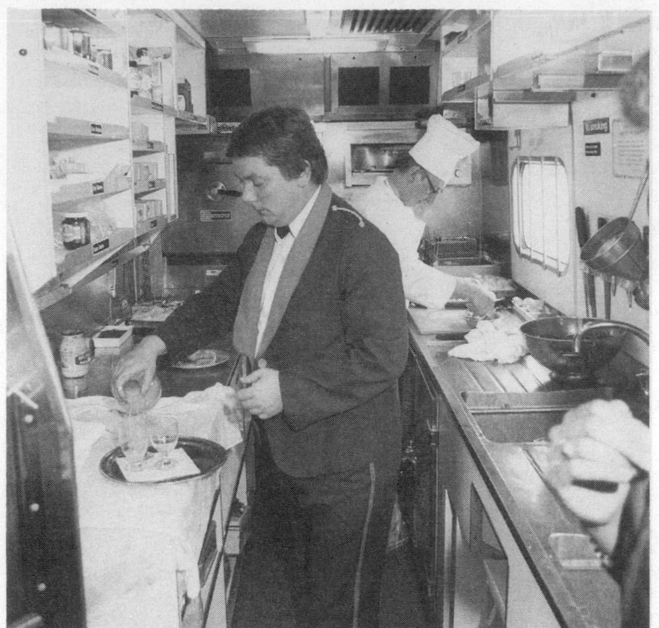

Fig. 11.12 Kitchen and servery on a high-speed train

Only after all the pre-planning of the job is complete comes the actual work itself.

Careful preparation of foods and equipment (a good mise-en-place) is essential if a busy service is to follow and is to be operated efficiently so that orders move out methodically without confusion.

The work to be done must be carefully planned so that the items requiring long preparation or cooking are started first. Where a fast production is required lining up will assist efficiency. Work carried out haphazardly, without plan or organisation, obviously takes longer to do than work done according to plan. There is a sequence to work that leads to high productivity and an efficient worker should learn this sequence quickly.

When preparing French beans they should all be topped and tailed, then cut – not topping, tailing then cutting each bean separately. When cutting food, articles to be cut should be on the left of the chopping board (for right-handed people), drawn with the left hand to the centre of the board, cut and pushed to the right. This should be a continuous, smoothly flowing process.

Food is often wasted by using bad working methods. For example: when preparing spinach, to tip a whole box of spinach into the sink of water, then pick off the stalks so that they drop back on to the unpicked spinach will always result in waste. This is a bad practice used by careless cooks because three-quarters of the way through the job the contents of the sink (including an amount of good spinach) are thrown away. This can happen in the preparation of other vegetables such as sprouts, potatoes, carrots.

These are just a few examples of how planning and working methodically can save time, energy and materials.

Further information
Currie, *Work Study* (Pitman, 1977); Jenkins, *Fast Food Operations* (Barrie and Jenkins).

12 Hygiene

Having read the chapter these learning objectives should be achieved.

General objectives Understand why hygienic practice is essential and know the causes of ill health resulting from failure to exercise sound hygienic principles. Be aware of the need to have a healthy positive attitude and to practise high standards to the benefit of customers, employees, and employers.

Personal hygiene

General objectives Appreciate the need for personal hygiene and know how to maintain good health. Understand why particularly those employed in the catering industry should acquire good hygienic habits. Develop a responsible attitude to hygienic practices.

Specific objectives State why personal hygiene is essential and describe how hygienic standards are achieved. Explain how germs may be transferred from the food handler to equipment, food and to other people in practical situations.

Germs or bacteria are to be found in and on the body and they can be transferred on to anything with which the body comes in contact. Personal cleanliness is essential to prevent germs getting on to food.

Personal cleanliness

Self-respect is necessary in every food-handler because a pride in one's appearance promotes a high standard of cleanliness and physical fitness. Persons suffering from ill-health or who are not clean about themselves should not handle food.

Bathing

It is essential to take a bath or shower every day (or at least two to three times a week); otherwise germs can be transferred on to the clothes and so on to food, particularly in warm weather.

1	**6**
Always wash your hands before touching food, and always after using the toilet.	Clean as you go in food rooms. Keep kitchen equipment and utensils clean.
2	**7**
Tell your supervisor at once of any skin, nose, throat or bowel trouble.	Keep food clean, covered and either cold or piping hot. Separate raw and cooked food.
3	**8**
Cover cuts and sores with waterproof dressings.	Keep your hands off food as far as possible.
4	**9**
Wear clean clothing and be clean.	Keep the lid on the dustbin.
5	**10**
Remember that smoking in a food room is illegal and dangerous. Never cough or sneeze over food.	Do not break the law – Tell your supervisor if you cannot follow the rules.

Always remember – Food Poisoning can kill.

Hands

Hands must be washed thoroughly and frequently; particularly after using the toilet, before commencing work and during the handling of food.

They should be washed in hot water, with the aid of a nail brush and bactericidal soap. This can be dispensed from a fixed container in a liquid or gel form and is preferable to bar soap, which can accumulate germs when passed from hand to hand. After washing, hands should be rinsed, and dried on a *clean* towel, suitable paper towel or by hand hot-air drier. Hands and finger-nails can be a great source of danger if not kept clean, as they can so easily transfer harmful bacteria on to the food.

Rings (except for a plain wedding band), watches and jewellery should not be worn where food is handled. Particles of food may be caught under a ring, and germs could multiply there until they are transferred onto food.

Watches should not be worn because foodstuffs, eg salads and cabbage, which have to be plunged into plenty of water may not be properly washed if a watch is worn. (Apart from this, the steam in a kitchen will ruin watches anyway.)

Jewellery should not be worn, since it may fall off into food, unknown to the wearer; small sleepers for pierced ears are, however, permissible.

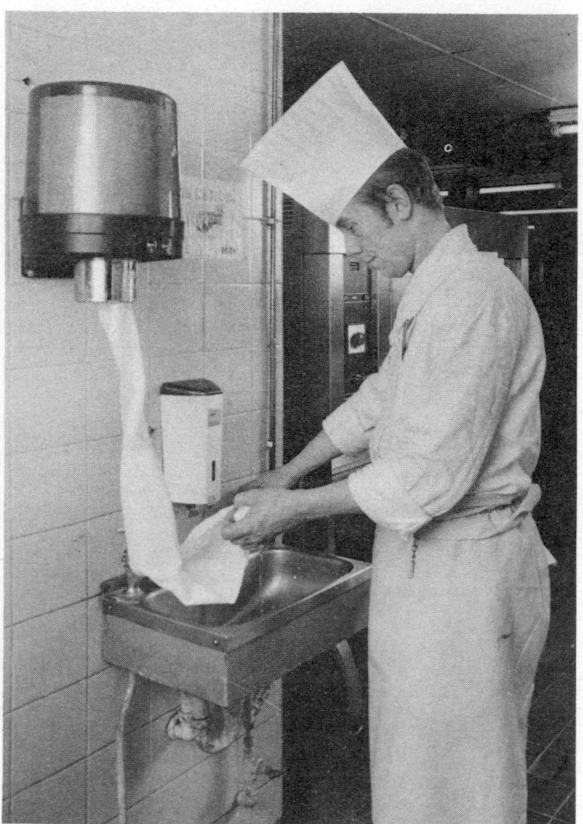

Fig. 12.1 Handwashing point

Finger nails

These should always be kept clean and short as dirt can easily lodge under the nails and be dislodged when, for example, making pastry, so introducing bacteria into food. Nails should be cleaned with a nail brush and nail varnish should not be worn.

Hair
Hair should be washed regularly and kept covered where food is being handled. Hair that is not cared for is likely to come out or shed dandruff which may fall into food. Men's hair should be kept short as it is easier to keep clean; it also looks neater. Women's hair should be covered as much as possible. Both men's and women's hair can be kept in place using hair lacquer or a hair net. The hair should never be scratched, combed or touched in the kitchen, as germs could be transferred via the hands to the food.

Nose
The nose should not be touched when food is being handled. If a handkerchief is used, the hands should be washed afterwards. Ideally, paper handkerchiefs should be used and then destroyed, and the hands washed afterwards. The nose is an area where there are vast numbers of harmful bacteria; it is therefore very important that neither food, people nor working surfaces are sneezed over, so spreading germs.

Mouth
There are many germs in the area of the mouth, therefore the mouth or lips should not be touched by the hands or utensils which may come into contact with food. No cooking utensils should be used for tasting food, nor should fingers be used for this purpose as germs may be transferred to food. A clean teaspoon should be used for tasting, and washed well afterwards.

Coughing over foods and working areas should be avoided as germs are spread long distances if not trapped in a handkerchief.

Ears
The ear-holes should not be handled while in the kitchen as, again, germs can be transferred.

Teeth
Sound teeth are essential to good health. They should be kept clean and visits to the dentist should be regular so that teeth can be kept in good repair.

Feet
As food-handlers are standing for many hours, care of the feet is important. They should be washed regularly and the toe-nails kept short and clean. Tired feet can cause general fatigue which leads to carelessness, and this results in a lowering of the standards of hygiene.

Cuts, burns and sores
It is particularly important to keep all cuts, burns, scratches and similar openings of the skin covered with a waterproof dressing. Where the skin is septic (as with certain cuts, spots, sores, and carbuncles) there are vast numbers of harmful bacteria which must not be permitted to get on food; in most cases people suffering in this way should not handle food.

Cosmetics
Cosmetics, if used by food-handlers, should be used in moderation, but ideally their use should be discouraged. Cosmetics should not be put on in the kitchen

and the hands should be washed well afterwards; they should be put on a clean skin, not used to cover up dirt.

Smoking

Smoking must never take place where there is food, because when a cigarette is taken from the mouth, germs from the mouth can be transferred to the fingers and so on to food. When the cigarette is put down the end which has been in the mouth can transfer germs on to working surfaces. Ash on food is most objectionable and it should be remembered that smoking where there is food is an offence against the law.

Smoking chef fined after health check

A chef carried on smoking as he cut up meat in front of a health investigator, a court heard this week.

The senior environmental officer said that a cat was allowed to walk around while food was being prepared and that staff were wearing dirty overalls.

On a later visit he found the chef smoking a cigarette as he chopped up chicken.

TV pub 'revolting'

A picturesque pub featured in a BBC programme was fined a total of £6,750 yesterday for food hygiene breaches. The magistrate hearing the case described the kitchen as 'absolutely revolting'.

Spitting

Spitting should never occur, because germs can be spread by this objectionable habit.

Clothing and cloths (see also pp. 337–8)

Clean whites (protective clothing) and clean underclothes should be worn at all times. Dirty clothes enable germs to multiply and if dirty clothing comes into contact with food the food may be contaminated. Cloths used for holding hot dishes should also be kept clean as the cloths are used in many ways such as wiping knives, wiping dishes and pans. All these uses could convey germs on to food.

Outdoor clothing, and other clothing which has been taken off before wearing whites, should be kept in a locker away from the kitchen.

General health and fitness

The maintenance of good health is essential to prevent the introduction of germs into the kitchen. To keep physically fit, adequate rest, exercise, fresh air and a wholesome diet are essential.

Sleep and relaxation

Persons employed in the kitchen require adequate sleep and relaxation as they are on the move all the time, often in a hot atmosphere where the tempo of work may be very fast. Frequently, the hours are long or extended over a long period of time, as with split duty, or they may extend into the night. In off-duty periods it may be wise to obtain some relaxation and rest rather than spend all the time energetically. The amount of sleep and rest required depends on each person's needs and the variation between one person and the next is considerable.

Exercise and fresh air
People working in conditions of nervous tension, rush, heat and odd hours need a change of environment and particularly fresh air. Swimming, walking or cycling in the country may be suitable ways of obtaining both exercise and fresh air.

Wholesome food and pure water
A well-balanced diet, correctly cooked, and pure water will assist in keeping kitchen personnel fit. The habit of 'picking' (eating small pieces of food while working) is bad; it spoils the appetite and does not allow the stomach to rest.

Meals should be taken regularly; long periods without food are also bad for the stomach. Pure water is ideal for replacing liquid lost by perspiring in a hot kitchen, or soft drinks may be taken to replace some of the salt as well as the fluid lost in sweating.

Fig. 12.2 Good restroom facilities for staff

Kitchen clothing

It is most important that people working in the kitchen should wear suitable clothing and footwear. Suitable clothing must be:

1 protective;
2 washable;
3 of a suitable colour;
4 light in weight and comfortable;
5 strong;
6 absorbent.

1 Protective

Clothes worn in the kitchen must protect the body from excessive heat. For this reason chefs' jackets are double-breasted and have long sleeves; they are to protect the chest and arms from the heat of the stove and to prevent hot foods or liquids burning or scalding the body.

Aprons: designed to protect the body from being scalded or burned and particularly to protect the legs from any liquids which may be spilled; for this reason the apron should be of sufficient length to protect the legs.

Chef's hat: designed to enable air to circulate on top of the head and thus keep the head cooler. The main purpose of the hat is to prevent loose hairs from dropping into food and to absorb perspiration on the forehead. The use of lightweight disposable hats is both acceptable and suitable.

Footwear: should be stout and kept in good repair so as to protect and support the feet. As the kitchen staff are on their feet for many hours, boots (for men) and clogs (for men and women) give added support and will be found most satisfactory. Modern industrial safety shoes are to be encouraged. Footwear such as sandals, training shoes etc are insufficient protection from spillage of hot liquids.

2 Washable

The clothing should be of an easily washable material as many changes of clothing are required.

3 Colour

White clothing is readily seen to be soiled when it needs to be changed, and there is a tendency to work more cleanly when wearing 'whites'. Chefs' trousers of blue and white check are a practical colour but also require frequent changing.

4 Light and comfortable

Clothing must be light in weight and comfortable, not tight. Heavy clothing would be uncomfortable and a heavy hat in the heat of the kitchen would cause headaches.

5 Strong

Clothes worn in the kitchen must be strong to withstand hard wear and frequent washing.

6 Absorbent

Working over a hot stove causes people to perspire; this perspiration will not evaporate in an inadequately ventilated atmosphere and so underclothes made from absorbent material, such as cotton, should be worn. The hat absorbs perspiration and the neckerchief is used to prevent perspiration from running down the body, for wiping the face and also to protect the neck, which is easily affected by draughts.

Summary of personal hygiene

The practice of clean habits in the kitchen is the only way to achieve a satisfactory standard of hygiene. These habits are as follows:

Hands must be washed frequently and always after using the toilet. Food should be handled as little as possible.

Bathing must occur frequently.

Hair must be kept clean and covered in the kitchen; it should not be combed or handled near food.

Nose and *mouth* should not be touched with the hands.

Cough and *sneeze* in a handkerchief, not over food; people with colds should not be in contact with food.

Jewellery, *rings* and *watches* should not be worn.

Smoking and *spitting* must not occur where there is food.

Cuts and *burns* should be covered with a waterproof dressing.

Clean clothing should be worn at all times and only clean cloths used.

Foods should be tasted with a clean teaspoon.

Tables should not be sat on.

Only healthy people should handle food.

Kitchen hygiene

General objectives Know why premises must be kept clean and understand the need for premises and equipment to be designed for ease of cleaning.

Specific objectives Specify the characteristics of well-designed premises which facilitate cleaning. State the methods for cleaning the various materials used for kitchen equipment and explain how the equipment is cleaned. List the procedure for hygienic and safe cleaning of electrically powered equipment.

Neglect in the care and cleaning of any part of the premises and equipment could lead to a risk of food infection. Kitchen hygiene is of very great importance to:

(a) those who work in the kitchen, because clean working conditions are more agreeable to work in than dirty conditions;
(b) the owners, because custom should increase when the public know the kitchen is clean;
(c) the customer – no one should want to eat food prepared in a dirty kitchen.

Cleaning materials and equipment

To maintain a hygienic working environment a wide range of materials and equipment is needed. These are some of the items which need to be budgeted for, ordered, stored and issued:

brooms	squeegee	flyspray
brushes	scrubbing machine	oven cleaner
buckets	wet suction cleaner	plastic sacks
cloths	dry suction cleaner	scouring powder
dusters	ammonia	soap
dustpans	detergent	soda
dustbins	disinfectant	steel wool
mops	dustbin powder	washing powder
sponges	floor cleaner	

Kitchen premises

Ventilation

Adequate ventilation must be provided so that fumes from stoves are taken out of the kitchen, and stale air in the stores, larder, still-room, etc, is extracted. This is usually effected by erecting hoods over stoves and using extractor fans.

Hoods and fans must be kept clean; grease and dirt are drawn up by the fan and, if they accumulate, can drop on to food. Windows used for ventilation should be screened to prevent entry of dust, insects and birds. Good ventilation facilitates the evaporation of sweat from the body, which keeps one cool.

Lighting
Good lighting is necessary so that people working in the kitchen do not strain their eyes. Natural lighting is preferable to artificial lighting. Good lighting is also necessary to enable staff to see into corners so that the kitchen can be properly cleaned.

Plumbing
Adequate supplies of hot and cold water must be available for keeping the kitchen clean, for cleaning equipment and for staff use. For certain cleaning hot water is essential, and the means of heating water must be capable of meeting the requirements of the establishment.

There must be hand washing and drying facilities and suitable provision of toilets, which must not be in direct contact with any rooms in which food is prepared or stored.

Hand-washing facilities (separate from food preparation sinks) must also be available in the kitchen with a suitable means of drying the hands, eg hot air or paper towels.

Cleaning of toilets and sinks
Toilets must never be cleaned by food-handlers. Sinks and hand basins should be cleaned and thoroughly rinsed.

Floors
Kitchen floors have to withstand a considerable amount of wear and tear, therefore they must be:

(a) capable of being easily cleaned;
(b) smooth, but not slippery;
(c) even;
(d) without cracks or open joints;
(e) impervious (non-absorbent).

Quarry tile floors, properly laid, are suitable for kitchens, since they fulfil the above requirements.

Thorough cleaning is essential: floors are swept, washed with hot detergent water and then dried. This can be done by machine or by hand, and should be carried out at least once a day. As a safety precaution, suitable warning signs should be used to alert staff if the floor is wet.

Walls
Walls should be strong, smooth, impervious, washable and light in colour. The joint between the wall and floor should be rounded for ease of cleaning. Tiling is the best wall surface because it is easily cleaned and requires little further maintenance.

Cleaning: clean with hot detergent water and dry. This will probably be done monthly, but frequency will depend on circumstances.

Ceilings
Ceilings must be free from cracks and flaking. They should not be able to harbour dirt.

Doors and windows
Doors and windows should fit correctly and be clean. The glass should be clean inside and out so as to admit maximum light.

Food lifts
Lifts should be kept very clean and no particles of food should be allowed to accumulate as lift shafts are ideal places for rats, mice and insects to gain access into kitchens.

Cafe boss fined over health risk

A CAFE owner was fined £2,150 after his shop was described as a 'health risk.' Town hall environmental health officers who investigated the cafe discovered there was no running hot water in the store room or kitchen.

Floors, walls and fridges were dirty and staff toilets lacked paper. The court was told that washroom towels were also dirty.

Kitchen equipment, including a bacon slicer, was stained with impregnated and decaying food. Kitchen tiles, shelving and cookers were dirty.

A faulty extractor fan also allowed insects to fly into the kitchen.

Environmental health officers visited the cafe last October as part of the council's Clean Food Campaign.

They recommended that the owner clean up the shop, but when they returned two days later they found virtually nothing had been done.

Hygiene of kitchen equipment (also see Chapter 7)

Kitchen equipment should be so designed that it can be:

(a) cleaned easily;
(b) readily inspected to see that it is clean.

Failure to maintain equipment and utensils hygienically and in good repair may cause food poisoning.

Material used in the construction of equipment must be:

hard so that it does not absorb food particles,
smooth so as to be easily cleaned,
resistant to rust,
resistant to chipping.

Containers, pipes and equipment made from toxic materials, such as lead and zinc, should not be in direct contact with food or drink or be allowed to wear excessively, for example copper pans that need retinning on the inside will expose harmful copper to food. Food must be protected from lubricants.

Easily cleaned equipment is free from unnecessary ridges, screws, ornamentation, dents, crevices or inside square corners, and has large smooth areas. Articles of equipment which are difficult to clean, for example mincers, sieves

Fig. 12.3 Pot and pan washer, specially designed for the proper cleansing of large equipment

and strainers, are items where particles of food can lodge so allowing germs to multiply and contaminate food when the utensil is next used.

Normal cleaning of materials

Metals: as a rule all metal equipment should be cleaned immediately after use.

(a) *Portable items:* remove food particles and grease. Wash by immersion in hot detergent water. Thoroughly clean with a hard bristle brush or soak till this is possible. Rinse in water at 77°C, by immersing in the water in wire racks.
(b) *Fixed items:* remove all food and grease with a stiff brush or soak with a wet cloth, using hot detergent water. Thoroughly clean with hot detergent water. Rinse with clean water. Dry with a clean cloth.

Abrasives should only be used in moderation as their constant scratching of the surface makes it more difficult to clean the article next time.
Marble: scrub with a bristle brush and hot water and then dry.

Wood: scrub with a bristle brush and hot detergent water, rinse and dry.
Plastic: wash in reasonably hot water.
China, earthenware: avoid extremes of heat and do not clean with an abrasive. Wash in hot water and rinse in very hot water.
Copper: remove as much food as possible. Soak. Wash in hot detergent water with the aid of a brush. Clean the outside with a paste made of sand, vinegar and flour. Wash well. Rinse and dry.

Alternatively, a proprietary copper cleaner may be used. Copper pans are gradually being replaced in commercial kitchens, mainly due to the expense involved in retinning.
Aluminium: do not wash in water containing soda as the protective film which prevents corrosion may be damaged. To clean, remove food particles. Soak. Wash in hot detergent water. Clean with steel wool or abrasive. Rinse and dry.
Stainless steel: stainless steel is easy to clean. Soak in hot detergent water. Clean with a brush. Rinse and dry.

Fig. 12.4 Hygienic storage of equipment

Tin: tin which is used to line pots and pans should be soaked, washed in detergent water, rinsed and dried. Tinned utensils, where thin sheet steel has a thin coating of tin, must be thoroughly dried, otherwise they are likely to rust.
Zinc: This is used to coat storage bins of galvanised iron and it should not be cleaned with a harsh abrasive.
Vitreous enamel: clean with a damp cloth and dry. Avoid using abrasives.
Equipment requiring particular care in cleaning (sieves, conical strainers, mincers, graters). Extra attention must be paid to these items, because food particles clog the holes. The holes can be cleaned by using the force of water from the tap, by using a bristle brush and by moving the article, particularly a sieve, up and down in the sink, so causing water to pass through the mesh.

Whisks must be thoroughly cleaned where the wires cross at the end opposite the handle as food can lodge between the wires. The handle of the whisk must also be kept clean.
Saws and choppers, mandolins: these items should be cleaned in hot detergent water, dried and greased slightly.
Tammy cloths, muslins and piping bags: after use they should be emptied, food particles scraped out, scrubbed carefully and boiled. They should then be rinsed and allowed to dry.

Certain piping bags made of plastic should be washed in very hot water and dried. Nylon piping bags should be boiled.

Cleaning of large electrical equipment (ovens, mincers, mixers, choppers, slicers)

1 Switch off the machine and remove the electric plug.
2 Remove particles of food with a cloth, palette knife, needle or brush as appropriate.
3 Thoroughly clean with hand-hot detergent water all removable and fixed parts. Pay particular attention to threads and plates with holes on mincers.
4 Rinse thoroughly.
5 Dry and reassemble.
6 While cleaning see that exposed blades are not left uncovered or unguarded and that the guards are replaced when cleaning is completed.
7 Any specific maker's instructions should be observed.
8 Test that the machine is properly assembled by plugging in and switching on.

Kitchen energy distribution systems

A system of this type operates from stainless steel housings (known as 'raceways') which are fastened to walls, floors, ceilings or may be island mounted. Inside the raceways are runs of electrical bus-bars or bus-wires and plumbing pipes. At intervals, appropriate for the kitchen equipment served, are switch or valve sockets, electrical, gas, water, steam etc.

Connecting flexible cords and pipes from the kitchen equipment plug into the sockets and are designed to hang clear of the floor and are smooth plastic coated for easy cleaning.

For maximum advantage from this idea, the hygiene, safety, flexibility, ease

Fig. 12.5 Identify the faults

of cleaning and maintenance etc, most of the kitchen equipment is mounted on castors.

Periodic cleaning is carried out by pulling the equipment out from the wall or island, unplugging all the services then moving the equipment away on its castors giving free access to all wall and floor surfaces as well as backs and sides of equipment.

Further information
Eurocaddy Systems Ltd, Powder Mill Lane, Dartford, Kent DA1 1NN.

Food hygiene

General objectives Understand the need to know how food may become contaminated and how to prevent this happening.

Specific objectives State the common methods whereby food may become a source of danger to health. List the ways food poisoning can be prevented. Specify the bacterial sources of contamination and the symptoms associated with each. Explain how bacterial growth is dependent on the factors of temperature, time, moisture and suitable food. Identify the foods most likely to need special care.

The most succulent mouth-watering dish into which has gone all the skill and art of the world's best chefs, using the finest possible ingredients, may look, taste and smell superb, yet be unsafe, even dangerous to eat because of harmful bacteria.

Fig. 12.6 Food plated when handler wears plastic gloves

It is of the utmost importance that everyone who handles food, or who works in a place where food is handled, should know that food must be both clean and safe. Hygiene is the study of health and the prevention of disease, and because of the dangers of food poisoning, hygiene requires particular attention from everyone in the catering industry.

There are germs everywhere, particularly in and on our bodies; some of these germs if transferred to food can cause illness and in some cases death. These germs are so small they cannot be seen by the naked eye, yet food which looks

Warning as food bug cases rocket

FOOD poisoning cases are soaring in Britain and the official figures represent only the 'tip of the iceberg' it was claimed yesterday.

There were 30,000 reported cases in 1987, up from 11,000 in 1978. To make matters worse, as many as 90 per cent of cases go unreported, said the director of food hygiene with the Public Health Laboratory Service.

"In most cases the problem lies in the kitchen and the immediate cause is the failure to observe simple rules of food hygiene," he told a seminar in London organised by the Food and Drink Federation.

He added: "There is an urgent need for more education on food hygiene issues, but bacterial food poisoning could be eliminated altogether if a few key points were followed."

He said people should keep the kitchen clean, wash their hands before preparing food, avoid cross-contamination between cooked and uncooked foods, always thaw, cook and reheat food adequately, and store food properly.

Most people did not realise storing food at room temperature could allow micro-organisms to grow, he said. And only half those questioned in a nationwide survey were aware of the possibility of one high-risk food dripping on to and contaminating another in the fridge.

Salmonella is present in about 60 per cent of raw and frozen chickens.

Thorough cooking destroys the bacteria. But if the bird has not been thawed properly in the fridge before cooking, the salmonella can survive and multiply, causing food poisoning.

And pre-cooked meals should not be stored beyond their recommended date.

The head of food science with the Ministry of Agriculture said that a Ministry survey of 2,000 households showed a widespread unawareness of basic rules of hygiene in the kitchen.

The Ministry of Agriculture is recommending that the Education Department introduces food hygiene into the school science curriculum, so that boys and girls learn the basics at the beginning.

clean and does not smell or taste bad may be dangerous to eat if harmful germs have contaminated it and multiplied.

The duty of every person concerned with food is to prevent contamination of food by germs and to prevent these germs or bacteria from multiplying.

Food-handlers must know the Food Hygiene Regulations, but no matter how much is written or read about food hygiene the practice of hygienic habits by people who handle food is the only way to safe food.

Food poisoning

Over twenty thousand people each year have been found by doctors to be suffering from food poisoning. This represents the average number of notified cases over the last few years, and there are thousands more who have not

25 hospital kitchens ban fresh eggs

FRESH eggs have been banned from the kitchen of 25 hospitals in one area because of fears that they may be a source of salmonella infection.

The health authority is switching its weekly order for 7,200 eggs to liquefied, pasteurised eggs after an outbreak of 78 cases of food poisoning.

The Government warned people last week against eating raw or undercooked eggs and researchers have since found that even cooked eggs may be a source of infection by a strain of bacteria called salmonella enteritidis.

A spokesman for the health authority said 'Until we get much clearer guidelines we are not going to take chances with the sick and the elderly.'

Farming practices had changed in recent years, he said, "and this bacterium is now a lot stronger that it was and is finding itself in a lot more places than before".

A spokesman for the Ministry of Agriculture said the risks from eggs were very small and described the area's action as "rather alarmist".

A Health Department spokesman said that caterers were advised to use pasteurised liquid egg.

The advice is reinforced by a study by Public Health Laboratory doctors of four cases of Salmonella enteritidis poisoning.

The foods blamed for the outbreaks included home-made ice cream containing raw egg, scrambled eggs, egg sandwiches and Scotch egg.

Writing in the *Lancet*, the doctors say all eggs should be regarded as possibly infected.

notified their doctor, but have suffered from food poisoning. This appalling amount of ill-health could largely be prevented. Failure to prevent it may be due to:

(a) ignorance of the rules of hygiene;
(b) carelessness, thoughtlessness or neglect;
(c) poor standards of equipment or facilities to maintain hygienic standards;
(d) accident.

Food poisoning can be prevented by:

1 High standards of personal hygiene.
2 Attention to physical fitness.
3 Maintaining good working conditions.
4 Maintaining equipment in good repair and in clean condition.
5 Adequate provision of cleaning facilities and cleaning equipment.
6 Correct storage of foodstuffs at the right temperature.
7 Correct reheating of food.
8 Quick cooling of foods prior to storage.
9 Protection of foods from vermin and insects.
10 Hygienic washing-up procedure.
11 Food-handlers knowing how food poisoning is caused.
12 Food-handlers not only knowing but carrying out procedures to prevent food poisoning.

What is food poisoning?

Food poisoning can be defined as an illness characterised by stomach pains and diarrhoea and sometimes vomiting, developing within one to 36 hours after eating the affected food.

Fig. 12.7 Poisoned any good customers lately?

60 workers hit by food bug in City

Bank and finance house workers from the City overwhelmed Bart's Hospital's casualty department yesterday after a food poisoning outbreak. The London ambulance service carried 26 victims to hospital and many others staggered in by themselves after lunch.

50 casualties with sickness, dizziness and diarrhoea were treated and another nine were at a neighbouring hospital.

City of London police said the source of the outbreak was believed to be a high-class mobile food firm which delivers to businesses.

A spokesman said: "It appears that all the workers had lunches from the same firm. We are not disclosing the firm's name at the moment, although we have been given it."

A spokesman said: "We are hoping to get most of the casualties out tonight.

"We are rushed off our feet and have had to call in back-up staff."

None was reported as being seriously ill.

Causes of food poisoning

Food poisoning results when harmful foods are eaten. They may be harmful because:

(a) *Chemicals* have entered foods accidentally during the growth, preparation or cooking of the food.
(b) *Germs* (harmful bacteria) have entered the food from humans, animals or other sources and the bacteria themselves, or the toxins (poisons) produced in the food by certain bacteria, have caused the foods to be harmful. By far the greatest number of cases of food poisoning is caused by harmful bacteria.

Chemical food poisoning

Certain chemicals may accidentally enter food and cause food poisoning.

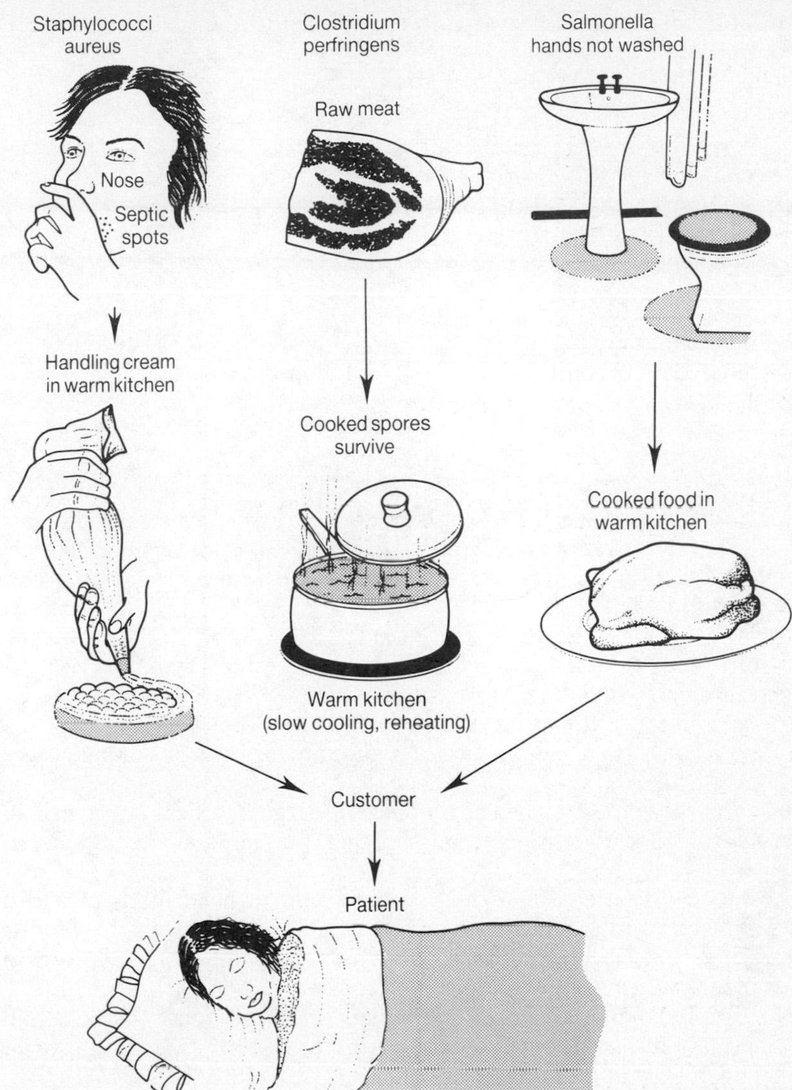

Fig. 12.8 How food poisoning may be caused

Arsenic is used to spray fruit during growth, and occasionally fruit has been affected by this poison.

Lead poisoning can occur from using water that has been in contact with lead pipes and then drunk or used for cooking.

Antimony or *zinc:* acid foods if stored or cooked in poor quality enamelled or galvanised containers can also cause poisoning.

Copper pans should be correctly tinned and never used for storing foods, particularly acid foods, as the food could dissolve harmful amounts of copper.

Certain *plants* are poisonous: for example, poisonous fungi. Rhubarb leaves and

the parts of potatoes which are exposed to the sun above the surface of the soil are also poisonous.
Rat poison may accidentally contaminate food.

Prevention of chemical food poisoning
Chemical food poisoning can be prevented by:

(a) using correctly maintained and suitable kitchen utensils;
(b) obtaining foodstuffs from reliable sources;
(c) care in the use of rat poison, etc.

Bacterial food poisoning
Food contaminated by bacteria (germs) is by far the most common cause of food poisoning.

Bacteria

Bacteria are minute, single-celled organisms which can only be seen under a microscope. They are everywhere in our surroundings, and as most bacteria cannot move by themselves they are transferred to something by coming into direct contact with it.

Some bacteria form spores which can withstand high temperatures for long periods of time (even 6 hours) and on return to favourable conditions become normal bacteria again which then multiply.

Some bacteria produce toxins outside their bodies so that they mix with the food; the food itself is then poisonous and symptoms of food poisoning follow within a few hours.

Other bacteria cause food poisoning by virtue of large numbers of bacteria in food entering the digestive system, multiplying further and setting up an infection.

Certain bacteria produce toxins which are resistant to heat; foods in which this toxin has been produced may still cause illness, even though the food is heated to boiling-point and boiled for half an hour. Some bacteria will grow in the absence of air (anaerobes), others need it (aerobes).

Bacteria multiply by dividing in two, under suitable conditions, once every 20 minutes. Therefore one bacterium could multiply in 10 to 12 hours to between 500 million and 1000 million bacteria.

Not all bacteria are harmful. Some are useful, for example, those used in cheese production; some cause food spoilage, for example souring of milk.

Some bacteria which are conveyed by food cause diseases other than food poisoning. These include typhoid, paratyphoid, dysentery and scarlet fever. In these cases the bacteria do not multiply in the food, they are only carried by it and the disease is known as a food-borne disease. With bacterial food poisoning the bacteria multiply in the food.

The time between eating the contaminated food (ingestion) to the beginning of the symptoms of the illness (onset) depends on the type of bacteria which have caused the illness.

Conditions favourable to bacterial growth
For the multiplication of bacteria certain conditions are necessary:

1 *Food* of the right kind.
2 *Temperature* must be suitable.
3 *Moisture* must be adequate.
4 *Time* must pass.

Food

Most foods are easily contaminated; those less likely to cause food poisoning have a high concentration of vinegar, sugar or salt, or are preserved in some special way (see Chapter 14).

Foods most easily contaminated: the following foods are particularly susceptible to the growth of bacteria because of their composition. Extra care must be taken to prevent them from being contaminated.

1 Stock, sauces, gravies, soups.
2 Meat and meat products (sausages, pies, cold meats).
3 Milk and milk products.
4 Eggs and egg products.
5 All foods which are handled.
6 All foods which are reheated.

Temperature

Food poisoning bacteria multiply rapidly at body temperature, 37°C. They grow between temperatures of 10°C and 63°C. This is a similar heat to a badly

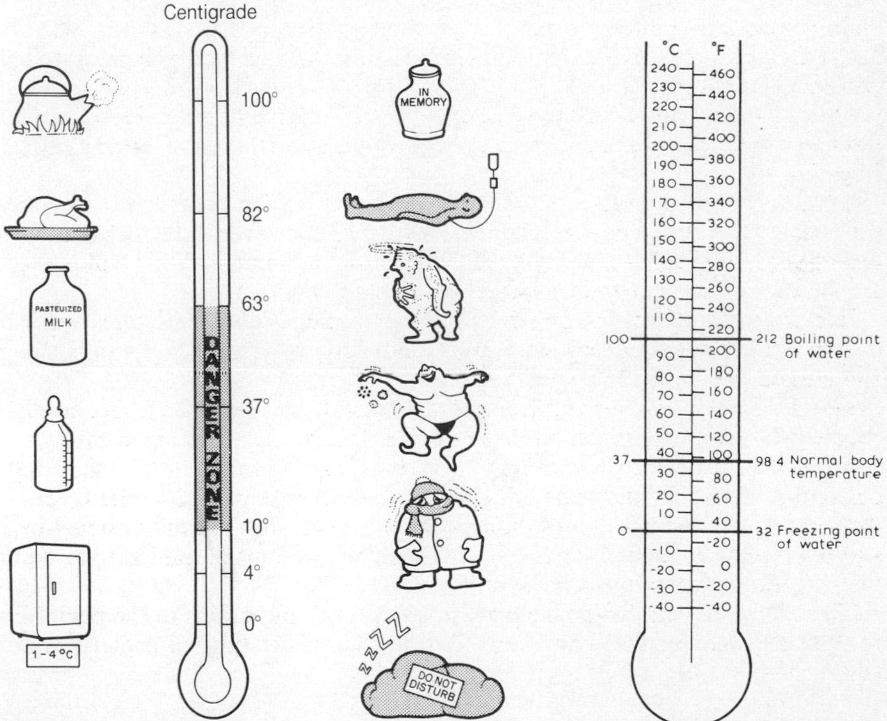

Fig. 12.9 Germometer

ventilated kitchen and for this reason foods should not be kept in the kitchen. They should be kept in the larder or refrigerator. Lukewarm water is an ideal heat for bacteria to grow in. Washing-up must not take place in warm water as bacteria are not killed and the conditions are ideal for their growth, therefore pots and pans, crockery and cutlery may become contaminated. Hot water must be used for washing up (see Fig. 12.9).

Boiling will kill bacteria in a few seconds, but to destroy toxins boiling for a half-hour is necessary. To kill the most heat-resistant of spores, 4 to 5 hours' boiling is required. It is important to remember that it is necessary not only to heat foods to a sufficiently high temperature but also for a sufficient length of time to be sure of safe food. Extra care should be taken in warm weather to store foods at low temperatures and to reheat thoroughly foods which cannot be boiled.

Bacteria are not killed by cold although they do not multiply at very low temperatures, for example in a deep freeze they lie dormant for long periods. If foods have been contaminated before being made cold, on raising the temperature the bacteria will multiply. Foods which have been taken out of the refrigerator, kept in a warm kitchen and returned to the refrigerator for use later on may well be contaminated.

Moisture

Bacteria require moisture for growth – they cannot multiply on dry food. Ideal foods for their growth are jellies with meats, custards, creams, sauces, etc.

Time

Under ideal conditions one bacterium divides into two every 20 minutes; in five

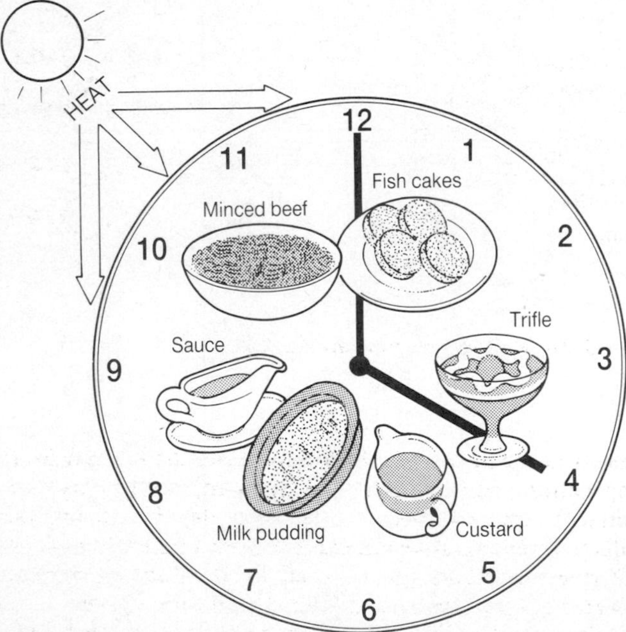

Fig. 12.10 Germs multiplying on moist foods in warm temperature over time

to six hours millions of bacteria will have been produced. Small numbers of bacteria may have little effect, but in a comparatively short time sufficient numbers can be produced to cause food poisoning. Particular care therefore is required with foods stored overnight, especially if adequate refrigerated space is not available.

Types of food poisoning bacteria

The commonest food poisoning bacteria are:

1 The *salmonella* group (cause food poisoning because of large numbers of bacteria in the food).
2 *Staphylococcus aureus* (causes food poisoning due to poison (toxin) production in the food).
3 *Clostridium perfringens* (causes food poisoning due to large numbers of bacteria producing toxins in the intestines).

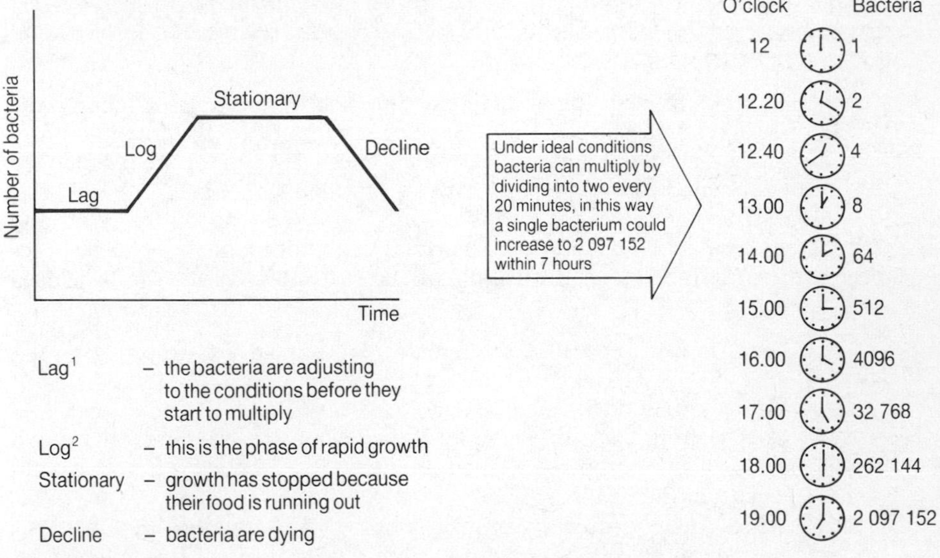

Fig. 12.11 Danger temperature at which germs can multiply

Salmonella group

These bacteria can be present in the intestines of animals or human beings; they are excreted and anything coming into contact directly or indirectly with the excreta may be contaminated, eg raw meat at the slaughter house or the unwashed hands of an infected person. Infected excreta from human beings or animals may contaminate rivers and water to be used for drinking purposes, although chlorination of water is very effective in killing harmful bacteria.

Salmonella infection is the result of human beings or animals eating food contaminated by salmonella-infected excreta originating from human beings or

Food poisoning hits conference

Doctors attending a conference on diabetes at the weekend were struck down with food poisoning, believed to be salmonella.

Four hundred clinicians, nurses and health specialists had eaten cold meats, meat pies, seafood and salad at Friday lunchtime.

That evening two of the delegates were admitted to the casualty department with severe vomiting and diarrhoea. The next day a further 23 people with suspected salmonella poisoning were admitted to the hospital.

By Saturday evening 35 people had been seen, some at neighbouring hospitals and 80 people had reported symptoms of food poisoning.

VIPs food poison alert

More than 150 VIPs at two banquets in the city of London are suspected victims of food poisoning.

Salmonella is believed to be the cause and suspicion has centred on a cheese and egg savoury – Canape Roquefort – which was on both menus.

animals, so completing a chain of infection. For example, when flies land on the excreta of a dog which has eaten infected dog-meat and the flies then go on to food, if that food is then left out in warm conditions for a time, the people who eat the contaminated food could well suffer from food poisoning.

Foods affected by the salmonella group: the most affected are poultry, meat and eggs (rarely processed egg products or duck eggs, although some hen's eggs have been found to be infected with salmonellae). Contamination can be caused by:

1 Insects and vermin, because salmonellae are spread by droppings, feet, hairs, etc.
2 The food itself may be infected (as, very occasionally, with duck eggs).
3 By cross contamination: for example, if a chicken is eviscerated on a board and the board is not properly cleaned before another food (for example, cold meat), is cut on the board.
4 The food could be infected by a human being who has the disease or who is a carrier (a person who does not suffer from food poisoning but who carries and passes on the germs to others).

Staphylococci aureus

These germs are present on human hands and other parts of the skin, or sores, spots, etc, and in the nose and throat.

Foods affected by staphylococci aureus: foods which have been handled are often contaminated because the hands have been infected from the nose or throat, cuts, etc. Brawn, pressed beef, pies and custards are foods frequently contaminated (either by food handlers or air-borne infection) because they are ideal foods for the multiplication of the bacterium.

Clostridium perfringens

These bacteria are distributed from the intestines of humans and animals and are found in the soil.

Foods affected by clostridium perfringens: raw meat is the main source of these bacteria, the spores of which survive light cooking.

Clostridium botulinum is another type of bacteria which causes food poisoning, but it is rare in the UK.

Campylobacter bacteria are a common cause of diarrhoea in the UK. Large numbers are not required to cause illness (see food-borne disease, p. 366); poultry and meats are the main foods infected but adequate cooking will kill the bacteria.

Bacillus cereus: this bacterium is found in soil where vegetables and cereals, like rice, may grow. Long, moist storage of warm cooked food, especially rice, allows the spores to revert to bacteria which multiply and produce toxin.

Listeria: bacteria from this genus are aerobic, non-sporing organisms which can cause serious food-borne disease, particularly in the elderly, the chronically sick or babies. These bacteria are found in soil, vegetables and animal feed. They are killed by correct cooking but grow at refrigeration temperatures and in mildly acidic conditions such as that found in soft cheeses where lactic acid is present.

There is particular concern over contamination of pre-packed salads and chilled raw chicken. Although it is unlikely that a small number of organisms would cause any harm to healthy people, the bacteria can cause illness in vulnerable groups – even infecting young babies in the womb.

Sources of infection

Food-poisoning bacteria live in:

(a) the soil;
(b) humans – intestines, nose, throat, skin, cuts, sores, spots, etc;
(c) animals, insects and birds – intestines and skin, etc.

Prevention of food poisoning from bacteria

To prevent food poisoning everyone concerned with food must:

(a) prevent bacteria from multiplying;
(b) prevent bacteria from spreading from place to place.

This means harmful bacteria must be isolated, the route of infection must be broken and conditions favourable to their growth eliminated. (The conditions favourable to their growth – heat, time, moisture and a suitable food on which to grow – are explained above.) It is also necessary to prevent harmful bacteria being brought into premises or getting on to food. This is achieved by a high standard of hygiene of personnel, premises, equipment and food-handling.

Spread of infection

1 Human: coughing, sneezing, by the hands.
2 Animals, insects, birds: droppings, hair, etc.
3 Inanimate objects: towels, dishcloths, knives, boards.

Human

People who are feeling ill, suffering from vomiting, sore throat or head cold must not handle food.

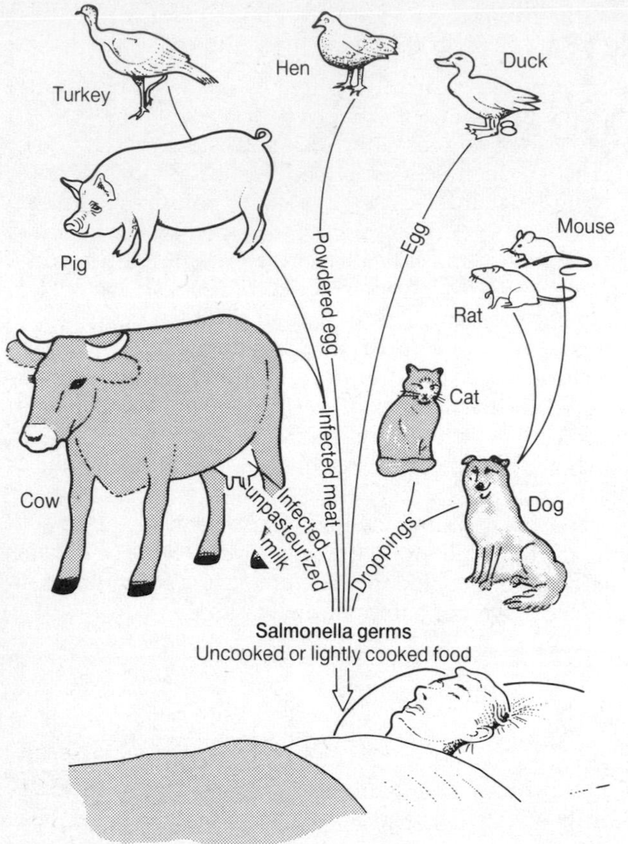

Fig. 12.12 Foods contaminated by salmonella germs if uncooked or lightly cooked may result in food poisoning

As soon as a person becomes aware that he or she is suffering from, or is a carrier of, typhoid or paratyphoid fever, or salmonella or staphylococcal infection likely to cause food poisoning or dysentery, the person responsible for the premises must be informed. He or she must then inform the Medical Officer for Health.

Standards of personal hygiene should be high at all times (see section on personal hygiene, p. 332).

Animal

Vermin, insects, domestic animals and birds can bring infection into food premises.

Rats and *mice* are a dangerous source of food infection because they carry harmful bacteria on themselves and in their droppings. Rats infest sewers and drains and, since excreta is a main source of food-poisoning bacteria, it is therefore possible for any surface touched by rats to be contaminated.

Rats and mice frequent warm dark corners and are found in lift shafts, meter

Poison curry starts epidemic alert

Health chiefs warned of a deadly food poisoning epidemic last night as they tried to trace more than 1,000 party guests who ate contaminated curry.

They fear many people who had the lamb dish may be unaware that they have caught para-typhoid fever.

The rare disease, which can cause fatal blood poisoning, could spread rapidly if any victims are employed in the food industry.

Already 40 of those who attended the party have been taken ill.

Eleven people are seriously ill in hospital.

Another nine suspected cases were reported yesterday as a team of 30 health visitors made house-to-house inquiries trying to track down the guests.

It is feared that as many as 200 people may have contracted the disease.

The food was prepared and left overnight in an old factory before it was taken to the party. Some of the guests ate vegetable curry, but many had lamb.

Para-typhoid, an extreme form of food poisoning, is rare in Britain. The symptoms are like flu and include feverishness, diarrhoea and headaches.

Officials fear that some family doctors may fail to recognise the symptoms.

The disease can be fatal in the very young and elderly and those already suffering from another illness.

The Environmental Medical Officer said: 'At worst there could be a national epidemic of frightening proportions.

'If someone infected was working in a dairy and contaminated bulk supplies of milk, who knows how many cases we might get.

'For that reason we are extremely anxious to trace everyone who attended the party.'

Fig. 12.13 Pests and the damage they cause

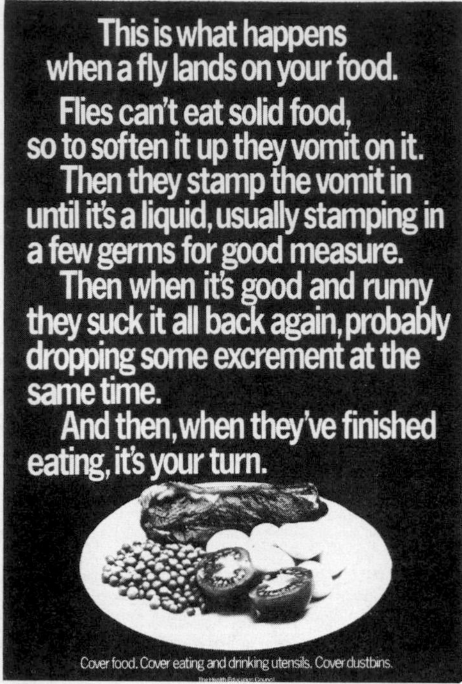

This is what happens
when a fly lands on your food.
Flies can't eat solid food,
so to soften it up they vomit on it.
Then they stamp the vomit in
until it's a liquid, usually stamping in
a few germs for good measure.
Then when it's good and runny
they suck it all back again, probably
dropping some excrement at the
same time.
And then, when they've finished
eating, it's your turn.
Cover food. Cover eating and drinking utensils. Cover dustbins.

Fig. 12.14 Food poisoning

cupboards, lofts, opening in walls where pipes enter, under low shelves and on high shelves. They enter premises through any holes, defective drains, open doorways and in sacks of food-stuffs.

Signs to look for are droppings, smears, holes, runways, gnawing marks, grease marks on skirting boards and above pipes, clawmarks, damage to stock and also rat odour. (See Fig. 12.13.)

Rats spoil ten times as much food as they eat and there are at least as many rats as human beings. They are very prolific, averaging ten babies per litter and six litters per year, so that under ideal conditions it is theoretically possible for one pair of rats to increase to 350 million in three years. To prevent infestation from rats and mice the following measures should be taken:

(a) Food stocks should be moved and examined to see that no rats or mice have entered the store-room.
(b) No scraps of food should be left lying about.
(c) Dustbins and swill-bins should be covered with tight-fitting lids.
(d) No rubbish should be allowed to accumulate outside the building.
(e) Buildings must be kept in good repair.
(f) Premises must be kept clean.

If premises become infested with rats or mice the environmental health inspector or a pest control contractor should be contacted.

Fig. 12.15 Electrical lamp equipment to attract, kill and collect winged insects

Insect infection

House flies are the foremost of the insects which spread infection. Flies alight on filth and contaminate their legs, wings and bodies with harmful bacteria, and deposit these on the next object on which they settle; this may well be food. They also contaminate food with their excreta and saliva. (See Fig. 12.14.)

To control flies, the best way is to eliminate their breeding place. As they breed in rubbish and in warm, moist places, dustbins in summer are ideal breeding grounds, therefore:

1 Dustbins and swill-bins must be kept covered at all times with tight-fitting lids and the surrounding area kept clean.
2 The bins must be kept clean and sprayed with insecticide.
3 Ideally, dustbins and swill-bins should not be kept. Rubbish should be burnt immediately if it cannot be disposed of through a waste-master.
4 Paper or plastic lined bins which are destroyed with the rubbish are preferable to other types of bin.

Other ways to control flies are to:

(a) Screen windows to keep flies out of kichens.
(b) Install ultra-violet electrical fly-killers.
(c) Use sprays to kill flies (only where there is no food).
(d) Employ a pest control contractor.

Cockroaches: cockroaches like warm, moist, dark places. They leave their droppings and a liquid which gives off a nauseating odour. They can carry harmful bacteria on their bodies and deposit them on anything with which they come into contact.

Silverfish: these small silver-coloured insects feed on starchy foods (among other things) and are found on moist surfaces. They thrive in badly ventilated areas and improving ventilation will help to control silverfish.
Beetles: beetles are found in warm places and can also carry harmful germs from place to place.

Insects are destroyed by using an insecticide, and it is usual to employ people familiar with this work. The British Pest Control Association has a list of member companies.

Cats and dogs

Domestic pets should not be permitted in kitchens or on food premises as they carry harmful bacteria on their coats and are not always clean in their habits. Cats also introduce fleas and should not be allowed to go into places where food is prepared.

Birds

Entry of birds through windows should be prevented as food and surfaces on which food is prepared may be contaminated by droppings.

Dust

Dust contains bacteria, therefore it should not be allowed to settle on food or surfaces used for food. Kitchen premises should be kept clean so that no dust can accumulate. Hands should be cleaned after handling dirty vegetables.

Washing up

The correct cleaning of all equipment used for the serving and cooking of food is of vital importance to prevent multiplication of bacteria. This cleaning may be divided into the pan wash (plonge) or scullery and the china wash-up.

Scullery

For the effective washing up of pots and pans and other kitchen equipment the following method of work should be observed:

1 Pans should be scraped and all food particles placed in a bin.
2 Hot pans should be allowed to cool before being plunged into water.
3 Pans which have food stuck to them should be allowed to soak (pans used for starchy foods, such as porridge and potatoes, are best soaked in cold water).
4 Frying-pans should be thoroughly wiped with a clean cloth, they should not be washed unless absolutely necessary.
5 Trays and tins used for pastry work should be thoroughly cleaned with a clean dry cloth, while warm.
6 Pots, pans and other equipment should be washed and cleaned with a stiff brush, steel wool or similar article, in hot detergent water.
7 The washing-up water must be changed frequently; it must be kept both clean and hot.
8 The cleaned items should be rinsed in very hot clean water to sterilise.
9 Pans, etc, which have been sterilised (minimum temperature 77°C) dry

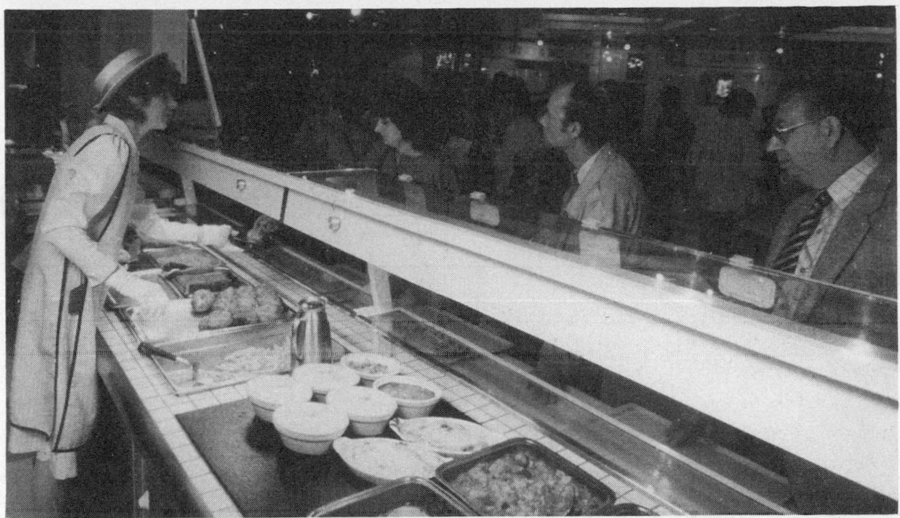

Fig. 12.16 Hygienic service at the hot food counter

quickly; if it has not been possible to rinse in very hot water they should be dried with a clean cloth.

10 Equipment should be stored on clean racks, pans should be stacked upside down.

China wash-up

The washing up of crockery and cutlery may be by hand or machine.

Handwashing:

1 Remove scraps from plates with a scraper or by hand.
2 Wash in water containing a detergent as hot as the hands can bear (whether gloves are worn or not).
3 Place in wire baskets and immerse them into water thermostatically controlled at 77°–82°C for at least 2 minutes.
4 The hot utensils will air-dry without the use of a drying cloth.
5 Both the washing and sterilising water must be kept clean and at the correct temperature.

Machine washing-up: there are several types of machines which wash and sterilise crockery. In the more modern machines the detergent is automatically fed into the machine, which has continuous operation. To be effective the temperature of the water must be high enough to kill any harmful bacteria and the articles passing through the machine must be subjected to the water for sufficient time to enable the detergent water to cleanse all the items thoroughly. The detergent used must be of the correct amount and strength to be effective. Alternatively low temperature equipment is available which sterilises by means of a chemical, sodium hypochlorite (bleach).

Where brushes are used they must be kept free from food particles.

Further information
Lever Industrial, Lever House, St James's Road, Kingston-upon-Thames, Surrey KT1 2 BA.

Hygienic storage of foods

One of the most important ways to prevent contamination of food is the correct storage of food (see also Chapter 6). Foodstuffs of all kinds should be kept covered as much as possible to prevent infection from dust and flies. Foods should be kept in a refrigerated cold room or refrigerator where possible.

Hot foods which have to go into a refrigerator must be cooled quickly. This can be done in several ways: by dividing large quantities of food into smaller containers; by cooling in a draught of air using fans or by raising the container and placing an article underneath, for example, a triangle or weight, so that air can circulate; or by placing the container in a sink with running cold water. If large quantities of food, for example minced beef, are left in one container the outside cools but the centre is still warm. When reheated the time taken to bring such a large quantity to the boil is sufficient to allow the bacteria to continue to multiply. If the food is not boiled long enough food poisoning can occur (see Temperature, p. 353).

Particular care must be taken to store foods correctly in the warmer months; food not refrigerated in hot weather does not cool completely and, furthermore, flies and bluebottles are numerous in the summer. It is not by chance that the vast majority of food poisoning cases occur in the summer months in the UK.

Foods requiring special attention

Meat

1 All made-up dishes, such as cottage pie, need extra care. They must be very thoroughly cooked.
2 Reheated meat dishes must be thoroughly reheated.
3 Pork must be well cooked (this is because pork may be affected by trichinosis, which is a disease caused by tapeworm).
4 Poultry which is drawn in the kitchen should be cleaned carefully; boards, tables and knives must be thoroughly cleaned afterwards, otherwise there is a danger of contamination from excreta.
5 Meat should be handled as little as possible. Minced and cut-up meats are more likely to become contaminated because of infection from the food-handler. Boned and rolled joints require extra care in cooking as inside surfaces may have been contaminated.
6 Sausages should be cooked right through.
7 Tinned hams are lightly cooked, therefore they must be stored in a refrigerator.

Fish

Fish is usually washed, cooked and eaten fresh and is not often a cause of food poisoning, except in reheated fish dishes. Care must be taken to reheat thoroughly such dishes as fish cakes, fish pie, coquilles de poisson, etc.

Some fish, such as oysters and mussels, have caused food poisoning because they have been bred in water which has been polluted by sewage. They are today purified before being sold. All shellfish should be used fresh. If bought alive, there is no doubt as to their freshness.

Eggs

Both hens' eggs and ducks' eggs have been implicated in causing food poisoning, and Department of Health guidelines now suggest that it would be prudent to avoid eating raw eggs or uncooked foods made from them, such as home-made mayonnaise, home-made mousses etc. If dried eggs are used they should be reconstituted and used right away, not left in this condition in a warm kitchen as they may have been contaminated in or after processing. Bulk liquid egg undergoes pasteurisation but may be contaminated after the container is opened. Hollandaise sauce which is made with eggs is an example of a food which should not be kept in a warm kitchen for long. If not used in the morning it should not be used in the evening.

Milk

When used in custards, trifles, puddings, etc, unless eaten soon after preparation, milk should be treated with care. If required for the following day these dishes must be refrigerated.

Watercress and other green salad

Watercress must be thoroughly washed, as it grows in water which could be contaminated by animals. All green salads and other foods eaten raw should be well washed.

Synthetic cream

Synthetic cream can be a cause of food poisoning if allowed to remain in warm conditions for long periods. It is easily contaminated by handling and from the air.

Particular care is required in the handling and holding at the correct temperature of soups, sauces and gravies because bacteria multiply more rapidly in these foods.

Reheated foods (*rechauffé*)

In the interests of economy a sound knowledge of handling left-over food is necessary. Many tasty dishes can be prepared, but care must always be taken to see that the food is thoroughly and carefully reheated. If care is not taken then food poisoning can result (see p. 354). Only sound food should be used ('if in doubt, throw it out').

After each meal service all unserved food should be cleared away in clean dishes, cooled quickly in the larder and placed in a cold room or refrigerator.

A good hors-d'œuvrier can make interesting dishes out of left-over meats, poultry, fish and certain vegetables by mixing them with foods such as rice, gherkins, tomatoes, chives, parsley and a well-seasoned dressing such as mayonnaise or vinaigrette.

Trimmings and bones of meat, game and poultry should be used for stock. Trimmings of meat fat cooked or uncooked should be minced and rendered down for dripping.

Fish: cooked kippers and haddock may be turned into savouries if freed from skin and bone, finely minced or pounded with anchovy essence and a little butter and used as a spread on toast.

Cold fish may be used in many interesting dishes. For example:

curried fish
fish cakes
fish cutlets or croquettes
fish pie
fish kedgeree
fish salad

Vegetables: cold left-over cooked vegetables such as peas, cauliflower, haricot beans, potatoes, may be mixed with vinaigrette or mayonnaise and used for salads. Cold boiled potatoes can be used for potato salad or for sauté potatoes. Cold mashed potatoes may be used for fish cakes or potato cakes.

Meat: left-over cooked items such as bacon, ham, tongue, kidneys or liver may be mixed with mince of any meat and used to give extra flavour to croquettes and rissoles.

Cold meats can be used for a number of dishes. For example:

minced for cottage pie
minced lamb or mutton
Cornish pasties
salad
miroton of beef

Left-over poultry, such as chicken, if cut into joints can be reheated carefully in a curry sauce.

If the skin and bone are removed the poultry can be used for:

salad
mayonnaise
cutlets or croquettes
vol-au-vent or bouchées

Rice, spaghetti, macaroni can be turned into mixtures for hors-d'œuvre with items such as chopped onion, chives, tomatoes, beetroot, cooked meat, haricot or French beans and a dressing of vinaigrette or mayonnaise.

Bread: trimming of crusts, etc, should be kept until dry, lightly browned in the oven, then passed through a mincer to make browned breadcrumbs (chapelure) which may be used for crumbling cutlets, croquettes of fish, etc.

Stale bread can also be used for bread pudding. Stale sponge cake can be used for:

trifles
cabinet puddings
queen of puddings

Cheese: left-overs of cheddar cheese can be grated or chopped and used for Welsh rarebit.

Food-borne diseases

Typhoid and paratyphoid are diseases caused by harmful bacteria carried in food or water. Scarlet fever, tuberculosis and dysentery may be caused by drinking milk which has not been pasteurised.

To prevent diseases being spread by food and water the following measures should be taken:

1 Water supplies must be purified.

2 Milk and milk products should be pasteurised.
3 Carriers should be excluded from food preparation rooms.

Food Hygiene Regulations

These regulations should be known and complied with by all people involved in the handling of food. A copy of the full regulations can be obtained from HM Stationery Office and an abstract can be obtained which gives the main points of the full regulations.

These points are as follows:

Equipment

This must be kept clean and in good condition.

Personal requirements

1 All parts of the person liable to come into contact with food must be kept as clean as possible.
2 All clothing must be kept as clean as possible.
3 All cuts or abrasions must be covered with a waterproof dressing.
4 Spitting is forbidden.
5 Smoking is forbidden in a food room or where there is food.
6 As soon as a person is aware that he is suffering from or is a carrier of such infections as typhoid, paratyphoid, dysentery, salmonella or staphylococcal infection he must notify his employer, who must notify the Medical Office of Health.

Requirements for food premises

Toilets

1 These must be clean, well lighted and ventilated.
2 No food room shall contain or directly communicate with a toilet.
3 A notice requesting people to wash their hands after using the toilet must be displayed in a prominent place.
4 The ventilation of the soil drainage must not be in a food room.
5 The water supply to a food room and toilet is only permitted through an efficient flushing cistern.

Washing facilities

1 Hand basins and an adequate supply of hot water must be provided.
2 Supplies of soap, nail-brushes and clean towels or warm air machines must be available by the hand basins.

First aid: bandages, waterproof dressings and antiseptics must be provided in a readily accessible position.
Lockers: enough lockers must be available for outdoor clothes.
Lighting and ventilation: food rooms must be suitably lit and ventilated.
Sleeping room: rooms in which food is prepared must not be slept in. Sleeping

rooms must not be adjacent to a food room.
Refuse: refuse must not be allowed to accumulate in a food room.
Buildings: the structure of food rooms must be kept in good repair to enable them to be cleaned and to prevent entry of rats, mice, etc.
Food temperatures: certain foods must be kept at temperatures below 10°C or at not less than 62.8°C. These foods include meat, fish, gravy, imitation cream, egg products, milk and cream.
Storage: Foods should not be placed in a yard, etc, lower than 0.5 metre (18 inches) unless properly protected.

Penalties

Any person guilty of an offence shall be liable to a heavy fine and/or a term of imprisonment. Under the Food and Drugs (Control of Food Premises) Act, unhygienic premises can be closed down by a local authority in 72 hours, on the advice of the Environmental Health Officer.

The Environmental Health Officer when visiting premises will probably check for:

- grease in ventilation ducts and on canopies
- long-standing dirt in less accessible areas
- cracked or chipped equipment
- provision for staff toilets and clothing
- 'now wash your hands' notice
- adequate and correct storage of food, eg cooked food stored above raw food if there is not separate refrigerated provision
- correct storage temperature of foodstuffs
- signs of pests and how they are prevented
- any hazards
- cleaning, training records and proper supervision.

Checklist for catering establishments

Entrances and exits unobstructed.
Fire doors undamaged and in operating position.
Escape routes clearly indicated.
Fire-fighting equipment visible and accessible.
Lighting good.
Suitable supply of hot and cold water.
Good ventilation.
Separate hand-washing basin.
Soap, nail-brush and towels by basin.
Floors in good repair, clean and dry.
Equipment operating correctly.
Guards on machines.
All surfaces undamaged and clean.
Staff trained to use machines.
Notice concerning use of machine close to it.
Suitable protective clothing worn.
Food, equipment and cleaning materials stored properly.
Rubbish bins covered and emptied regularly.
Staff work in accordance with safety guidelines.

Summary of food hygiene

Dangers to food

Chemical (copper, lead, etc).
Plant (toadstools).
Bacteria (cause of most cases of food poisoning).

Bacteria

Almost everywhere; not all are harmful.
Must be magnified 500–1000 times to be seen.
Under ideal conditions, they multiply by dividing in two every 20 minutes.

Sources of food-poisoning bacteria

Human – nose, throat, excreta, spots, cuts, etc.
Animal – excreta.
Foodstuffs – meat, eggs, milk, from animal carriers.

Method of spread of bacteria

Human – coughs, sneezes, hands.
Animals – excreta (rats, mice, cows, pets, etc), infected carcasses.
Other means – equipment, china, towels.

Factors essential for bacterial growth

Suitable temperature.
Time.
Enough moisture.
Suitable food.

Method of control of bacterial growth

Heat – Sterilisation, using high temperatures to kill all micro-organisms.
– Pasteurisation using lower temperatures to kill harmful bacteria only.
– Cooking.

Cold – Refrigeration (3°–5°C) stops growth of food poisoning bacteria and retards growth of other micro-organisms.
– Deep freeze (−18°C) stops growth of all micro-organisms.

Foods commonly causing food poisoning

Poultry.
Made-up meat dishes.
Trifles, custards, synthetic cream.
Sauces.
Left-over foods.

Prevention of food poisoning

Care of person

1 Washing of hands.
2 Handle food as little as possible.
3 Cover cuts and burns with waterproof dressing.
4 Clean clothes and clean habits.

Care of food

1 Keep food cold during storage.
2 Cook meat and eggs thoroughly.
3 Cook and eat foods same day. 'Warmed-up' foods must be thoroughly reheated.
4 Protect foods from flies, rats, mice, etc.

Care of environment

1 Provide spacious well-lighted and well-ventilated premises.
2 Adequate washing and cleaning facilities.
3 Ample cold storage.
4 Suitable washing-up facilities.

Definition of terms

Antibiotic	Drug used to destroy pathogenic bacteria within human or animal bodies.
Antiseptic	Substance that prevents the growth of bacteria and moulds, specifically on or in the human body.
Bactericide	Substance which destroys bacteria.
Carrier	Person who harbours, and may transmit, pathogenic organisms without showing signs of illness.
Cleaning	Removal of soil, food residues, dirt, grease and other objectionable matter.
Contamination	Occurrence of any objectionable matter in food.
Danger zone of bacterial growth	Temperature range within which multiplication of pathogenic bacteria is possible (from 10°C to 63°C).
First-aid materials	Suitable and sufficient bandages and dressings, including waterproof dressings and antiseptic. All dressings to be individually wrapped.
Food handling	Any operation in the production, preparation, processing, packaging, storage, transport, distribution and sale of food.
Gastroenteritis	Inflammation of the stomach and intestinal tract that normally results in diarrhoea.
Germicide	Agent used for killing micro-organisms.
Incubation period	Period between infection and the first signs of illness.
Mildew	Type of fungus similar to mould.
Moulds	Microscopic plants (fungi) that may appear as woolly patches on food.
Optimum	Best.

Pathogen	Disease-producing organism.
Pesticide	Chemical used to kill pests.
Residual insecticide	Long-lasting insecticide applied in such a way that it remains active for a considerable period of time.
Sanitiser	Chemical agent used for cleansing and disinfecting surfaces and equipment.
Spores	Resistant resting-phase of bacteria protecting them against adverse conditions, such as high temperatures.
Steriliser	Chemical used to destroy all living organisms.
Sterile	Free from all living organisms.
Sterilisation	Process that destroys all living organisms.
Toxins	Poisons produced by pathogens.
Viruses	Microscopic pathogens that multiply in living cells of their host.
Wholesome food	Sound food, fit for human consumption.

Further information

The Royal Society for the Promotion of Health, 13 Grosvenor Place, London SW1X 7EN.

Royal Institute of Public Health and Hygiene, 28 Portland Place, London W1N 4DE.

The Institution of Environmental Health Officers, Chadwick House, Rushworth Street, London SE1 0QT.

Local Environmental Health Departments.

Health and Safety Executive, Baynards House, 1 Chepstow Place, Westbourne Grove, London W2 4FT.

Health Education Authority, Hamilton House, Mabledon Place, London WC1H 9TX.

Health and Safety Executive, Regina House, Old Marylebone Road, London NW1.

Royal Society of Health, 38A St George's Drive, London SW1V 4BH.

Food Hygiene Bureau Ltd, Wychwood House, Charlbury, Oxford OX7 3QR.

Betty C Hobbs and Diane Roberts, *Food Poisoning and Food Hygiene*, Fifth Edition (Edward Arnold).

Food Hygiene Regulations (HM Stationery Office).

Food Hygiene Codes of Practice (HM Stationery Office).

Clean Catering (HM Stationery Office).

Aston and Tiffney, *A Guide to Improving Food Hygiene* (Northwood Publication).

C M Lucas, *Hygiene in Buildings* (Rentokil, 1982).

Guidelines on Pre-cooked Chilled Foods (HM Stationery Office).

Clean Food: Health Service Catering (HM Stationery Office).

Hygiene: Health Service Catering (HM Stationery Office).

Richard A Sprenger, *The Food Hygiene Handbook* (The Institution of Environmental Health Officers, Highfield Publications).

13

Elementary nutrition and food science

Having read the chapter, these learning objectives, both general and specific, should be achieved.

General objectives Understand the basic principles of nutrition and know the reasons why it is necessary to have this understanding so as to be able to apply this knowledge.

Specific objectives Explain the digestive system and state the function of nutrients. List the foods containing the various nutrients and state the effect of heat upon those nutrients. Explain basal metabolism and specify the value of foods in the diet.

Food and nutrients

A food is any substance, liquid or solid, which provides the body with materials:

(a) for heat and energy;
(b) for growth and repair;
(c) to regulate the body processes.

The materials are known as *nutrients*. They are:

proteins	vitamins
fats	minerals
carbohydrates	water

The study of these nutrients is termed nutrition. Only those substances containing nutrients are foods (alcohol is an energy-provider but it also has the effects of a drug, so it is not listed under the nutrients). Most foods contain several nutrients; a few foods contain only one nutrient, for example sugar.

For the body to obtain the maximum benefit from food it is essential that everyone concerned with the buying, storage, cooking and serving of food and the compiling of menus should have some knowledge of nutrition.

Digestion

This is the breaking down of the food and takes place:

1 In the mouth, where food is mixed with saliva, and starch is broken down by the action of an enzyme in saliva.

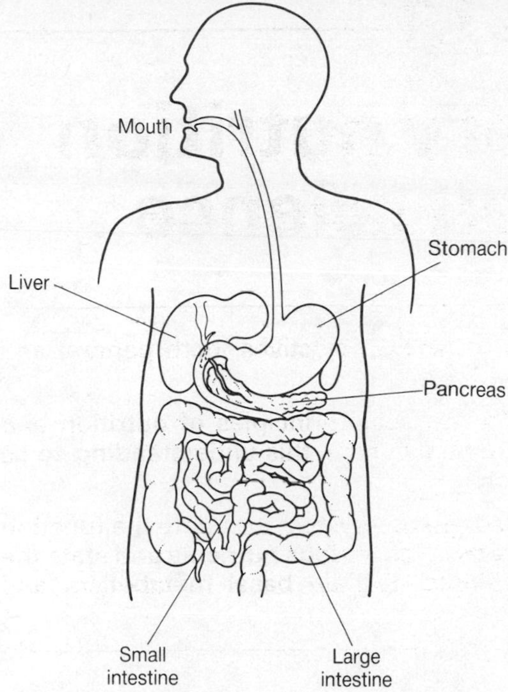

Fig. 13.1 The digestive tract

2 In the stomach, where the food is mixed and gastric juices are added, and proteins are broken down.
3 In the small intestine, where proteins, fats and carbohydrates are broken down further and additional juices are added.

Absorption

To enable the body to benefit from food it must be absorbed into the bloodstream; this absorption occurs after the food has been broken down; the product then passes through the walls of the digestive tract into the bloodstream.

This occurs in:

(a) The stomach where simple substances, such as alcohol and glucose, are passed through the stomach lining into the bloodstream.
(b) In the small intestine where more of the absorption of nutrients takes place due to a further breakdown of the food.
(c) In the large intestine, where water is re-absorbed from the waste.

For the body to obtain the full benefit from foods it should be remembered that to stimulate the flow of saliva and gastric juices food must smell, look and taste attractive.

When the full benefit is not obtained or there is a lack of one or more nutrients then this leads to a state of malnutrition.

The main function of nutrients

Energy	*Growth and repair*	*Regulation of body processes*
carbohydrates	proteins	vitamins
fats	minerals	minerals
proteins	water	water

For a summary, see also the table on p. 389.

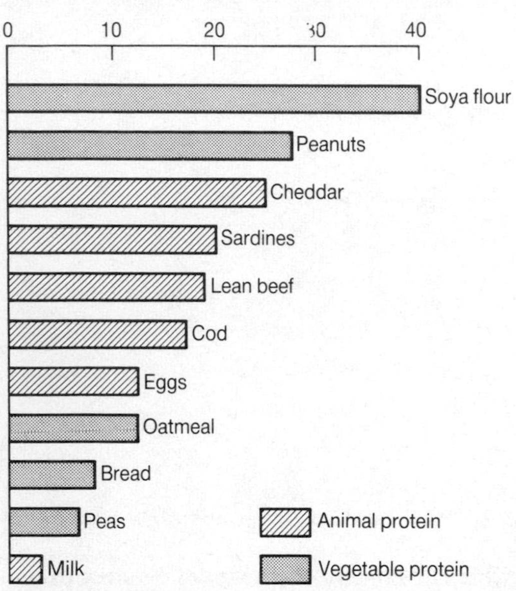

Fig. 13.2 Proportion of protein in some foods

Proteins

Protein is an essential part of all living matter; it is therefore needed for the growth of the body and for the repair of body tissues.

There are two kinds of protein:

1 Animal protein, found in meat, game, poultry, fish, eggs, milk, cheese, eg myosin, collagen (meat, poultry and fish), albumin, ovovitellin (eggs), casein (milk and cheese).

2 Vegetable protein, found mainly in the seeds of vegetables. The proportion of protein in green and root vegetables is small. Peas, beans and nuts contain most protein and the grain of cereals, such as wheat, have a useful amount because of the large quantity eaten, eg gliadin and glutenin forming gluten with water (wheat and rye).

Figure 13.3 (opposite) represents the main sources of protein and the contribution made by different protein foods in the typical Western diet. The proportion of animal foods contributing to the total would be very much reduced in the Third World countries.

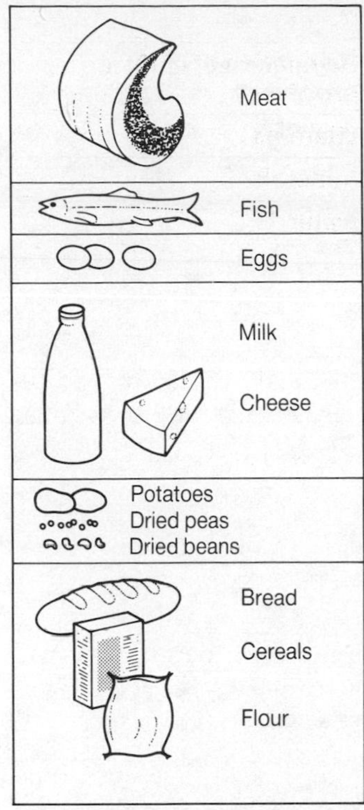

Fig. 13.3 Main supply of protein in the average diet

It follows that, because protein is needed for growth, growing children and expectant and nursing mothers will need more protein than other adults, whose requirements are mainly for repair. Any spare protein is used for producing heat and energy. In diets where the protein intake is minimal, it is important that there is plenty of carbohydrate available so that protein is used for growth and repair, rather than for energy purposes.

What is protein?

Protein is composed of different amino-acids; so the protein of cheese is different from the protein of meat because the number and arrangement of the acids are not the same. A certain number of these amino-acids are essential to the body and have to be provided by food. Proteins containing all the essential amino-acids in the correct proportion are said to be of high biological value. The human body is capable of converting the other kinds of amino-acids to suit its needs.

It is preferable that the body has both animal and vegetable protein, so that a complete variety of the necessary amino-acids is available.

During digestion protein is split into amino-acids; these are absorbed into the bloodstream and used for building body tissues and to provide some heat and energy.

Effects of cooking on protein

On being heated, the different proteins in foods set or coagulate at different temperatures; above these temperatures shrinkage occurs, and this is particularly noticeable in grilling or roasting meat. Moderately cooked protein is the most easy to digest: for example, a lightly cooked egg is more easily digested than a raw egg or a hard-boiled egg.

Fats

There are two main groups of fats, animal and vegetable. The function of fat is to protect vital organs of the body, to provide heat and energy, and certain fats also provide vitamins.

Fats can be divided into:

(a) solid fat;
(b) oils (fat which is liquid at room temperature).

Fats are obtained from the following foods:

animal origin: dripping, butter, suet, lard, cheese, cream, bacon, meat fat, oily fish;
vegetable origin: margarine, cooking fat, nuts, soya-beans.

Oils are obtained from the following foods:

animal origin: halibut and cod-liver oil;
vegetable origin: from seeds or nuts.

Composition of fats

Fats are composed of glycerol to which is attached three fatty acids (hence the name triglyceride). Fats differ because of the fatty acids from which they are derived. These may be, for example, butyric acid in butter, stearic acid in solid fat, such as beef suet, oleic acid in most oils. These fatty acids affect the texture and flavour of the fat.

To be useful to the body, fats have to be broken down into glycerol and fatty acids so that they can be absorbed; they can then provide heat and energy.

The food value of the various kinds of fat is similar, although some animal fats contain vitamins A and D.

The contribution of animal fat in the Western diet is gradually changing as healthy eating policies encourage a reduction in the total fat intake, particularly animal fats. There has been a swing towards skimmed milk, leaner cuts of meat, cooking with vegetable oils and a reduced market for eggs, high fat cheeses and butter.

Fats should be eaten with other foods such as bread, potatoes, etc, as they can then be more easily digested and utilised in the body.

Certain fish, such as herrings, mackerel, salmon, sardines, contain oil (fat) in the flesh. Other fish, such as cod and halibut, contain the oil in the liver.

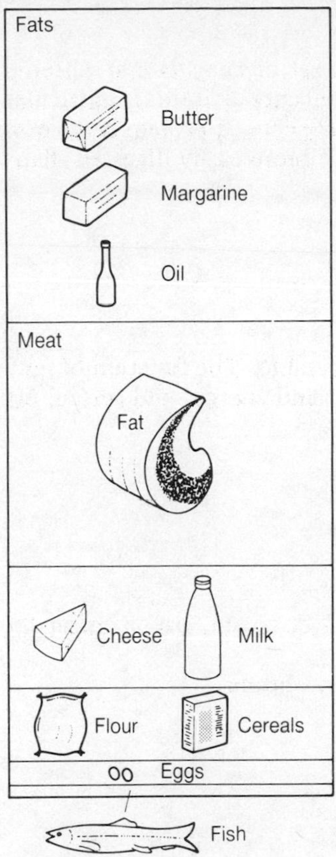

Fig. 13.4 Main supply of fat in the average diet

Vegetables and fruit contain very little fat, but nuts have a considerable amount.

Effects of cooking on fat

Cooking has little effect on fat except to make it more digestible.

Carbohydrates

There are three main types of carbohydrates:

(a) sugar;
(b) starch;
(c) cellulose.

The function of carbohydrates is to provide the body with most of its energy. Starch is composed of a number of glucose molecules (particles), and during digestion starch is broken down into glucose.

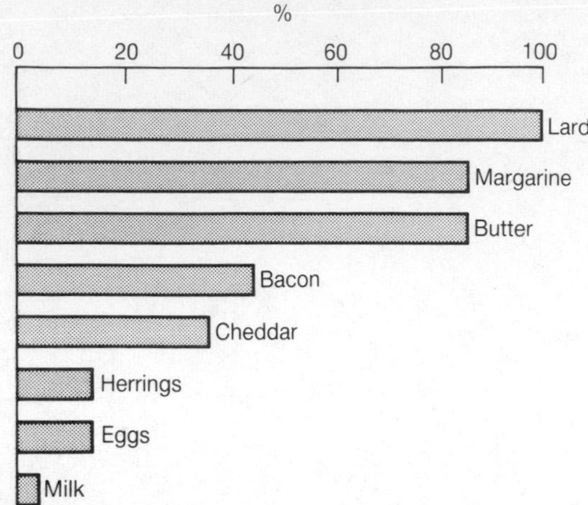

Fig. 13.5 Proportion of fat in some foods

(a) Sugar

There are several kinds of sugar:

glucose: found in the blood of animals and in fruit and honey.
fructose: found in fruit, honey and cane sugar.
sucrose: found in beet and cane sugar.
lactose: found in milk.
maltose: produced naturally during the germination of grain.

Sugars are the simplest form of carbohydrate and the end-products of the digestion of carbohydrates. They are absorbed in the form of glucose and simple sugars and used to provide heat and energy.

(b) Starch

Starch is present in the diet through the following foods:

whole grains: rice, barley, tapioca.
powdered grains: flour, cornflour, ground rice, arrowroot.
vegetables: potatoes, parsnips, peas, beans.
unripe fruit: bananas, apples, cooking pears.
cereals: cornflakes, shredded wheat, etc.
cooked starch: cakes, biscuits.
pastas: macaroni, spaghetti, vermicelli.

Cooking effects on starch
Uncooked starch is not digestible.

Foods containing starch have cells with starch granules, covered with a cellulose wall which breaks down when heated or made moist. When browned, as with the crust of bread, toast, roast potatoes, skin on rice pudding, etc, the

Fig. 13.6 Main supply of carbohydrate in the average diet

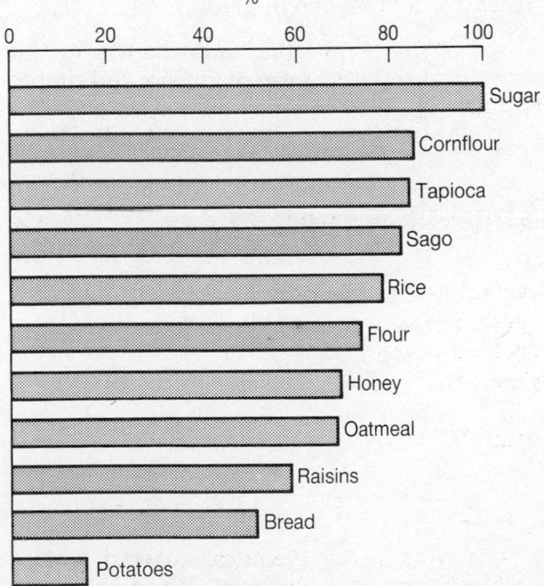

Fig. 13.7 Proportion of carbohydrate in some foods

starch forms dextrins and these taste sweeter. On heating with water or milk, starch granules swell and absorb liquid, thus thickening the product, eg thickened gravy or cornflour sauce. This thickening process is known as gelatinisation of starch.

(c) Cellulose

Cellulose is the coarser structure of vegetables and cereals which is not digested but is used as roughage in the intestine. It is often now referred to as dietary fibre.

Vitamins

Vitamins are chemical substances which are vital for life, and if the diet is deficient in any vitamin, ill-health results. As they are chemical substances they can be produced synthetically.

General function of vitamins

To assist the regulation of the body processes, eg:

1 To help the growth of children.
2 To protect against disease.

Vitamin A

Function

1 Assists in children's growth.
2 Helps the body to resist infection.
3 Enables people to see better in the dark.

Vitamin A is fat soluble, therefore it is to be found in fatty foods. It can be made in the body from carotene, the yellow substance found in many fruits and vegetables.

Dark green vegetables are a good source of vitamin A, the green colour masking the yellow of the carotene. Carotene is gradually destroyed by light (hence the fading of orange coloured spices and vegetables on prolonged storage).

Foods in which vitamin A is found

halibut-liver oil
cod-liver oil
kidney
liver
butter
margarine (to which vitamin A is added)
cheese
eggs
milk
herrings
carrots
spinach
watercress
tomatoes
apricots

Fish-liver oils have the most vitamin A. The amount of vitamin A in dairy produce varies. Because cattle eat fresh grass in summer and stored feeding-stuffs in winter, the dairy produce contains the highest amount of vitamin A in the summer.

Kidney and liver are also useful sources of vitamin A.

Vitamin D

Function

Vitamin D controls the use the body makes of calcium. It is therefore necessary for healthy bones and teeth.

Like vitamin A it is fat soluble.

Sources of vitamin D

An important source of vitamin D is from the action of sunlight on the deeper layers of the skin (approximately 75 per cent of our vitamin D comes from this source). Others include:

- fish-liver oils
- oily fish
- egg yolk
- margarine (to which vitamin D is added)
- dairy produce

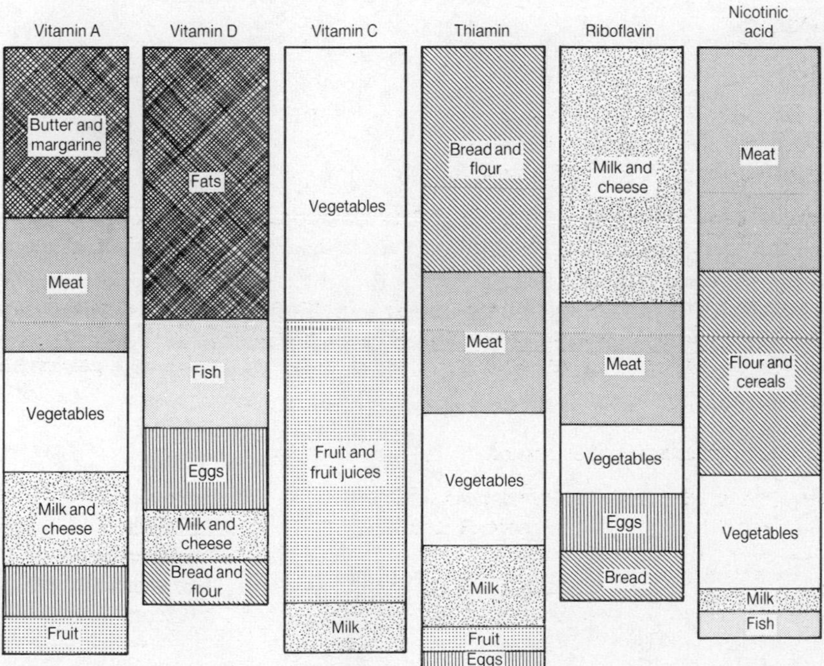

Fig. 13.8 Main supply of vitamins in the average diet

Vitamin B

When first discovered vitamin B was thought to be one substance only; it is now known to consist of at least eleven substances, the three main ones being:

thiamin (B_1)
riboflavin (B_2)
nicotinic acid, or niacin

Others include folic acid and pyridoxine (B_6).

Function

Vitamin B is required to:

1 Keep the nervous system in good condition.
2 Enable the body to obtain energy from the carbohydrates.
3 Encourage the growth of the body.

Vitamin B is water-soluble and can be lost in cooking water.

Some foods containing vitamin B

Thiamin (B_1)	*Riboflavin (B_2)*	*Nicotinic acid*
yeast	yeast	meat extract
bacon	liver	brewers' yeast
oatmeal	meat extract	liver
peas	cheese	kidney
wholemeal bread	egg	beef
bacon		

Vitamin C (ascorbic acid)

Function

1 Vitamin C is necessary for the growth of children.
2 Assists in the healing of cuts and uniting of bones.
3 Prevents gum and mouth infection.

Vitamin C is water-soluble and can be lost during cooking or soaking in water. It is also lost by bad storage (keeping foods for too long, bruising, or storing in a badly ventilated place) and by cutting vegetables into small pieces.

Some foods containing vitamin C

blackcurrants	potatoes	Brussels sprouts and other greens
strawberries	lemons	oranges
grapefruit	tomatoes	bananas
fruit juices		

The major sources in the British diet are potatoes and green vegetables.

Mineral elements

There are nineteen mineral elements, most of which are required by the body in very small quantities. The body has at certain times a greater demand for certain mineral elements and there is a danger then of a deficiency in the diet. Calcium, iron and iodine are those most likely to be deficient.

Calcium

Calcium is required for:

1 Building bones and teeth.
2 Clotting of the blood.
3 The working of the muscles.

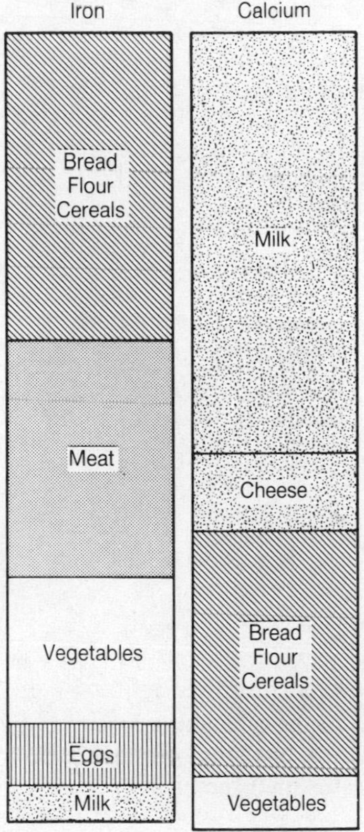

Fig. 13.9 Main supply of iron and calcium in the average diet

The use the body makes of calcium is dependent on the presence of vitamin D.

Sources of calcium
Milk and milk products.
The bones of tinned oily fish.
Wholemeal bread and white bread (to which calcium is added). *Note* It is still the practice to add calcium, iron, thiamin and nicotinic acid to flour despite the

DHSS report No. 23 (1981) which recommended that it should be discontinued.
Vegetables (greens).
It may also be present in drinking water.

Although calcium is present in certain foods (spinach, cereals) the body is unable to make use of it as it is not in a soluble form and therefore cannot be absorbed.

Owing to extra growth of bones and teeth, infants, adolescents, expectant and nursing mothers have a greater demand for calcium.

Phosphorus

Phosphorus is required for:

1 Building the bones and teeth (in conjunction with calcium and vitamin D).
2 The control of the structure of the brain cells.

Sources of phosphorus
Liver, kidney
Eggs, cheese
Bread, fish

Iron

Iron is required for building the haemoglobin in blood and is therefore necessary for transporting oxygen and carbon dioxide round the body.

Sources of iron
Lean meat, offal
Egg yolk
Wholemeal flour
Green vegetables
Fish

Iron is most easily absorbed from meat and offal, its absorption is helped by the presence of vitamin C.

Iron may also be present in drinking water and obtained from iron utensils in which food is prepared.

As the haemoglobin in the blood should be maintained at a constant level, the body requires more iron at certain times than others, eg after loss of blood.

Sodium

Sodium is required in all body fluids, and is found in salt (sodium chloride). Excess salt is continually lost from the body in urine. The kidneys control this loss. We also lose sodium in sweating, a loss over which we have no control.

Sources of sodium
Many foods are cooked with salt or have salt added (bacon and cheese) or contain salt (meat, eggs, fish).

Iodine

Iodine is required for the functioning of the thyroid gland which regulates basal metabolism (see p. 387).

Sources of iodine
Sea foods
Vegetables grown near the sea
Drinking water obtained near the sea
Iodised salt

Other minerals

Potassium, magnesium, sulphur and copper are some of the other minerals required by the body.

Water

Water is required for:

1 All body fluids.
2 Digestion.
3 Absorption.
4 Metabolism.
5 Excretion.
6 Secretion.
7 Playing a part in regulation of body temperatures by evaporation of perspiration.

Sources of water

(a) Drinks of all kinds.
(b) Foods, such as fruits and vegetables, meat, eggs etc.
(c) Combustion or oxidation: when fats, carbohydrates and protein are used for energy a certain amount of water (metabolic water) is produced within the body.

The cooking of nutrients

Protein

When protein is heated it coagulates and shrinks. Too much cooking can spoil the appearance of the food, eg scrambled eggs, as well as causing destruction of certain vitamins. See p. 376 for cooking effects on protein.

Carbohydrate

Unless starch is thoroughly cooked it cannot be digested properly (for example, insufficiently cooked pastry or bread). When cooked, the starch granules swell, burst and then the starch can be digested. (This is called gelatinisation of starch). See also pp. 378–80.

When sugar is heated it melts and with further heating loses water, gradually turning brown, dark brown and then black. This is known as the caramelisation of sugar.

Fat

The nutritive value of fat is not affected by cooking. During cooking processes a certain amount of fat may be lost from food when the fat melts, for example, in the grilling of meat.

Mineral elements

There is a possibility of some minerals being lost in the cooking liquor, so diminishing the amount available in the food. This applies to soluble minerals, such as salt, but not to calcium or iron compounds which do not dissolve in the cooking liquor.

Iron

Iron may be acquired from foods cooked in iron utensils. The iron in foods is not affected by the cooking.

Calcium

Cooking foods in hard water may very slightly increase the amount of calcium in food.

Vitamins

Vitamins A and *D* withstand cooking temperatures, and they are not lost in the cooking.

Vitamin B_1 (thiamin) can be destroyed by high temperatures and by the use of bicarbonate of soda. It is soluble in water and can be lost in the cooking. Vitamin B_2 (riboflavin) is not destroyed easily by heat but bright sunlight can break it down.

Vitamin C is lost by cooking and by keeping food warm in a hot place. It is also soluble in water (the soaking of foods for a long time and bruising are the causes of losing vitamin C). It is unstable and therefore easily destroyed in alkaline conditions (bicarbonate of soda must not be used when cooking green vegetables).

Food requirements

Energy is required to enable the heart to beat, for the blood to circulate, the lungs and other organs of the body to function, for every activity such as talking, eating, standing, sitting and for strenuous exercise and muscular activity.

Young and active people require a different amount of food from elderly, inactive people because they expend more energy, and this energy is obtained from food during chemical changes taking place in the body.

The energy value of a food is measured by a term called a kilocalorie or Calorie (this term should be written with a capital C although popularly is often written with a small c). This is the amount of heat required to raise the temperature of 1000 grammes of water from 15° to 16°C.

A new unit is now gradually replacing the Calorie. This is the joule. Since the joule is too small for practical nutrition, the kilojoule (kJ) is used.

1 Calorie = 4.18 kJ

(Both units will be given here and for ease of conversion 1 Calorie will be taken to equal 4.0 kJ.)

Foods contain certain amounts of the various nutrients, which are measured in grams.

The energy value of nutrients is as follows:

1 gram carbohydrate produces 4 Calories (16 kJ);
1 gram protein produces 4 Calories (16 kJ);
1 gram fat produces 9 Calories (36 kJ).

The energy value of a food, diet or menu is calculated from the nutrients it contains; for example, 28 grams of food containing:

10 grams carbohydrate	will produce	$10 \times 4 =$	40 Calories (160 kJ)
2 grams protein	will produce	$2 \times 4 =$	8 Calories (32 kJ)
5 grams fat	will produce	$5 \times 9 =$	45 Calories (180 kJ)
	Total		93 Calories (372 kJ)

Foods having a high fat content will have a high energy value; those containing a lot of water, a low energy value. All fats, cheese, bacon and other foods with a high fat content have a high energy value.

Men require more Calories (kJ) than women, big men and women require more than small men and women, and people engaged in energetic work require more Calories (kJ) than those with sedentary occupations.

Basal metabolism

Basal metabolism is the term given to the amount of energy required to maintain the functions of the body and to keep the body warm when it is still and without food. The number of Calories (kJ) required for basal metabolism is affected by the size, sex and general condition of the body. The number of Calories (kJ) required for basal metabolism is approximately 1700 per day.

In addition to the energy required for basal metabolism, energy is also required for everyday activities, such as getting up, dressing, walking, etc, and the amount required will be closely related to a person's occupation.

The approximate energy requirements per day for the following examples are:

Clerk	2000 Calories (8 000 kJ)
Carpenter	3000 Calories (12 000 kJ)
Labourer	4000 Calories (16 000 kJ)

The table overleaf indicates the recommended daily allowance of Calories to provide a healthy diet for the categories of people shown.

Recommended daily intake of calories

Age and sex	*Calories*	*Kilojoules*
Boys and girls:		
0–1 year	1000	4000
2–6 years	1500	6000
7–10 years	2000	8000
Boys:		
11–14 years	2750	11000
15–19 years	3500	14000
Men:		
20+ years (for average activity)	3000	12000
Girls:		
11–14 years	2750	11000
15–19 years	2500	10000
Women:		
20+ years (for average activity)	2500	10000

Value of foods in the diet

Milk

Cows' milk is almost the perfect food for human beings; it contains protein, carbohydrate, fat, minerals, vitamins and water.

When milk is taken into the body it coagulates in the same way as in the making of junket. This occurs in the stomach when digestive juices (containing the enzyme rennin) are added. Souring of milk is due to the bacteria feeding on the milk sugar (lactose) and producing lactic acid from it, which brings about curdling.

Composition of milk

The approximate composition is as follows:

- 87 per cent water
- 3–4 per cent proteins (mostly casein)
- 3–4 per cent fat
- 4–5 per cent sugar
- 0.7 per cent minerals (particularly calcium)
- Vitamins A, B and D

(There are legal minimum requirements for the various grades of milk. In the Channel Islands the percentage of fat is 4 per cent, all others is 3 per cent.)

Milk, therefore, is a body-building food because of its protein, an energy food because of the fat and sugar, and a protective food as it contains vitamins and minerals. Because of its high water content, while it is a suitable food for babies, it is too bulky to be the main source of protein and other nutrients after the first few months of life. It is also deficient in iron and vitamin C.

Foods containing the various nutrients and their use in the body

Name	*Food in which it is found*	*Use in body*
Protein	Meat, fish, poultry, game, milk, cheese, eggs, pulses, cereals	For building and repairing body tissues. Some heat and energy
Fat	Butter, margarine, cooking-fat, oils, cheese, fat meat, oily fish	Provides heat and energy
Carbohydrate	Flour, flour products and cereals, sugar, syrup, jam, honey, fruit, vegetables	Provides heat and energy
Vitamin A	Oily fish, fish-liver oil, dairy foods, carrots, tomatoes, greens	Helps growth. Resistance to disease
Vitamin B_1 – thiamin	Yeast, pulses, liver, whole grain cereals, meat and yeast extracts	Helps growth. Strengthens nervous system
Vitamin B_2 – riboflavin	Yeast, liver, meat, meat extracts, whole grain cereals	Helps growth, and helps in the production of energy
– nicotinic acid (niacin)	Yeast, meat, liver, meat extracts, whole grain cereals	Helps growth
Vitamin C – ascorbic acid	Fruits such as strawberries, citrus fruits, green vegetables, root vegetables, salad vegetables, potatoes	Helps growth, promotes health
Vitamin D (sunshine vitamin)	Fish-liver oils, oily fish, dairy foods	Helps growth. Builds bones and teeth
Iron	Lean meat, offal, egg yolk, wholemeal flour, green vegetables, fish	Building up the blood
Calcium (lime)	Milk and milk products, bones of fish, wholemeal bread	Building bones and teeth, clotting the blood, the working of the muscles
Phosphorus	Liver and kidney, eggs, cheese bread	Building bones and teeth, regulating body processes
Sodium (salt)	Meat, eggs, fish, bacon, cheese	Prevention of muscular cramp

However, it may be included in everyone's diet as a drink and it can be used in a variety of ways.

Skimmed milk, which has had the cream layer removed, is increasing in popularity. Not only does it provide a lower Calorie intake for those watching their weight, but also the potentially harmful animal fat has been removed.

Cream

Cream is the fat of milk and the minimum fat content of single cream is approximately 18 per cent, for double cream 48 per cent and clotted cream 60 per cent.

Cream is therefore an energy-producing food which also supplies vitamins A and D. It is easily digested because the fat is in a highly emulsified form (ie the fat globules are very small).

Butter

Butter is made from the fat of milk and contains vitamins A and D, the amount depending on the season. Like cream it is easily digested.

Composition of butter

The approximate composition is:

82 per cent fat
13 per cent water
1 per cent salt
vitamins A and D

Butter is also an energy-producing food and a protective food in so far as it provides vitamins A and D.

Margarine

Margarine, which is made from animal and/or vegetable oils, and skimmed milk, has vitamins A and D added to it. The composition and food value of margarine are similar to butter.

Cheese

Cheese is made from milk; its composition varies according to whether the cheese has been made from whole milk, skimmed milk or milk to which extra cream has been added.

The composition of cheddar cheese is:

35 per cent fat
30 per cent water
25 per cent protein
calcium
vitamins A and D

The food value of cheese is exceptional because of the concentration of the various nutrients it contains. The minerals in cheese are useful, particularly the calcium and phosphorus. Cheese is also a source of vitamins A and D.

It is a body-building, energy-producing and protective food because of its protein, fat and mineral elements and vitamin content.

Cheese is easily digested, provided it is eaten with starchy foods and eaten in small pieces as when grated.

Meat, poultry and game

Meat consists of fibres which may be short, as in a fillet of beef, or long, as in the silverside of beef. The shorter the fibre the more tender and easily digested the meat. Meat is carved across the grain to assist mastication and digestion of the fibres.

Hanging the meat helps to make the flesh of meat more tender; this is because acids develop and soften the muscle fibres. Marinading in wine or vinegar prior to cooking also helps to tenderise meat so that it is more digestible. Expensive cuts of meat are not necessarily more nourishing than the cheaper cuts.

Meat contains proteins, variable amounts of fat, and water, also iron and thiamin. (Bacon is particularly valuable because of its thiamin, and pork and pork products are especially rich in thiamin.) Tripe, in addition to its protein, is a good source of calcium as it is treated with lime during its preparation. It is also easily digested. Meat of all kinds is therefore important as a body building food.

Fish

Fish is as useful a source of animal protein as meat.

The amount of fat in different fish varies: oily fish contain 5–18 per cent, white fish less than 2 per cent.

When the bones are eaten calcium is obtained from fish (eg tinned sardines or salmon).

Oily fish is not so easily digested as white fish because of the fat; shellfish is not easily digested because of the coarseness of the fibres.

Fish is important for body building, and certain types of fish (oily fish) supply more energy and are protective because of the fat and vitamins A and D contained in the fish.

Eggs

Egg white contains protein known as egg albumin and the amount of white is approximately twice the amount of the yolk.

The yolk is more complex; it contains more protein than the white, also fat, vitamins A and D, thiamin, riboflavin, calcium, iron, sulphur and phosphorus. Lecithin (an emulsifying agent) and cholesterol are also present.

Composition of eggs (approximate percentage)

	Whole egg	*White*	*Yolk*
Water	73	87	47
Protein	12	10	15
Fat	11		33
Minerals	1	0.5	2
Vitamins			

Because of the protein, vitamins, mineral elements and fat, eggs are a body-building, protective and energy-producing food.

Fruit

The composition of different fruit varies considerably; for example, avocado pears contain about 20 per cent fat, whereas most other fruits contain none. In unripe fruit the carbohydrate is in the form of starch which changes to sugar as the fruit ripens.

The cellulose in fruits acts as a source of dietary fibre.

Fruit is valuable because of the vitamins and minerals it contains. Vitamin C is present in certain fruits, particularly citrus varieties (oranges, grapefruit) and blackcurrants and other summer fruits. Dried fruits such as raisins and sultanas are a useful source of energy because of their sugar content, but they contain no vitamin C.

Composition of fruit

Approximately:

water	85 per cent
carbohydrate	5–10 per cent
cellulose	2–5 per cent
minerals	0.5 per cent
vitamin C	

Very small amounts of fat and protein are found in most fruits.

Fruit is a protective food because of its minerals and vitamins.

Nuts

Nuts are highly nutritious because of the protein, fat and minerals they contain. Vegetarians may rely on nuts to provide the protein in their diet.

Nuts are not easily digested because of their fat content and cellulose.

Vegetables

Green vegetables

Green vegetables are particularly valuable because of their vitamins and minerals; they are therefore protective foods. The most important minerals they contain are iron and calcium. Green vegetables are rich in carotene, which is made into vitamin A in the body.

The greener the vegetable the greater its nutritional value. Vegetables which are stored for long periods, or are damaged or bruised, quickly lose their vitamin C value, therefore they should be used as quickly as possible.

Green vegetables also act as a source of dietary fibre in the intestines.

Root vegetables

Compared with green vegetables most root vegetables contain starch and sugar; they are therefore a source of energy. Swedes and turnips contain a little vitamin C and carrots and other yellow-coloured vegetables contain carotene, which is changed into vitamin A in the body.

Potatoes

Potatoes contain a large amount of starch (approximately 20 per cent) and a small amount of protein just under the skin. Because of the large quantities eaten, the small amount of vitamin C they contain is of value in the diet.

Onions
The onion is used extensively and contains some sugar, but its main value is to provide flavour.

Peas and broad beans
These vegetables contain carbohydrate, protein and carotene.

Cereals

Cereals contain from 60 to 80 per cent carbohydrate in the form of starch and are therefore energy foods. They also contain 7–13 per cent protein, depending on the type of cereal, and 1–8 per cent fat.

The vitamin B content is considerable in stoneground and wholemeal flour, and B vitamins are added to other wheat flours, as are calcium and iron salts.

Oats contain good quantities of fat and protein.

Sugar

There are several kinds of sugar, such as those found in fruit (glucose), milk (lactose), cane and beet sugar (sucrose).

Sugar, with fat, provides the most important part of the body's energy requirements.

Saccharine, although sweet, is chemically produced and has no food value.

Liquids

Water
Certain waters contain mineral salts; for example, hard waters contain soluble salts of calcium. Some spas are known for the mineral salts contained in the local water. Bottled natural mineral waters are sold in many places (particularly supermarkets), and are being used more widely in the catering industry and in the home. Fluoride may be present naturally in some waters, and makes children's teeth more resistant to decay.

Fruit juices
In recent years there has been a tremendous increase in the consumption of fruit juices sold in cartons as a chilled drink or in a 'long-life' form which will keep almost indefinitely before being opened. In addition, freshly squeezed orange juice is a popular alternative drink in many places, including airport and rail terminal restaurants.

Beverages
Tea and coffee have no food value in themselves, but they do act on the nervous system as a stimulant.

Cocoa contains some fat, starch and protein, also some vitamin B and mineral elements.

Because tea, coffee and cocoa are usually served with milk and sugar they do have some food value.

Balanced diet and healthy eating

A balanced diet provides adequate amounts of the various nutrients for energy, growth and repair and regulation of body processes.

In order to be healthy the body must have sufficient but not too much of all the nutrients which are present in foods. Provided the diet provides enough food energy to satisfy the demands for basal metabolism and all other activities, and includes a good mixture of foods, all the requirements for the different nutrients will be met.

We all know when we are eating too much food, because we put on weight, and unfortunately this is a very common problem both for the young and for older people. Carrying too much weight not only looks unattractive but is also a health hazard as it puts extra strain on the body. An overweight person should cut down on their intake of high energy foods such as butter, fried food, cakes, pastries etc, and also be careful to avoid too many purely energy-providing foods such as sweets and fizzy drinks. In this way energy intake will be reduced but not at the expense of the important body-building and protective foods.

Many diseases are linked to poor diet; we know for instance that too little vitamin C will eventually result in scurvy, but also there are many diseases that occur commonly in wealthy countries but which are rare in poorer areas of the world. Many people in developed countries (eg the UK) tend to have a way of life that includes smoking, a relatively high alcohol intake and a diet which is high in fat, low in dietary fibre (especially that from cereals), and contains too much energy. A better diet would contain less fat (particularly dairy fats), less sugar in sweets, chocolate, puddings and beverages, and more bread and potatoes. Wholemeal bread and cereals are particularly beneficial to increase the amount of fibre in our diets.

On the whole people in the West eat plenty of protein and could well look to using some vegetable foods, such as peas, beans, nuts and lentils, for providing protein as a change from animal protein foods.

There is controversy about whether we eat too much salt, and certainly food manufacturers are starting to use less in their tinned products, infant foods etc.

Nutritional guidelines

When compiling menus for institutions, industrial catering etc, the following guidelines should be considered:

1 Spread the calories fairly evenly through the day.
2 Provide a dish which is a good source of protein in at least two meals of the day.
3 Fruit and vegetables (including potatoes) should be available each day.
4 Incorporate high fibre cereals whenever possible, eg brown rice, a proportion of wholemeal flour in pastry, wholemeal bread, wholemeal pastas etc.
5 Use the minimum of salt in cooking.
6 Grill rather than fry.
7 Let appetite determine the energy-producing food requirements.

Food additives

These can be divided into 12 categories, and except for purely 'natural' substances, their use is subject to certain legislation.

1 Preservatives: for example, natural ones include salt, sugar, alcohol and vinegar; synthetic ones are also widely used.
2 Colouring agents: natural, including cochineal, caramel and saffron, and many synthetic ones.
3 Flavouring agents: synthetic chemicals to mimic natural flavours, for example monosodium glutamate to give a meaty flavour to foods.
4 Sweetening: for example, saccharin, sorbitol and aspartame.
5 Emulsifying agents (to stop separation of salad creams, ice cream etc); examples are lecithin and glyceryl monostearate (GMS).
6 Antioxidants: to delay the onset of rancidity in fats due to exposure to air, for example vitamin E and BHT.
7 Flour improvers: to strengthen the gluten in flour, for example vitamin C.
8 Thickeners:
   (a) animal – gelatine;
   (b) marine – agar-agar;
   (c) vegetable – gum tragacanth (used for pastillage), pectin;
   (d) synthetic products.
9 Humectants: to prevent food drying out, for example glycerine (used in some icings).
10 Polyphosphate: injected into poultry before rigor mortis develops. It binds water to the muscle and thus prevents 'drip', giving a firmer structure to the meat.
11 Nutrients: for example vitamins and minerals added to breakfast cereals, vitamins A and D added to margarine.
12 Miscellaneous: anti-caking agents added to icing sugar and salt; firming agents (for example calcium chloride) added to tinned fruit and vegetables to prevent too much softening in the processing; mineral oils added to dried fruit to prevent stickiness.

Further information

Mottram and Barasi, *Human Nutrition*, Fourth Edition (Edward Arnold, 1987).
Stretch and Southgate, *The Science of Catering* (Edward Arnold, 1986).
Manual of Nutrition (HM Stationery Office).
Eating for Health (HM Stationery Office).
Pyke, *Success in Nutrition* (John Murray, 1975).
Kilgour, *Science for Catering Students* (Heinemann).
Gaman and Sherrington, *Science of Food* (Pergamon).

Nutrition Society, Grosvenor Gardens House, 35–37 Grosvenor Gardens, London SW1H 0BX.

14
Preservation of foods

Having read the chapter, these learning objectives, both general and specific, should be achieved.

General objectives Understand how foods are preserved and be aware of the various methods used. Appreciate the value of preserving foods and know which foods are preserved and by which method.

Specific objectives Explain in a simple manner the methods of preserving food. State which foods are preserved by which method. Give examples of the uses of preserved foods.

Food spoilage

Unless foods are preserved they deteriorate; therefore, to keep them in an edible condition it is necessary to know what causes food spoilage. In the air there are certain micro-organisms called moulds, yeasts and bacteria which cause foods to go bad.

Moulds

These are simple plants which appear like whiskers on foods, particularly sweet foods, meat and cheese. To grow, they require warmth, air, moisture, darkness and food; they are killed by heat and sunlight. Moulds can grow where there is too little moisture for yeasts and bacteria to grow, and will be found on jams and pickles.

Although not harmful they do cause foods to taste musty and to be wasted, for example, the top layer of a jar of jam should be removed if it had mould on it.

Correct storage in a dry cold store prevents moulds from forming.

Not all moulds are destructive. Some are used to flavour cheese (stilton, roquefort) or to produce antibiotics (penicillin, streptomycin).

Yeasts

These are single-cell plants or organisms larger than bacteria, which grow on foods containing moisture and sugar. Foods containing only a small percentage of sugar and a large percentage of liquid, such as fruit juices and syrups, are liable to ferment because of yeasts. Although they seldom cause disease yeasts do increase food spoilage; foodstuffs should be kept under refrigeration or they may be spoiled by yeasts. Yeasts are also destroyed by heat. The ability of yeast to feed on sugar and produce alcohol is the basis of the beer and wine-making industry.

Bacteria

Bacteria are minute plants, or organisms, which require moist, warm conditions and a suitable food to multiply. They spoil food by attacking it, leaving waste products, or by producing poisons in the food.

Their growth is checked by refrigeration and they are killed by heat. Certain bacterial forms (spores) are more resistant to heat than others and require higher temperatures to kill them.

Pressure cooking destroys heat-resistant bacterial spores provided the food is cooked for a sufficient length of time, because increased pressure increases the temperature; therefore heat-resistant bacterial spores do not affect canned foods as the foods are cooked under pressure in the cans. Acids are generally capable of destroying bacteria, for example, vinegar in pickles.

Dehydrated foods and dry foods do not contain much moisture and, provided they are kept dry, spoilage from bacteria will not occur. If they become moist then bacteria can multiply; for example, if dried peas are soaked and not cooked the bacteria present can begin to multiply.

Other causes

Food spoilage can occur due to other causes, such as by chemical substances called enzymes, which are produced by living cells. Fruits are ripened by the action of enzymes; they do not remain edible indefinitely because other enzymes cause the fruit to become over-ripe and spoil.

When meat and game are hung they become tender; this is caused by the enzymes. To prevent enzyme activity going too far, foods must be refrigerated or heated to a temperature high enough to destroy the enzymes. Acid retards the enzyme action; for example, lemon juice prevents the browning of bananas or apples when they are cut into slices.

The acidity and alkalinity of foods

The level of acidity or alkalinity of a food is measured by its pH value. The pH can range from 1–14, with pH 7 denoting neutral (neither acid nor alkaline).

1	2	3	4	5	6	7	8	9	10	11	12	13	14
strong acid lemons vinegar rhubarb			medium acid pears bananas carrots tomatoes		weak acid		weak alkali some mineral waters hard water		medium alkali egg white bicarbonate of soda		strong alkaline		

Most micro-organisms grow best at near neutral pH. Bacteria (particularly harmful ones) are less acid tolerant than fungi, and no bacteria will grow at pH less than 3.5. Spoilage of high acid foods such as fruit is usually caused by yeasts and moulds. Meat and fish are more susceptible to bacterial spoilage, since their pH is nearer neutral.

The pH may be lowered so that the food becomes too acidic (less than pH 1.5) for any micro-organisms to grow, for example, the use of vinegar in pickling. In the manufacture of yogurt and cheese bacteria produce lactic acid; this lowers the pH, and retards the growth of food poisoning and spoilage organisms.

Methods of preservation

Foods may be preserved by:

(a) removing the moisture from the food, eg drying, dehydration;
(b) making the food cold, eg chilling, freezing;
(c) applying heat, eg canning, bottling;
(d) radiation, using X- or gamma- (γ) rays;
(e) chemical means, eg salting, pickling, crystallising;
(f) vacuum packing.

Preservation methods:

1	drying or dehydration	5	bottling	9	chemical
2	chilling	6	pickling	10	gas storage
3	freezing	7	salting	11	radiation
4	canning	8	smoking (curing)	12	vacuum packing

Drying or dehydration

This method of preserving is achieved by extracting the moisture from the food, thus preventing moulds, yeasts and bacteria from growing. In the past this was done by drying foods, such as fruits, in the sun; today many types of equipment are used, and the food is dried by the use of air at a regulated temperature and humidity.

Freeze drying

This is a process of dehydration whereby food requires no preservation or refrigeration yet, when soaked in water regains its original size and flavour. It can be applied to every kind of food. The food is frozen in a cabinet, the air is pumped out and the ice vaporised. This is called freeze drying and it is the drying of frozen foods by sublimation under conditions of very low pressure. Sublimation is the action of turning from solid to gas without passing through a liquid stage; in this case it is ice to steam without firstly turning to water.

When processed in this way the food does not lose a great deal of its bulk, but it is very much lighter in weight. When water is added the food gives off its natural smell.

Advantages of drying

(a) If kept dry, food keeps indefinitely.
(b) Food preserved by this method occupies less space than food preserved by other methods. Some dried foods occupy only 10 per cent of the space that would be required when fresh.
(c) Dried foods are easily transported and stored.

(d) The cost of drying and the expenses incurred in storing are not as high as other methods of preservation.
(e) There is no waste after purchase, therefore portion control and costing are simplified.

Foods preserved by drying
Vegetables: peas, onions, beetroot, beans, carrots, lentils, cabbage, mixed vegetables, potatoes.
Herbs
Eggs
Milk
Coffee
Fruits: apples, pears, plums (prunes), apricots, figs, grapes (sultanas, raisins, currants).
Meat
Fish

Vegetables
Many vegetables are dried; those most used are the pulse vegetables, eg beans, peas and lentils, which are used for soups, vegetable purées and many vegetarian dishes. Usually potatoes are cooked, mashed and then dried. The other dried vegetables are used as a vegetable, eg cabbage, onions.

Pulse vegetables may be soaked in water before use, then washed before being cooked. Vegetables which are dehydrated (having a lower content of water as more moisture has been extracted) are soaked in water.

Dehydrated potatoes are in powder form and are reconstituted with water, milk, or milk and water. They usually have manufactured vitamin C added as dehydration results in loss of vitamin C.

Herbs
Herbs are tied into bundles and allowed to dry out in a dry place.

Fruits
Sultanas, currants and raisins are dried grapes which have been dried in the sun or by hot air. Figs, plums, apricots, apples and pears are also dried by hot air. Apples are usually peeled and cut in rings or diced and then dried.

All dried fruits must be washed before use, and fruits such as prunes, figs, apricots, apples and pears are cooked in the water in which they are soaked.

Little flavour or food value is lost in the drying of fruits, with the exception of loss of vitamin C.

Milk
Milk is dried either by the roller or spray process. With the roller method the milk is poured on to heated rollers which cause the water to evaporate; the resulting powder is then scraped off. This method is not widely used now as it damages the milk proteins and results in a less soluble dried product, which is more difficult to reconstitute. With the spray process the milk is sent through a fine jet as a spray into hot air, the water evaporates and the powder drops down. The temperature is controlled so that the protein in the milk is not cooked.

Use: milk powder may be used in place of fresh milk mainly for economic purposes (especially skimmed milk powder) and is used for cooking purposes such as custard, white sauce, etc.

Eggs

Eggs are dried in the same way as milk, and although they have a food value similar to fresh eggs, dried eggs do not have the same aerating quality. When reconstituted the eggs should be used at once; if left in this state in the warm atmosphere of the kitchen bacteria can multiply and food poisoning may result because, although pasteurised before drying, the mixture may be contaminated in the kitchen and it is a very suitable food for the growth of bacteria.

Use: dried eggs are mainly used in the bakery trade.

Chilling and freezing (see also Chapter 10)

Refrigeration is a method of preservation where the micro-organisms in food are not killed; they are only prevented from multiplying. The lower the temperature the longer foods will keep. Refrigerators kept at a temperature between 0°C–7°C prevent foods from spoiling for only a short time; most frozen foods can be kept at −17°C for a year and at −28°C for two years. Foods must be kept in a deep freeze until required for use.

Cold chilled storage of fresh foods merely retards the decay of the food; it does not prevent it from eventually going bad. The aim of chilling is to slow down the rate of spoilage; the lower the chill temperature within the range −1°C and +8°C the slower the growth of micro-organisms and the bio-chemical changes which spoil the flavour, colour, texture and nutritional value of foods. Lowering the temperature to this range also reduces food poisoning hazards although it is important to remember that the food must not be contaminated before chilling.

If frozen slowly, large uneven crystals are formed in the cells of food. The water in each cell contains the minerals which give flavour and goodness to food; if frozen slowly, the minerals are separated from the ice crystals which break through the cells; on thawing, the goodness and flavour drain away. Quick-freezing is satisfactory because small ice crystals are formed in the cells of food; on thawing, the goodness and flavour are retained in the cells.

Figure 14.1 (opposite) shows how only small ice crystals are formed when the temperature falls rapidly through zero, whereas in the second curve, the slower fall results in large ice crystals.

Meat

Chilling: meat which is chilled is kept at a temperature just above freezing-point and will keep for up to one month. If the atmosphere is controlled with carbon dioxide the time can be extended to 10 weeks.

Freezing: imported lamb carcasses are frozen; beef carcasses are not usually frozen because owing to the size of the carcass it takes a long time to freeze and this causes ice crystals to form which, when thawed, affect the texture of the meat. Frozen meat must be thawed before it is cooked.

Quick-freezing of raw food and cooked foods

During the cooking and freezing process, foods undergo physical and/or

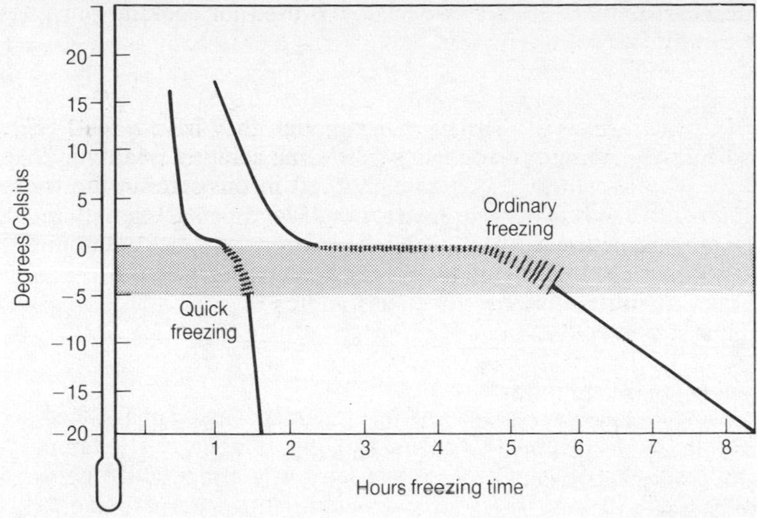

Fig. 14.1 Speed of freezing

chemical changes. If it is found that these changes are detrimental to the product, then recipe modification is required. The following products require some modification: sauces, casseroles, stews, cold desserts, batters, vegetables, egg dishes.

Conventional recipes normally use wheat flour for thickening, but in the cook-freeze system this will not give an acceptable final product because separation of the solids from the liquids in the sauce will occur if the product is kept in frozen storage for more than a period of several weeks. To overcome this problem it is necessary to use wheat flour in conjunction with any of a number of classically modified starches, eg tapioca starch, waxy maize starch. Many recipes prove successful with a ratio of 50 per cent wheat flour with 50 per cent modified starch.

Rapid freezing of foodstuffs can be achieved by a variety of methods using different types of equipment, for example:

1 Plate freezer.
2 Blast freezer.
3 Low-temperature immersion freezer.
4 Still-air cold room.
5 Spray freezer (using liquid nitrogen or carbon dioxide). Known as *cryogenic* freezing this is a method of freezing food by very low temperature. It also freezes food more quickly than any other method. The food to be frozen is placed on a conveyor belt and passes into an insulated freezing tunnel. The liquefied nitrogen or carbon dioxide is injected into the tunnel through a spray, and vaporises, resulting in a very rapid freezing process.
6 Freeze flow. This is a system which freezes food without hardening it.

Foods which are frozen

A very wide variety of foods are frozen, either cooked or in an uncooked state.

Examples of cooked foods: whole cooked meals; braised meat; vol-au-vents; éclairs; cream sponges; puff pastry items.

Examples of raw foods: fillets of fish; fish fingers; poultry; peas; French beans; broad beans; spinach; sprouts; broccoli; strawberries; raspberries; blackcurrants.

With most frozen foods, cooking instructions are given; these should be followed to obtain the best results.

Fillets of fish may be thawed out before cooking; vegetables are cooked in their frozen state. Fruit is thawed before use and as it is usually frozen with sugar the fruit is served with the liquor.

Advantages of using frozen foods

(a) Frozen foods are ready-prepared, therefore saving time and labour.
(b) Portion control and costing are easily assessed.
(c) Foods are always 'in season'.
(d) Compact storage.
(e) Additional stocks to hand.
(f) Guaranteed quality.
(g) Very little loss of vitamin C from fruits and vegetables even after several months in a deep freeze.

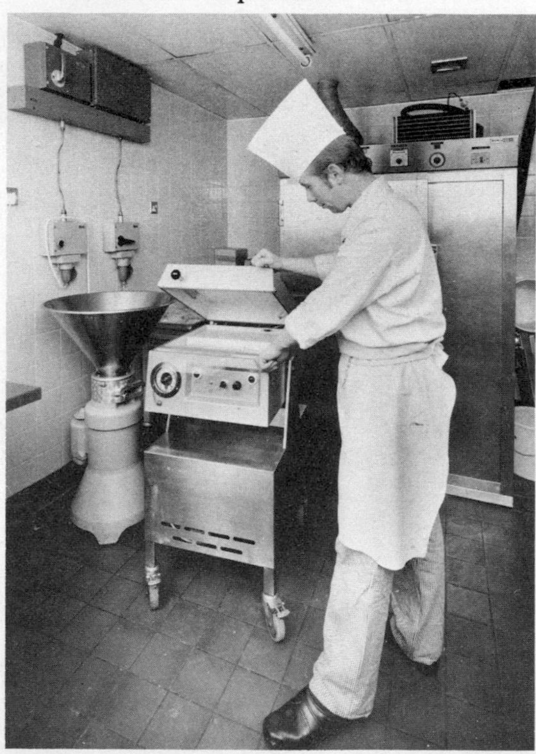

Fig. 14.2 Hotel ready-food kitchen: left to right: high-speed mixer, vacuum packer and blast freezer

Canning and bottling

Bottled and canned foods are sealed in airtight bottles or tins and heated at a high enough temperature for a sufficient period of time to destroy harmful organisms.

Dented cans which do not leak are safe to use, but blown cans, that is those with bulges at either end, must not be used (see p. 196).

Tinned hams are canned at a low temperature in order to retain their flavour and avoid excessive shrinkage in the can and therefore should be stored in a refrigerator and consumed soon after purchase. Other tinned foods are kept in a dry, cool place and the table below indicates the advised storage time.

Storage of tinned foods

Type of tinned food	*Advised storage time*
Fruit	up to 12 months
Milk	up to 12 months
Vegetables	up to 2 years
Meat	up to 5 years
Fish in oil	up to 5 years
Fish in tomato sauce	up to 1 year

Foods are canned in tins of various sizes, see table below.

Tin sizes

Size	*Approx. weight*	*Use*
	142 g	baked beans, peas
	227 g	fruits, meats, vegetables
A 1	284 g	baked beans, soups, vegetables, meats, pilchards
14Z	397 g	fruits, vegetables
A 2	567 g	fruits, vegetables, fruit and vegetable juices
A 2½	794 g	fruits, vegetables
A 10	3079 g	fruits, vegetables, tongues

The advantages of canned foods are similar to those of frozen foods, but a disadvantage is that due to the heat processing a proportion of the vitamin C and B_1 (thiamin) may be lost.

Preservation by salt, salting and smoking

Micro-organisms cannot grow in high concentrations of salt. This method of preservation is used mainly to preserve meat and fish, and the advantage lies chiefly in the fact that a wider variety of dishes with different flavours can be put on the menu.

Meats

Meats which are salted or 'pickled' in a salt solution (brine) are brisket, silverside of beef, ox tongues, legs of pork.

Fish

Fish are usually smoked as well as being salted and include: salmon, trout, haddock, herrings, cods' roes.

The amount of salting varies. Bloaters are salted more than kippers and red herrings more than bloaters.

The salt added to butter and margarine and also to cheese acts as a preservative.

Preservation by sugar

A high concentration of sugar prevents the growth of moulds, yeasts and bacteria. This method of preservation is applied to fruits in a variety of forms: jams, marmalades, jellies, candied, glacé and crystallised.

Jams are prepared by cooking fruit and sugar together in the correct quantities to prevent the jam from spoiling. Too little sugar means the jam will not keep.

Jellies, such as red-currant jelly, are prepared by cooking the juice of the fruit with the sugar.

Marmalade is similar to jam in preparation and preservation, citrus fruits being used in place of other fruits.

Candied: the peel of such fruit as orange, lemon, grapefruit and lime, and also the flesh of pineapple, are covered with hot syrup, the syrup's sugar content is increased each day until the fruit is saturated in a very heavy syrup, then it is allowed to dry slowly.

Crystallised: after the fruit has been candied it is left in fresh syrup for 24 hours. It is then allowed to dry slowly until crystals form on the fruit. Angelica, ginger, violet and rose petals are prepared in this way.

Glacé: the fruit, usually cherries, is first candied, then dipped in fresh syrup to give a clear finish.

Preservation by acids (see p. 397 for explanation of pH)

Foods may be preserved in vinegar, which is acetic acid diluted with water. In the UK malt vinegar is most frequently used, although distilled or white wine vinegar is used for pickling white vegetables such as cocktail onions and also for rollmops (herrings).

Foods usually pickled in vinegar are: gherkins, capers, onions, shallots, walnuts, red cabbage, mixed pickles and chutneys.

Preservation by chemicals

A number of chemicals are permitted by law to be used to preserve certain foods such as sausages, fruit pulp, jam, etc. For domestic fruit bottling, Campden preserving tablets can be used.

Preservation by gas storage

Gas storage is used in conjunction with refrigerators to preserve meat, eggs and fruit. Extra carbon dioxide added to the atmosphere surrounding the foods increases the length of time they can be stored. Without the addition of gas these foods would dry out more quickly.

Preservation by radiation

When foods are irradiated they are exposed to material that emits gamma rays (radioactive material) which kill surface bacteria and moulds. The effect is to prolong the keeping quality of, for example, fruit and vegetables, thereby reducing wastage and extending storage time. Although the system is recommended by such influential bodies as the World Health Organisation, irradiation of foods is a contentious issue. As yet this method of preservation is not permitted in the UK.

Preservation by vacuum packing

Sealing cooked food in an airtight package in conditions where air is removed will preserve the food for longer and retain its flavour and colour. The *sous-vide* system of food preservation employs sterile conditions in the vacuum packing and hence the shelf-life of the cooked food is very much prolonged.

Further information

Guidelines on Pre-cooked Chilled Foods (HMSO).

Freeze Production Electricity Council, 30 Millbank, London SW1.

Education Department, Unilever Ltd, Unilever House, Blackfriars, London EC4.

15

Service of food

Having read the chapter, these learning objectives, both general and specific, should be achieved.

General objectives Appreciate the need for co-operation between kitchen and food service staff. Develop the attitude of good service through understanding from the point of view of the customer and of the food service personnel.

Specific objectives List the points that assist serving and food service staff to serve food supplied from the kitchen. Specify the various ways food may be served to the customer.

This chapter deals with the service of food from the kitchen and considers the different methods which are used to enable the customer to receive the meal.

Fig. 15.1 Service with a smile

The mode of service will depend on the type of establishment, and in some places more than one kind of service will be used, often from one kitchen. The cost of operating these methods varies, but the final objective is the same: that is, the food, when presented to the customer, should look attractive, should be of the right temperature, it should be as ordered and give value for money.

Types of service

The kinds of service that are used are:

waiter or waitress service,
cafeteria service,
hatch and counter service,
snack bar, buffet service, take away.

The kind of service to be provided, will depend to some extent upon the type of people to be served, the number of people to be served, the dining accommodation, the number of sittings and the amount of time and money to be spent on the meal.

Waiter/waitress service

This method of service is the most costly to operate; it is used extensively in many kinds of restaurants. The waiter or waitress takes the order from the customer, then the food ordered is collected from the hot plate by the waiting staff and served to the customer.

For the kitchen staff the following points are of importance:

(a) The food ordered by the waiter should be ready when it is required.
(b) Food should leave the kitchen at the correct temperature (hot if it should be hot, cold if it is meant to be cold), so that it can be presented correctly to the customer by the waiter.
(c) Orders received from the waiting staff should be dealt with in strict rotation and must go from the hot plate in the same order. (However, the waiter should not expect food to be on the hot plate before a reasonable period of time.)
(d) The correct kitchen accompaniment to dishes should be sent from the hot plate with the appropriate dish and the vegetables, as ordered, should be ready to go with the main dishes.

Co-operation between the kitchen and restaurant staff is essential for the successful service of food. The teaching of waiting to young people training to work in the kitchen is invaluable, since they are given an opportunity to see beyond the hot plate and to appreciate the waiters' problems. The need to serve portions of equal size becomes more obvious when a customer complains that the person opposite paying the same money has a portion larger than his or her own. The difficulty of sharing five potatoes between two people or trying to bone an insufficiently cooked sole in front of the customer should cause the kitchen brigade to be careful in the way they prepare and serve the food.

Waiting staff will be used for à la carte and table d'hôte menu service (see Chapter 4), also for banquets and for club service.

Points to note

In serving food the kitchen staff should remember these points:

1 That it is necessary to dress the dish in such a way that the waiter may effectively transfer the food from the dish to the customer's plate.
2 To serve the food on the correct dish, which should be clean and of the right temperature.
3 The food should be arranged attractively; this is very important.
4 The dish should be clean after the food has been added to it and the correct amount should be placed on the dish.
5 Food which is served on a plate should be arranged neatly.
6 Hot foods (except those which are deep fried and would go limp and soft) should be covered with a lid.

Fig. 15.2 Room service

Fig. 15.3 Cafeteria service counter

Cafeteria service

Cafeteria service is used mainly in popular restaurants, industrial canteens and similar establishments (Fig. 15.3).

The customer proceeds alongside the service counter, choosing food from the selection displayed. The counter contains bains-marie and has sections for hot and cold foods; usually one part is for beverages. The food is served and replenished by counter-hands.

The customer collects his or her own cutlery, and therefore staff are required only to clear tables. In some places the tables are laid; the customer then has only to choose his food and take it to the table.

When a large number of people have to be fed in a limited time, several counters would be provided, and the customers' meal times in industrial establishments would be staggered so as to reduce queuing.

The advantage of this method of service is speed, and it is therefore necessary for the kitchen to keep the counter supplied with food and not to cause a hold-up in the service by keeping the counter-hands waiting. The arrangement of the food should be such that the cold dishes are collected first and hot items placed towards the end of the service counter.

Hatch service

When high-speed service of meals is required this method may be used. Hatches connect the kitchen and dining-room. These hatches will be numbered and the numbers correspond to items numbered on the menu. The customer makes up his or her mind at the entrance and goes to the appropriate hatch and collects the meal.

Fig. 15.4 Afternoon tea

Another form of this method of service is to provide the main course at the hatch and a selection of vegetables to be provided. This of course is a slower method of service because, as soon as a choice is provided, service slows down. This type of service is also referred to as counter service.

Snack bars

Snack bars usually provide beverages, sandwiches, salads, fruit, pastries and pies which are suitable for people requiring something quickly or something light. Seating accommodation is provided at the service counter as well as in the room and there may also be provision for take-away food.

Buffets

All kinds of foods may be provided at full buffets, some requiring carving or skilled service; full buffets are usually served from behind the buffet by members of the kitchen staff. Customers will help themselves to those foods not requiring the service of the staff. For such functions it is usual for the kitchen to replenish the buffet as required and to keep the buffet tables attractive.

For cocktail parties all the foods are dressed on dishes and the customers help themselves. When hot foods are served they are sent into the room while the customers are there so as to be still hot when waiters pass them round or when people help themselves.

Automatic vending

Because of the increased cost of labour there has been a considerable development in the use of vending machines; this is because their use does not require labour to serve, labour is only required to maintain and replenish the machines. Complete meal service can be achieved by using prepared meals held in a refrigerated compartment and used in conjunction with a microwave oven and a vending machine for drinks. This aspect of service can be of considerable importance to catering, particularly to replace or supplement existing catering services.

Some advantages of automation are:

1 Foods are available for 24 hours of the day.
2 Machines can relieve pressure of normal service at peak periods.
3 Staff are not required to serve from machines.
4 Clearing and washing-up are dispensed with because disposable cartons are used.
5 Refreshments are available on the job so reducing tea breaks.

Fig. 15.5 Self-service restaurant: general merchandisers vending complete cook-chill dishes for reheating in adjacent microwave ovens, plus hot and cold drinks – all coin- or card-operated

Speciality restaurants

Moderately priced speciality eating houses are in great demand and have seen a tremendous growth in recent years. In order to ensure a successful operation it is essential to assess the customers' requirements accurately and to plan a menu that will attract sufficient customers to give adequate profit. A successful caterer is the one who gives customers what they want and not what the caterer thinks the customers want. The most successful catering establishments are those which offer the type of food thay *can* sell, which is not necessarily the type of food they would *like* to sell.

Well-cooked fish and chips have always been popular in the UK and probably always will be; and it is interesting to note that one of the most successful speciality restaurant developments in the USA (the home of speciality restaurants) has been the English fish and chip shop, complete with the food served in a bag made from a copy of *The Times* of the year 1778.

The Wimpy House, McDonald's, Texas Pancake House, Pizzaland, the health food restaurant, Kentucky Fried Chicken, the sandwich bar, plus

Fig. 15.6 Food service

numerous others, are examples of speciality catering houses offering food and drink at moderate prices with menus carefully planned to fit their estimated markets.

Take away

Customer demand for prepared and cooked food to take away has increased over the years (particularly ethnic food) and the enterprising caterer looking for the opportunity to increase his turnover would be well advised to explore any potential market demand for his products. Suitable greaseproof containers need to be available for the service and carrying away of the food.

Ganymede dri-heat

This is a method of keeping foods either hot or cold. It is used in some hospitals as it ensures that the food which reaches the patients is in the same fresh condition as it was when it left the kitchens.

A metal disc or pellet is electrically heated or cooled and placed in a special container under the plate. The container is designed to allow air to circulate round the pellet so that the food is maintained at the correct service temperature.

This is used in conjunction with conveyor belts and special service counters and helps to provide a better and quicker food service.

Further information

Lillicrap, *Food and Beverage Service* (Edward Arnold).

The Vending Book, Third Edition (The Automatic Vending Association of Britain).

Fig. 15.7 Refrigerated counter service

16

The use of computers

Having read the chapter, these learning objectives, both general and specific, should be achieved.

General objective Be aware of the use of computers in the catering industry and understand their use.

Specific objectives Explain how computers can be used in a variety of ways to provide accurate and timely information for caterers. Be able to use correctly the basic terminology associated with computers.

Introduction

All students should be aware of the increasing use of computers in everyday life within the catering and hotel industry. The huge advances in technological developments over the last decade have brought tremendously powerful micro-computers to a price and size that everyone can afford and manage. (Even the catering course being followed by the student will probably have been planned to some degree by a computer of some sort!) As the general pace of life increases, so the hospitality industry needs to respond to the changing demands of its customers; and the speed with which it can change will often affect the cost of providing the service and the profitability of the venture.

The task of the catering manager is in acquiring, collating and manipulating information in order to make faster and more accurate decisions within the establishment. Information is thus a prime and essential resource in effective management, ranking in importance with people, materials and energy resources. Good caterers have to plan for the future and this means managing information effectively.

Any catering business will have to overcome the normal problems associated with the collection of information:

(a) not enough information
(b) too much of the wrong kind
(c) information in the wrong place
(d) important information which is missing
(e) information which arrives too late
(f) information which is expressed in the wrong way for it to be used.

It is here that the computer becomes of value to those in the catering industry. If the computer is used to collect all the information within the organisation, it can make sure it is able to provide any information, in any format, when and where it is needed, and provide it in a systematic way for different managers in the organisation, eg chefs, head housekeepers, food and beverage managers and restaurant managers. Increased use of Information Technology (IT) has meant the change from recording and communicating information on paper to digital electronic recording using computers.

In this chapter we will be looking at how the computer works and how it can be used as a tool in a variety of ways by those in hospitality and institutional management.

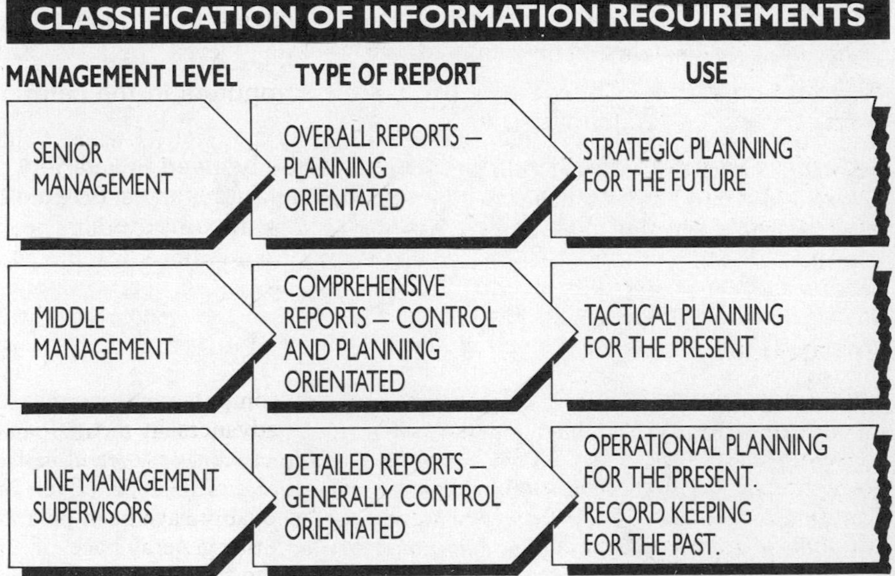

CLASSIFICATION OF INFORMATION REQUIREMENTS
MANAGEMENT LEVEL
TYPE OF REPORT
USE
SENIOR MANAGEMENT
OVERALL REPORTS – PLANNING ORIENTATED
STRATEGIC PLANNING FOR THE FUTURE
MIDDLE MANAGEMENT
COMPREHENSIVE REPORTS – CONTROL AND PLANNING ORIENTATED
TACTICAL PLANNING FOR THE PRESENT
LINE MANAGEMENT SUPERVISORS
DETAILED REPORTS – GENERALLY CONTROL ORIENTATED
OPERATIONAL PLANNING FOR THE PRESENT. RECORD KEEPING FOR THE PAST.

Fig. 16.1

Computers still come in all shapes and sizes but are usually measured in terms of how much information they can store and 'digest' at any one time. The computer's functions include storing information (data) and using that data to provide fresh information or data. This requires the computer to process the information and gives rise to the term 'data processing' or (DP), around which a vast industry has developed over recent years.

In the same way that a cassette recorder requires the tape to be inserted before it can play the music, or have sounds recorded on it, so the computer equipment (hardware) requires a tape or some medium containing instructions before it can be brought into use. These instructions (software) are written in special computer language (there are several different languages that can be used) so that they can be understood by the hardware; they are written in chapters just like a book and these are called programs. Consequently, those who write programs are referred to as programmers.

Computing and IT is a complicated subject and may be more difficult because the computer industry has invented new words and created a jargon of its own, without which it is not possible to understand fully how the computer is able to help the catering industry.

Hardware

Hardware refers to the manufactured equipment which goes to make up a computer. It cannot work at all without instructions (programs or software) and usually requires several different pieces of equipment linked together to enable it to function.

For the computer to be of use in catering we have to be able to put data 'in' and take data 'out'; data also has to be stored until it needs to be used. This will determine the main components of the computer. Each piece of equipment (or device) can be classified as an 'input device', 'output device' or a 'storage device'.

The television screen with a keyboard like a typewriter is often the most distinctive feature of the computer. Data is input to storage by means of the keyboard and may be checked on the screen (Visual Display Unit or VDU) before it is stored away. In this way it becomes an 'input device'. It can also be used to take information out of storage and so is then used as an 'output device'. The size and style of the VDU and keyboard vary from one manufacturer to another and some computers require no VDU at all and rely only on a printer as an output device. Others will allow the use of an ordinary television, but these are usually small domestic computers and less powerful than those used in industry.

The printer is like a typewriter without a keyboard. It types in different ways, either using little dots joined together to form letters or like a traditional typewriter with characters on a wheel known as a 'daisy wheel'. Many popular printers type at speeds of 120–200 characters per second (CPS) and some can type at speeds of 3000 CPS or more. Generally speaking, the price of the printer will depend on the speed and the quality of the typed print.

The silicon chip, or collection of many chips, which makes all this possible is called the central processing unit (CPU). These come in different sizes and are measured by how many characters can be stored at any given moment. These characters are counted in thousands (kilobytes or Kb) and are referred to as the 'random access memory' (RAM) of the computer. It is essential to know the size of the computer's RAM, because this will determine what 'processing power' it has and what exactly the computer can do if programmed correctly. The bigger the CPU, the more expensive the computer. Domestic and other small computers need a 64 Kb RAM, larger computers can increase to 256 and 512 Kb – all the way up to 4000 Kb (or 4 Megabyte) and beyond.

Data is not always required to be instantly available; it can be unloaded from the RAM on other kinds of storage such as magnetic tape or discs. The magnetic tape acts in the same way as the tape in a tape recorder and the various kinds of discs perform in just the same way but are a different shape. This 'off-line' storage is also measured by the number of characters that can be stored and we measure them in 'megabytes' (millions/Mg). Most commonly used are the 'floppy discs' which are like small magnetic records similar to those used on a modern stereo record player. For larger volumes of storage, these become 'hard' or 'fixed discs' and even small computers can have up to 20 Mg of off-line (or secondary) storage for data.

Each piece of hardware is connected by wires to the CPU and with the use of British Telecom equipment connections between computers can be made from one side of the globe to another. As computer science progresses, and computers become more widely used, so they become cheaper, while technological developments over the last decade have also made them smaller and smaller. Complicated computers costing hundreds of thousands of pounds which might have taken up a whole room in an office building at one time can now be bought for a fraction of the price and sit neatly on a desk top.

Software

As we know, without instruction the computer will not work and programs have to be devised which will make the hardware perform the required tasks. The same hardware can do different jobs almost at the same time (in fact, it deals with each task in turn but does it so fast that it appears to happen at the same time).

The instructions are written in special forms so that the computer will understand what should happen next. New 'high level' languages mean that programmers can write in English and use other programs to convert what they have written into machine language or 'compiled code'. Programmers must not only create the code but must understand what they want to happen and how they want the computer to react to their instructions.

In this way software can be made to suit different applications and it is common for companies to specialise in providing software programs for only one industry, such as catering or hotels. It should not be necessary to understand all the internal process of the computer before being able to use it, and if the software is helpful, most people can learn to use it after only a few hours of training. Great care is needed when buying a computer, in order to be sure that the software will perform all the tasks which the user requires and that it is easy to use, giving help to anyone who needs it. It is, therefore, a combination of reliable and dependable hardware, with helpful and dynamic software, which forms the basis of a good computer system. Finally, the important information which is provided by the computer depends heavily upon how much and which information was put in, just as a recipe depends on the right ingredients. In the next section we shall consider how computers help those in the catering industry.

Catering controls

Wherever meals are provided in quantity, it is necessary to examine the costs which occur and to ensure that some control exists to monitor payments to suppliers and staff, and to ensure that these costs are accounted for. At the end of the day, profit levels can therefore be calculated. Additionally, institutional caterers must be in a position to be able to compare costs against allowances, so that over-spending does not occur. For example, the additional expense of 1p per meal per person, becomes very significant in a factory feeding 10000 people twice daily, five days a week; at the end of the year, this represents the sum of £52 000, as shown:

$$10000 \text{ people} \times 2 \text{ meals} \times 5 \text{ days} \times 52 \text{ weeks} \times £0.01 = £52000$$

Stock control

In Chapter 6, we learnt how food costs have been calculated manually. The main element in calculating what food costs have been incurred over a period of time is stocktaking. The simple formula for calculating the cost of each item is shown here:

No.	*Item*	*Opening Stock*	*Receipts of + purchases*	*Closing − stock*	*Consumption = £*
001	Bacon	244.00	+ 105.00	− 165.00	= 184.00
002	Eggs	169.00	+ 92.00	− 145.00	= 116.00
		413.00	+ 197.00	− 310.00	= 300.00

From this simple example, we can see that at the beginning of the period there was an opening stock of £413.00 and during the period £197.00 more bacon and eggs were purchased. On the last day of the period, there was only £310.00 worth of eggs and bacon and it was therefore possible to calculate exactly how much stock had been used. In this case it was £300.00.

Of course, the bacon and eggs had to be counted before the value of the closing stock could be worked out. The bacon would have been weighed and then valued at a cost per pound or kilogram. The eggs would have been counted and multiplied by their price. If this has to be done every week or every month for six hundred or a thousand stock items, it means a lot of paperwork. It is very time consuming finding the right price of each item and multiplying it by the quantity which was left. It is likely, therefore, that the caterer would work the

Fig. 16.2 The back office computer system of a large hotel

opening stock, receipts and closing stock by measurement of weight, volume or numbers and only express the consumption in monetary value. So:

No.	Item	*Opening* stock	+ *Receipt of* purchases	– *Closing* stock	= *Consumption* £
001	Bacon	225 lb 15 oz	+ 97 lb 4 oz	– 152 lb 13 oz	= 170 lb 6 oz
002	Eggs	3755	+ 2044	– 3221	= 2578 eggs

No.	Item	Consumption	(times)	Unit price	= Value
001	Bacon	170 lb 6 oz	×	108p/lb	= £184.00
002	Eggs	214 doz 10/12th	×	54p/doz	= £116.00
					£300.00

Check the arithmetic for the bacon to see just how difficult it can be to get a precise result. Furthermore, these calculations would be far more complicated if the caterer wanted to know the value of the receipts or closing stock. Other figures might also be added to these to make allowances for transfers from one kitchen to another, or to 'write-off' food items which have been spoilt or wasted through over-production.

It was obvious that these calculations should become the first job for computerisation. All the prices can be stored in the program and everything can be measured in terms of money and, if necessary, converted to weights and measures. Conversely, if given the weights and measures the computer could express them in monetary value. It does not relieve the caterer from the tedium of having to count every item at the end of the period, but it does reduce the amount of work because the computer can prepare the papers with all the information printed on them and then it only requires the caterer to enter the amounts of the closing stock in figures, decimals or fractions.

Receipts, of course, are gathered on a daily basis as goods are received. The invoices are entered into the system against each item, so that at the end of each period not only can the value of receipts be calculated but also the caterer is in a position to make exact payments to each supplier. The price of each ingredient is collected from each invoice so that the system can value all the items at the correct price.

Those involved in new technology are now turning their attention to the collection of information for closing stock. Small hand-held terminals with special light-sensitive pens can read the stock number of items and allow the stocktaker to enter the quantities on a small keyboard just like a calculator. This information can then be put straight into the system for processing, thus reducing even further the amount of work to be done by the operator. Stocks which were manually calculated required ten to fourteen days for completion, whereas with the help of the computer the entire process can be completed in an hour or two.

It is also possible to arrive at the value of stock consumed by another method: namely by dividing the quantities of the different ingredients by the number of portions each recipe provides, and then multiplying that quantity by the number of portions prepared or sold. This will give a 'notional' or 'theoretical' stock consumption figure. To make these theoretical projections, the computer must have not only the recipes which have been used but also it must store details of the number of portions provided by each recipe.

Production control

Recipe report sheets present a second major area for the application of computers for caterers. Since details of all ingredients are already in the system for stocktaking purposes, these same records could be used as a source of data from which recipes could be made. Of course, ingredients are rarely used in the same measures as they are purchased and it is therefore necessary to have a complete set of conversion tables, so that if an ingredient is bought by the pound or kilo it can be used in recipes by the gram or by the ounce. Furthermore, these units of measure would have to be abbreviated to make the system easy to use.

This would allow the operator to build up a group of ingredients into recipes and express each recipe in cost per portion. The caterer could see the cost of each recipe and, should the price of any ingredient change, so too would the cost of all the recipes using that ingredient. This application is generally referred to as 'production control' and presents very major advantages to the caterer.

First, the caterer can obtain from the computer comparisons on his *actual* consumption with his *notional* consumption and give the variance, or difference, in terms of money and quantity. This enables him to see clearly not only what he actually used but what he should be using if the recipes are followed correctly. Of course, explanations would have to be sought for large variances but the computer can indicate for the first time which ingredients should be investigated.

Secondly, by putting in a series of menus for some days ahead the caterer can ask the system what ingredients are required for the next period.

This breaking down of menus and recipes into ingredients is called an 'explosion' and by creating such 'recipe explosions' the caterer can gauge his orders more accurately and so ensure a reasonable delivery system. Where food-cost management and food production have to be highly accurate these tasks have been performed manually for many years.

In school meals and hospital catering, pupil and patient requirements can be analysed and converted into ingredients extremely quickly by means of a card-reading device. This device can identify which dishes have been selected from a menu and give precise information to the caterer on what must be produced for the next meal and, in the case of a central kitchen supplying various locations, to where the food should be despatched at the time of service.

From here it is only a short step to work out that, if a list of suppliers were maintained alongside the recipes and ingredients' files, then the computer could easily produce a purchase order list exactly to the specification required by the caterer.

In airline 'in-flight' catering, it may be necessary to write an invoice for meals supplied to passengers aboard a particular flight; or, for one of the large industrial contract caterers, to bill each of the customers in turn for what they have consumed. Yet more data is needed for this function since the system requires the selling price of each portion of food supplied, on which an invoice can be based. Sometimes it may be necessary to have more than one selling price for each item, so that a complex marketing policy can be followed.

In the case of stock systems required for managing liquor stocks in bars, it is quite common for the same beer to be more expensive in one bar than another although the purchase price costs the same.

Thus the various computer applications can be expended to provide a wide range of information against which the caterer can make plans for the future and obtain results on past activity with little or no delay. By making budgets for the future and keeping figures from the past, performance can be compared with objectives and important management decisions are based on reliable information.

Point of sale

Wherever goods are sold it is desirable to record sales and keep cash or credit card payments in a 'cash register'. This provides somewhere safe for the money and provides some control in case mistakes are made.

The new 'electronic points of sale' (EPOS) work in much the same way as has been described for computer systems and because they both use electronics they can be linked together (interfaced) to exchange information. It may be necessary to have a number of registers in different areas, such as the restaurant, the bar or room service, all reporting back to the main computer in order to provide important sales information or to charge the cost of a meal to the bill of a hotel guest.

This equipment can also pass information rapidly to other departments and it is commonplace for orders taken in the restaurant to be transmitted electronically to the kitchen which receives their instructions on a small printer.

The quality of the information available also improves with the new equipment. For example, EPOS systems can record not only which soup was sold and by whom, but it can also provide the time at which it was sold, in order to enable better planning for the next day. Professional caterers often study the relationship between 'profit and popularity'. It may be important to know why certain dishes are popular or why the organisation makes a loss on some. How to make the recipes popular and profitable requires a great deal of information not only from the kitchen but also from the customers.

Fig. 16.3 Using EPOS in one of the bars of a large conference centre

Dietary analysis

In recent years there has been a general trend towards a more healthy diet: people eating out in restaurants require low fat, low sugar, high fibre or vegetarian meals; parents demand wholesome foods for their children in school; workers who depend on their company for their main meal of the day want to have a nutritionally balanced diet. Hospital caterers have long since had the advice of a dietitian to help them plan special diets for patients in hospitals, recognising that a good diet is important in ensuring a quick recovery from illness.

It is now possible to link the dietary values of nutrients, such as vitamins, minerals and carbohydrates, to the recipes on the computer. The computer can then provide detailed or simplified information to advise the caterer or customer what each dish contains. It can dispose of the time-consuming mathematics associated with the manual calculations necessary for accurate dietary information and make it possible for even inexperienced caterers to say which dishes contain a high number of calories or are low in carbohydrates or fat.

Hotel management software

With different software programs, computers are also invaluable to hoteliers. Records of detailed information can be kept for all advanced bookings, so that the hotel knows who to expect, when the guest will arrive or depart, and what kind of room is required.

The computer can also assist by writing the confirmation letters, keeping messages for guests and advising the hotel manager about regular guests, so improving the level of service the hotel offers. When the guest arrives at the hotel the same information can be used to produce a range of information for other departments. For example, it is helpful for those who answer the telephone to know who is in each room and to be able to offer a fast and friendly service.

The housekeeper also needs to know which rooms are being vacated, so that linen can be changed and the room prepared for the next arrival. If a room is not to be let for some time the housekeeper can be advised, to ensure that the heating is turned off or that maintenance or repairs are carried out during this period. It is often the mark of a professional housekeeper to know the names of regular guests and their individual preferences. These are often the little details which make people feel welcome and will ensure that they return on another occasion, and the computer can help by keeping all this information up to date.

The computer is a particularly valuable tool in the accounts office. A great deal of accurate financial information is required for any organisation if it is to be run correctly. Accounts clerks and managers need to know who owes them money and to whom the hotel owes money. Details of debtors and creditors play an important part in business management and managers often rely on computers to ensure that there is sufficient money in the bank to pay suppliers or to provide wage packets at the end of each week or month. Computerised payroll systems in many organisations can be linked to computers at the bank and weekly or monthly wages or salaries can be translated electronically into employees' bank accounts.

It is often important that systems used in the different areas of an organisation, whether in hotels or catering establishments, can be brought together to exchange information and to avoid having to re-enter the same information twice. Much of today's developments in computing are concerned with 'interfacing' one system with another and thereby speeding up the task of information collection.

Fig. 16.4 The front office computer in use in a small hotel

Glossary

Central processing unit (CPU)	Nerve centre of the computer.
Chips, silicon	Combination of electronic circuits built on to a slice of silicon.
Compiled code	Instructions for the computer, translated into a machine language.
CPS	Characters per second.
Daisy wheel	Metal wheel bearing characters for the typing of documents.
Data	Information stored in the system which is not part of the program.
Data processing	Usually applied to the manipulation of information and figures by the computer.
Domestic computers	Small computers, generally considered unsuitable for business use.
Fixed disc	Solid, flat disc which is covered in magnetic material, used for storing programs and data.
Floppy disc	Flexible, flat disc also used for storing programs and data.
Hard disc	Same as a fixed disc but may be removable or interchangeable.
Hardware	Collection of computer equipment.
Input device	Piece of equipment which allows information to be put into the computer.
Main frames	Large installations of computers.

Megabyte	One million sets of binary digits, usually used to measure the amount of storage.
Micro-computer	Smallest type of computers.
Mini-computer	Intermediate type of computers.
Off-line storage	Means of keeping information for the computer which is filed away and not brought into the system until required.
Output device	Piece of equipment which can take information out of the system.
Processing	Manipulation of data by the computer.
Programmers	People who write instructions for computers.
Programs	Computer instructions.
RAM	Random access memory is the form of instant memory available without going to the storage facilities.
Software	Complete sets of programs required to make the computer system function.
Storage device	Equipment used for storing data and programs usually in the form of fixed or floppy discs but also as tapes.

Further information

P R Gamble, *Small Computers and Hospitality Management* (Hutchinson Educational, 1984).

S Godowski, *Microcomputers in the Hotel and Catering Industry* (Heinemann, 1986).

M L Kasavana, *Hotel Information Systems* (CBI Publishing Co. Inc, USA, 1978).

P Zorkoczy, *Information Technology: An Introduction* (Pitman, 1985).

17

Industrial relations

General objectives To have a knowledge and understanding of what is meant by industrial relations in the catering industry and an awareness of the basic legal requirements in the working environment. To create an appropriate attitude towards the responsibilities and the rights of people at work.

Specific objectives To relate legislation to specific examples in the catering industry. To explain the common terms used in committee procedure in industrial relations. To define the specific problems associated with the industry. To state the role and outline the purpose of the trade unions.

Effective relationships in industry depend upon:

(a) co-operation between employee and employer;
(b) knowing the laws passed by Parliament (legislation);
(c) having the right attitude towards those laws.

This brief introduction to industrial relations is intended to produce just such an attitude so that students and employees will work harmoniously and efficiently and thus obtain job satisfaction. Good industrial relations are created when employees and employers know both their responsibilities and their rights and use this knowledge to their mutual benefit and to the advantage of those they serve in the catering industry.

However, the nature of the catering industry means that good industrial relationships are not easy to create for the following reasons:

1 Labour turnover is often high.
2 A vast majority of establishments are small.
3 Many employers take pride in the relationship they have with their employees and do not favour unions.
4 Few employees are union-minded.
5 No one union is solely concerned with the industry.
6 Many employees are foreign and do not speak English.
7 Many establishments are seasonal and operate for only part of the year.
8 Many part-time workers are employed.
9 Unsocial hours are worked.
10 The industry has a history of poor conditions, poor wages and low status.

Legal aspects

A range of legislation since 1970, affecting employers and employees, has gradually been helping to improve the situation in the industry. This legislation includes:

Equal Pay Act 1970,
Trade Union & Labour Relations Act 1974,
Sex Discrimination Act 1975,
Employment Protection Act 1975,
Race Relations Act 1976,
Health and Safety at Work Act 1974 (see p. 311).

Industrial tribunals

In order to administer and enforce the implementation of the Acts, *industrial tribunals* have been set up to settle disputes over unfair dismissal, redundancy and cases of alleged discrimination. The intention has been to protect the individual employee and to strengthen and encourage good relationships between employers and the trade unions.

Communication

In effect, communication channels between staff and management should exist with opportunities and facilities for trade union meetings so that employees have greater participation in the establishment's organisation. To be effective communication often needs to be written and, by law, staff working 16 hours a week or more are entitled to a written statement of terms and conditions of employment. An example of such a statement can be seen below:

Name of establishment
Address
Employee's name .... Address ....
Job title ....
....
Date of commencement .... Remuneration ....
Terms & conditions of holidays and holiday pay
Sick pay arrangements
Pensions & pension schemes
Disciplinary rules
Grievance procedure
Previous service
Length of notice to terminate contract
Other specific conditions

Trade unions and the catering industry

Those employed in the catering industry who join trade unions mainly belong to the Transport and General Workers Union or the General and Municipal Workers Union. The primary aim of unions is to look after the interests of their members at work, in particular, hours of work, conditions and pay. Their

Fig. 17.1 Co-operation

function is to negotiate on behalf of their members with the employers through their local officials. In the event of disagreement between the unions and the employers the Advisory Conciliation and Arbitration Service (ACAS) could be used.

For example, a shop steward in a kitchen should listen to any employee who is a member of the union if he or she has a grievance which seems justified. On their behalf the shop steward could approach the chef or catering manager to resolve the issue. The shop steward may obtain the advice of the branch or district union officer before taking up the case. The role of the trade union is to look after members' interests and this includes the smooth running of a hygienic and safe kitchen.

Women in employment

A female employee who is pregnant and who has been working for a stated period of time for the same employer may not be dismissed because of her pregnancy unless her condition makes it impossible to work competently. An employee who leaves work to have a baby is entitled to her job back after the baby is born, provided she has the required minimum service, has continued to work up to the specified time before confinement and before her absence informs her employer of her intention to return. Maternity pay is paid to employees complying with the stated conditions.

Details are obtainable from the Department of Social Security and Citizens Advice Bureaux.

Equal Pay Act 1970

This Act specifies that pay must be the same for men and for women doing like work or work that is graded as similar. For example, a man or a woman employed to wash-up are both, by law, entitled to the same pay. This would also apply if a female chef de partie for the pastry was employed; the pay would be the same as for a male chef de partie of equal competence and experience.

Sex Discrimination Act 1975

Within the terms of this Act it is unlawful to discriminate on the grounds of a person being male or female, or being married when selection, appointment, transfer, dismissal or promotion are being considered. This means that both men and women should be assessed and decisions made according to their ability, competence, reliability etc, and not according to gender. For example if a kitchen supervisor and a storekeeper are required, both positions should be available to men and women; it is against the law to restrict the posts to male or to female applicants.

Race Relations Act 1976

This Act makes it illegal to discriminate against a person because of their race. However, factors which could affect employment issues relate, for example, to language and religion. The potential waiter, unable to make himself understood or to understand the language of the customers, or the cook whose religion restricts the handling of certain foods, may well jeopardise the opportunity for obtaining and keeping employment. But a person cannot be discriminated against solely because of their race.

Employment Protection Act 1975

The purpose of this Act is to prevent the unfair dismissal of a member of staff. It is essential to know what are considered to be fair reasons for dismissal of staff as well as some reasons considered to be unfair.

Fair reasons for dismissal could include:

(a) incompetence – such as lack of skill, lack of technical or academic qualifications;
(b) misconduct – eg stealing or flagrant breach of hygiene rules;
(c) illegality – eg a foreign worker without a work permit;
(d) genuine redundancy.

Unfair dismissal would include:

(a) for being a member of, or proposing to join, a trade union;
(b) unfair selection for redundancy.

Glossary

The following is a list of some of the terms used in negotiations and committees:

Abstain Voting neither for nor against, effectively not voting.

Abstention This is a vote which is cast neither for nor against.

Address the Chair When speaking at a meeting members must speak to the Chair and not to other members.

Adjourn When the meeting or part of the business is delayed until later.

Ad hoc committee A committee formed to do a specific job which ceases to exist when this special work is complete.

Against A vote in disagreement with the motion.

Agenda The list of items to be discussed by the committee.

Amendment This is a proposition to change the wording of a motion. The amendment needs a proposer and a seconder; it is then put to the vote and if carried (has a majority vote for it), the motion as amended replaces its original form. If the amendment is defeated then the original motion stands. More than one amendment can be put forward; each is discussed separately and then voted on in the order received.

AGM Annual General Meeting.

AOB Any other business. Usually the last item on the agenda for the matters not included on the agenda. Should be used as little as possible since matters need to be considered before discussion.

Arbitration When, in a dispute, agreement cannot be reached and the decision of an independent person or persons is accepted.

Check-off Union dues deducted by the employer who then pays the dues to the union.

Closed shop This is the situation where individuals must be a member of the same union to which the other workers belong, or when new employees must join the union. The agreement of both the employer and the trade union is required to operate a closed shop.

Collective agreement Agreements made between several trade unions and several employers or employers' associations.

Collective bargaining Negotiations to result in collective agreement regarding conditions of work, allocation of work, discipline, facilities for trade union officials and procedures for consultation.

Chair, Chairman or Madam Chairman The person conducting the meeting.

Consensus The general feeling of the meeting.

Conciliation A process whereby an outside party brings opposing parties in dispute together to settle the dispute.

Constitution A formal document which states the aims of the organisation, its membership and how it should be managed.

Co-opted member A person invited to join a committee by its members because of special assistance he or she can bring to the committee.

Correction of minutes When minutes of the previous meeting are due to be signed as a correct record it is sometimes found necessary to correct them if the meeting agrees to the correction.

Defeated Said of a motion which has been voted on and decided against.

Delegate A person authorised by a committee or organisation to represent it on its behalf.

Ex officio Means 'because of his or her office' for example the Chair of an organisation is usually a member (ex officio) of all its committees because of being the Chair.

For A vote in favour of the motion.

Job evaluation A term used to determine the value of jobs in a way acceptable to those in the job.

Joint consultation When employees and employers discuss before decisions are taken.

Legislation The law, having legal authority.

Lobby Recognised way of persuading people to support an idea.

Lost Said of a motion when it has been voted and decided against.

Minutes The written record of a committee's decisions. All resolutions, amendments and decisions, including votes, must be recorded. Discussions may be summarised.

Motion A statement which will be discussed and then may be put to the vote.

Move The proposer of a motion is said 'to move it' when he or she asks that it be put to the vote.

Nem con 'No one against'. A motion is passed 'nem con' when some vote for, none against, but some abstain.

Nomination The giving of the name of a person for office or to be a member of a committee.

Out of order Not conforming to the rules of procedure or the proper conduct of the meeting.

Point of order When a member requests the Chair to correct or bring the running of the meeting to comply with the Rules of Procedure.

Proposer The principal speaker for the motion.

Proxy A person given authority to exercise a member's vote, to vote instead of that member.

Quorum The minimum number of members required to be present for business. The number should be stated in the Rules of Procedure. If insufficient members attend then the situation is described as inquorate.

Resolution	The actual wording of a motion.
Ruling	The Chair's decision on a matter of procedure which must be followed without discussion.
Shop steward	The trade union member elected by the department or section he or she represents. He or she communicates management proposals to his or her colleagues and represents their views to management.
Status quo	If a change causes a dispute then the original situation is reverted to until agreement is reached.
Seconder	The next person to support a motion following the proposer.
Substantive agreement	An agreement which determines, for example, rates of pay, hours of work, holiday arrangements.
Trade dispute	A dispute between employers and employees or between employees and employees.
Unanimous	When all members present vote for the motion.

Further information

'Industrial Relations' Guide No. 7 (HCTB).
The Acts of Parliament, (HM Stationery Office).

18

Guide to study and employment

Most students can be successful with their studies provided they wish to succeed in the catering industry and are determined to work reasonably hard throughout the course. A problem which is presented to many students is *how* to get the best out of their course, because it may be the first time they have entered an educational establishment where much of the responsibility for learning lies with them. Therefore some suggestions follow which may be helpful in guiding students towards how to study and how to cope with the various assessment techniques used in education.

The successful catering student is one who not only achieves the required standard of techniques but, equally important, has the right attitude to other students, teaching staff, customers and the industry.

Right attitude includes such qualities as reliability, conscientiousness, willingness, co-operativeness, honesty, loyalty, punctuality and courtesy, and the student who is to be successful needs to develop these qualities.

Successful studying

Catering is a very practical occupation, nevertheless there is a considerable amount of study needed for the learning of the theoretical aspects of catering courses and the following comments may be of assistance:

1 Learning requires effort and hard work, but thorough preparation gives confidence.
2 Studying in a quiet place, such as the local library's reading room, is effective for most people and can give the best results.
3 Studying is more efficient when students are not tired.
4 The careful rewriting of lesson notes aids learning.
5 Do not leave revision until too near the examination but revise throughout the course, because spaced-out learning is more effective than 'cramming'.
6 Study consistently throughout the course.
7 Organise regular times for both study and revision.
8 Practice in answering previous examination questions can be useful at appropriate stages of the course.

Most students need to know how they are progressing on the course of study, both in relation to other members of the course and the standards required of the course. This information is obtained from teachers and various methods of evaluating students are used. It is essential that students know during the course as well as at the crucial stages, such as at the end of the year, if they are working in the best manner to reach the required standard.

What to study

The syllabus of most catering courses is written in objective terms, which enables the student to know precisely what should be known and what they should be able to do at the end of the course. An advantage of having the course content expressed in this way means that the student and the teacher are both aware of the depth and breadth to which the course will be examined. Towards the end of the course students should check the syllabus for any omissions in their knowledge; the sensible student then accepts responsibility to remedy any gaps by further study and revision.

Evaluation procedures

Students are subjected to various techniques designed to assess what has been learned and therefore it is helpful to consider those methods in which catering students will be involved, although all students will not necessarily use all the methods. They include the evaluation of theoretical aspects by:

(a) subjective-type examination (brief answer and essay type);
(b) objective-type examination;
(c) continuous assessment.

It is essential for students to understand that, although the theoretical and practical aspects of the course may be assessed separately, theory and practice cannot be separated, because the understanding of the theory is necessary for achieving good results in the practical class.

Continuous assessment

One purpose of continuous assessment is to enable students to know how they are progressing during the course, this is achieved by periodic evaluations or assessments. The advantage of this system is that a person does not fail on one particular occasion as could occur with a single examination. Furthermore the student and the teacher can become aware of weaknesses early in the course and steps can be taken to remedy them.

Continuous assessment of theory work

Some students may be expected to present work throughout the course in place of, or as well as, an examination. This work may include homework, work completed in the class, projects, etc and the marks awarded for these can be used in place of an examination mark. Again the student benefits from this system; for example, if the student is away or unwell on the day of an examination this can cause a problem, but with work spread over the course this problem does not occur.

Theory examinations

The object of a theory examination is to find out if the candidate knows the answers. The students have to convey to the examiner the required answers and this is usually done by objective-type questions (short answer) or subjective-type questions, which may range from a brief answer to a short essay or the use of both.

Objective-type questions

When answering objective-type questions it cannot be too strongly emphasised that students must *carefully* read the question, decide which is correct, then mark the paper accordingly. If the student is not *sure* of the answer it is wise to proceed to the next question. Having considered all the questions in this way, the student can then carefully re-read the questions which have not been answered and mark the paper in the appropriate box.

For most students it will be unwise to review the questions they have answered straight away (provided the question has been carefully read); this is because with multiple-choice questions the distractors should be plausible and doubts might come into the student's mind.

Finally, more than adequate time is allowed for objective-type examinations; since time is not a limiting factor there is no urgency to complete the paper quickly – accuracy is the key to success.

Examples of objective-type questions can be found in *Questions on Practical Cookery* (Edward Arnold) and *Questions on Theory of Catering* (Edward Arnold).

Subjective-type questions

As with objective-type questions it is essential that care is taken when reading the question. With essay-type questions it is also necessary to take care in producing the answer and the following points should be considered.

1 *Writing:* this must be readable. The easier it is to read, the more favourable is the impression given of the student's paper.

2 *Spelling:* the facts are what the examiner wants, but if there are many words spelt wrongly an unfavourable impression is given. French words should be correct. It is better to use correctly spelt English words than misspelt French words.

   Extra care must be taken not to misspell words which are similar in French and English, eg filet and fillet, carotte and carrot.

   Simple words are often spelt wrongly, such as gravy, plaice, gherkin, lettuce, etc.

3 *Answering questions:*
   (a) The meaning of the answer must be clear to the examiner.
   (b) The question should be understood and answered to the point.
   (c) The answer should be precise, with no padding.
   (d) No essential facts should be omitted from the answer.
   (e) All parts of a question should be answered.
   (f) Avoid using first person singular, eg 'Braising is a nice method of cooking, but I like fried steak'.
   (g) Avoid slang expressions and terms which are not good English.
   (h) Avoid vagueness and inaccurate phrases, eg 'Spot of water'.

(i) Use correct terms and words, eg sugar is not *diluted*, but dissolved. Gelignite does not go into bavarois!
(j) Use accepted abbreviations for weights and measures, but avoid marge, veg, fridge.
(k) Answer only the number of questions asked for. No extra marks will be gained if more are answered, but be certain to answer the required number of questions.
(l) Answer questions in any order, but number them clearly.
(m) Re-read the answers carefully when the paper is completed.

4 *Layout:* a paper laid out clearly creates a favourable impression. The following points may be helpful:
(a) Leave a generous margin.
(b) Tabulate answers where suitable.
(c) If an essay form answer is necessary give an introduction and have a good concluding paragraph.
(d) Name the recipe, underline the heading.
(e) Where diagrams can be used these should be drawn carefully.

Summary: it is necessary to know the facts and to present them clearly. The writing must be legible, the English and spelling correct, the layout neat and the information to the point.

Examination advice

Hints on examinations

A problem which has to be faced by many people is nerves: these may only be controlled to a certain degree according to each individual. Confidence in one's own ability helps, and this confidence comes from knowledge; provided candidates have done their utmost to learn, there need be no excessive nervousness.

Preparation for examinations

1 Revise throughout the course, but in addition revise the whole course prior to the examination.
2 Determine when revision is most effective for you; some people prefer early morning, others late evening.
3 Near the examination, practise answering past examination questions in the same time allowed as in the actual examination.
4 Do not rely only on past examination questions.

Examination day prior to the examination

1 Allow plenty of time so as to arrive punctually.
2 Have an adequate number of pens.
3 If you wish to chew sweets select those without wrappings so that you do not disturb others.
4 Most examinations occur in the summer, therefore wear suitable clothes.

The examination

If there is a choice of questions then take extra care reading them so that you fully understand the question; you can then select those you can answer best.

Most candidates' nerves disappear as soon as they start writing in the theory examinations. Some people, however, find their minds go blank; in this case it may help to concentrate on one small part of the question, particularly questions on practical cookery. The student who may not have learnt a particular recipe by heart can often, by thinking hard of the practical preparation, arrive at a sufficiently sound answer to satisfy the examiner.

Obtaining employment and building a career

Having chosen to come into catering, it is to be hoped that prior to or during the course students will have worked in the industry and have seen the different types of work available. If possible try to obtain experience in a variety of different establishments, eg hotels, hospitals, industrial, restaurants etc. You may find you wish to specialise in the pastry, for instance, or that to work in a hospital appeals to you. People do best that which interests them most, so try to find out what appeals to you.

Points to consider prior to obtaining employment

1 Keep an accurate record of all employment, including part-time and college-sponsored work.
2 Keep all certificates together in a safe place.
3 Maintain an accurate record of all education received.
4 Prepare a curriculum vitae (CV), ie a comprehensive and correct account of yourself and your achievements to include:
   (a) date of birth;
   (b) address;
   (c) educational establishments attended, both school and college, full-time and part-time, with dates;
   (d) educational achievements, not only academic but also sporting, musical etc.
   (e) employment – stating period of time worked, and how employed;
   (f) interests – eg youth clubs, Scouts, Guides, boys' or girls' brigades etc, first aid, sports, community work, travel, music, reading etc. Any awards, such as Duke of Edinburgh's, Queen's Guide or Scout, first aid certificates, should be mentioned.
5 Ask two people to act as referees for you and to be prepared to provide references if required by potential employers. These referees are not to be relatives, but two people who know you from different situations, eg minister of religion, youth leader, former employer, as well as college tutor. Not all employers require or take up references but it is courteous to inform anyone that is prepared to give a reference that you have applied for a job, in case the reference is requested. This is particularly important as your career progresses.
6 Keep up to date with job vacancy advertisements; use libraries for journals and periodicals containing this information.

7 Attend student careers conventions.
8 Write to companies for details of their career and employment information.
9 Discuss your interests with teaching staff and obtain their advice.
10 Develop the attitudes and qualities required to make you a good prospect for an employer ('employable'), for example, that you are willing to:
   - work and learn, and to improve and progress;
   - accept constructive criticism;
   - work with others (porters as well as the chef de partie);
   - be co-operative, courteous, reliable, punctual, loyal, honest, hard-working and cheerful;
   - be confident and flexible.

How to obtain employment

1 Direct contact:
   (a) many colleges receive requests for staff from employers (jobs may be displayed on a noticeboard);
   (b) some college staff have personal contact with catering establishments and vacancies;
   (c) through part-time employment and/or college placements in industry;
   (d) through friends and relatives, and former students who have contacts in the industry.
2 Answering advertisements: vacancies are advertised in national and local newspapers and in magazines and periodicals. Use public and college libraries to obtain access to these publications.
3 Using agencies: Jobcentres and private employment agencies are important sources of job vacancies. The Services have their own recruitment offices.

Preparing for an interview

First read the advertisement carefully and if it seems a suitable job then find out about the establishment before applying for the job. If possible speak to someone employed there, but remember that their comments will be subjective.

Consider the following points:

1 When writing for an application form use handwriting.
2 Complete the application form accurately and neatly, and have it typed if possible.
3 On no account give any false information.
4 If names of referees are required inform the referees that you have applied for the job, having previously obtained their permission.
5 If a photo is required, send a recent head and shoulders passport-type photo.
6 If your CV is required send a photocopy of it.

Going for an interview

1 Prepare in advance any questions you may wish to ask.
2 Have any certificates available in case they are required.
3 Make certain you know where the interview is taking place, how to get there and how long it takes.

4 Leave extra time so that should there be delays because of traffic or transport problems you arrive on time.
5 Take with you the letter stating the address and phone number of where the interview is to be held, so that if you are delayed then you can phone and explain the situation.
6 Dress neatly and cleanly.
7 Avoid excessive jewellery and make up.
8 Remember that clean hands and finger nails are essential.

At the interview

1 Be reasonably confident but not over-confident.
2 You may be nervous, but this is to be expected. (It may not show.)
3 When seated, sit up and do not lounge.
4 If you normally smoke – *don't*.
5 A natural smile, not a grin, is helpful.
6 Speak up when answering questions and keep to the point.
7 You should be given the opportunity to ask questions at the end of the interview; if this has not happened then say you wish to ask a question(s).
8 Do not be surprised if you are asked about what you hope to do in the future – you need to have thought this out before the interview and have some idea of what to say.

After the interview

1 If you get the job: congratulations!
2 If you do not, then consider how the experience was worthwhile.
3 Evaluate why you did not get the job:
   (a) were other applicants more suitable?
   (b) did your interview go badly? (For example, because you were too nervous, did not know the answers, felt unwell, did not like the interviewer etc.);
   (c) perhaps you did not suit the employer's needs etc?
4 Remedy any shortcomings you discover in yourself.
5 Apply again for other jobs until you succeed.

Building a career

Having got on the ladder, the following points may be considered when trying to get up it:

1 Do not get off one ladder until you have got onto another one; in other words make certain you have a job to go to before leaving present employment.
2 It is generally advisable to stay with your first employer for at least one year, and to spend at least a year in subsequent jobs.
3 It is desirable to keep in continuous employment; gaps do not present employers with the view of a stable employee.
4 Advancement is more likely if one keeps within one area of catering, eg contract, hospital, restaurants, so that experience gained can be of benefit to employers.

5 However, some careers need people experienced in several aspects of the industry, eg teaching.
6 Know where you are going and have attainable goals. However, if a real mistake has been made and a move has been wrong then a change may be for the best.

In evaluating the need to progress, these factors need to be considered apart from the money: value of new experience, establishment's reputation, conditions and hours of work, opportunities for advancing in existing establishment, facilities offered for self development, eg further courses, overseas experience etc.

If possible, when leaving college or any employment endeavour to leave in such a way that you can return at any time. The catering industry needs people who are prepared to work hard, to enjoy their work and to work together as a team.

Index

aboyeur, 285
absorption, 373
accelerated freeze drying, 400
accident report form, 313
accidents, 313
acidity of foods, 397
additives in food, 394
administration, 287
aerobes, 352
African cookery, 20
agar agar, 170
albumin, 376, 391
alkalinity, 397
allspice, 164
almonds, 135, 136
alternating current, 252
aluminium equipment, 120, 236
American cookery, 14
amino acids, 375
anaerobes, 352
anchovies, 111
anchovy essence, 170
angelica, 171
animal fats, 146
anise, 165
antioxidants, 395
apples, 132
apricots, 132
arrowroot, 154
artichoke, globe, 129
  Jerusalem, 126
artificial respiration, 319
asafoetida, 165
ascorbic acid, 382
asparagus, 129
aspic jelly, 171
atmospheric steamers, 215
aubergines, 128
Austrian cookery, 12
automatic boiler, 226
automatic vending, 410
avocado pear, 128

bacon, 87, 95
bacteria, 352, 397
bain-marie, 219
Baisakhi Day, 10
baking powder, 155
balanced diet, 394
ball valve, 268
bananas, 133
Bangladeshi cookery, 16
banquet menus, 67
barley, 152
basal metabolism, 387
basil, 162
bass, 116
bay leaves, 162
bean sprouts, 129
beans
  broad, 128
  butter, 128
  dried, 161
  haricot, 161, 240
  runner, 128
beef, 85
  food value, 84, 159
  French terms, 91
  storage, 84, 157
  uses, 89
beetroot, 126
beverages, 393
bilberries, 131
bin cards, 199
blackberries, 131
blackcurrants, 131
blackjack, 69
blenders, 224
blueberries, 131
boiling pans, 217

Bombay duck, 171
bones, 98
borage, 162
brains, 98
brassicas, 127
bratt pan, 216
brawn, 171
Brazil nuts, 135
breakfast menus, 55
bream, 117
brill, 113
brine, 403
British cookery, 10
British Thermal Unit (BTU), 245
broccoli, 127
Brussels sprouts, 128
Buddhist influences, 10
buffets, 410
bulb vegetables, 127
burns, prevention of, 315
burst pipes, 273
butchers' blocks, 221
butter, 390
butyric acid, 376
buying, 181

cabbage, 128
  red, 128
  savoy, 128
cafeteria service, 409
calcium, 383
Calor gas, 251
Calorie, 387
calorie requirement, 387
canning, 403
Cape gooseberries, 131, 175
capers, 174
capsicums, 165
carambola, 131
caraway, 165
carbohydrate, 377
cardamom, 165
careers in catering, 436
Caribbean cookery, 15
carotene, 380
carp, 117
carrots, 126
casein, 374
cash account, 203
cash discount, 202
cashew nuts, 136
cassia, 165
cast aluminium, 236
cauliflower, 128
caviar, 110, 171
cayenne, 168
celeriac, 126
celery, 129
celery seed, 162
cellulose, 380
Celsius (temperature scale), 353
centralised production, 301
ceps, 129, 171
cereals, 150, 393
cervelat, 172
chanterelles, 130
charcoal, 251
cheese, 147, 390
chemical food poisoning, 350
cherries, 133
  cocktail, 175
chervil, 162
chestnuts, 135
chicken, 101
chicory, 127
chillies, 165
chilling, 400
chill-rooms, 197, 230
Chinese cabbage, 127
Chinese cookery, 17
Chinese five-spice, 165
Chinese leaves, 127
Chinese menus, 17
chippers, 225
chives, 163
chlorination, 262
chlorine dioxide, 150
chocolate, 158
chocolate vermicelli, 175
cholesterol, 395
chollah, 10
chopping boards, 238
chow-chow, 171
Christian influences, 9
Christmas, 9
cinnamon, 165
cisterns, 269
cleaning materials, 340
clementines, 133
clostridium botulinum, 357

clostridium perfringens, 356
clothing (and hygiene), 337
cloths, 241
cloves, 166
clubs, 23
cochineal, 169
cockles, 118
cockroaches, 361
cocktail cherries, 175
cocoa, 158
coconut, 135
cod, 117
coffee, 159
cold rooms, 197, 230
cold water systems, 264
coley, 117
collagen, 374
colourings, 169
combustion, 385
commanding (supervising), 289
commercial documents, 201
commodities list, 178, 180
communicating, 291
comparison of fuels, 257, 259
computer glossary, 423
computers, 414
condiments, 167
conduction, 244
conger eel, 111
contact grills, 220
contamination, 350
contract catering, 35
control cycle, 192
controlling (supervising), 290
convection, 244
convection oven, 209
cook-chill, 296
cook-freeze, 301
cooking fat, 144
copper (and nutrition), 385
copper equipment, 235
coriander, 166
corn on the cob, 128
corn salad, 127
cornflour, 153
cost control, 188
courgettes, 128
couscous, 14
couverture, 158
crab, 119
cranberries, 133
crawfish, 119
crayfish, 119
cream, 141, 365, 389
credit notes, 201
cross contamination, 351
cryogenic freezing, 401
crystallised fruits, 131
cucumber, 129
cumin, 166
currents, electric, 252
curriculum vitae, 436
curry powder, 167
custard powder, 153
cutting boards, 238
cuttle fish, 122
cuts, prevention of, 314, 318
cyclical menus, 38

dab, 113
daily stores issue sheet, 203
damsons, 132
Danish cookery, 13
dates, 133
deep fat-fryers, 217
deep freezers, 230
defrosting, 232
delegation, 290
delicatessen goods, 170
delivery note, 201
design of menu, 40
diet balance, 394
dietary fibre, 380
dietitians, 25
digestion, 373
dill, 163
dill seeds, 166
dinner menu, 63
discount, 262
dishwashing machine, 232
Divali, 9
dog fish, 117
drainage of water, 273
dried vegetables, 399
dripping, 146
Dublin Bay prawns, 119
duck, 102
  wild, 105
dysentery, 358

earthenware, cleaning of, 343
Easter, 9
Eastern European cookery, 12
eel, 112
eggs, 136, 365, 391
elastin, 84
electric cookers, 209
electric shock, 319
electrical equipment, large, cleaning of, 345
electrical fuses, 254
electrical plugs, 253
electrical terms, 252
emotional needs (and food), 2
employment, 437
Employment Protection Act, 428
energy conservation, 260
English cookery, 10
environmental health officer, 312
enzymes, 397
Equal Pay Act, 428
Escoffier, 279
essences, 170
ethnic cultures, 8
examinations, 435
explosions, 316
extracts, 172

Fahrenheit (temperature scale), 353
fainting, 318
fast food menus, 76
fats, 144, 376
fennel, 163
fennel seeds, 166
fenugreek, 166
figs, 133
filberts, 135
fines-herbs, 164
finishing kitchen, 298
fire blanket, 321
fire extinguishers, 323
fire precautions, 319
first aid, 317
first aid box, 317, 106
fish
  composition, 391
  food value, 109, 391
  French names, 108
  garnishes, 53
  offal, 122
  preservation, 110
  seasons for, 108
  storage, 107, 110
flavourings, 170
floors, kitchen, 316
flounder, 114
flour, 151
fluoride, 393
flushing systems, 268
foie gras, 172
foil, 242
folic acid, 382
fondant, 176
food additives, 394
food-borne diseases, 366
food
  and society, 1
  buying, 181
  choppers, 224
  costing, 188
  hygiene, 347
  ideas, 2
  images, 3
  mixers, 223
  poisoning, 348
  preservation, 399
  regulations, 367
  requirements, 387
  resources, 3
  slicers, 224
  spoilage, 396
  storage, hygienic, 364
  summary, 369
  values, 388
  waste disposers, 233
forecasting, 193, 288
Frankfurt sausage, 172
freezing of pipes, 271, 400
French cookery, 11
French garnishes, 53
French grammar, 43
French terms, 47
frogs' legs, 172
fromage frais, 150
frozen foods, 400
frozen pipes, 271
fructose, 377
fruit, 130
  food value, 130, 391
  French names, 133

juices, 393
preservation, 131
purchasing points, 130
quality, 130
seasons for, 130
storage, 130
fry plates, 220
fuels, comparison of, 257
fuses, 255

galantine, 172
game, 103
Ganymede, 412
garam masala, 166
garlic, 123
gas
bills, 247
equipment, 248
meter, 246
gate valve, 266
gelatine, 172
gelatinisation, 380
German cookery, 12
ghee, 16
gherkins, 173
ginger, 166
gliadin, 374
glossary of French terms, 47
glucose, 377
gluten, 374
glutenin, 374
glycerol, 376
glyceryl mono stearate, 395
goose, 102
gooseberries, 132
granadillas, 134
grapefruit, 132
grapes, 134
gravlax, 13
grease traps, 274
Greek cookery, 13
green vegetables, 124
greengages, 131
griddle plate, 220
grills, 220
grocery goods, 170
grouse, 105
guavas, 134
gudgeon, 117
guinea fowl, 102
gum tragacanth, 176

habit, 1
haddock, 117
haggis, 173
hake, 118
halibut, 114
halogen hobs, 214
hams, 87, 173
Hanukkah, 10
hare, 104
hatch service, 409
hazel-nuts, 135
heads, calves', 97
Health and Safety Act, 311
healthy eating, 394
healthy menu (sample), 32
hearts, 99
herbs, 162
herrings, 112
Hindu influences, 9
historical background (food), 5
Holi, 9
honey, 176
horseradish, 173
hospital catering, 24
hot air rotary fryers, 218
hot cupboards, 219
hotels, 22
humectants, 395
Hungarian cooking, 12
hunger, 1
hygiene, 323
hygiene terms, 370

ice-cream, 176
Idd-ul-Fitar, 9
induction cookers, 213
industrial catering, 33
industrial relations, 425
industrial relations terms, 429
industrial tribunals, 426
infection
sources, 357
spread, 357
insect infection, 361
interviews, 437
invoices, 204
iodine, 385
Irish cookery, 11

iron, 384
iron, equipment, 233
  (mineral), 384
Italian cookery, 11
Italian pastes, 151

jam, 176
Janam Ashtami, 9
Japanese cookery, 18
jelly bag, 240
jelly, piping, 177
jelly, redcurrant, 177
Jewish influences, 10
John Dory, 115
joule, 387
Judaism, 10
juniper berries, 166

kale, 125
kidney, 98
kilocalorie, 387
kilojoule, 387
kitchen
  clothing, 337
  cloths, foils, papers, 241
  French, 43
  hygiene, 340
  lighting, 341
  organisation, 277
  premises, 340
  staff, 279
  supervisors, 286
  utensils, 233
  ventilation, 340
kiwi fruit, 131
kohlrabi, 129
kosher, 10
kumquats, 133

lactic acid, 388
lactose, 388
lamb, 86
  quality, 86
  uses, 92
lard, 146
lecithin, 395
leeks, 127
legal aspects, 426
legislation, 427
lemons, 132
Lent, 9
lentils, 161
lettuce, 127
licensed house (pub) catering, 35
lifts, food, 342
lighting, kitchen, 341
ling, 115
liquidiser, 224
liquids, 393
listeria, 357
liver, 98
liver sausage, 172
lobster, 119
loganberries, 131
lovage, 163
lunch menus, 57
luncheon clubs, 34
lychees, 134

mace, 166
mackerel, 112
maize, 153
maltose, 378
mandarins, 133
mandolins, 237
mangetout, 128
mango, 134
  chutney, 174
mangosteens, 134
marble, cleaning of, 343
margarine, 145
marjoram, 163
markets, 186
marmalade, 176
marrons glacés, 176
marrow, 129
  beef, 98
marzipan, 176
masher, hand or electric, 225
matzo, 10
meat
  composition, 83, 390
  garnishes, 54
  preservation, 364
  storage, 364
mechanical equipment, 222
media influences, 4
Mediterranean cookery, 13
megrim, 114
melon, 134

menu balance, 42
menus
  banquet, 67
  breakfast, 55
  colour, 42
  cyclical, 38
  dinner, 63
  fast food, 76
  French, 43
  functions, 69
  hospital, 26
  industrial catering, 78
  light buffets, 72
  luncheon, 57
  planning, 41
  school, 30
  structure, 39
  supplies, 41
  tea, 61
  wording, 43
metabolism, 387
meter reading, 246
Mexican cookery, 15
microwave ovens, 211
Middle Eastern cookery, 13
milk, 140, 365, 388
mincemeat, 176
mineral elements, 382
mint, 163
mixed spice, 167
mixers, 223
monkfish, 115
monosodium glutamate (MSG), 395
mooli, 126
morels, 130
Mormons, 9
mortadella, 220
motivation, 291
moulds, 396
mullet, 117
mushrooms, 129
Muslim influences, 9
muslin, 240
mussels, 121
mustard, 168
myasin, 374

niacin, 382
nicotinic acid, 382
non-dairy cream, 143
non-stick equipment, 237
Norwegian cookery, 13
nose bleeds, 319
nutmeg, 166
nutrients, 372, 385
nutrition
  and food science, 372
  fats, 376
nuts, 135, 393

oatmeal, 152
oats, 152
octopus, 122
offal, 97
ohms, 252
oils, 144
oily fish, 111
okra, 128
oleic acid, 376
olives, 173
onions, 127
oranges, 132
order book, 200
oregano, 163
organisation, 289
outside catering, 35
ovens, 209
ovovitellin, 374
oxidation, 385
oxtail, 97
oysters, 120

Pakistani cookery, 16
papaya (paw-paw), 134
paper
  greaseproof, 241
  kitchen, 241
paprika, 168
paratyphoid fever, 358
parsley, 163
parsnips, 126
partie system, 279
partridge, 105
passion fruit, 134
pastillage, 177
pâté maison, 173
peaches, 132
peanuts, 136
pearl barley, 152

pears, 132
  avocado, 128
peas
  fresh, 128
  green split, 161
  marrowfat, 161
  yellow split, 161
pecan nuts, 135
pectin, 395
Pentecost, 10
pepper, 168
perch, 115
persimmon, 131
personal hygiene, 332
pH, 397
pheasants, 105
phosphorus, 384
pickles, 173
pigeon, 103
pike, 115
pilchards, 112
pimentos, 129
pineapple, 131
piping bag, cleaning of, 240
piping jelly, 177
pistachios, 135
plaice, 114
planning menus, 36
plastic, cleaning of, 345
plums, 132
pods and seeds, 123, 128
Polish cookery, 12
pollack, 115
polyphosphate, 395
pomeloes, 133
poppadums, 174
poppy seeds, 167
pork, 86, 94
portion control, 182
  equipment, 183
potato flour, 154
potato peelers, 222
potatoes, 126
potted shrimps, 174
poultry, 100, 390
  quality, 101
  storage, 101
  types of, 101
  uses, 102
poussin, 101
prawns, 118
preservation of food, 396
pressure fryers, 218
pressure governor, gas, 247
price lists, 180
production system, 293
protein, 374
pulses, 161
pumpkin, 129
purchasing, 181
purchasing specification, 186
pyridoxine, 382

quails, 105
  eggs, 140
quark, 150
quick freezing, 400
quorn, 88

rabbit, 104
Race Relations Act, 428
radiation, 244, 405
radiccio, 127
radishes, 126
raising agents, 155
Raksha Bandha, 9
Ramadan, 9
raspberries, 133
raw eggs, 357
redcurrant jelly, 177
redcurrants, 133
redfish, 116
refrigerants, 229
refrigeration, 197, 227
refrigerators
  absorption, 228
  compression, 228
  maintenance, 232
regeneration, 300
reheated food, 365
relationships, 2
religious influences, 8
rennet, 177
rennin, 388
requisition book, 200
residential establishments, 33
restaurants, 22
rhubarb, 133
riboflavin, 382
rice, 153

rockfish, 116
roe, 122
rollmops, 174
root vegetables, 126
rosemary, 163
rotary fryers, 218
Russian cookery, 12

safety, 311
safety at work, 311
saffron, 167
sage, 163
sago, 154
Saint Nicholas, 9
salamander, 220
salami, 172
salmon, 112
  smoked, 174
salmon trout, 112
salmonella, 355
salsify, 126
salt, 167
salting, 403
saltpetre, 174
sardines, 112
satsumas, 133
sauerkraut, 174
sausage, Continental, 172
scalds, prevention of, 315
scallops, 121
scampi, 119
Scandinavian cookery, 13
scarlet fever, 352
school meals service, 29
scorzonera, 126
Scottish cookery, 11
scratches, prevention of, 314
sea kale, 129
sea urchin, 122
semolina, 151
service of food, 406
sesame seeds, 167
Sex Discrimination Act, 428
shallots, 127
shark, 116
sharon fruit, 131
shellfish
  food value, 118
  French names, 120
  seasons, 120
  storage, 120
shock, 318
shrimps, 116
  potted, 174
Sikh influences, 10
sinks, 221
skate, 114
smelt, 116
smetana, 144
smoked fish, 110
smoked salmon, 174
smoking of food, 403
smörgäsbord, 13
smørrëbrod, 13
snack bars, 410
snails, 174
snapper, 116
snipe, 105
sodium, 384
soft fruit, 132
sole, 114
sous-vide cookery, 305
South American cookery, 15
South East Asian cookery, 19
Spanish cookery, 13
speciality restaurants, 411
spending power, 3
spices, 164
spinach, 127
sprats, 112
squash, 129
squid, 121
stainless steel equipment, 237
standard purchasing specifications, 187
standard recipe, 187
staphylococci, 356
starch, 378
statements, 201
steamers, 215
stearic acid, 376
stems and shoots, 129
sterilisation, 232
stock sheets, 200
stone fruits, 132
stopcock, 265
storekeeper's duties, 198
storekeeping, 195
  ledger, 199

stores, 195
strawberries, 132
studying, 432
sublimation, 398
sucrose, 377
suet, 98
sugar, 157, 378, 393
sulphur, 385
supervision, 286
surmac seeds, 167
swedes, 126
Swedish cookery, 12
sweetbreads, 99
sweetcorn, 128
Swiss chard, 123
Swiss cookery, 12

tables, 221
take-away, 412
tammy cloth, cleaning of, 240
tandoor oven, 16
tangelos, 131
tangerine, 133
tapioca, 154
taps, 266
tarragon, 164
taste, 1
tea, 160
tea menus, 61
teal, 105
temperature (bacteria), 353
terms
  computer, 423
  French, 47
  hygiene, 370
  industrial, 429
textured vegetable protein (tvp), 88
Thanksgiving, 9
theory examinations, 434
thermostat, 246
thiamin, 382
thyme, 164
tin
  cleaning of, 234
  steel equipment, 237
tomatoes, 129, 175
tongues
  lamb, 99
  ox, 99
toxins, 350
trade discount, 202
trade unions, 426
transference of heat, 243
trichinosis, 363
triglyceride, 376
tripe, 97
tropical fruits, 133
trout, 113
truffles, 175
tuber vegetables, 123, 126
tuberculosis, 366
tuna (tunny), 113
turbot, 115
turkey, 102
turmeric, 167
turnips, 126
types of catering, 21
typhoid, 358

ugli fruit, 133
utensils, 233

vacuum packing, 405
value of foods in diet, 388
vanilla, 177
veal
  garnishes, 92
  joints, 91
  quality, 86
  uses, 92
vegetables, 122, 126, 392
  EC grading, 124
  food value, 124
  preservation, 125, 399
  purchasing, 124
  quality, 124
  season, 125
  storage, 125, 198
  types, 123
  uses, 126
venison, 104
ventilation, kitchen, 340
vertical high speed cuttermixer, 223
Vesak, 10
vindaloo, 16
vinegar, 168
vitamin A, 380
vitamin B, 382
vitamin C, 382
vitamin D, 381

vitamins, 380
vitreous enamel, 345
volts, 252

wafers, 177
walls, kitchen, 341
walnuts, 135, 173
washing up, 326
water, 262, 385, 393
  boiling appliances, 225
  filtration, 262
  systems, 263, 269
  taps, 266
  treatment, 270
watercress, 127
watts, 252
welfare, 291
welfare catering, 23
Welsh cookery, 11
whitebait, 113
whiting, 109
wholemeal flour, 151
winkles, 122
wiring of plugs, 256
witch, 115
wood, cleaning of, 238
wood pigeon, 103
woodcock, 105
wooden equipment, 237
Worcester sauce, 175
work study, 328
working methods, 327

yams, 127
yeast, 155
yogurt, 143

zinc, cleaning of, 345

LAMBETH ACCORD:

THE THEORY OF CATERING